The Turn to Biographical Methods in Social Science

Comparative issues and examples

**Edited by Prue Chamberlayne,
Joanna Bornat and Tom Wengraf**

London and New York

1006184513

First published 2000
by Routledge
2 Park Square, Milton Park, Abingdon, Oxon, OX14 4RN

Simultaneously published in the USA and Canada
by Routledge Inc
270 Madison Ave, New York NY 10016

Routledge is an imprint of the Taylor & Francis Group

Transferred to Digital Printing 2005

© 2000 Prue Chamberlayne, Joanna Bornat and Tom Wengraf

Typeset in Goudy by Taylor & Francis Books Ltd

British Library Cataloguing in Publication Data
A catalogue record for this book is available from the British Library

Library of Congress Cataloging in Publication Data
The turn to biographical methods in social science : comparative issues
and examples /
edited by Prue Chamberlayne, Joanna Bornat, and Tom Wengraf.
p. cm. – (Social research today)
Includes bibliographical references and index.
1. Social sciences–Biographical methods. 2. Social sciences–Research. I.
Chamberlayne, Prue. II. Bornat, Joanna. III. Wengraf, Tom. IV. Series.

H61.29.T87 2000
300'.7'2–dc21
                                                              99-048261

ISBN 0–415–22837–9 (hbk)
ISBN 0–415–22838–7 (pbk)

Contents

Illustrations

Figures

Tables

Contributors

Molly Andrews is Senior Lecturer in psychosocial studies at the University of East London. Her research interests include the psychological bases of political commitment, psychological challenges posed by societies in transition to democracy, gender, and ageing. She is the author of *Lifetimes of Commitment: Ageing, Politics, Psychology* (Cambridge: Cambridge University Press, 1991). She conducted her research in East Germany as an associate Research Fellow at the Max Planck Institute in Berlin.

Ursula Apitzsch is Professor of Sociology and Political Science at the J.W. Goethe University, Frankfurt/Main and Director of the Institute of Cultural Studies and Social Psychology. She has been President of the Biographical Research section within the German Sociological Association since 1995 and board member of the Research Committee, Biography and Society, of the International Sociological Association since 1997. She has been Co-ordinator of the international European Union project 'Self-employment Activities Concerning Women and Minorities' since 1994. Within this project she has developed methods of biographical analysis and has published broadly in the fields of migration, culture, ethnicity, education and biographical analysis.

Daniel Bertaux is Research Director of Sociology at the Centre National de la Recherche Scientifique (CNRS). He has extensively published on class structure and social mobility, artisanal trades such as bakery, anthroponomics, and on qualitative methods, especially life stories. He is the author and/or editor of *Destins personnels et structure de classe* (Paris: Presses Universitaires de France, 1977); *Biography and Society* (London: Sage, 1981); *La Mobilité sociale* (Paris: Hatier, 1998), *Les Récits de vie* (Paris: Nathan, 1998). He now studies the everyday struggles of the poor.

Joanna Bornat is a Senior Lecturer in the School of Health and Social Welfare at the Open University. She is joint editor of the journal *Oral History*. She has published an edited collection, *Reminiscence Reviewed: Perspectives, Evaluations, Achievements* (Milton Keynes: Open University Press, 1994) and is joint editor of *Oral History, Health and Welfare* (London: Routledge, 1999). She also has an interest in the impact of family change on older people and, with colleagues, has researched and written on this topic.

Prue Chamberlayne is Director of the Centre for Biography in Social Policy at the University of East London, where she also teaches European Social Policy. Her research has centred on the ESRC-funded (Economic and Social Research Council) 'Cultures of Care' project (1992–6) and the seven-country EU-funded study of 'Social Strategies in Risk Society' (SOSTRIS, 1996–9). Both are comparative studies using biographical methods. Recent publication work includes the jointly edited *Welfare and Culture in Europe* (London: Jessica Kingsley Publishers, 1999), the jointly authored *Cultures of Care* (Policy Press, 2000), and articles in *Social Politics* (1995), *Sociology* (1996) and *The Sociology of Health and Illness* (1997).

Andrew Cooper is Professor of Social Work at the Tavistock Clinic and at the University of East London. Since 1991, he has worked on a series of comparative studies of European child protection systems and practices. With Rachael Hetherington and others, he is the author of *Positive Child Protection: A View from Abroad* (1991) and *Protecting Children: Messages from Europe* (1997) both published by Russell House Publishing, Lyme Regis.

Catherine Delcroix teaches sociology as 'Maitre de Conférences' at the Versailles Saint Quentin en Yvelines University. She specialises in ethnic, urban and family studies. Her books include: *Espoirs et réalités de la femme arabe: Algérie, Egypte* (Paris: L'Harmattan, 1986); *Double mixte, la rencontre de deux cultures dans le mariage* (Paris: L'Harmattan, 1992); and *Médiatrices dans les quartiers fragilisés: le lien* (Paris: La Documentation Francaise, 1996).

Brian Dimmock is a Senior Lecturer in the School of Health and Social Welfare at the Open University where he is Chair of the national Open Learning Diploma in Social Work Programme. He is also Chair of the National Stepfamily Association.

Wolfram Fischer-Rosenthal is Professor of Sociology and Methods of Case Reconstruction at the University of Kassel. He held previous professorships at the Technical University of Berlin (general sociology) and at the universities of Giessen and Mainz (medical sociology). During 1980–2, he was a research fellow with Anselm Strauss at the University of California, San Francisco. He was President of the biographical research sections of the ISA (International Sociological Association) in 1990–4, and of the DGS (German Sociological Association) in 1990–6. His research interests include the sociology of knowledge, biographical research, living with chronic illness, forced migration and health, professional interventions, and qualitative methods.

Anthony Hazzard's working life has been spent as a clinician in the National Health Service. A general practitioner for more than thirty years, he started one of the first counselling services in primary care. He is also a chartered counselling psychologist and has worked as a hospital-based psychotherapist. A tutor for the Royal Free Hospital School of Medicine, he is involved in the training and supervision of both psychological and medical practitioners. He is at present a Research Fellow in philosophy at the University of East London, working on the relevance of hermeneutics for the clinical encounter.

Helen Hewitt lectures part time in the School of Nursing at Nottingham University. Her nursing experience and academic studies of psychology led to the completion of a Ph.D. in 1997 at Loughborough University in the Department of Human Sciences on the use of life story work in transitions of care for people with profound learning difficulties. Her current main research interest is in developing the use of life story work in the long-term care of people with severe difficulties in communication.

Wendy Hollway is a Reader in Gender Relations in the Department of Psychology, University of Leeds. She has researched and published on questions to do with subjectivity, gender, sexuality, parenting, anxiety, the history of work psychology and gender relations in organisations. Her published works include *Changing the Subject* (2nd edn, with Henriques, Urwin, Venn and Walkerdine, London: Routledge, 1998), *Mothering and Ambivalence* (co-edited with Featherstone, London: Routledge, 1997), *Work Psychology and Organizational Behaviour* (London: Sage, 1991), and *Subjectivity and Method in Psychology* (London: Sage, 1989). With Tony Jefferson, she is writing *Doing Qualitative Research Differently: Free Association, Narrative and the Interview Method* (London: Sage, 2000).

Lena Inowlocki is Associate Professor of Sociology at the J.W. Goethe

University in Frankfurt/Main. She has been active in the Research Committee, Biography and Society, of the International Sociological Association since it was initiated in 1978 and joined the board as a member in 1990. Since 1994 she has been one of the two Vice Presidents of the section Biographical Research of the German Sociological Association. Her research and publications concern right-wing extremist group membership, immigrant families, issues of migration and transculturality and life-worlds of women in families of Jewish Displaced Persons.

Tony Jefferson is a Professor of Criminology in the Department of Criminology, University of Keele. He has researched and published widely on questions to do with youth subcultures, the media, policing, race and crime, masculinity, and the fear of crime. His published works include *Masculinities, Social Relations and Crime* (1996, Special Issue of the *British Journal of Criminology*, edited with Pat Carlen), *The Case Against Paramilitary Policing* (Milton Keynes: Open University Press, 1991), *Policing the Crisis* (London: Macmillan, 1978, with Stuart Hall et al.) and *Resistance through Rituals* (London: Hutchinson, 1976, edited with Stuart Hall). Joint work with Wendy Hollway includes work on methodology, sexuality and anxiety and fear of crime. Their forthcoming book is entitled *Doing Qualitative Research Differently: Free Association, Narrative and the Interview Method* (London: Sage, 2000).

Chris Jones is a Researcher in the Centre for Social Work and Community Research at the University of Hertfordshire. She was a researcher on the Cultures of Care Project at the University of East London between 1995 and 1996. Her research interests include applying narrative methods to understanding marginalised groups in Britain and she is currently involved in work with disaffected young people and people with drug-related problems.

David Jones is a Lecturer in the Faculty of Applied Social Sciences and Humanities at Buckinghamshire University College.

Annette King has worked as a researcher in the fields of social and health care. Her interests lie in comparisons of welfare regimes, the interface of social and health care issues and in qualitative methods in social policy and health services research, particularly case-study approaches and methodologies. She was first introduced to biographical methods in the 'Cultures of Care' project, a social policy project about informal caring in Germany and Britain, at the University of East London. She has since moved to health care and organisational research and is currently located at the London School of Hygiene and Tropical Medicine.

Eva Maedje is Special Advisor for Social Policy for the German parliamentary group Bündnis 90/Green Party. She did her doctoral research at the Free University of Berlin and worked as a researcher there and at the Martin Luther University in Halle-Wittenberg.

David Middleton is a Reader in Psychology at Loughborough University in the department of Human Sciences. He is a member both of the Discourse and Rhetoric Group and the Developmental Studies Group at Loughborough. His current main research interest is the social organisation of succession and change in paediatric settings. Work in this and related areas includes co-editing with Derek Edwards *Cognitive Remembering* (London: Sage, 1990) and (with Yjro Engeström) *Cognition and Communication at Work* (Cambridge: Cambridge University Press, 1996).

Claudia Neusüss studied political science, psychology and economic geography in Bonn, where she was Women's Speaker, and at the Free University of Berlin, where she taught and did her doctoral degree. She has been involved in various East–West projects regarding the transformation process. In 1987 she co-founded the women's co-operative *WeiberWirtschaft*, of which she was executive director during 1991–96. Since August 1996 she has been a member of the executive board of the Heinrich-Böll-Foundation (a political foundation associated with the Green Party). She is author of various articles, especially on the relationship between women and the welfare state.

Sheila Peace is a Senior Lecturer in the School of Health and Social Welfare at the Open University. Prior to joining the School in 1990 she was a Senior Research Officer and founder member of the Centre for Environmental and Social Studies in Ageing at the University of North London. She has been involved in a wide range of research with older people, particularly in areas of residential care and environment.

Susanna Rupp was a Research Fellow at the Centre for Biography in Social Policy at the University of East London from 1995 to 1998, first on the Cultures of Care project, then on SOSTRIS (Social Strategies in Risk Society). Currently she is working as researcher and research consultant in Darmstadt (Germany). She has been working with biographical methods since 1984, with a focus on the effects of the Nazi past on biographies, on generations and on education. Recent publications include biographical studies from the SOSTRIS project (published as *SOSTRIS Working Papers*) and on the role of education in a biographical context 'Zur biographischen Bedeutung von Bildung in der enttrationalisierten Gesellschaft', published in B. Schmitt *et al. Über Grenzen* (Frankfurt, 1998)

Michael Rustin is Professor of Sociology at the University of East London and a visiting professor at the Tavistock Clinic. He is the author of *The Good Society and the Inner World* (London: Verso, 1991) and many published articles on psychoanalytic and sociological topics. He has been working on the EU Social Strategies in Risk Society project over the last three years. He is co-editor of the magazine *Soundings*.

Martina Schiebel is conducting her doctorate on 'East German Women's Biographies in Institutionalised Welfare Work' as a scholar of the Hans-Böckler Foundation at the Institute for Applied Biographical and Lifeworld Research, University of Bremen. Her fields of work include right-wing extremism, the process of transformation in East Germany, qualitative methods, and biographical research.

Astrid Segert studied philosophy in Berlin and then worked as a sociologist at the Institute for Sociology and Social Policy of the Academy of Science in the former GDR. She is currently working in the Department of Social Sciences at Potsdam University. Her special fields of interest are biographical studies, the analysis of social transition in East Germany, and research into environmental behaviour. Recent publications include co-authoring *Sozialstruktur und Milieuerfahrungen: Aspekte des alltagskulturellen Wandelssystem in Ostdeutschland* (Westdeutscher Verlag, 1997), and 'Problematic Normalisation: East German Workers Eight Years after Unification' (*German Politics and Society*, 1998).

Antonella Spanò, born in Italy in 1955, is Researcher at the Department of Sociology of the Federico II University of Naples, where since 1991 she has also been teaching sociology. Her two main fields of interest are social exclusion (especially poverty and unemployment in southern Italy) and gender issues. She uses the biographical method and more general qualitative approaches.

Corinne Squire is at the University of East London. She is the author (with Ellen Friedman) of *Morality USA* (Minnesota: Minnesota University Press, 1998) and the editor of *Culture in Psychology* (London: Routledge, 2000), *Women and AIDS* (London: Sage, 1994) and, with Molly Andrews, Shelley Sclater and Amal Treacher, *Lines of Narrative* (London: Routledge, 2000). She is currently doing research on HIV and citizenship.

Tom Wengraf is Senior Lecturer at Middlesex University, having specialised successively in sociology, cultural studies, communication studies and social research methodology. He has conducted research into the sociology of Algeria just after independence, and into the experiences of students at university, and has been involved in the EU-funded SOSTRIS project 'Social Strategies in Risk Society'. As Director of the Higher Education Action Research and Design unit he researched performance indicators of staff consultation, empowerment and satisfaction (PISCES). He has taught and used qualitative research methodology for a number of years, specialising in semi-structured and narrative interviewing on which he is currently completing a textbook for Sage.

Irene Zierke studied cultural sciences in Berlin and worked as a sociologist at the Institute for Sociology and Social Policy of the Academy of Science in the former GDR. She is currently working in the Department of Social Sciences at Potsdam University. Her special fields of interest are biographical studies, the analysis of social transition in East Germany, and research into environmental behaviour. Recent publications include co-authoring *Sozialstruktur und Milieuerfahrungen: Aspekte des alltagskulturellen Wandelssystem in Ostdeutschland* (Westdeutscher Verlag, 1997), and 'Zwischen Distanz und Nähe: Zu alltagskulturellen Wurzeln ostdeutscher Bürgerbewegungen' (in the *Forschungsjournal Neue Soziale Bewegungen*, 1995).

Introduction
The biographical turn

Prue Chamberlayne, Joanna Bornat and
Tom Wengraf

The burgeoning of biographical methods

Our choice of the phrase 'the turn to biographical methods' for the title of
this collection is a statement about the scope and influence of a shift in
thinking which is currently shaping the agenda of research and its applications across the social science disciplines. This shift, which amounts to
a paradigm change (Kuhn 1960) or a change of knowledge culture
(Somers 1996), affects not only the orientations of a range of disciplines,
but their interrelations with each other. In general it may be characterised
as a 'subjective' or 'cultural' turn in which personal and social meanings,
as bases of action, gain greater prominence.

There is also by now a wide recognition that social science, in its
longues durées of positivism, determinism and social constructionism, has
become detached from lived realities. And although structuration theory
conceptualised the reproduction of social structures and cultures through
the social action of subjects, debates about the relative effects of structure
and agency, which have been vigorous, have remained abstract (Giddens
1990; Mouzelis 1995; Archer 1995). Even less did the concerns of postmodernism with, on the one hand, individual, multiple and floating
identities, and, on the other, the discursive constitution of the social,
clarify the interconnections between the personal and social.

Perhaps it was inevitable that concerns with reflexivity, individualism
and identity would lead back to a more structural level of analysis, and on
to a preoccupation with the conditions and efficacy of agency. Certainly
the late 1990s have seen an intensified search to take better account of
the interweaving of human and socio-political development (Newton
1999: 411) and to find research tools which could 'prise open the different
dimensions of lived totality' (Gottfried 1998: 452), and reconnect with
'the vitality' and the 'bedrock reality' of everyday lives (Crook 1998: 524).
It is this concern to link macro and micro levels of analysis which

explains, it seems to us, the burgeoning interest and development in biographical methods. For biographies, which are rooted in an analysis of both social history and the wellsprings of individual personality, reach forwards and backwards in time, documenting processes and experiences of social change (Giele 1998; Bertaux and Thompson 1998). And biographical methods, with their long and diverse genealogy (e.g. Mills 1967), provide a sophisticated stock of interpretive procedures for relating the personal and the social.

One feature of this book is to place developments in biographical methods within a history of social theory, and a second is to provide working examples of processes of interpretation, laying bare the methodological premises of particular protocols. Until now the constitutive effects of interpretive practices (at least in Britain) have remained relatively too immune from reflexive questioning; comparative research forces attention on differences in research traditions, not just at the level of the interview, but at the level of theorisation of data. This book seeks to impel such questioning forward, creating opportunities both for hybridity and for more discerning selectivity.

A third feature of the book lies in its consideration of the push-and-pull relationship between developments in policy and the turn to biographical methods. It was oral historians, some of whom were or became social practitioners, who already in the early 1980s adopted life-history methods as an emancipatory tool, and launched the concept of 'empowerment' as a key concept in welfare practice. Yet despite the relevance of biographical methods to life course work which was prominent in social work training, such approaches remained relatively marginalised in academic social policy in the 1980s. In the sociology of medicine, by contrast, interpretive methods were widely used. Gerontology, which spans medicine and social policy, was an exception here (see *Ageing and Society* 1996.) By the late 1990s, however, biographical approaches had become widely accepted, even sought out, by policy makers as 'useful'. Principles of user involvement had become officially sanctioned, even mandated, although whether the effect was one of genuine democratisation might be disputed. A cynical view would see the 'turn' as a figleaf for off-loading collective responsibilities and for the more selective targeting of resources. But perhaps policy makers were at last responding to the requirements of a more differentiated and reflexive society and the need to realign policy with the realities and strategies of everyday lives.

Antecedents

What are the antecedents of this 'biographical turn' in social science? It is within the shifting boundaries between history and sociology that some of the most telling and stimulating debating issues have emerged. Attempts to account for individual agency, whether in relation to shifting power balances over time, or measured against broad structural determinants in societies, have drawn historians and sociologists towards evidence that is rooted in autobiography, eye-witness statements or straightforward personal narrative. In each discipline, the status of personal accounts, unless drawn from more powerful actors in the case of history, raised questions of reliability, subjectivity and representativeness. Where historians elevated the document and its provenance as reliable evidence, sociologists sought evidence in quantitative measures of social events. Nevertheless, Paul Thompson, in his classic text on the roots of oral history, *The Voice of the Past* (1978), found evidence of historians making use of personal testimony over the centuries, and Ken Plummer's search for the origins of a 'humanistic method' in sociology identified diaries, letters, photographs and life histories as typical source materials of nineteenth- and early twentieth-century social investigators (Plummer 1983).

While the antecedents have long histories, a more modern and decisive shift to embrace personal accounts can be located within the latter half of the twentieth century. Beginning in the 1960s and 1970s a more political and populist turn within history and sociology led to a recognition that the personal account provides a means to reaching those sections of society, both in the present and the past, whose experience could not be directly tapped through documentary or formal survey sources.

Plummer, writing in 1983, argues for Thomas and Znaniecki's *The Polish Peasant*, published from 1918–20 onwards, as the first substantive sociological engagement with 'the individual and the social' (p.40). Their distinction between the '*objective* factors of the situation and the *subjective* interpretation of that situation' (p.41, his emphasis) he holds as being of fundamental significance. Paul Thompson (1978) defines this shift in historiography as one of both method and meaning. Engaging with personal accounts meant valuing and finding ways of eliciting and analysing the spoken and written words of people who, earlier, had been seen as marginal to history making or to sociological explanation. Immigrant Poles, moving between Europe and the United States, were perceived as a social problem in the first decades of the century, but their personal experience was not used as a part of the explanation of the ensuing social change. Similarly, the new history of the mid century, as it turned to include the voices of people whose marginalisation and resistance had contributed to the effects of industrial change a hundred years earlier, was to alter both the methods and the content of history making.

As the historian E.P. Thompson explained in *The Making of The English Working Class*, he was demonstrating that: 'Their aspirations were valid in terms of their own experience...' (1963: 13).

In giving value to subjective experience, historians and sociologists were discovering common ground, although the fine work of developing explanations around telling and remembering, and their functions in relation to agency and meaning had yet to be explored. However, such issues were beginning to be recognised. In 1982, the French sociologist Daniel Bertaux, a contributor to this volume, was arguing that what he chose to call 'anthroponomy' (p.142), the identification of the ways human beings act on society and how the actions of past generations shape and form a basis for current action, was 'a fundamental philosophical question' (p.149).

Early 1980s: the questioning of memory and identity

In Britain, biographical methods have been enriched by a number of interrelated influences. While the points in time when these were acknowledged and accepted continue to be debated, their significance and contribution is not. Here we look briefly at the significance and contribution of three main influences: debates about memory, feminism, and postmodernism and identity.[1] All three have challenged approaches to working with biographies, both in terms of method and meaning.

Debates about memory preoccupied oral historians in the early 1980s as they responded to criticisms of their emergent method. In seeking validation alongside traditionally more trusted sources such as documents and evidence from representative surveys, there was a tendency to emphasise the quality and orginality of data, while at the same time setting up sampling procedures and advocating interview methods to ensure representivity and lack of bias (Thompson 1978; Lummis 1987; Thomson *et al.* 1994: 33). This emphasis left the new method open to criticism for its lack of attention to subjectivity and for neglecting social and psychological influences on remembering. A significant assault came from the Popular Memory Group at the Centre for Contemporary Cultural Studies in Birmingham. Their 1982 essay attacked oral history's empiricism, its unquestioning validation of the individual, its alleged epistemologically impoverished presentation of the past, and its lack of engagement with the political nature of research as based in an unequal relationship between interviewer and interviewee (Popular Memory Group 1998).

These criticisms, despite their exaggeration in many respects, set an agenda for oral history, and by association with biographical methods debates, which have continued to be productive over subsequent years.

The issue of subjectivity had already been exposed by Luisa Passerini, an Italian oral historian. Her exploration of working-class communities in Turin during the Fascist period deliberately emphasised the rewards of an emphasis on subjectivity and ambivalence in remembering, rather than staying with the apparent security of more 'positivist and historicist' approaches, in order to account for contradictions and silences in interviews (Passerini 1979). Similarly, Alessandro Portelli, was recommending oral history precisely because 'it tells us less about events than about their meaning' and because it can 'force on the historian...the speaker's subjectivity' (Portelli 1981: 99). Identifying individual meaning and giving weight to the changing perspective of the interviewee has remained an abiding focus for oral historians and others who are keen to understand the tensions between stability and instability and between public genre and individual experience in remembering. So, for example, Al Thomson, in his study of Anzac veterans, has traced how public narratives of the Australian experience of the First World War combine with the events of individuals' life histories to affect remembering in very late life (Thomson 1994).

While the Popular Memory Group's criticisms were telling, they were ultimately bypassed by developments in feminism. Feminist historians in the early 1970s drew from oral and biographical sources to substantiate arguments about marginalised histories inaccessible through conventional documentary sources. Early works by writers such as Elizabeth Roberts (1975), Mary Chamberlain (1975), Sheila Rowbotham and Jean McCrindle (1977), Jill Liddington and Jill Norris (1978), Catherine Hall (1977), Di Gittins (1977), Thea Thompson (1981) and others opened up to research scrutiny topics such as everyday domestic life, women's industrial labour, maternity, sexuality and birth control. However, given feminism's political drive, this was not simply a question of redressing an imbalance in the making and telling of history. These new agendas for historical research were also a means to establish continuities with women's oppression in the present. This meant that understanding what was meant by the past shifted as feminists redrew the maps of responsibilities and power, challenging assumptions with accounts which used women's words, women's knowledge and women's stories. From here, the move to seeing the interview itself as both a positive and negative force, as misrepresenting through inequality, or as empowering by giving voice to individual experience of oppression, was only a short step (Oakley 1981; Personal Narratives Group 1989; Gluck and Patai 1991). Debates about the ethics of telling, hearing and representing have continued to dominate in English oral history and biographical work.

The third area which we identify as contributing to the shaping of biographical work is the turn to reflexivity, identified by Anthony Giddens as a key diagnostic feature of the postmodern state (1991). In tandem with feminists such as Liz Stanley and her exploration of *The Auto/-Biographical 'I'* (1992), an emphasis on self-construction, life review and the fashioning of identity made its own impact on the development of biographical methods. Tracing reflexivity in the process of interviewing and being interviewed has resulted in the exposure of often quite raw emotions, misconceptions and even traumatic remembering, bringing oral history and biographical work close to an identification with therapeutic processes, far distant from their originating antecedents (see *Sociology* 1993; *Oral History* 1998). Nevertheless, such work has maintained a continuing commitment to changing perspectives in social science, adding a critically personal edge to what had earlier been defined as simply 'history', 'society' or 'policy'.

The 1980s postmodernist movement against positivist social science saw the celebration of the freedom and arbitrariness of subjectivity and a denial of the determinisms of alleged 'social structures', including the determinisms of class but also of other 'positioning categories'. Taken up in the 'linguistic-textualist turn' of that time, a significant minority of sociologists developed a canon of 'qualitative inquiry' which focused completely or almost completely on 'the point of view of the actor', while simultaneously coming to assert the extreme fragility of any particular actor's identity or point of view. This was a new version of the earlier 'structuralist' assertion (attacked by E.P. Thompson 1978) that individual actors were nothing more than the expression of ideological and social-structural determinations playing upon them. An extreme version of this postmodernist scepticism and refusal to make inferences from text were those who denied that actors had any coherent 'point of view' or any stable 'identity' that could be expressed by what they said or did. Given sufficient emphasis on the incoherence of the alleged points of view in the text and on any alleged 'identity' that the text might be deemed to express, the safest position was to celebrate the text as a momentary expression of transient and precarious pseudo-coherence. A present-time analysis of the 'text of the moment' was all that could be achieved without falling into any inferences about alleged continuities of point of view, identity, etc.

Previous grand narratives about the collective agents of class and nation had been decomposed and subverted by the industrial transformations in modern societies after the 1970s, by what may be loosely called globalisation and the crisis of the nation-state, and in particular by the collapse of Communism in Soviet Russia and its satellites. Newer collective identities of 'women' and 'blacks' were proposed but were soon 'deconstructed' in their turn. Associated with this apparent 'world transformation', there spread very widely in society and in the social sciences a denial of the relevance of history, a denial originally put forward by the archetypical capitalist Henry Ford ('History is bunk'), by Marxist structuralists in the 1970s, and then in the Western euphoria generated by the collapse of Communism (in for example Fukuyama 1992). The 'end of history' – the biggest rupture possible in the grand meta-narrative – for some implied the end of the relevance of doing historically minded research work.

The 1990s: 'historical' and 'cultural' understanding of agents and actions

During the 1980s, however, alongside the postmodernist belief in 'situational freedom', there developed a counter-movement which was deeply sceptical of declarations that we had reached the end of history and useful historical-mindedness. This counter-movement, which has increased in its relative strength in the 1990s as the limits of postmodernist description and neoliberal market self-celebration have became more apparent, takes account of the earlier structuralist and later postmodernist critiques of essentialist or determinist positions, but is doing so in order to deepen its historical and cultural approach to structures and agencies.

To understand oneself and others, we need to understand our own histories and how we have come to be what we are. We make our own history but not under conditions of our own choosing, and we need to understand these conditions of action more if our future making of our own history is to produce outcomes closer to our intentions and projects. Fischer-Rosenthal, in this volume, argues that, in the contemporary epoch, modernisation has and will foreground individualisation and 'the individual'. This, together with a historical movement in society and in social science may well lead – both on the part of the individual actor and on the part of the researcher attempting to understand the individual actor – to a biographical approach.

We welcome our discovery of considerable convergence between our concern for reflexivity in our interviewees and in ourselves with that of a research tradition not particularly focused towards biography. McDonald (1996) in a mid-1990s collection has a discussion of a general turn towards history in the human sciences with a beautiful formulation which could be our own: 'The notion...of historically self-conscious analysts reconstructing fully contextualized historical actors and representing them in a theoretically-sophisticated narrative that takes account of multiple causes and effects is at the heart of the vision of the historic turn' (1996: 10).

Biographical social researchers in the 1990s are increasingly attempting to describe people as historically formed actors whose biographies are necessary to render fully intelligible their historical action in context – its conditions, meanings and outcomes, whether such conditions, meanings and outcomes be conscious or unconscious.

Consequently, while the historical turn in the social sciences does not have to be a biographic turn, to introduce biographising into social science is to accentuate a historical orientation. We are now seeing more and more understandings of the evolutions of structures, agencies and actions as historically formed and historically forming. These accounts tend to move to higher levels of sophistication and depth of analysis both of intra-psychic and of societal-context realities. This book is part of that movement.

Staying with the 'British story' for the moment, we consider four areas of change which result from and contribute to this general shift in perspective in the 1990s. These are movements in the relationship between psychoanalysis and social sciences, a new orientation to 'culture' in social policy, the use of narrativity in gerontology, and the 'officialising' of 'empowerment'. All these changes are illustrative of mutations in social science in the 1990s and are interrelated with the new burgeoning of biographical methods.

Until very recently, the psychoanalytic tradition was kept very firmly apart from sociology and from the practice of biographising in the social sciences (Rustin, this volume). A key paper in Bertaux's 1981 volume, by Ferrarotti, regretfully concluded that, at that time, 'no intrapsychic or relational model of the social individual' existed for sociological use.

However, to attempt to deepen our understanding of individual agency as *historical* means avoiding an excessively present-centred and function-alist 'over-socialised concept of man' (Wrong 1961). It is not surprising then that the turn to subjectivity has meant for some sociologists a turn towards a particular view of, or model of, subjectivity, that presented by psychoanalysis. Fitting the turns to subjectivity and to history, psycho-analysis provides a 'thick description' of the historical evolution of the individual as acted-upon agent: it accounts for subjectivity in a historical way.

It is true that this 'classic model' of psychoanalysis – one in which personal self-understanding moves from self-defensive unconscious mysti-fication to self-aware understanding of real personal history, from illusion to truth – was challenged strongly in the 1980s by postmodernism within the psychoanalytic tradition. Schafer (1976) and Spence (1982) in different ways argued that psychoanalysis did not discover any truths, but only produced a more coherent and a more personally accepted narrative. What was important was 'narrative truth', however historically untrue it might be. This version of psychoanalysis could then be freely used for 'understanding' the subjective texts of postmodernist narrations. Under this regime of pseudo-knowledge, as the oxymoronic concept of 'narrative truth' suggests, the researcher's account and understanding of the life-history narration only needed to be 'coherent and attractive' and need not worry about its historical truth.

Despite this postmodernist challenge, the presupposition that *all actors are incompletely conscious* of the conditions, meanings, and outcomes of their actions remained strong in both psychoanalysis and in social science, and the 1990s has seen increased use and assimilation by biographic researchers of psychodynamic and psychoanalytic structures of understanding. One of the strengths of the biographical-interpretive method, which is strongly represented in this volume, is precisely its ability to explore latent levels of personal meaning. Ferrarotti's regret for the absence of an 'intrapsychic or relational model of the social individual', if it was ever justified, now seems increasingly out of place (see, in this volume, Rustin, Hollway and Jefferson, and Chamberlayne and Spano).

Another shift across the social sciences, which biographical methods both reflect and impel, lies in the rediscovery of 'culture'. There is an understanding that in social policy, for example, material policies and practices are lived out or 'filtered' through networks of relationships and shared assumptions and meanings which vary greatly between societies. Such explorations of the cultural underpinnings of welfare systems, and the relating of theory to experience and practice, bring anthropological methods to the fore. The social order is not just transmitted, in the way cultural studies might emphasise, but experienced and explored. Formal systems are played out in interaction with informal cultures and structures and through the lives and strategies of individuals.[2] The productive potential for reworking social policy through a cultural approach is explored in the volume *Welfare and Culture in Europe*, in which several of the contributors to his collection have also been involved (Chamberlayne *et al.* 1999). Such an orientation to culture can paradoxically draw little from cultural studies, which has tended to focus on the study of youth and on 'representation' rather than 'agency'. 'Cultural sociology' rather than 'cultural studies' is what is needed.[3]

Narratologists who work in gerontology argue that storying, story-telling and narrative maintenance play an important role in personal adjustment in later life. Seen in this way, biographising becomes a normal human activity, contributing to the maintenance of identity, the presentation of self and the passing on or transference of key cultural and personal elements: even a guarantee of immortality at the end of life (Coleman 1986; Biggs 1993: 61–6; McAdams 1993; Phillipson 1998: 23–8). Identifying the characters, plots and archetypes employed in narratives is more than simply a question of classification of types. Bruner argues for the role of the autobiography, as the basis for 'negotiability', the process whereby an individual presents him or herself to the world through a storied version of their life (1995: 169). Indeed Coleman *et al.*, drawing on data from a longitudinal study of older people, see story-telling as one of the most enduring themes of late old age (1993). This very social function of the narrative act is also detected in studies of narration among elderly people living in residential care, where the life story, as told, may be a product of the social context in which someone lives, a version of a life made ready for public consumption in a situation where identity is at risk from the negative stereotypes of frailty and the processes and procedures of caring (Dobroff 1984; Wallace 1992/3; Gubrium and Holstein 1995a and 1995b).

Though talk about past experience is accepted as a normal part of everyday life, its role in work with vulnerable children and adults has only recently been legitimated. Work with life story books, where adults with learning disabilities are moving from institutional care to community settings, in care planning with older people or with children separated from their birth parents, now has established sets of procedures including ethical guidelines. Such practices have emerged in tandem with philosophies of care which now focus on the individual as a consumer rather than a recipient of services. Working with the 'whole person' calls for knowledge of that person's past as well as their current needs and preferences. How that past is presented, in what detail and with what emphases is a relevant issue. It may include hitherto unrevealed aspects of identity, it may be incompletely communicated where there is cognitive impairment (Middleton this volume). Whatever form it takes, its presentation provides an opportunity for the development of appropriate and sensitive care practice and interventions and the promotion of more socialised and empowering perceptions of the self in circumstances when stigma, segregation and disempowerment may have been a more common experience (Atkinson 1997; Adams *et al.* 1998; Ryan and Walker 1999).

The provenance of the book

Although strong international networking had already developed by the early 1980s,[4] there was at that time little cross-fertilisation between research practices in Germany, France and Britain. Even now there remain underlying difficulties in mutual comprehension which often provoke sharp exchanges at international conferences. It is of course a paradox that closer European collaboration sharpens understandings of difference, which then necessitate further investigation. A return to first principles, which is a feature of paradigm shifts, is also impelled by comparative work in which researchers confront each others' mind-sets and working contexts.

Our aim in assembling this collection is to provide readers with exemplars of work within the traditions identified, to facilitate an appreciation of the strengths of these different approaches to biographical analysis, and thereby support more confident collaboration and experimentation. In asking researchers to spell out their conceptual premises our purpose has been to mediate between traditions, increase accessibility and to facilitate the expansion of repertoires within qualitative research. In our view, and despite the self-evidently 'European' nature of classical sociology, such processes of exchange are at an early stage, and our contribution tentative and preliminary. We do however perceive a decisive change in the 1990s, with the growth of practical collaboration which has been bolstered by the late twentieth-century process of Europeanisation.[5] This volume arises out of that development.

Joanna Bornat, as editor of *Oral History*, was involved in the earlier history of international debate, and the shifting of focus among oral historians towards perceiving the interview as a social event as much as an act of memory retrieval. At the same time, retaining its original notion of the interview as an emancipatory act, oral history has persisted in its commitment to breaking down the boundaries between the academy and everyday understandings and evaluations of history and society (Grele 1985; Bornat 1989; Frisch 1990; Portelli 1991; Walmsley 1995).

Prue Chamberlayne's first engagement with biographical-interpretive methods began with the ESRC-funded Cultures of Care project (1992–6), which was conducted in East and West Germany and in Britain. The same method was used in the EU-funded SOSTRIS project (Social Strategies in Risk Society 1996–9), which she convened, and in which Roswita Breckner played a leading role as research consultant. Tom Wengraf joined the SOSTRIS work in 1997. This project brought together teams from seven countries in ongoing discussion and practice of biographical methods (*SOSTRIS Working Papers 1–9*; see Chamberlayne and Spanò in this volume).

During these two projects four meetings were held in London to pursue issues which emerged in the course of the use of biographical methods in comparative analysis. The first, in 1994, invited researchers from Britain, Germany and France to present accounts of their interpretive practices. The focus lay particularly in the theoretical underpinnings in moving from single case studies to their comparison. The second meeting in 1995 arose from a request from British researchers at the first seminar for a training workshop in biographical-interpretive methods. This workshop was led by Roswita Breckner and Bettina Voelter, from Quatext in Berlin. Quatext is a training school established by Gabriele Rosenthal and Wolfram Fischer-Rosenthal, which uses procedures drawn from a number of currents in German use of biographical methods (Rosenthal 1993; Breckner 1998). The third event was a conference entitled 'Subjectivity Revisited' (May 1997), which explored commonalities and differences between phenomenological, discourse and psychoanalytical approaches to subjectivity. And the fourth was a conference 'Biographical Methods in the Social Sciences' held in September 1998. While exploring the wider sociological uses of biographical methods, this conference particularly compared grounded sociological forms of inference and interpretation with those arising in psychoanalytical uses of case-study material.

The editorial collaboration for the current volume has facilitated some fascinating and creative exchanges as the common quests and overlaps in what at times feel like separate and yet parallel universes in sociology and oral history, and in pure and applied social sciences, have become manifest.

As editors we are, of course, not 'neutral'. The very selection of contributors derives from particular network configurations, which have their own history, though our research experience is widely based, in comparative social policy and the informal sphere, in oral history and community care, in cultural studies and research into student learning. We inevitably mediate towards and mainly address English-speaking researchers, and bring to the volume our own cultural capital, subjective understandings and questions. And while this volume originated from seminars organised to promote dialogue between practitioners of biographical methods, the very task of producing a book written in English has involved a shift from the two-way dialogue of the workshop to the English-centred focus of the book. It combines English researchers presenting their work to an Anglophone readership and German researchers working through a translation process to present their work to that same readership.

As mediators between research traditions, we need to hold a balance between seeking commonalities between approaches and deepening understanding of differences, the latter being vital to appreciating and negotiating debates. A danger of 'Euro-speak' is that researchers talk past each other in a semblance of common terminology, overriding more subtle and deep-rooted cultural meanings (Chamberlayne 1997). The process of translating and editing these papers is a case in point. Out of concern to make the language and thinking of the Continental contributions accessible to an English-speaking audience it may well be that, despite our efforts, editing has been excessive, 'flattening out' cultural and philosophical differences.

Cross-national borrowing and comparative work

It is possible that the 'subjective', 'cultural' and 'biographical' turn in the social sciences is specific to Britain. Certainly the shift towards biographical methods occurred earlier in France and Germany. Heinritz and Rammstedt (1991), in a review of biographical work, dated the 'craze' (*mode galopante*) for it in France to the early 1970s, and the international collection edited by Bertaux (1981) on *Biography and Society* spoke already of a 'biographical movement', whose impact had been considerable in shifting sociological perspectives.

The key aim of this collection is to encourage changes in the nature and direction of both the theoretical and the methodological traffic of biographical research. In particular it contributes to bridging the intellectual gaps which have developed between German and either French or British intellectual traditions in postwar years, as these bear on biographical and narrative work. For while collaboration between German and British research and social policy has been increasing (Leisering and Walker 1998; Clasen et al. 1998), British sociology has in many ways been more strongly inspired by French structuralism and post-structuralism in recent decades, and increasingly detached from German phenomenology. Much 'realist' French work using life histories, on the other hand, is more influenced by the Chicago School than by post-structuralism and 'narrativism', despite the influence of Ricoeur's *Time and Narrative* (1984). An interest in the construction of identity through narrative is shared by both discourse theorists and phenomenologists. Yet approaching identity through biographical reconstruction (which is inherently historical) or through the structures of language and cultural representation (especially if these are treated situationally) is very different.

The 'realism' of the Chicago School approach as a means of researching social processes and social change has 'entered' and re-entered different European sociological traditions at different times. Apitzsch and Inowlocki (in this volume) trace this history with regard to German sociology, while also bringing into view a greater variety of contributory influences to biographical work in Germany than is captured by a narrower emphasis on its roots in phenomenological interpretation and meaning. There are of course many aspects to the Chicago School. Apitzsch and Inowlocki stress the interest of Fritz Schütze, as a key figure in the development of German biographical methods, in the symbolic interactionism and the grounded-theory analytical procedures of Anselm

Strauss and in the group methods and detailed supervision of students used by the Chicago School. They also highlight his interest in suffering and disorderly social processes, and hence his interest in 'trajectories' as a means of comparing responses to traumatic events.[6]

In France, the re-burgeoning of interest in the Chicago School in the 1990s, has centred rather on its study of social relations, and 'the historical fabric of social relations which underlies practical behaviour' (Heinritz and Rammstedt 1991: 353, quoting Bertaux and Bertaux-Wiame). Likewise, in this volume, Bertaux and Delcroix argue for the cross-generational study of families, combining history and sociology, as a means of identifying inter-generational transmission. As compared with the concept of social reproduction as used by Bourdieu, this is a far more particularised approach, which takes account of individual initiative as well as socio-cultural determinations (Heinritz and Rammstedt 1991: 353, 358).

As Heinritz and Rammstedt (1991) point out, however strong and prolific the realist tradition in French biographical work, there are others in France who regard narratives as artefacts, and there is a wide spectrum in between. A well-known text by Demazière and Dubar (1997), for example, which draws on Greimas (1986), makes a sociological analysis of the structural categories used by young unemployed men and women from all over France in narrative interviews, using a process of inductive typologising.

In British traditions of biographical analysis there has predominently been an emphasis on the social relations of the interview understood in terms of power and positioning. Chapters by Cooper and Hazzard in this collection draw on French and German studies respectively, highlighting differences between British and 'Continental' approaches.

By focusing on biographical work, we as editors tell a story of any national tradition from a particular viewpoint, and may even influence its course of development. The introduction of biographical interpretive methods in Britain has catalysed some new orientations (see Hollway and Jefferson in this volume). On the other hand, as we emphasised above, we see our intervention as occurring within a wider set of paradigm changes. Whether similar 'paradigm changes' are in train in France or Germany is beyond the scope of this introduction – the question itself and the difficulty of answering it confirm our argument of the need for more work in this field – hopefully this collection will add impetus to such a development.

The structure of the book

The book is divided into two parts. The chapters in Part 1, 'Issues of methodology and theory', explore reasons why the development of both society and social science has produced a new interest and excitement in biographical methods. Exploring historical and philosophical contexts, the authors discuss the relevance of reflective 'biographical work', both within everyday life and for the epistemology of social science research and comparative analysis (see Chamberlayne *et al.* 1999). Part 2, 'Examples of biographical methods in use', illustrates 'constituting practices' in biography-based research. Thus the rich synthesis in the UK between, on the one hand, post-structuralist analyses of the construction of reality through text and narrative with, on the other, issues of power, voice, content and representation is illustrated in chapters by Hollway and Jefferson, Squire, King and Bornat *et al.* Other chapters, by Schiebel and by Neusüss and Maedje for example, demonstrate the theoretical bases and working procedures used in analysing materials, drawing on aspects of research practice which tend to be more explicit and theorised in German traditions.

In both parts of the book, each of the chapters illustrates how the 'biographical turn' has led to the development of analyses and investigations across a wide range of settings and topics. So, for example, among the issues which our contributors have addressed are: single mothers in Berlin; HIV status and identity construction; care transitions and profound learning disability; anxiety and fear of crime; the provision of home care; right-wing attitudes; responses to modernisation; experiences of family change. Very different topics, yet there is also shared space and a common focus on the contribution which the presentation of an individual life can make to understanding and interpreting the reach and penetration of structural change and to clarifying the implications of deconstructing influences for meaning and identity in different contexts and life stages.

Subjectivity and the social world

In this volume contributors have been asked to make explicit the conceptual armoury from which their interpretation of biographical material proceeds. Such expositions inevitably lead back to founding debates within sociology concerning the relationship between the individual and society and around the nature of subjectivity. Such terrain is indeed explored within the more historical contributions by Rustin, Apitzsch and Inowlocki, Fischer-Rosenthal, and Hazzard. Taken together, these chapters suggest the deep rifts which traverse the social sciences, intra-nationally as well as internationally, and also the complex lineages of biographical methods, which cross both national and discipline boundaries in patterns of exodus and return. The historical examples of creative hybridisation form a supportive backcloth for those more recently embarking on social science uses of biographical methods. The contributions in the second part of the book by Hollway and Jefferson, King, and Chamberlayne and Spanò provide examples of the daunting while exciting nature of such breaking of boundaries.

Debates concerning subjectivity are both greater and smaller than might be expected. Apitzsch and Inowlocki firmly refute the notion that there is a 'German' school of biography rooted in idealism, showing the contributory currents within biographical work in Germany of American pragmatism, ethnography, and the Chicago School, and asserting the transcending of any opposition between 'objective social reality' and 'subjective accounts'. They cite Kafka's 'K' to illustrate the impact of institutionalised 'process structures' on subjectivity, and Habermas' insistence that all communication requires that a person 'objectify belonging in the life world'. They show how Fritz Schütze drew on conversation analysis to arrive at a technique for uncovering 'identity work' in the formal, 'objective' features of interview texts. They also quote Alfred Schutz on the 'common sense constructs of the reality of everyday life...these thought objects which determine (their) behaviour, define the goal of (their) action, the means available for attaining them'. At the same time Hazzard spells out the philosophical development of hermeneutics as an intersubjective process of understanding which is the special preserve of phenomenology.

For Hollway and Jefferson, it is the notion of the (psychoanalytically derived) 'defended subject' together with the 'intersubjective provenance' of the biographical interview which are so richly productive for research and provide the grounds to arbitrate between different interpretations. This clashes sharply both with the elusiveness of subjectivity within auto/biographical approaches which confine themselves to 'intertextuality' and with the opposite view that the subject is closer to the truth about his/her life than the researcher can ever be.

If phenomenology and discourse theory share a common concern with the ways in which society is reproduced, and even with institutionalised aspects of that process of reproduction, there are nevertheless great differences between the 'biographical' and 'discursive' reproduction of social forms. Phenomenology is more concerned with personalised, inner worlds of meaning, how the external world is received and processed. The story of 'K' emphasises the nature of his experience, even if his 'problem' is that he tries to perpetuate his expectations of 'everyday normality' in greatly changed circumstances. In the Jones and Rupp chapter, despite the 'determining' nature of 'external' factors such as migration, racism and marriage, the key focus is on Mrs Rajan's inner world as marked by closure until the turning point of a 'healthy son' allows her to become more outgoing and open to outside support. In Schiebel's chapter on racist youth in West Germany, which has powerful implications for youth work and for schools, the point of interpretation remains the inner orientations of the two youths, their search for self-esteem and social bonding amidst alienated parental relationships, and the meticulous uncovering of such readings through textual interpretation, using the biographical-interpretive method. In Chamberlayne and Spanò's chapter, which compares the biographical resources on which workers may draw in making major social transitions, the analysis centres on highly individualised experiences and personally rooted meanings of work, however socially structured those may also be.

In the discourse approach, by contrast, the point of interest is less the personalised world of experience, but rather the structuring of that external world which impacts on the individual and on collectivities. Its prime interest is *what* impacts on the individual, rather than on *how* it does so in an experiential sense. The external apparatuses that are related to power and are themselves forms of power are often linguistic. In Squire's chapter, an HIV-infected man adopts the knowledge and language of medicine as a contingent form of identity. By avoiding forms of questioning that would allow the donning of pre-formed genres of discourse, the researcher enables data to emerge that suggests the discontinuities of identity within individuals and HIV communities. The influence of political ideology on memory and therefore identity is the key theme in Andrews' chapter on the 'reconstructing' of lives in 1989 in East Germany. The importance of narrative as a tool towards citizenship is explored in the chapter by Middleton and Hewitt which concerns the significance for the parents and the impact on professionals of marking out and registering the remembering of an act of volition in a very disabled young man, and the function of narrative in facilitating and sustaining the effectivity of this action.

Biographical research in Britain is concerned both with the personalised world of experience and the structuring of the externalities impinging on individuals and collectivities: it also bears its own distinctive marks, as in the prominence of issues of power and democracy. The chapters by Squire and by Middleton and Hewitt illustrate how the emphasis within discourse analysis on 'external' social constructionism within Britain becomes fused with concerns for citizenship, representation, and empowerment. Bornat *et al.*'s chapter explores narrative coherence as a means of resisting negative public discourse on divorce and maintaining personal identity in the face of family fragmentation. In the German hermeneutic tradition the relationship between the researcher and the interviewee is often investigated in order to set it aside: the goal is to clarify the frame of reference of the subject, in order to access the inner world. In British work, it is more likely that the relationship between the researcher and the researched person remains a prime object of study. While such work can lead to narcissistic navel-gazing, it has also been used to great purpose in professional-service user relationships, to enhance user empowerment.

In the hands of British researchers biographical-interpretive methods have been used to emphasise power and class aspects of context, whether at a local-level (King) or a macro-level (Chamberlayne and Spanò). In contrast with phenomenology, whose special strength lies in the analysis of subjectivity, for British sociology 'engaging with the subject' has been fraught with difficulty (see Rustin). Posing the relationship of the individual and society in terms of agency and structure has quickly led to issues of class power (Giddens 1984; Archer 1996; Mouzelis 1989), whereas the formulation of 'basic structural processes of social reality' in Germany in such middle-range terms as 'career models', the 'life course', or 'developments and changes in social worlds, social milieus and social movements' (Apitzsch and Inowlocki), from a British perspective, can seem functionalist and abstract. Functionalism has been undergoing a revival in Germany, as Fischer-Rosenthal's discussion of Luhmann makes clear. Apitzsch and Inowlocki also explain a new emphasis on institutions in German sociology as a reaction to the excessive rationalism and intentionalism of action theory. But functionalism produces its own resistance. Segert and Zierke's research reasserts a degree of East German continuity of culture and life strategies in the face of a West German hegemonic view that East Germany must 'catch up with modernity'; and Neusüss and Maedje claim that single mothers' negotiations of welfare are creating a new mode of social reproduction in which the patriarchal breadwinner form is no longer dominant.

Research procedures

If the clarification of subject–object and individual–society relations is one prerequisite of biographical work, knowledge of practical procedures is another. Contributors to the section on 'Examples of biographical methods in use' were asked to spell out their practical as well as their conceptual approaches to the interpretation of biographical material. The purpose was to 'prise open' what has often remained the 'black box' of emergent interpretation and theorising. Authors have been commissioned to integrate, with their substantive research focus, explicit discussion of methodological problems of the individual researcher and research panels as they struggle for the best interpretation/theorisation of their material. We think that this provides clarity for the reader as to how the complex activity of interpretation and inference actually happens.

Inevitably, though, accounting for interviewing procedures is an integral part of interview analysis, since the form of the material is dependent on the interviewing approach and technique. It is not the intention of the book to cover all aspects of biographical research; the question of theoretic as opposed to quota sampling, for example, is not discussed (Lummis 1987: ch. 4), nor are questions of 'ownership' or feedback to interviewees.

The straight 'narrative interview' is a feature of several reports. Wengraf describes the influential biographic-interpretive methodology (BIM) of analysing primarily narrative interviews and identifies a precise form of the 'single question' asking for a life story. A more selective, and more complex, narrative question is discussed in Jones and Rupp, together with the means of handling and using such complexity. Bornat *et al.* also discuss the strength of the interviewee's agenda as a primary determinant of the direction of the interview. Topic-centred semi-structured interviewing was used by Bornat *et al.*, while Hollway and Jefferson combine standardised questions with asking for biographic narratives.[7] While much of the work reported here is based on single-interviewer interviews, some used joint interviewers. Hollway and Jefferson discuss how they alternated the task of interviewing and analysis between them in a team of two.

The longest-running, post-1945 attempt to lay down procedures for the process of interpretation of qualitative data such as life-history interviews is that of the (now splitting) 'grounded theory school' invented in its current formulation by Glaser and Strauss (1967), documented in great detail by Strauss (1987), but then recently codified by Strauss and Corbin (1990) in a way then strongly criticised by Glaser (1992) as a betrayal. Some uses of that approach has fed into much British qualitative research (e.g. Coffey and Atkinson 1996) if only to provide a justification for allowing theory to emerge and change during analysis and to provide a stimulus to thinking about and exposing the act of interpreting qualitative data.

The understanding of the biographies of particular historical agents in particular historical contexts requires some mode or other – and there is a variety – of combining relatively objective and relatively subjective data. This needs to be done in a way that makes sense as a result of a process of analysis and interpretation that is, as far as possible, publicly inspectable and publicly debatable.

The BIM school, the philosophy of which is outlined in Fischer-Rosenthal and in Wengraf, has an elaborate procedure for 'case reconstruction'. This centres on an account of the interaction of the 'lived life' and the 'told story', constructed from two separate and contrasting analyses: a 'biographical data analysis' and the 'thematic field analysis' of the text (Schiebel, Jones and Rupp, Chamberlayne and Spano). Apitzsch and Inowlocki give an account of how Schütze came to focus on formal textual features as a means of uncovering the informant's 'autobiographical theory', and the 'identity work achieved in argumentation'. They also detail the four 'process structures' which he found operating, whether singly or in combination, in narrative interviews. Hollway and Jefferson stress the importance of 'narrations' (in the sense of dramatised stories) in revealing the 'defences' of the interviewee, which provides the means of going beyond the 'autobiographical theory' put forward by the interviewee.

Other methods of analysis are illustrated in several chapters. King departed in her research on caring regimes from the full 'case structure' analysis of the BIM method in favour of a greater emphasis on 'class, welfare systems, and family relationships'. Hollway and Jefferson's mode of analysing their cases is governed by the decision to explore certain theoretical questions relating to anxiety and fear of crime, and a consonance between Kleinian theory and their methodological as well as their theoretical concerns. Rustin also argues for the importing of psychoanalytically informed models and forms of description into biographical research, but Squire is more cautious, warning about the danger of those not trained in psychoanalysis making 'psychoanalytic statements' about people they have not psychoanalysed but have only 'narratively' or 'semistructuredly' interviewed. Squire is more oriented to genre analysis, and Bornat *et al.* are also concerned with negotiations between public and private forms of discourse.

The use of group workshops for the collective analysis of data, which poses important questions for research resourcing and organisation, is often influenced by Strauss (1987). Highlighted in all the BIM work and in the cross-cultural study described by Cooper, the rationale of collective analysis is briefly discussed in Wengraf.

Typically, the 'object of study' being illuminated by biographical research is that of the individual. However Bertaux and Delcroix take the 'family case history' as the unit of analysis, and Bornat *et al.* are also concerned with family change over time, and with the different perspectives of different generations. In the second phase of the SOSTRIS project a biographical approach has been applied in agency studies, to illuminate the 'life' of an organisation (*SOSTRIS Working Paper 8: Innovative Social Agencies in Europe*).

The context-situatedness of any researched life is discussed by Apitzsch and Inowlocki who stress the 'embeddedness of the biographical account in social macro-structures' and by Wengraf who discusses the mutual implication of lives, stories, contexts and subjectivities in any analysis of a given life. However, for many purposes, the identification of a unique case is not and cannot be sufficient, and generally the single case as presented for publication has been selected from others. Indeed Bertaux and Delcroix argue that the study of a single case cannot and should not be sufficient for sociological research, while Wengraf asserts that even the study of a single case involves mobilising tacit or explicit knowledge about other cases – including fictional representations, as Rustin argues powerfully.

Yet to understand lives and the conditions of living, sociologically oriented biographical research can be interested in their 'unique individuals' as illustrating typical patterns or mechanisms, worlds and processes: Bertaux explored the lives of bakers (Bertaux 1981, 1997); Rosenthal *et al.* explored the lives of three generations, the families of victims and perpetrators of Nazi persecution (Rosenthal 1998). In this volume, the worlds of 'carers' are explored in Germany by King and in Britain by Jones and Rupp and, differently, by Middleton and Hewitt. The effectiveness of using individual case analysis in the study of large-scale social transformations, in which continuities of context may well occur, is illustrated in the transition from Communism of the former East Germany (Andrews, Segert and Zierke), and from traditional occupations to post-Fordism (Chamberlayne and Spanò). Bertaux and Delcroix make reference to studies of family experiences after the Russian Revolution of 1917. Bertaux (1997) has used the term 'ethnosociology' to refer to biographical research oriented towards and used for analysis of social structures, mechanisms and processes, and the SOSTRIS project has characterised its adaptation of the biographic-interpretive method in comparative work as 'socio-biography'.

Although the material may be gathered by means of biographical research, that which is being studied may not be the lives of 'whole persons' at all: Bertaux and Delcroix use studies of linked lives to cast light on 'networks of relationships', and on the 'transmission of cultural capital'. Drawing on Bourdieu, Segert and Zierke are interested in the continuities and discontinuities of types of *habitus* in former East Germany. The SOSTRIS project has been concerned to discuss the interrelationship between societal strategies, and the strategies of individuals or families in a socially precarious situation.

Since the essence of case-study analysis all too often lies in particularised detail, and since the 'validity' of the analysis is usually shown through the detailing of the analysis, there are inevitable constraints on the number of cases which can be presented. In this volume Segert and Zierke, and Neusüss and Maejde, are concerned to develop typologies, or at least a range of types. In both instances the cases are used as illustrative material in developing theory. Wengraf discusses types and typologies in general (see also Demazière and Dubar 1997). There is one single case study (Jones and Rupp), but more usually chapters present two contrasting cases, as in Chamberlayne and Spanò, Schiebel, Hollway and Jefferson.

Clearly a theory-driven (Pawson 1996) and theory-generating research programme will always move beyond the level of description, but Chamberlayne and Spano stress that 'generating insights into social processes' is not the same as 'generalising about them'. Issues of cross-cultural comparison are more fully explored in Cooper. Some expositions are explicitly focused on the advancing of theory: Bornat *et al.* and Hollway and Jefferson. Other expositions are concerned to use the 'orienting concepts' (Layder 1998) of theory, but do not aim primarily or solely to produce a 'conclusion' where 'theoretical significance' can be summed up in 'proven propositions'. Chamberlayne and Spanò discuss the way in which initial concepts of modernisation were enriched and questioned by the cases of lived experience – 'attention to particularity at the micro-level was a powerful means of enriching macro-level conceptualisation, generating more differentiated thinking'.

Applications

In making a case for the theoretical and methodological relevance of biographical research we are also mindful of the need to emphasise the social relevance of this approach. The method itself is suggestive of ways of working which foreground the individual and which lay stress on valuing knowledge of a personal history in arriving at an understanding of the choices which people make and the constraints and assumptions as well as the decisions which structure their lives. At the same time, theorising from biographical evidence can lead to fresh insights and creative approaches in work with disadvantaged or vulnerable groups and individuals.

While the chapters included here illustrate the theoretical significance of the 'biographical turn' for the continuing development of social science practice, in most cases, they also demonstrate an accompanying concern: a commitment to relevance and use. Biographical analysis is, by definition, person-centred, and perhaps for this reason a tendency to link research to application and to establish a connection with social policy outcomes should not be unexpected. An approach which seeks to understand the link between individual agency and wider social structures and processes has relevance for professional practice, highlighting as it does the lived experience of empowering policies or of poverty and social exclusion. This 'applied' tendency contributes in relation to issues of process, difference and outcome. Each of these has implications for practice and policy which are highly significant.

Some chapters provide examples of a method which is primarily informed by classical theories of *verstehen* and the construction of individual meaning (see Hazzard on Dilthey). Narrative interviewing and objective hermeneutics provide the means to maintain the detachment and systematisation of observations which are to be elicited from text. Under such conditions, though the objective is the understanding and representation of individual lives, the issue of authorship is straightforwardly simple. There is an assumed detachment, temporally, physically, socially and emotionally, between the subject, the data and the interpreter. Authorship ultimately rests with the interpreter. Fischer-Rosenthal's chapter argues for a 'neutral position', for example, suggesting that biographical research can play a role in mediating the divergent interests and respective blindspots of professional and service user worlds and understanding the limiting and enabling nature of structures for service users.

Other chapters suggest a less clear-cut distinction and a more difficult process. Authorship, like identity, is something to be contested and established. It emerges through the process of biographical interviewing. So, for example, Hazzard demonstrates a specialised example of inter-subjective empathy and understanding in a clinical setting, making explicit the possibility of mutual understanding. Under the influence of this perspective a biographical account is seen as emergent from the interview situation, this latter being an added factor in interpretation. This perspective is observed through the interview and incorporated through a range of methods owing much to the grounded theory methodology developed by Glaser and Strauss (1967). Among chapters included here, those by Middeton and Hewitt, Hollway and Jefferson and by Squire best illustrate an awareness of interview process. Bornat *et al.* offer an additional dimension, the framing of biographical narrative by the preoccupations of later life.

Approaches to biographical work which allow for difference in the making and interpretation of accounts are also suggestive of a perspective which goes beyond simple categorisation. So, for example, chapters by Segert and Zierke, King and Chamberlayne and Spanò draw out issues from case-study approaches which include resource inequality, social positioning and political heritage. In each case links are made to social problems of adjustment, change and management which have direct implications for the emergence of sensitive and relevant social policy development and implementation. Neusüss and Maedje present the example of service users understanding and using services differently, challenging official ideologies, rendering them obsolete, perhaps even creating a 'new model of social reproduction'. They illustrate the need for finely tuned timing in the use of benefits to suit particular, and different, life strategies and constraints.

Finally the issue of outcomes in biographical work. Why should social policy researchers concern themselves with the detailed reconstruction of individual life stories? In the past, the systems that emerged in the two Germanys each gave rise to a need to challenge bureaucracy and to give expression to ordinary people. Also, there was a desire to achieve self-understanding in the context of the gross disruptions and inhumanities of the twentieth century. Biography in Germany, as the chapters by Andrews, Schiebel and by Segert and Zierke demonstrate, became a means to deal with the system and with history, a way of defining need in broadly humanistic terms, a way to identify opportunities and choices for the future. Schiebel, for example, demonstrates the gains to be made from helping youths to reinterpret their familial, political and social contexts and in maintaining a sense of personal connection with them. She argues that it is the alienation of the familial world and a drive to censoriousness which has driven them into right-wing group membership.

Despite a different history, those writing in a British context demonstrate a similar drive. Here too, biography is seen as an alternative narrative, the voice of the non-professional, the user of services and a means to challenge a system which substitutes efficiency for sociability, economy for need, and public panic for individual experience. Biography seen in these contexts becomes a precondition for effective human agency both for welfare subjects and the professionals working with them. So, for example, Jones and Rupp illustrate the importance of sensitive understanding of inner-worlds and emotional blockages and the interaction of those with complex cultures and contexts (of families, migration, services), in order for professional interventions to be effective. Narrative interviews introduce the possibility of such disclosures and self-understandings becoming manifest. Similar possibilities emerge from chapters by Bornat *et al.*, Middleton and Hewitt, and Squire.

For many professionals and practitioners working in human service settings the need to make sense of the interaction between social mechanisms and social arrangements on individual life strategies is an abiding preoccupation. Bertaux and Delcroix's chapter, with its focus on the significance of the historical and sociological determinants and the repertoires available to individuals and families, makes a powerful case for the relevance of, and potential contribution of, biographical methods to the knowledge and skill bases of professionals and practitioners whose concern is the empowerment of the people they work with. (For an example see also Murard 1999, and a discussion in *SOSTRIS Working Paper 9: Final Report*.)

The authors writing in this collection are taking part in a continuing dialogue, which, as we have suggested, spans national cultures, academic traditions, discipline barriers and academic discourses, and which has raised issues of purpose and ethics in qualitative research. We see the book's publication as maintaining the momentum of the 'biographical turn' while sustaining its critical force well into the twenty-first century. In positioning ourselves in this way, we are mindful of all the people who have engaged with us as we assembled and edited the chapters. In particular we acknowledge the help of Zoe Fearnley in preparing the manuscript and much else. We'd also like to thank Judy Gahagan for difficult translation work, and the participants at countless workshops, seminars and conferences, locally, nationally and internationally, who have engaged in the discussions and debates which have contributed to this volume.

Notes

1 Community history was another important contributory strand to the development of biographical methods.
2 The importance of such thinking has been belatedly recognised in the case of German unification, where the 'imposition' of the Federal system of welfare on East Germany cut across and failed to utilise existing East German social infrastructures and forms of social capital (Pollack and Pickel 1998; Chamberlayne 1998).
3 An argument made by Andrew Blaikie at the IVth World Congress of Gerontology in Berlin, July 1999.
4 See for example the four volume series *The International Yearbook of Oral History and Life Stories*, Passerini (ed.) 1992; Bertaux and Thompson (eds) 1993; Benmayor and Skotnes (eds) 1994; Leydesdorff *et al.* (eds) 1996.
5 In 1978 the *ad hoc* biography group of the Ninth World Congress of the International Sociological Association had, according to Bertaux (1981: 1), some twenty papers presented by sociologists from fifteen countries, and almost as many approaches. By 1998, within the well-established Biography and Society Research Committee at the Fourteenth World Congress, there were over eighty papers scheduled from twenty-five countries.
6 It may be understandable that a nation in which public and ritual grieving for sufferings under Nazism have been repressed, should be particularly preoccupied by issues of suffering and disorder.
7 Elsewhere Hollway and Jefferson (1997) provide a personal account of shifting from semi-structured interviewing to biographical-narrative interviewing.

References

Adams, J., Bornat, J. and Prickett, M. (1998) 'Discovering the Present in Stories about the Past', in A. Brechin, J. Walmsley, J. Katz and S. Peace (eds), *Care*

Matters: Concepts, Practice, Research in Health and Social Care, London: Sage.

Ageing and Society (1996) 'Special Issue on Ageing, Biography and Practice' 16(6).

Archer, M.S. (1995) *Realist Social Theory: The Morphogenic Approach*, Cambridge: Cambridge University Press.

—— (1996) 'Social Integration and System Integration: Developing the Distinction', *Sociology* 30(4): 679–99.

Atkinson, D. (1997) *An Auto/Biographical Approach to Learning Disability Research*, Aldershot: Ashgate.

Benmayor, R. and Skotnes, A. (eds) (1994) *Migration and Identity*, Oxford: Oxford University Press.

Bertaux, D. (ed.) (1981) *Biography and Society: The Life History Approach in the Social Sciences*, London: Sage.

—— (1982) 'The Life Course Approach as a Challenge to the Social Sciences', in T. Hareven and K.J. Adams (eds), *Ageing and Life Course Transitions: An Interdisciplinary Perspective*, London: Tavistock.

—— (1997) *Les Récits de Vie*, Paris: Nathan.

Bertaux, D. and Kohli, M. (1984) 'The Life Story Approach: A Continental View', *Annual Review of Sociology* 10: 215–37.

Bertaux, D. and Thompson, P. (eds) (1993) *Family Models, Myths and Memories*, Oxford: Oxford University Press.

—— (1998) *Pathways to Social Mobility*, Cambridge: Cambridge University Press.

Biggs, S. (1993) *Understanding Ageing, Images, Attitudes and Professional Practice*, Buckingham: Open University Press.

Bornat, J. (1989) 'Oral History as a Social Movement: Reminiscence and Older People', *Oral History* 17(2): 16–20.

Breckner, R. (1998) 'The Biographical-Interpretive Method: Principles and Procedures', *SOSTRIS Working Paper 2: Case Study Materials: The Early Retired*, London: Centre for Biography in Social Policy, University of East London.

Bruner, J. (1995) 'The Autobiographical Process', *Sociology* 43(2/3): 177–9.

Chamberlain, M. (1975) *Fenwomen: A Portrait of Women in an English Village*, London: Quartet.

Chamberlayne, P. (1997) 'Social Exclusion: Sociological Traditions and National Contexts, *SOSTRIS Working Paper 1: Social Exclusion in Comparative Perspective*, London: Centre for Biography in Social Policy, University of East London.

—— (1998) 'Changing Cultures of Care: Underlying Ideologies, Policies and Practices in Post-Communist and Post-Fordist Societies', in S. Ramon (ed.), *The Interface Between Social Work and Social Policy*, Birmingham: Venture Press.

Chamberlayne, P., Cooper, A., Freeman R. and Rustin, M. (1999) *Welfare and Culture in Europe: Towards a New Paradigm in Social Policy*, London: Jessica Kingsley Publishers.

Clasen, J., Gould, A. and Vincent, J. (eds) (1998) *Voices Within and Without: Responses to Longterm Unemployment in Germany, Sweden and Britain*, Bristol: Policy Press.

Coffey, A. and Atkinson, P. (1996) *Making Sense of Qualitative Data: Complementary Research Strategies*, Thousand Oaks, CA: Sage.

Coleman, P. (1986) *Ageing and Reminiscence Processes*, Chichester: Wiley.

Coleman, P.G., Ivani-Chalian, C. and Robinson, M. (1993) 'Self Esteem and its Sources: Stability and Change in Later Life', *Ageing and Society* 13(2): 171–92.

Crook, S. (1998) 'Minotaurs and Other Monsters: Everyday Life in Recent Social Theory', *Sociology* 32(3): 523–40.

Demazière, D. and Dubar, C. (1997) *Analyser les entretiens biographiques: l'exemple de récits d'insertion*, Paris: Nathan.

Dobroff, R. (1984) 'A Time for Reclaiming the Past', *Journal of Gerontological Social Work* 7(1–2): xvii–xix.

Frisch, M. (1990) *A Shared Authority: Essays on the Craft and Meaning of Oral and Public History*, Albany, NY: State University of New York Press.

Fukuyama, F. (1992) *The End of History and the Last Man*, London: Hamish Hamilton.

Giddens, A. (1984) *The Constitution of Society*, Cambridge: Polity.

—— (1990) 'Structuration Theory and Sociological Analysis', in J. Clark, C. Modgil and S. Modgil (eds), *Anthony Giddens: Consensus and Controversy*, Brighton: Falmer.

—— (1991) *Modernity and Self Identity: Self and Society in the Late Modern Age*, Cambridge: Polity Press.

Giele, J. (1998) 'Innovation in the Typical Life Course', in J.Z. Giele and G. Elder (ed.), *Methods of Life Course Research: Qualitative and Quantitative Approaches*, Thousand Oaks, CA: Sage.

Gittins, D. (1977) 'Women's Work and Family Size Between the Wars', *Oral History* 5(2): 84–100.

Glaser, B. (1992) *The Basics of Grounded Theory Analysis: Emergence Versus Forcing*, Mill Valley: Sociology Press.

Glaser, B. and Strauss, A. (1967) *The Discovery of Grounded Theory: Strategies for Qualitative Research*, New York: Aldine de Gruyter.

Gluck, S.B. and Patai, D. (eds) (1991) *Women's Words: The Feminist Practice of Oral History*, New York and London: Routledge.

Gottfried, H. (1998) 'Beyond Patriarchy? Theorising Gender and Class', *Sociology* 32(3): 451–68.

Greimas, A.J. (1986) *Semantiques Structurales*, Paris: Presses Universitaires de France.

Grele, R. (1985) *Envelopes of Sound: The Art of Oral History*, Chicago, IL: Precedent Publishing.

Gubrium, J. and Holstein, J. (1995a) 'Life Course Malleability: Biographical Work and Deprivatization', *Sociological Inquiry* 65(2): 207–23.

—— (1995b) 'Biographical Work and New Ethnography', in R. Josselson and A. Lieblich (eds), *Interpreting Life Experience: The Narrative Study of Lives*, vol. 3, London: Sage.

Hall, C. (1977) 'Married Women at Home in Birmingham in the 1920s and 1930s', *Oral History* 5(2): 62–83.

Heinritz, C. and Rammstedt, A. (1991) 'L'Approche Biographique en France', *Cahiers Internationaux de Sociologie* 91: 330–70.

Hollway, W. and Jefferson, T. (1997) 'Eliciting Narrative through the In-depth Interview', *Qualitative Inquiry* 3(1): 53–70.

Kuhn, T. (1960) *The Structure of Scientific Revolutions*, Chicago, IL: Chicago University Press.

Layder, D. (1998) *Sociological Practice: Linking Theory and Social Research*, London: Sage.

Leisering, L. and Walker, R. (eds) (1998) *The Dynamics of Modern Society: Poverty, Policy and Welfare*, Bristol: Policy Press.

Leydesdorff, S., Passerini, L. and Thompson, P. (eds) (1996) *Gender and Memory*, Oxford: Oxford University Press.

Liddington, J. and Norris, J. (1978) *One Hand Tied Behind Us: The Rise of the Women's Suffrage Movement*, London: Virago.

Lummis, T. (1987) *Listening to History: The Authenticity of Oral Evidence*, London: Hutchinson.

McAdams, D. (1993) *The Stories We Live By: Personal Myths and the Making of the Self*, New York: Morrow.

McDonald, T.J. (ed.) (1996) *The Historical Turn in the Human Sciences*, Ann Arbor, MI: University of Michigan.

Mills, C.W. (1967) *The Sociological Imagination*, Oxford: Oxford University Press.

Mouzelis, N. (1989) 'Restructuring Structuration Theory', *Sociological Review* 37(4): 613–35.

—— (1995) *Sociological Theory: What Went Wrong?*, London: Routledge.

Murard, N. (1999) 'From Confidence in Biographic Narratives to Confidence in Social Policy', *SOSTRIS Working Paper 8: Innovative Social Agencies in Europe*, London: Centre for Biography in Social Policy, University of East London.

Newton, T. (1999) 'Power, Subjectivity and British Industrial and Organisational Sociology: The Relevance of the Work of Norbert Elias', *Sociology* 33(2): 411–40.

Oakley, A. (1981) 'Interviewing Women: A Contradiction in Terms', in H. Roberts (eds), *Doing Feminist Research*, London: Routledge.

Oral History (1998) Issue entitled 'Memory Trauma and Ethics' 26(2).

Passerini, L. (1979) 'Work Ideology and Consensus under Italian Fascism', *History Workshop* 8: 84–92.

—— (ed.) (1992) *Memory and Totalitarianism*, Oxford: Oxford University Press.

Pawson, R. (1996) 'Theorizing the Interview', *Journal of Sociology* 47(2): 295–314.

Personal Narratives Group (eds) (1989) *Interpreting Women's Lives: Feminist Theory and Personal Narratives*, Bloomington, IN: Indiana University Press.

Phillipson, C. (1998) *Reconstructing Old Age: New Agendas in Social Theory and Practice*, London: Sage.

Plummer, K. (1983) *Documents of Life: An Introduction to the Problems and Literature of a Humanistic Method*, London: George Allen and Unwin.

Pollack, D. and Pickel, G. (1998) 'Die Ostdeutsche Identitaet: Erbe des DDR-Sozialismus oder Produkt der Wiedervereinigung?', *Aus Politik und Zeitsechichte* B 41–2: 9–23.

Popular Memory Group (1998) 'Popular Memory: Theory Politics and Memory', in R. Perks and A. Thomas (eds), *Oral History: a Reader*, London: Routledge.

Portelli, A. (1981) 'The Peculiarities of Oral History', *History Workshop* 12: 96–107.

—— (1991) *The Death of Luigi Trastulli and Other Stories*, New York: State University of New York Press.

Ricoeur, P. (1984) *Time and Narrative*, Chicago, IL: University of Chicago Press.

Roberts, E. (1975) 'Learning and Living: Socialisation Outside School, *Oral History* 3(2): 14–28.

Rosenthal, G. (1993) 'Reconstruction of Life Stories: Principles of Selection in Generating Stories for Narrative Biographical Interviews', in R. Josselson and A. Lieblich (eds), *The Narrative Study of Lives*, 1, Thousand Oaks, CA: Sage, pp.59–91.

—— (ed.) (1998) *The Holocaust in Three Generations: Families of Victims and Perpetrators of the Nazi Regime*, London: Cassell.

Rowbotham, S. and McCrindle, J. (eds) (1977) *Dutiful Daughters: Women Talk about their Lives*, London: Allen Lane.

Ryan, T. and Walker, R. (1999) *Life Story Work*, London: British Agencies for Adoption and Fostering, 3rd edn.

Schafer, R. (1976) *A New Language for Psychoanalysis*, New Haven, CT: Yale University Press.

Sociology (1993) Special Issue 'Auto/Biography in Sociology' 27(1).

Somers, M. (1996) 'Where is Sociology after the Historic Turn? Knowledge Cultures, Narrativity, and Historical Epistemologies', in T.J. McDonald (ed.), *The Historical Turn in the Human Sciences*, Ann Arbor, MI: University of Michigan.

SOSTRIS Working Papers (1988–1999) vols 1–9, London: Centre for Biography in Social Policy, University of East London.

SOSTRIS Working Paper 8: Innovative Social Agencies in Europe (1999) London: Centre for Biography in Social Policy, University of East London.

SOSTRIS Working Paper 9: The Final Report (1999) London: Centre for Biography in Social Policy, University of East London.

Spence, D. (1982) *Narrative Truth and Historical Truth: Meaning and Interpretation in Psychoanalysis*, New York: Norton.

Stanley, L. (1992) *The Auto/Biographical I: Theory and Practice of Feminist Auto/Biography*, Manchester: Manchester University Press.

Strauss, A. (1987) *Qualitative Analysis for Social Scientists*, Cambridge: Cambridge University Press.

Strauss, A and Corbin, J. (1990) *Basics of Qualitative Research: Grounded Theory, Procedures and Techniques*, Newbury Park, CA: Sage.

Thomas, W.I. and Znaniecki, F. (1958) *The Polish Peasant in Europe and America*, New York: Dover.

Thompson, E.P. (1963) *The Making of the English Working Class*, London: Gollancz.

—— (1978) *The Poverty of Theory*, London: Merlin Press.

Thompson, P. (1978) *The Voice of the Past*, Oxford: Oxford University Press; 2nd edn, 1988; 3rd edn, 2000.

Thompson, T. (1981) *Edwardian Childhoods*, London: Routledge and Kegan Paul.

Thomson, A. (1994) *Anzac Memories: Living with the Legend*, Oxford: Oxford University Press.

Thomson, A., Frisch, M. and Hamilton, P. (1994) 'The Memory and History Debates: Some International Perspectives', *Oral History* 22(2): 33–43.

Wallace, J.B. (1992/3) 'Reconsidering the Life Review: The Social Construction of Talk about the Past', *The Gerontologist* 32(1): 120–5.

Walmsley, J. (1995) 'Life History Interviews with People with Learning Disabilities', *Oral History* 23(1): 71–7.

Wrong, D. (1961) 'The Over-socialised Concept of Man in Modern Sociology', *American Journal of Sociology* 26(2): 183–93.

Part 1
Issues of methodology and theory

1 Reflections on the biographical turn in social science

Michael Rustin

Contemporary theories of individualisation (Beck 1992; Giddens 1991, 1992) argue that modern society is giving a new importance to individuals. Where earlier agrarian and industrial societies provided social scripts, which most individuals were expected to follow, contemporary societies throw more responsibility on to individuals to choose their own identities. Social structures – classes, extended families, occupational communities, long-term employment within a firm – which formerly provided strong frames of identity, grow weaker. Simultaneously, society exposes individuals to bombardments of information, alternative versions of how life might be lived, and requires of individuals that they construct an 'authentic' version of themselves, making use of the numerous identity-props which consumer-society makes available. The transition from *The Hidden Injuries of Class* (1972) in Richard Sennett and Jonathan Cobb's classic book of that title, to Sennett's recent study of the children of that generation *The Corrosion of Character* (1998) provides one description of this transition, which Sennett represents as involving as much loss as gain in terms of psychic and moral wellbeing.

Some theorists of this new 'individualised' order view it as embodying the possibility of emancipation. 'Reflexivity' – the possibility to understand and choose the circumstances and rules of one's life – is for some the realisation of a prospect of human emancipation. Although the uncertainties and 'risks' of this situation are recognised, and anxieties are expressed about the social bonds and solidarities that might be necessary to sustain the meaning of individual lives, some writers celebrate this new world of freedom and choice.

Others view individualisation more critically. Foucault noted that individuals were 'produced' through social procedures which were in their own way as coercive as the more collectivised routines of the previous social era. Critics of consumer capitalism have long seen the choices between commodities and the identities packaged with them as superficial, masking dependence on a system which exploits, without satisfying, a human need for authenticity. The concepts of 'risk' and 'individualisation' are viewed by some as a way of celebrating what for the majority is a condition of increased anxiety and insecurity, the consequence of a transfer of economic risk from the owners of capital to those without its advantages. While those better positioned in the labour or capital markets, and able to exploit the opportunities they provide for the management of uncertainty, may gain from this situation, many members of society lose, and might prefer, if offered a choice, a situation where risks were better contained.

Whatever view one takes of the phenomenon of 'individualisation', it is not surprising that a new focus on individuals is having influence on the methods of the social sciences. In such a climate, the time seems right for a fresh methodological turn towards the study of individuals, a turn to biography.

A historical paradox

Individual subjects were 'discovered' (some would say invented or constructed), and became the principal focus of cultural attention, at an earlier stage in modern history. This first happened in the culture and society of early modern Europe. From the late sixteenth century, with increasing momentum, European society became interested in individuals, in their differences from one another, in their imputed psychological depth, their moral value, their capacity for change and development. 'To thine own self be true' Polonius tells his son Laertes in *Hamlet*, echoing in his banal homily the fashionable ideas of the time. The portraits and self-portraits of Rembrandt convey a new dimension of self-reflectiveness and of the passage of time. The printed word, the first and most important kind of disembedding of information from its local context, allowed individuals to make their own sense of other people's experiences, initially in the vernacular translation of the Bible and then in many other kinds of writing. Protestantism required of individuals an intense capacity for self-scrutiny and self-purification. The philosophy of the seventeenth century took as the foundation of knowledge the sensory experiences (Berkeley, Locke, Hume) or the introspected ideas (Descartes, Spinoza) of individuals. The emergence of the novel, in the eighteenth century, enabled readers to reflect on the meaning of lives of persons like themselves and those around them. One of the most influential of these early novels, *Robinson Crusoe*, imagined the life of a person living in a state of virtual isolation and self-sufficiency, giving an emblematic foundation to the idea of the individual. Lyric poetry established the idea of individual sensibility, a subjectivity based on discriminated states of feeling. In Wordsworth's *The Prelude* the idea of a spiritual autobiography achieved its canonical modern form. In Germany, in the same period, the '*bildungsroman*', or narrative of personal development (notably in Goethe's *Wilhelm Meister's Apprenticeship*), established a parallel view of the world through the life-experience of a representative individual. Later on, the drama which had been originally in the forefront of the cultural 'discovery' of the individual (in the plays of the ancient Greek tragedians and in England and France in the sixteenth and seventeenth centuries) reemerged as a significant form of exploration of the complexities of individual life, in the work of Ibsen, Strindberg and Chekhov, and in a succession of later dramatists from Miller to Beckett. From its inception, the cinema became an exceptionally powerful and popular means of establishing images of individual identity, worth and beauty, popularising the idealisation of the individual through its invention of 'the star'. These various kinds of images and reflections of individual lives are in the broadest sense 'biographical', even though the biographies they construct and represent are for the most part 'imaginary' or 'fictional' in quality.

The paradox is that, while a variety of forms of Western cultural representation have been preoccupied with individuals, and have been working in various imaginative biographical registers for centuries, social science has generally not been sympathetic to these approaches, and has mostly filtered biography out of its fields of interest.[1] Why is this?

The explanation of this paradox, and also of the new possibility of escaping from its grip, lies in the prescriptive conceptions of scientific method which have dominated social scientific inquiry until recently. The power of the natural sciences lay in their methods of generalisation and abstraction, in their capacity to view phenomena through particular perspectives capable of generating knowledge, while blanking out all others. Plainly, in studying the solar system, or natural species, or human bodies, or the chemical elements, filtering out the prior texture of mythical, religious, cultural and emotional associations which such phenomena had for members of a culture was fundamental in enabling them to be seen in new and transformative ways.[2] The capacity to reinterpret, and thereby to gain a new control of, the natural world, required the rejection of previous 'common-sense' understandings, in which religious, aesthetic and moral meanings were as important as factual description and causal explanation.

A particularly sharp conjunction of 'modern' and 'pre-modern' ways of experiencing and analysing the natural world is described by Robert Sack's (1986) work on the North American settlers' understanding of land and

place. What for the indigenous Indian population were places deeply invested with cultural meaning were for the settlers mere tracts of territory,
measured by their potential economic yields. It was difficult for the communities holding these two world-views even to understand one another.

The extreme high (or low) point of this insistence on impersonal
objectivity and generality was the philosophical doctrine of logical positivism, developed under the intellectual sway of physics in the early part
of this century. This argued that statements which referred neither to
observable facts, nor logical relations between their elements, were
without meaning (Ayer 1936).

Thus, modelling themselves on the natural scientists, human biologists
and psychologists set out to construct models of body and mind which
described uniformities and regularities, and which enabled human
behaviour to be understood 'objectively', that is in terms of its abstracted
common attributes. Interests in individual idiosyncrasy and variation were
seen as impediments to this ambition to create a generalising science of
man. To explain the aspect of behaviour and social organisation that
interested them, the economists constructed an ideal-typical model of
rational actors which similarly abstracted from the full range of human
motives and meanings, with powerful explanatory effect. The intellectual
ancestors of both scientific psychology and economics were the empiricist
philosophers – Hobbes, Locke, Hume and the utilitarians – who had
earlier stripped human motivation down to what they deemed to be its
fundamental atomistic elements.

Exceptions to scientism: phenomenology and psychoanalysis

There were two major exceptions to this dominant approach in the
human sciences. The first of these was a minority idealist or subjectivist
tradition within sociology originating with Dilthey. This influenced the
mainstream of sociology through Max Weber, leading to the compromise
between idealist and empiricist methodologies embodied in his prescription that explanation should be 'adequate at the level of cause and
adequate at the level of meaning'. The idealist tradition, especially in
German philosophy, had a continuing influence on the social sciences via
phenomenology and hermeneutics. This tradition influenced American
interactionist sociology, via Husserl and Alfred Schütz, and Husserl's
influence was also significant in France, via Sartre, Merleau-Ponty, and
Ricoeur. Although rationality ruled in England via a dominant philosophy of empiricism, in German-speaking culture these issues were more
contested, even though the rival idealist and empiricist perspectives had

both to be sustained in exile, and then renewed in the Federal Republic after the war (Adorno *et al.* 1976). In France, the idea of subjectivity was marginalised in a different way, through the structuralist and post-structuralist movements, whose intellectual programme was to insist on the construction of individual subjects through systems of language and culture. Even where sociologies of action and practice remained important, as in the work of Pierre Bourdieu, questions of individual subjectivity were subordinated to the mapping of social structures, which were seen to shape the competition of collective actors by allocating resources of material, social and cultural capital. This idealist or phenomenological tradition has been the primary source of biographical approaches in social science, both directly through its absorption by sociologists in Germany and France, and indirectly via its hybridisation with symbolic interactionist perspectives in the United States. These connections are explored elsewhere in this volume.

A second important exception to the dominant anti-subjectivist current of social science was psychoanalysis, which was unusual among the social sciences in rejecting the opposition between scientific and imaginative methods, between typification and the investigation of the particular. Freud wanted to develop a new psychological science which would provide causal explanations of mental states, and to connect these to their biological basis in instinctual drives. He saw himself as a scientist, yet his primary method of investigation was the case study, seen as the history elicited from patients and those around them, and more particularly as what could be learned through the method of psychoanalytic treatment, with its distinctive method of interpretation of dreams and free associations. Freud constructed his typified models of psychic structures from individual cases. Other psychoanalysts tested Freud's findings both through investigation of the application of his theoretical models to their clinical experience, and through identifying similarities and differences between their own cases and those described by Freud and other analysts. The development of psychoanalysis post-Freud has followed this method. The investigations of cases in the consulting room, making increasing use of the transference and counter-transference as sources of understanding, have been the main empirical resource for the development of psychoanalytic theories and techniques. The transmission and reproduction of psychoanalytic ideas has always taken place to a great extent through clinical examples, through the 'family resemblances' between one instance of a typical psychic structure in the consulting room and another. Without such clinical illustration and exemplification, psychoanalytic theories appear scarcely intelligible abstractions, and where the field relies too heavily on abstracted theory, it does not make much progress.

In its insistence on the 'whole person' as the object of study, and on the necessity to understand non-rational aspects of mental life as constitutive of human nature, psychoanalysis refused to accept the legitimacy of prevailing orthodoxies in the human sciences. The claims made by Freud for the scientific status of psychoanalysis were vigorously disputed, and psychoanalysis gained little influence in academic psychology or psychiatry, in Britain at least. But, on the other side of the 'two cultures' divide, it was extremely influential. The resources that psychoanalysis provided for reflecting on disturbing and poorly understood aspects of the self were widely taken up, in particular in cultural metropolises such as Vienna, Berlin, London, New York, Paris and Buenos Aires where the educated congregated in the most contested and open cultural spaces. The fact that psychoanalysis could be sustained wherever individual patients were willing to pay psychoanalysts to analyse them made it possible for psychoanalysis, like modernist literature and art, to flourish even if universities and scientific establishments had little time for it (Rustin 1997, 1999). In fact, psychoanalytic ideas became part of everyday life, and were particularly influential in the arts, where the idea that the mind might not be transparent to itself and that communication often took place in unintended, over-determined, or metaphorical ways, was a stimulus to imaginative work. Since production in the arts did not usually take the form of following explicit rules and protocols, and often took as its subject-matter experiences which seemed to fall outside the domain of scientific understanding, psychoanalysis' doubtful and ambiguous status as a scientific discipline was little obstacle to its influence in the arts and humanities.

In fact, argument about the scientific status of psychoanalysis has continued to take place within the psychoanalytic movement, as well as between psychoanalysts and scientific psychologists. While Freud himself was emphatic that he wished to create a science whose theories would be testable, and which would enable causal relations to be discovered, many psychoanalysts felt more comfortable working with ideas of meaning rather than of causal determination. The organisation of personality by reference to instincts, drives and desires, which had been important in Freud's early work, developed into a theory of personality governed by structures of relationship to internal and external objects. This development began in Freud's own work – for example, his paper *Mourning and Melancholia* is based on the idea of relation to an internalised concept of a loved person – and was developed further by his successors. Melanie Klein's concept of the paranoid-schizoid and depressive positions is based on the idea of a relation to 'internal objects' as providing an unconscious template which shapes individuals' relationships to persons in their external world, and is in turn shaped and constituted by their experiences of such others especially in early life. These unconscious structures of mind are the primary theoretical objects of this school of psychoanalysis. Some argue that such structures embody causal hypotheses; others prefer accounts which describe patterns of thought and action, and think of psychic structures in terms of meaning and coherence, not cause and effect.

It is clear in any case that the essence of all psychoanalytic method depends on the interpretation of descriptions of states of mind or mental acts (dreams, desires, actions) in terms of more abstract models of mind. Psychoanalysis moves between the phenomenological details of what patients say, as these are understood and interpreted by their analysts, and more generalised concepts and classifications of states of mind. An analysand will be understood at a given moment to be in a state of projective identification, or in a state of Oedipal jealousy, or to be narcissistic in libidinal or destructive ways, or to be experiencing persecutory or depressive anxiety. Or an individual, a child for example, may be deeply affected by the state of mind of loved persons, intruded into by their depression or anxiety, or deprived of emotional nourishment by their withdrawal of responsive attention.

States of mind and relationship that psychoanalysts have tried to map conceptually, by classifications which one might think of as the psychoanalytic equivalent of ideal-types,[3] have at the same time been the imaginative subject of poets, novelists and artists. While the psychoanalysts were exploring the extreme and often unconscious responsiveness of individuals to the states of mind of others, writers such as D.H. Lawrence, Virginia Woolf, Samuel Beckett, or Sylvia Plath, were describing parallel susceptibilities as states of mind which they located in particular imagined persons. Works of 'fiction' have paradoxically been able to come closer to the truths of subjective experience than either generalising works of science, which fail to capture the particularity and immediacy of lived lives, or factual descriptions of individuals, whose common defect is a lack of coherence and connectedness, a sufficient sense of 'the essential'. It is for this reason that many people's understanding of the human world, and the store of ideas they have for making sense of it, has probably been more shaped by so-called 'fictional' works – including films, plays, novels, television serials – than by works of social science, whether theoretical or descriptive. It has been said that American gangsters learned how to behave 'in role' by going to the movies. Most people can probably remember moments in which they looked for some external definition of this kind for their own uncertain identities. This seems to be one of the main social functions of the cultural industries, promoting fashions not only in commodities but also in life-styles and self-presentations.

The 'cultural turn' in the social sciences

The relatively firm boundaries between 'scientific' and 'imaginative' ways of understanding human lives and the societies in which they were lived began to be undermined in the 1960s, by a number of currents of thought. T.S. Kuhn's *The Structure of Scientific Revolutions* (1962) itself initiated something like a revolution in the understanding of science, demonstrating that scientific understanding was itself the outcome of a social process like any other, and that the apparent objectivity and unanimity of 'science' in relation to its objects of study did not stand up well to investigation of the development, through argument and conflict, of actual scientific beliefs. Kuhn, and subsequent researchers in the field of the sociology and anthropology of science, introduced a new pluralism to the understanding of scientific knowledge, showing that scientific knowledge came in many varieties, and that its warrants to truth always depended on the consensus of particular scientific communities. Fierce arguments continue between defenders of the objectivity and absolute truth of science, and those who infer from Kuhn's sociological account that all such claims are relative to the interests and norms of those who make them. Bruno Latour (1987; Latour and Woolgar 1986), one of Kuhn's most important successors in the sociology of science, suggests that this choice is falsely posed. He argues that truths about the world are necessarily mediated by human perceptions. Even though nature has its own existence and attributes, and the effects of these enable us to discriminate between true propositions and false ones, there can be no direct revelation of these truths. What scientists bring to scientific inquiry unavoidably contributes to what science discovers.

The effect of this sociological approach was to broaden the understanding of science, and expose its actual diversity. It became easier as a result to recognise the validity of methodologies, including qualitative and interpretive approaches in the human sciences, hitherto deemed to belong more to the field of the arts than of science, the social sciences having occupied what had seemed to be an uneasy no man's land between them.

While the absolutist claims of science were being called into question, a development was taking place in some of the arts and humanities that converged with it, to bring about the broad change in the social sciences known as the 'cultural' or 'linguistic turn' (Rorty 1967; Chaney 1994; Jameson 1998). This development, in literary and cultural theory, sought to question absolutist claims which were the obverse of those made on behalf of the hard scientists. While science had insisted on the objectivity of nature, humanists had asserted the authenticity and autonomy of the individual subject. Structuralist and post-structuralist literary and cultural critics began in the 1960s to adopt a more systematic or 'scientific' approach to the analysis of language and other symbolic systems. They observed that meaning is always constructed through conventions and expectations of particular kinds, and is not the spontaneous creation of autonomous individuals. An extreme version of this asserted the 'death of the author', and looked instead to interpret works of art as the synthesis of a variety of culturally given genres or 'scripts'. Just as the sociological critique of science had undermined the idea of an Archimedean point of objective understanding of nature, so structuralist and post-structuralist accounts of textual determination undermined the idea of an absolute individual authenticity, the mirror-opposite of scientism.

These linked paradigm shifts – that were also sustained by idealistic and pragmatist developments in philosophy, which gave priority to 'forms of life' (Wittgenstein 1953) and to consensus based on shared interests and norms as the main legitimation of belief (Rorty 1980) – gave a new weight to cultural norms as the reality through which all understanding had to be reflexively mediated.

The recognition of the cultural variability or relativity of understandings reflected, as major intellectual revolutions usually do, changes in the world as well as in the models by which it was interpreted. The principal change was the widespread challenge to cultural authority which took place from the 1960s onwards, as new 'voices' of generation, gender, class, ethnicity and value demanded to be heard. Dominant 'enlightenment' world-views which had legitimised the 'improving' missions of imperialism, and which were institutionalised in two opposed versions in the Cold War, began to be undermined. Established cultural elites started to lose some of their power, and affluence, information flows and mass education brought about the beginnings of a kind of cultural democracy. The 'cultural turn' provided resources for reflecting on emergent differences of world-view.[4]

From the cultural to a biographical turn?

It is at this juncture that we must consider the place of biographical method in the social and cultural sciences, and its possibilities. It by no means follows, because a cultural and linguistic turn has taken place, that a biographical turn necessarily follows. The history of biographical methods in the social sciences seems to have been one of fits and starts, moments of creativity having usually been followed by a return to a normal marginal position. And as we have shown, the cultural turn is by no means automatically convergent with a subjectivist or biographical approach. An initial effect of the cultural turn was to deconstruct ideas of individual autonomy and authenticity which had hitherto been the main ground by which the 'imaginative' disciplines of the humanities maintained their distinction from the sciences. Once all the decodable attributes of individual expression have been identified and traced to their cultural context, the individual can seem to be a vanishing-point, a residue that lies beyond explanation or specification.[5] Not all students of literature and film have been pleased to discover that the authors or *auteurs* whom they thought they had come to university to study did not, as a matter of theoretical principle, exist.

What do we expect from the study of individuals and of subjectivity? It seems we must necessarily expect connections to be made between individual life stories and wider frameworks of understanding. Where biographical studies become wholly an investigation and celebration of individual lives *per se*, they seem unlikely to be either assimilable or compelling. There are too many lives, too many particulars, too many differences, for their mere elaboration and depiction to be in itself memorable. Social scientists, with their inherent leanings towards an understanding of representative or typical social facts, are particularly inclined to take this view. An approach which confines itself to the accumulation of facts is no less limited where the facts in question are those of subjective experience, life stories, or oral histories. Understanding involves the attribution of meaning, causal connection, typicality, and not merely detailed description. What else then should we want from the biographical method, in addition to the capturing of the particularity of lives which is its epistemological foundation?

A return to the two precedents of literary representation and psychoanalysis can help us to explore the particular senses of 'the representative' which will be needed if biographical methods are to establish themselves in the mainstream of the social sciences. Aesthetic realists, from Aristotle in his *Poetics* onwards, have argued that 'fictional' representations achieve, as a measure of their quality, a truth which we think of in terms of typicality,[6] in the representation of hitherto unrecognised aspects of human experience. 'Typicality' is represented in art not in the form of abstract generalisations, but as imagined instances of particular configurations of experience. Truth is recognised by identification, by the recognition of identity or similarity. This perception of identity is achieved by the representation of an imaginable life, or episodes in a life. Audiences recognise that any woman, placed in the position of Medea in Euripedes' tragedy could have murdered her children – thus what at first seems monstrous becomes understandable. It is the verisimilitude of the particular case (constructed and interpreted through signifying conventions) that enables the general significance of what is displayed to be recognised. As we have said, this mode of representation, discovery and understanding is one of the most powerful and definitive in our culture, perhaps in all imaginable human cultures.

Psychoanalysis adopts strategies of investigation which are both similar to and different from the imaginative. Its empirical method is the investigation of the individual case, but its concept of the representative is theoretically defined, cumulative and systematic. This discipline has sought to learn and teach by individual example (the case history, the case-narrative), but by theoretical generalisation and abstraction as well as by the heuristic and communicative power of its individual case examples. Psychoanalytic investigation of individual lives has been undertaken from a theoretically specific point of view. This presupposes the existence of an inner world or unconscious mind, which is not transparent to individuals, whose structures and processes can be illuminated, both for analysts and their patients, by psychoanalysis. The moral driving force of this process of inquiry has been the existence of mental pain, and the desire, by analysands and analysts alike, to alleviate it where possible. (There is an obvious derivation from the concern of medicine to prevent or alleviate physical suffering.)

The kinds of mental and emotional ill-being to which psychoanalysis has responded have evolved during its history, probably reflecting changes in socially constructed kinds of typical individual experience. Psychoanalytic patients are today less likely to present themselves with hysterical symptoms recognisable as the outcome of sexual repression than in Freud's day,[7] and more likely to appear saying that their lives are without meaning, and that they feel incapable of love or of lasting attachments. The field has developed both in its theories and its techniques, in attempts to widen its scope of understanding to individuals with many kinds of disturbance, to group processes, to institutions and, through the method of unobtrusive naturalistic observation, to normal infants in their families.[8] All of these methods of psychoanalytic work combine the empiricism of the case study with a commitment to the typification and generalisation of psychic attributes.

By contrast, the individual has been a largely subordinate preoccupation of sociology. Indeed the field in part constituted itself in the nineteenth century by opposition to disciplines (classical economics, psychology) which took the individual as their point of departure, and has yet fully to recover a capacity to take the individual seriously. The object of sociology as a field of knowledge has been to develop valid generalisations about societies, their component structures and processes and their development. The understanding of individuals has been subordinated to this task, and the effect of this has been to make it difficult, within this discipline, to do justice either to the particularity of human lives, or to their actual and potential agency.

The priority given to the social over the individual was most emphatic within the functionalist tradition, whose aim was to understand how different equilibrium states were maintained within societies, and how different elements of the social order contributed to this. Individuals, in such models, were of interest in so far as they fulfilled the normative requirements of the social structures in which they took their places. Individuals were defined as place-holders, necessary to fill the slots provided by social roles, but contributing little autonomously to them. Psychoanalysis was invoked by Talcott Parsons to explain how individuals came to conform, by means of normal childhood socialisation, to these expectations. Interesting issues did arise where such obligations were found to be in conflict with each other, where it seemed impossible for role incumbents to follow an unambiguous script. Within the functionalist tradition, this situation was interpreted as 'role strain', and Robert Merton (1957) developed an important typology of modes of adaptation of typical individuals to such situations.[9]

Parsons was also able to identify areas of individual and social stress, for example in adolescence, through tracking the passage of typical individuals through the roles and expectations set out for them. The idealised conformity attributed to role-incumbents was one of the main points of departure from functionalist sociology by its symbolic interactionist critics. Once they began to theorise roles as being 'made' rather than 'taken', and to give attention to the interactions through which individuals found their ways through social structures, a different sociology became possible (Rose 1962). It is out of this 'break' that much of the socio-biographical tradition in America in particular has emerged.

The alternative sociological framework of 'action theory', which traces its origins back to Max Weber, gave more scope to agency, and with this to individual subjectivity. Weber's ideal types are types of 'social action', in which typical configurations of ends and means are the building blocks of models of social structure. Emblematic individuals (Calvin, Benjamin Franklin) are described in Weber's work for their exemplary significance, and even for their causal agency, in defining norms of action. The debate between 'structure and agency' continues to be a defining polarity of sociological theory, with important attempts now being made to resolve it once and for all (Giddens 1984; Archer 1995; Mouzelis 1995). But the 'agency' to which the voluntaristic and subjectivist school of sociology gives priority is more that of collective than of individual actors. Despite the current interest in individualisation and reflexivity, there has so far been little interest taken in studying these forms of being as they are experienced by individuals. It seems almost definitional of sociology that the social comes first, and although the consequences of social forms for character and personality have been memorably described by many sociologists (e.g. in studies of bureaucratic personalities, amoral familism, total institutions, liminal experiences), the systematic study of individual biographies has rarely been important to this. Yet a biographical turn, if it occurs in social science on a significant scale, requires that methodologies be developed (the main topic of this book) which enable societies and cultures to be studied from the individual 'upwards', rather than from the social structure 'downwards'. This is a heuristic strategy that both the representational arts of imaginative literature, and psychoanalysis, have had no difficulty in following. What is necessary if sociology is to find its own uses for biography?

Biographical methods in sociology: the individual as agent

The essential problem for a biographical sociology is both to keep hold of an essentially sociological frame of reference and to demonstrate that original knowledge of social structure and process can be derived from the study of individual life stories (Rustin 1998). Just as the strength of the psychoanalytic method has come from its conjunction of the particular case study with a theoretical frame of reference (identifying characteristic defences against anxiety, developmental positions, psychic processes and their formative presences in the lives of individuals), so a biographical method in sociology must not forget its own primary frame of reference of sociological theory.

What has to be demonstrated is that sociological theory can be developed from the study of individual cases, in contrast to the usual sociological practice by which individual lives are shown to have meaning by their framing within previously established sociological categories. For such a methodology to be sociological, it is necessary to demonstrate that a life trajectory, or individual mode of being, is socially representative. It must enable us to understand, by inference or resemblance, other instances of the same kind. What is different in a biographical sociology (as is already the case in the knowledge-forms of psychoanalysis and the novel), is that the point of discovery, the ground from which inferences can be made, and similarities and differences identified, is the individual subject.

A much more radical argument can be made, about the *effectivity* of the individual. Changes in method often involve changes in ontology as well as in epistemology – that is, not only in how we come to know reality, but also in what reality consists of, and what has causal powers within it. In the case of the 'cultural turn', this change led to an epistemological focus on language and signs, and to an ontological belief that language and culture made a difference, shaped social reality. An earlier example of a transformation of this kind, in which changes in epistemology and ontology were linked, was the emergence of sociology, which both postulated a new category of 'social facts' and demonstrated their causal effectivity. Recent developments in geography, as it developed a post-Marxist theoretical basis, and challenged historicist assumptions in social theory, led to equally important heuristic claims, a change of perspective summarised in the axiom, 'space matters'. Similarly, the foundational idea in the development of psychoanalysis was that the unconscious exercised a determining influence on mental life, and it was from this assumption that psychoanalytic methods of investigation and clinical intervention developed.

If a 'biographical turn' is to take place in sociology, one expects it to have an ontological dimension as well as the new epistemology of socio-biographical research methods explored in this book. The ontological assumption must be that individuals have agency, that biographies make society and are not merely made by it. Unless it can be shown that individuals make a difference, that they have effectivity, there will in the end seem little to be gained from studying the social world from a biographical point of view.

The idea that individuals do (increasingly) embody agency is inherent in the contemporary ideas of 'individualisation' and 'reflexivity', ideas which thus seem to be awaiting their appropriate methods of research.[10] This of course is an idea already deeply encoded in Western imaginative literature, whose heuristic value derives from its repeated demonstrations that though individuals interact with others, and with a social world, they do so as agents. This is the case for the central characters of novels, from Fielding or Jane Austen to Conan Doyle or John Le Carré, of drama, from Euripides to Athol Fugard, and their near parallels in cinema or television, where detectives, gangsters, private eyes and Western heroes and villains represent potent images of agency. To represent individuals as essentially lacking the power of agency, as in the plays of Beckett or Chekhov, is usually to draw attention to a condition of crisis and pain.

This has not been an uncontested position. Developments initially associated with the cultural turn demonstrated the shaping power of language, discourses, and sign-systems. They were anti-humanist and critical of the idea of the individual subject. But the later development of post-structuralism has taken a somewhat different course. Once the endless complexity of discourse and language comes to be recognised, the idea that it wholly determines individual and social experience becomes untenable. First, because individuals (and collective agents) find themselves at points of intersection and choice between competing and contradictory discourses, and therefore obliged to make choices. And second, because languages are after all spoken, improvised, renewed. They are not invariant templates merely stamping out utterances (or the individuals who speak them) like the identical products of a die.

The early structuralist version of the cultural turn was a highly rationalist one, attributing (in the work of Lévi-Strauss and Althusser) to ideologies and cultural systems the power to reproduce themselves without the intervention of agents – somewhat like the algorithms of computer programs.[11] But as the complexities of discourse came to be recognised, a new post-structuralist emphasis was given to contingency, and to what lay outside language. The process of 'coming into being' of categories and modes of thought, and their instrumental role as forms of power (that is as the effects of agency) became the object of attention in Foucault's work and in the renewed interest in Nietzsche. We might say that a perspective dominated by the clash of two great ideological systems was replaced by one in which contingency, and the critique of power itself, came to be objects of attention. Post-structuralism also opened the way, in a return to a more anarchic modernist spirit, to recognition of the 'irrational preconditions of reason', the substratum of experience which has to be reflected on before rational discourses emerge.[12] The recovery of the 'pre-rational' and therefore contingent (which echoes the fundamental insights of psychoanalysis, and was indeed nourished by it, in Lacan's contribution to post-structuralism) is one resource for the recognition of individual agency, as the process of self-construction and self-recognition.

Whereas the early structuralist phase of the 'cultural turn' was deliberately antithetical to the idea of the individual subject, its later post-structuralist phase has thus opened a space for the rediscovery of individual agency, though the individual in this new context is no longer the unified subject of classical humanism.

These developments clear the theoretical ground for investigations which begin with the identification in individuals of distinctive life-strategies, trajectories, or kinds of self-recognition, as building blocks from which a larger understanding of society can be imagined. Recognition of contingency, of the spaces within which individuals create meaning and devise strategies for their lives, is critical if a biographical perspective is to escape from an ultimate social reductionism.

Socio-biographical accounts usually seek to identify in individual utterances elements which are socially recognisable, which are typical of some social form or other. We may think of these as segments of 'social script' (Harré 1979), or forms of self-presentation derived from existing social repertoires. Scheff's (1997) useful description of qualitative methodologies as focused on the links between parts and wholes describes one way in which social context is established. Essential as they are, there is still the risk that such interpretive procedures will merely deconstruct subjects into their socially derived elements, much like deconstructive textual procedures sometimes had the effect of dismantling the original work of art, transferring authority from its creator to its critic. The inherent tendency in sociology to hold the society to be the shaping force, and the individual subject as its product, will always threaten to push biographical methods in this direction.

This tendency can only be avoided if the individual case becomes the point of discovery and the starting-point for inferences about social structure. Biographical methods in social science need to develop a lexicon from the empirical investigation of lives, of biographies which are exemplary not in a moral sense, but as instances of representative kinds of lives.[13] A tradition of such work (a socio-biographical 'canon') can be constructed from existing classics in the field,[14] and needs to be further developed through new work.

Case examples have always been important sources of discovery, in sociology, and among its most memorable 'inscription devices'.[15] The 'thick descriptions' recommended, and provided, by Clifford Geertz, and in the ethnographies of Paul Willis, are examples of the conveying of sociological truths through holistic, particular kinds of report, from which theoretical generalisations are only subsequently inferred. Such case studies describe social agency in action. Historians normally work in this way, from particular cases. Knowledge of many social phenomena are contained and transmitted through memory of such instances, as well as through theoretical generalisation. A classic example is the idea of revolution and its dependence on the case (exemplary for both social scientists and revolutionaries) of the French Revolution. François Furet's (1981) *Interpreting the French Revolution*, gave a postmodern theoretical cogency to this particularist approach, rejecting theories which explained the revolution by reference to 'external' social forces (notably those of class conflict) and explaining it instead as a process which evolved from its own discourse, in an episode of pure emergent collective agency. This process of learning from social particulars is the holistic or ethnographical equivalent of the biographical method.

Just as ethnographies have provided exemplary descriptions of social life, from which an understanding of its essential attributes is derived, so socio-biographies can do this from an individual perspective. This has been a normal form of knowledge-generation in psychoanalysis, via its case studies. But it is through imaginative writing that understanding has been most often achieved through the description of individual life stories. Oedipus the King, Medea, Macbeth and Lady Macbeth, Faust, Anna Karenina, Raskolnikov, Hedda Gabler, Nora, Estragon and Vladimir, are points of common reference in European culture because their creators have identified in them some previously unrecognised but nevertheless representative kind of social being. While it may seem from a scientific point of view that social truths are established only by abstract general propositions or laws, in fact understanding of the social world has been equally accomplished through the luminosity of single cases. Ethnography and biography explore process, rather than merely structure. It is because it is through single cases that self-reflection, decision and action in human lives can best be explored and represented that the case study is essential to human understanding.

Epilogue on sociological education

It seems to be a long time since sociology inspired the majority of its students, as the bearer of a uniquely illuminating and liberating way of seeing the world. It has, since its moment of greatest euphoria in the 1960s, been through countless minor theoretical revolutions, seen many of its best ideas and methods adopted by neighbouring fields of study, and has suffered some disillusion in discovering that its insights did not, after all, seem to change the world in the direction of greater equality of voice and participation. (Or perhaps they did help to do so, in a general delegitimation of social and cultural authority, but not in the ways most of the sociologists had expected.)

A 'biographical turn' may now provide a fresh opportunity for sociologists to capture the interest and enthusiasm of their students. In an 'individualised' world, in which many social identities, of class, gender, race and generation, are being rendered uncertain or contested, one might expect that to start the investigation of society with the individual's own experience would have its appeal. The idea that the production as well as the reproduction of social identities takes place at an individual, subjective level, should be of interest to many who must be concerned to understand what spaces exist in which meaningful lives and careers can be made. Any theoretical and methodological programme will benefit from defining an associated field of practice. Gramscian neo-Marxists identified the practices of 'organic intellectuals' (those of teachers, nurses, journalists), whose work involved articulating social experiences on behalf of various collective subjects. For neo-liberals, the prescribed activity was to join the enterprise culture. A biographical turn in social science might offer a more exploratory form of action, in which students can explore how people make their world in the interaction with others, the sources of individuals' pain and satisfaction, and about how inspiration can be found in the lives of others.

'Undertake a socio-biographical interview, and through it explore the life story of an individual (for example, of one of your grandparents)' might be a rewarding initial research assignment for a sociology student.

Notes

1 Within the humanities, and among historians, biographies have always been a major form, from Plutarch's *Lives* and Vasari's *Lives of the Artists* onwards. It is the social sciences that have mostly avoided a biographical approach.

2 This was a theme of much of Ernest Gellner's work, e.g. *The Legitimation of Belief* (1975).

3 Hinshelwood (1989) is a valuable reference source for Kleinian concepts and theories. The two-volume collection edited by Spillius (1988) describe contemporary developments in this tradition.

4 Bauman's *Legislators and Interpreters* (1987) called attention to the authoritarian assumptions of enlightenment ways of thinking, and advocated a greater respect for difference.

5 Either, in other words, subjectivity is unintelligible, beyond the reach of reason, or it has already been wholly socialised. This stark choice summarises the position of Lacan.

6 The issue of 'typicality' was central to the adaptation of phenomenology to sociological inquiry in the United States, for example in the work of Alfred Schutz (1970).

7 This is an example of Anthony Giddens' 'double hermeneutic' – the 'discovery' of sexual repression in Freud's work contributed to a change in the social recognition and admissibility of sexuality, which is still proceeding. This of course does not abolish sexual repression, which remains a fact of normal development, but changes its forms and manifestations.

8 Psychoanalytic infant observation research is described in Miller *et al.* 1989; Reid 1997; and in *The International Journal of Infant Observation*.

9 Conformity or non-conformity on the dimensions of means and ends generated the illuminating four-fold typology of conformity, innovation, rebellion and retreatism.

10 The title 'Social Strategies in Risk Society' which was given to an EU-research project for the biographical study of social exclusion – see Chamberlayne and Spano, this volume – inches towards this insight, though 'social strategies' perhaps begs the question of where agency is believed to lie.

11 Not even genetic reproduction takes place without a substantial element of randomness, contingency and variation.

12 This insight has derived philosophically mainly from the phenomenological tradition of Husserl and Heidegger, and has demanded recognition in social science of the 'irrational' substratum and precursor of the rational. It has been

the outcome of a varied intellectual development, including developments of pragmatist philosophy in the United States (Richard Rorty), ethnomethodology, or the phenomenological tradition in sociology (Garfinkel), Derrida's post-structuralist philosophy in France and its wide take-up in the field of literary criticism in the United States and Britain, and Lacanian psychoanalysis, which brought together Freud's own attention to the 'irrational' with a Hegelian philosophical discourse also attentive to historical transformations of meaning and the problematic nature of fixed norms and ideals. In the Kleinian tradition of British psychoanalysis, Bion's attention to the experienced moment in the consulting room, had a similar effect in displacing given models of psychic structure with a focus on the ways understanding emerged and evolved.

13 Socio-biography studies the lives of socially-representative persons, not the lives of 'great men' (or women) the main subjects of biography as ordinarily understood. Although a socio-biographical (or psychobiographical) approach can and should inform biographies of this more conventional kind, what is explored here is the socio-biography of the everyday citizen, the normal subjects of social science.

14 Denzin (1989) provides a brief overview.

15 The concept of an 'inscription device' is Bruno Latour's.

References

Adorno, T.W. (1976) *The Positivist Dispute in German Sociology*, London: Heinemann.

Archer, M.S. (1995) *Realist Social Theory: the Morphological Approach*, Cambridge: Cambridge University Press.

Ayer, A.J. (1936) *Language, Truth and Logic*, London: Gollancz.

Bauman, Z. (1987) *Legislators and Interpreters*, Cambridge: Polity.

Beck, U. (1992) *Risk Society*, London: Sage.

Chamberlayne, P.,"Cooper A., Freeman, R. and Rustin, M. (eds) (1999) *Welfare and Culture*, London: Jessica Kingsley Publishers.

Chaney, D. (1994) *The Cultural Turn: Scene-setting Essays on Contemporary Cultural History*, London: Routledge.

Denzin, N. (1989) *Interpretive Biography*, London: Sage.

Furet, F. (1981) *Interpreting the French Revolution*, Cambridge: Cambridge University Press.

Geertz, C. (1975) *The Interpretation of Cultures*, London: Fontana.

Gellner, E. (1975) *The Legitimation of Belief*, Cambridge: Cambridge University Press.

Giddens, A. (1984) *The Constitution of Society*, Cambridge: Polity.

—— (1991) *Modernity and Self-Identity*, Cambridge: Polity.

—— (1992) *The Transformation of Intimacy*, Cambridge: Polity.

Harré, R. (1979) *Social Being*, Oxford: Blackwell.

Hinshelwood, R.D. (1989) *A Dictionary of Kleinian Thought*, London: Free Association Books.

Jameson, F. (1998) *The Cultural Turn: Selected Writings on the Postmodern, 1983–1998*, London: Verso.

Kuhn, T.S. (1962) *The Structure of Scientific Revolutions*, London: Chicago Univesity Press.

Latour, B. (1987) *Science in Action: How to Follow Scientists and Engineers through Society*, Milton Keynes: Open University Press.

Latour, B. and Woolgar, S. (1986) *Laboratory Life: the Construction of Scientific Facts*, 2nd edn, Princeton, NJ: Princeton University Press.

Merton, R.K. (1957) *Social Theory and Social Structure*, Glencoe, IL: Free Press.

Miller, L., Rustin, M.E., Rustin M.J. and Shuttleworth, J. (eds) (1989) *Closely Observed Infants*, London: Duckworth.

Mouzelis, N. (1995) *Sociological Theory: What Went Wrong?*, London: Routledge.

Reid, S. (1997) *Developments in Infant Observation*, London: Routledge.

Rorty, R. (ed.) (1967) *The Linguistic Turn: Recent Essays in Philosophical Method*, London: University of Chicago Press.

—— (1980) *Philosophy and the Mirror of Nature*, Oxford: Blackwell.

Rose, A.M. (1962) *Human Behavior and Social Processes: an Interactionist Approach*, London: Routledge and Kegan Paul.

Rustin, M.J. (1997) 'Give Me a Consulting Room', *British Journal of Psychotherapy* 13(4), 527–41.

—— (1998) 'From Individual Life Histories to Sociological Understanding', *SOSTRIS Working Paper 3*, Centre for Biography in Social Policy, University of East London.

—— (1999) 'Psychoanalysis: the Last Modernism?', in D. Bell (ed.), *Psychoanalysis and Culture: a Kleinian Perspective*, London: Duckworth.

Sack, R.D. (1986) *Human Territoriality: Its Theory and History*, Cambridge: Cambridge University Press.

Scheff, T.A. (1997) *Emotions, the Social Bond, and Human Reality: Part/Whole Analysis*, Cambridge: Cambridge University Press.

Schutz, A. (1970) *Alfred Schutz on Phenomenology and Social Relations: Selected Writings*, London: University of Chicago Press.

Sennett, R. (1998) *The Corrosion of Character*, London: Norton.

Sennett, R. and Cobb, J. (1972) *The Hidden Injuries of Class*, Cambridge: Cambridge University Press.

Spillius, E. (1988) *Melanie Klein Today: Vol. 1: Mainly Theory. Vol. 2: Mainly Practice*, London: Routledge.

Willis, P. (1977) *Learning to Labour: How Working Class Kids Get Working Class Jobs*, Farnborough: Saxon House.

Wittgenstein, L. (1953) *Philosophical Investigations*, Oxford: Blackwell.

2 Biographical analysis

A 'German' school?[1]

Ursula Apitzsch and Lena Inowlocki

Introduction: a brief historical sketch

Positions about biographical research have been taken by referring to a
'German School',[2] an allegedly 'idealist' approach which has little concern
for a sociological understanding of social reality and, instead, an overly
complicated methodological interest in single case analysis. While such
methodological care might still be acceptable for supplying the sociological community with special techniques for the effective explanation of
single cases, such as providing material examples of what happens in situations of societal transformation and insecurity, what the findings *mean*
would only be explainable by more general theoretical orientations. Thus,
while biographical research has become of interest to a number of sociologists, a certain impatience with the methodological aspects of biographical
analysis, as well as a seemingly weak theoretical benefit from such efforts,
have led to some critical judgements, mainly concerning Fritz Schütze's
concepts of 'cognitive figures' and 'process structures' in the analysis of
narratives (Kupferberg 1998).

First of all, biographical research is neither representative of, nor even
part of, mainstream sociology in Germany. Furthermore, such research is
not 'German', since it has emerged from sociological traditions both
transatlantically and intra-continentally. Both Fritz Schütze and Gerhard
Riemann, two of the most cited researchers in this area, strongly refer to
concepts which are rooted in the North American traditions of interpretive sociology, such as the Chicago School, pragmatism, symbolic
interactionism, ethnomethodology, (early) conversation analysis, socio-
linguistics and grounded theory. These theoretical resources have also
informed a number of other sociologists in Germany, who have developed
different ways of doing biographical analysis. The work and friendship of
Anselm Strauss has guided, among others, Fritz Schütze, Gerhard

Riemann, Christa Hoffmann-Riem, Wolfram Fischer-Rosenthal, Hans-Georg Soeffner, Bruno Hildenbrand.

Another prominent interpretive approach in Germany is represented by Ulrich Oevermann (1987), whose 'objective hermeneutics'[3] constitute an elaboration of genetic structuralism, with its roots in France (Lévi-Strauss, Bourdieu), Switzerland (Piaget), Northern American pragmatism (Peirce) and symbolic interactionism (Mead).

Maintaining strong relations with Northern American and Western European theoretical traditions is neither an accidental nor a recent phenomenon. The background and productiveness of the qualitative-interpretive approach, especially within biographical research, is not tied to the subjective hermeneutics of the German 'Geisteswissenschaften' (human sciences), but derives its characteristics and potential rather from a history of import and export and re-importing of thought, and also from a process of migration. This is exemplified in the work of Alfred Schütz, Georg Simmel and Karl Mannheim, which first became prominent in the United States after the Second World War, before it became a major influence in qualitative-interpretive sociology in Europe.

Our choice of this profile of theoretical resources and references is not because they exemplify qualitative-interpretive research in general, but because it seems that they provide the 'missing link' between method and theory. In fact we shall try to show not so much the interaction between, but rather the mutual embeddedness of, method and theory.

In 1899, the reporter and student Robert Ezra Park went from Harvard to Berlin and listened to Georg Simmel's lectures on sociology. In what became much later known as the 'Chicago School of Sociology', Park, as one of its central figures, extensively referred to Simmel's ideas (Park and Burgess 1924). Not accidentally, it seems to us, did Park, then Hughes and Lindesmith, later Becker and Strauss, as some of the main representatives of the different generations of the Chicago School, and also ethnomethodologists like Garfinkel[4] refer to the work of Simmel, Schütz and Mannheim. The work of these authors, with all the differences between them, reflects their position as outsiders through the social and societal exclusion they experienced as Jews, by being denied an academic career as in the case of Simmel and later, as in the case of Schütz and Mannheim, by their forced migration from Austria and Germany with the onset of the National-Socialist rise to power. It was these very inquiries into the conditions and consequences of human interaction that were then reformulated by the North American sociologists in terms of their own background: the enormous social transformation which they had witnessed. Eventually, these fundamental questions of how society is constituted became more radical questions about the very conditions that

make society possible. It is not surprising, therefore, that much qualitative-interpretive research, and especially biographical analysis, does not
presuppose social normality but rather asks about experiences during times
of social transformation and in moments and times of crisis, and the emergence of needs for new social practices to prevent further exclusion or the
complete breakdown of individual or social life.

A brief recent history

In the following, we can only give a limited overview of how the concept
of biographical analysis has been introduced into the social sciences in
Germany. Since the 1970s, research by means of collecting and analysing
biographical documents, especially interviews, has multiplied and developed in various directions. The volumes edited by Martin Kohli,[5] for
example, show the shift from the 'life course' concept to 'biographical
research'. The reprinting of Karl Mannheim's essay 'The Problem of
Generations', which was first published in 1928 in the collection
Soziologie des Lebenslaufs (Kohli 1978), gave a significant impetus to innovative conceptualisations of biography. This was because Mannheim, in
raising the basic question of the mutual interference of subjective perspectives, the impact of incisive historical events on subjectivity, and the
change of collective world views in successive generations, made it clear
that biographical research is not concerned with 'single cases' in the sense
of being restricted to individual case studies.

It is characteristic of the development of German biographical research
that important conceptual debates took place within the International
Sociological Association's *ad hoc* group 'Biography and Society', which
was initiated by Daniel Bertaux[6] in 1978 and became recognised as a
Research Committee in 1984. The German working group 'Biographie-
forschung' (biographical research) was then founded in 1979 by Martin
Kohli, Klaus Eder and Leopold Rosenmayer and was accepted by the
German Sociological Association in 1986 as a Research Section.
Researchers from Germany have been active in 'Biography and Society'
from the beginning. Within the educational sciences, biographical
researchers constituted a working group ('Erziehungswissen-schaftliche
Biographieforschung') in 1994.

While oral history and biographical research constitute separate areas,
discussions and controversies have helped to raise some fundamental
methodological issues. A documentation of some of this discussion, as
well as of the developments within biographical research in Germany, can
be found in the twice-yearly journal *Bios*, published since 1988.[7]

Within the historical sciences, oral history has figured in Germany as in the other European and Anglo-Saxon countries as a critical intervention through workers' history, or 'history from below', as a counter-hegemonic attempt to give a voice to formerly excluded protagonists of the historical process. However, disputes concerning the nature of testimonies and their relation to historical reality remain (Portelli 1991), and they especially came to the fore within the context of German history.

Referring to autobiographical narration in present-day Germany about life under National Socialism, Kohli (1981) emphasised the relevance within each particular study of our 'knowledge of the structural properties of autobiographical texts'. Biographical involvement in the Nazi era is characterised by 'silences, justifications and lies'[8] (Fischer-Rosenthal 1995). Accounts cannot be accepted at their face-value but have to be critically interpreted in their relation to historical events and experience (Rosenthal 1993). Also as a consequence of these considerations, the sociological analysis of biographical documents became more and more sophisticated, taking into account the formal features of narration, such as the distinction between narration and argumentation, or the degree of abstractness.

Within the social sciences the grounds for analysing biographical interviews were heavily attacked by researchers themselves. It was argued that there 'is hardly another kind of data collection which comes closer to spying and investigation'.[9] The possibility of encountering a 'neurotic narrator'[10] was raised. Martin Osterland, who had previously used biographical testimonies in his study on workers' consciousness, warned against colluding with 'retrospective illusions' and the 'mythology' of narration: 'The sociologist as the reader or listener of life histories is basically unable to determine whether a description of a past life is of what really happened, or what the subject only imagines his or her past to be' (Osterland 1983). Thus Osterland fundamentally doubts that historical truth can derive from biographical accounts.

A second order of objections that have been raised against biographical analysis concerns the relation between a single case and its relation to other cases. Even if we were to solve the problem of self-mythology versus historical truth, how would we be able to generalise our findings? And even if we were to resolve the problem of generalisability, what would we find out about society and social processes? In other words: how do we establish the sociological significance of our findings?

These are the objections most often raised in relation to biographical research, and we propose to look at them in the light of the broader theoretical traditions which have been mentioned above, such as phenomenology and symbolic interactionism, tracing through how they have been 'absorbed' and further developed in Germany since the early 1970s.

The life-world approach and the problem of reconstructed social reality

A phenomenological reconstruction of social interaction distinguishes between, on the one hand, the meaning given by social actors to their activities and experience as common-sense constructs, and, on the other, the interpretive activities of researchers studying such instances. Yet the scientific constructs of researchers themselves correspond to a special achievement of everyday communication, in which social actors create interpretive categories. It is these categories which researchers are concerned to interpret, in 'constructs of the second degree' (Alfred Schütz 1962: 6).[11] This complex argumentation has been misunderstood in ways which are, interestingly, diametrically opposed to one another. The first misunderstanding we have already encountered in the example of Osterland's rejection of any possible truth value of subjective accounts. From such a position, there is no sense in analysing meaning as having been *systematically* produced (a perspective we shall discuss further on), given the possible illusionary nature of subjective views.

The second misunderstanding lies in the objection raised against researchers over-interpreting actors' accounts, instead of relying on the truth-value these accounts contain as testimonies of social reality. This second objection has recently been voiced by Daniel Bertaux in his criticism of a 'narrativistic' interpretive orientation: 'The assertion that life stories do not faithfully describe lived experiences is speculative and lacks empirical justification' (Bertaux 1996: 4). However, with his insistence on a 'realist approach' (ibid.: 5), Bertaux also states, 'What we do need is a reasonable number of cases in order to compare instances of how accounts of lived experiences are systematically deformed after a period of ten years' (ibid.: 4). In his and Isabelle Bertaux-Wiame's long-term study on bakery workers, as well as Bertaux-Wiame's separate study of bakers of the same cohort who had meanwhile established their own bakeries, a systematic distortion, or colouring of the accounts of apprenticeship could be discerned according to whether the narrators had remained dependent workers or whether they had established their own bakeries.[12] In this conception of 'the truth', the social definition of the situation centres on the experience of certain 'objective conditions'. Thus, while Bertaux concedes that 'each account constitutes an interpretation, with some being more loyal, more clarifying, or more profound than others' (ibid.: 5), he sees socio-historical realities as existing 'independently of the conscious minds of actors' (ibid.: 2), who only mirror this already identified reality more or less faithfully. The study of the *systematically* produced distortion of lived experience in this view relies on a sufficient number of cases, in which different kinds of experience can come to the fore. In this perspective, while researchers might want to use first-hand accounts of social experiences to get at the 'objective conditions' of social reality behind these accounts, the production of such accounts of experience is not accepted *as being a part of*, and as constituting objective social reality.

Nevertheless, Osterland's as well as Bertaux's type of criticisms of narrative analysis point at some real problems in the hermeneutic interpretation of social interaction, which have been the subject of ongoing discussion. In Germany, the issues raised were taken up and elaborated mainly through the 'Arbeitsgruppe (working group) Bielefelder Soziologen', and through Ulrich Oevermann's elaboration of 'objective hermeneutics'.

The publication of *Alltagswissen, Interaktion und gesellschaftliche Wirklichkeit* (Knowledge of Everyday Life, Interaction and Social Reality) by the Bielefeld group in 1973, which introduced the different areas of interpretive research in the United States to German readers, such as symbolic interactionism, ethnomethodology, cognitive anthropology and ethnography of communication, also contributed to the debate. Fritz Schütze (1987) describes this transfer as facilitated by a similarity in the theoretical thought and research of symbolic interactionism (Blumer), the phenomenological social philosophy of Alfred Schütz, and the traditions of pre-war sociology of knowledge in Germany (Scheler, Mannheim). The social philosophy of George Herbert Mead, which had been an informal resource for the research monographs of the Chicago School of Sociology in the 1920s and 1930s, also gained renewed relevance for doing social research in Germany in the 1970s.

These research traditions were passed on especially through personal encounters, collaboration and friendships between 'third generation Chicagoans' like Anselm Strauss, Aaron Cicourel, Howard Becker, Erving Goffman, and ethnomethodologists like Harvey Sacks, Harold Garfinkel, Edward Rose and their German colleagues. These contacts created the possibility of a broad and dynamic confrontation between empirical research in the pragmatist tradition with a new orientation towards its theoretical and methodological foundations. The problem of representation of social reality in sociological inquiry was reformulated, in an attempt to transcend an oppositional positing of 'objective' social reality and 'subjective' accounts.

The most prominent application and elaboration in this direction with regard to biographical research can be found in Fritz Schütze's work. With reference to qualitative research in the Chicago tradition, Schütze developed new key concepts, in order both to unravel social phenomena which had been neglected also in German sociological research, such as processes of suffering and social disorder, and to refine the methods of analysis. His work shows how sociological understanding and knowledge rely both on the elaboration of theoretical concepts and the adequacy of data collection and analysis.

Schütze advocates that single case documents 'are not only rigorously sequentially analysed with regard to their contents but also concerning their procedures of reference and accounting' (1987: 544). What is first hidden in the technically recorded and transcribed materials becomes empirically and systematically analysable. Empirically based, systematically analysable concepts are, for example, 'process structures' in autobiographical narrative interviews. Four kinds of process structures within biographical accounts were identified by Fritz Schütze (1984):

1   those in which planning, initiative and action are dominant ('action schemes');
2   those in which institutional expectations and orientations are in the foreground;
3   those which indicate a (potential) loss of control over the life because of extraneous conditions ('trajectory', or 'trajectory potential');
4   those which suggest an unexpected or unaccountable turn towards a creative transformation in the biography.

These process structures correspond to experiences, and are represented in distinctive ways in the course of autobiographical accounts. They can figure as dominant or as recessive, as, for example, in the case of a trajectory potential underlying an action scheme. Dominant and especially recessive process structures can be hidden from the biographical narrator's awareness.

In questioning the 'taken-for-granted' action orientation of many sociological theories, including symbolic interactionism, 'trajectories' are of special sociological interest (Schütze 1987). Trajectories represent a concept of social reality, which refers both to situations which are objectively (potentially) threatening *and* to the interactive production and reproduction of threat, marginalisation and exclusion. Under the influence of, as well as in parallel with Anselm Strauss' work on interactions between institutional processes and terminally ill patients, Schütze and Riemann formulated a theory of biographical and collective trajectories (Riemann and Schütze 1991). This theory states that certain basic aspects of social reality are usually not recognised by actors in everyday life:

(a) the complex symbolic aspects of social reality and social interaction cannot be understood in everyday or routine situations and communication,

(b) social situations are not only expressive of social order, but can suddenly imply extensive suffering and disorder at different levels of social reality,

(c) the deepest suffering within such disorder arises from the removal of the basis of co-operation, solidarity and reciprocity in interaction (Schütze 1995: 116).

As an intriguing example of anomic life situations, which have not been paid much attention in sociology, Schütze (1995) quotes Franz Kafka's novel *The Trial* and reconstructs the paradoxical interaction between Franz K and his landlady Frau Grubach after the threatening announcement of his impending arrest. Paradoxically, it is *in asking for* the reassurance of normality in the reproduction of routine everyday interactions, following the fateful and incisive intrusion of a hostile force into K's life, that his exclusion from social life is brought about. Since the situation has fundamentally changed, these routines inevitably create a phantom normality. While those involved in the interaction cannot recognise the mechanisms that are producing anomie, the procedures of such social interaction can be analysed to reveal how the 'process structure' of 'trajectory' took over.

Process structures are not restricted to individual cases but can characterise groups or collectives as well, through the experience of totalitarian regimes, natural or 'man-made' catastrophes, war, or drastic social transformation. Schütze (1992) refers to such cases of collective breakdown of orientation as 'collective trajectories'. This leads us to the problem of what the analysis of a single case can tell us about a number of cases and, furthermore, how sociological theory can emerge from the analysis of individual cases.

Generalising from the biographical analysis of a single case?

What are the reasons for spending extended time on the analysis of each case? And what is it in a single case that we can count on as a basis for generalising? The analysis of biographical narration was motivated by a fundamental methodological problem which both Cicourel (1964) and Habermas (1967, 1981) encountered. The problem these authors tackled was the uncontrolled relationship between social theory and social data, for example the supposed correspondence between social reality and statistical records, or statements of interviewees in sociological inquiries. The 'truth' of social data was more often than not a product of the conditions of collecting and analysing it. This consideration led Habermas to the conclusion that the chronologically ordered content of a narration is less interesting for sociological research than the 'perspective of possible interpretation' (Habermas 1967: 167ff.). In his *Theory of Communicative Action* Habermas focused on the social meaning of the analysis of narration: it 'has a function with respect to the self-definition of persons, who must objectify their belonging to their life-world in terms of their active role as participants in communication' (Habermas 1981, II: 206). Habermas thus departs from the traditions of subjective hermeneutics and their 'hermeneutic idealisation of the lifeworld speaker' (Habermas 1981, II: 233ff.).[13]

How can autobiographical analysis escape the trap of being restricted to subjectively represented life worlds? As the approach developed by Schütze and others shows, the focus of analysis is not the reconstruction of intentionality that is represented as an individual's life course, but the embeddedness of the biographical account in social macro-structures, such as hierarchically controlled social situations (as evidenced by, for example, forced communication in police or court interrogations, or politically motivated bureaucratic decision-making), and other heteronomous social conditions leading to exclusion, such as unemployment, deviance, or alcoholism. The point is that the processes and mechanisms of biographical 'exposure' of oneself to the world, both as experienced and as accounted for, do not take place 'outside of' interaction and communication. However, since the predominant sociological theories are either biased towards rationalist or intentionalist interpretations, the more interesting phenomena of the biographical reproduction of social structures tend to be overlooked.

Theoretical positions often become more comprehensible when it is explained how one thing led to another, just as a biographical account can help to understand the positions a person takes. We would therefore like to explore a little the history of Fritz Schütze's discovery of the theoretical and methodological potential of autobiographical narratives. Upon his return to Germany in August 1979 after a year of working with Anselm Strauss, he was asked why in talking about his research he was oscillating between considerations of method and theory, and also about what he thought the impact of this research in communicative and narrative theory would be. He answered in terms of his own 'research biography', and began with the problem that sociological theory was usually conceptualised independently of concrete social phenomena. Also, open research procedures were needed to let informants speak extensively and freely. However, there remained the problem of how informants' accounts were related to the factual reality of action.

These theoretical and methodological considerations came into focus in a concrete piece of research on political and administrative procedures in a particular community. In interviewing politicians, standard questions would not have elicited talk about their conflicts of interests and involvement in shifts of power. Schütze thus had the idea of asking for a narrative account of their involvement in and contribution to the community project. Concentrating first on questions of interview technique, he noticed in observing the informants, the other interviewer and himself, how their communicative activities were led again and again by the same internal mechanisms of narrating and listening, phenomena which Schütze later described as 'narrative constraints' and 'cognitive figures'. Informants invariably either tried to escape from the unfolding narrative or spontaneously became involved in more marginal background narratives or explanations, hiding interest coalitions by less detailed representation; interviewers always asked further questions when there was vagueness or a lack of plausibility. Obviously, this had something to do with a 'communicative scheme' of narration.

Schütze then began a conversation analysis of the dynamics of narratives which he had recorded in a different project on 'naturally occurring' interactions (i.e., not researcher elicited), in court and in other institutions. By gaining insight into the elementary rules of the narrative scheme, he could understand the regularities of behaviour in a narrative interview. He used the regularities found in conversation analysis for sociological text analysis, and succeeded in systematically connecting some basic theoretical sociological phenomena with these textual phenomena. In a next step, Schütze went on to use the narrative interview to elicit individual biographical accounts of alcoholism, unemployment and homelessness. While action schemes could be clearly discerned in these interviews through the analysis of external events and courses of action, it was not possible by these means to reconstruct what had happened with the informant when, following a period of suffering, a positive transformation took place. It became apparent that the theoretical aspects of biographical narration had to be investigated. This meant analysing the overall autobiographical organisation, which was neither confined thematically (such as to the time of having been an alcoholic), nor limited textually to narrative sequences, since argumentative sequences embedded in the narrative contained the autobiographical theory of the informant. Through conversation analysis, the 'identity work' achieved in argumentation could be uncovered.

Thus he returned to the interviews, analysing them completely

through a formal conversation analysis. This analysis, together with considerations concerning the substantive content of the interviews, led to his
theory of the trajectory, as a sequential structure of suffering and disorderly processes. It became apparent that the development of the trajectory
can only be discerned in the text by 'symptomatology', since the informant is at least partially unaware of the trajectory process. Besides the
analysis of narratives and interactions concerning actually occurring
trajectories (of cancer patients), Schütze analysed literary presentations of
trajectories (especially in the work of Dostoevsky, Kafka, Handke).
Schütze concluded by emphasising the particular strength of 'formal'
conversation text analysis in leading to the further identification of
phenomena of substantive concern, as had been the case with discovering
'action scheme' and 'trajectory', and in providing 'pathways towards
generalisation' for a substantive theory. A formal text analysis without
such interest in sociological topics and initial substantive considerations
would not be very fruitful. The exploration of possibly relevant substantive dimensions together with sociologically important aspects can be
seen as the first abductive generalising step of the research process.[14]

This informal account was rendered at length, because it shows the
interconnection of methodological and theoretical observations which
went into the discovery of the autobiographical narrative interview as a
research method, and the implications of this for sociological theory and
its conventional bias towards an action orientation.

Some conclusions

Our intention has been to show that biographical research is not a
'method' in need of a 'theory', and that it derived not from a subjective
hermeneutic approach in the tradition of idealist philosophy, but on the
contrary from the rediscovery of wider theoretical and methodological
sources, including those which were excluded from sociology in Germany
in the 1930s. For different reasons, disregard continued up until the
1970s, mostly because of the predominance of survey research, and of
non-empirical theoretical studies. In reconstructing the process of rediscovery, we highlighted the problem of the relation between biographical
analysis and social reality, as well as the grounds for generalising from
single case studies. Our key point has been that a very detailed and
sophisticated formal analysis of different sorts of text revealed the impact
of social macro-structures in the single case, and that substantive concerns
with macro-structural conditions and processes directed research interests
and activities.

In teaching research related to the Chicago School tradition, and using the guidelines of 'grounded theory' (Glaser and Strauss 1967; Strauss and Corbin 1990), with students collecting and analysing data in different social and institutional contexts and settings, Riemann and Schütze (1987) found that certain theoretical models were regularly generated in the different kinds of research projects. Formulated as 'basic structural processes of social reality', these theoretical models were organised in certain 'theoretical building blocks', such as 'career models' (concerning institutionalised patterns of expectation within biographies), models of 'structural processes in the life course' (referring to the dynamics of biographical processes, such as trajectories), or models 'of developments and changes in social worlds, social milieus, and social movements'. Thus, even the few cases which students analysed in their research projects highlighted typical features of these social arenas, since the cases had been selected not randomly, but by the 'theoretical sampling' procedures of 'grounded theory', and because the findings could be structurally integrated into theoretical models which by these means then themselves became further elaborated.

The fertility of this theoretical and methodological approach is evidenced by the large number of empirical research contexts and projects that have worked with it and further elaborated it. A few recent examples include studies: on unemployed marginalised youth (Alheit 1994), on the reconstruction of historical and generational experience (Rosenthal 1998), on the changed East–West confrontation in Europe (Breckner 1994; Völter 1996), on gendered structures (Dausien 1996), on bodily experience (Fischer-Rosenthal 1999), on illness (Hanses 1996), on professional development (Jost 1997), on paradoxes in social work (Schütze 1996), on institutional counselling (Riemann 1997), on migration and inter-culturality (Apitzsch 1997, 1999a, 1999b), on the traditionality of life-worlds (Inowlocki 1993, 1997).

Examples of areas of research which have been developed in the associated context of the 'objective hermeneutics' approach, include, for example, studies on news media and the public (Oevermann 1996a), on professionalisation (Oevermann 1996b), on religious conversion (Wohlrab-Sahr 1995), on family structures (Hildenbrand et al. 1992). Of course, some approaches have been inspired by both objective hermeneutics and by biographical-narrative analysis (Rosenthal 1998), or by their critical review, for example, in research on the institutional framing of biography (Hoerning and Corsten 1995), or on the ageing of a cohort (Bude 1995).

While there are differences in their respective conceptualisations of social structures, both Schütze's and Oevermann's concepts rely on a specific way of connecting phenomenological traditions and the pragmatist logic of abduction, as first outlined by Peirce. Abductive logic (see note 14) takes account of the capacities of individual and collective actors to create solutions through practical action.[15] This presents social science with the task of defining the underlying problem structure. Thus, biographical research, in different phenomenologically and pragmatically inspired ways, can discover and show what is emerging as a new structure of social praxis in a specific situation of crisis resolution. Such research is different from attitudinal studies or from the glorifying of marginalisation, and has the advantage that empirically analysed and theoretically grounded findings can be critically reintroduced into the social praxis of actors.

Notes

1 We would like to thank Gerhard Riemann for his helpful suggestions.
2 Tom Wengraf refers to this debate in 'Representations of interpreted autobiographies in contexts: general concepts and unique cases' (paper presented at the ISA World Congress, Montreal, July 1998: 3). For the debate, see Daniel Bertaux (1996), as well as earlier and later issues of the ISA RC 38 *Newsletter*.
3 We cannot give a more detailed account of 'objective hermeneutics' in this paper. Its interpretive basis is shared by biographical analysis:

> [the purpose of] objective hermeneutics is to explicate structures of action with as much discrimination as possible. Thus there are methods in everyday life for quickly decoding meanings and for understanding motives. These procedures generate the most probable interpretations. For the time being we shall refer to these interpretive methods of everyday life as features of practical action assuring its economy and efficiency. We include among these those basic systems of relevance that make intersubjective understanding possible. The phenomenological tradition within sociology has been particularly interested in them.
>
> (Oevermann *et al.* 1987: 446)

4 Robert E. Park and E.W. Burgess (1924); Everett C. Hughes (1994); Alfred Lindesmith (1965); Howard Becker (1998); Anselm L. Strauss (1959); Harold Garfinkel (1967).
5 Martin Kohli (1978, 1981); Martin Kohli and Günther Robert (1984).
6 In 1981, Daniel Bertaux edited a state-of-the-art collection *Biography and Society*, which included Kohli's paper on 'Biography: Account, Text, Method', together with accounts of Italian, French, Canadian, US, Polish, Hungarian, Brazilian and British traditions within biographical research.
7 Published by Leske and Budrich. (Former) editors include Werner Fuchs, Charlotte Fuchs-Heinritz, Armin Nassehi.
8 'Schweigen-Rechtfertigen-Umarbeiten'.
9 Werner Fuchs (1979), according to Peter Alheit (1994: 10).
10 Bude (1985).

66 Ursula Apitzsch and Lena Inowlocki

11 As Schütz (1962: 6) explains:

> The social world...has a particular meaning and relevance structure for the human beings living, thinking, and acting therein. They have pre-selected and preinterpreted this world by a series of common-sense constructs of the reality of every-day life, and it is these thought objects which determine their behaviour, define the goal of their action, the means available for attaining them – in brief, which help them to find their bearings within their natural and socio-cultural environment and to come to terms with it. The thought objects constructed by the social scientists refer to and are founded upon the thought objects constructed by the common-sense thought of man living his everyday life among his fellow men. Thus, the constructs used by the social scientist are, so to speak, constructs of the second degree, namely constructs of the constructs made by the actors on the social scene, whose behaviour the scientist observes and tries to explain in accordance with the procedural rules of his science.

12 The dependent workers remembered the hardship and humiliation of their apprenticeship, while the independent bakers glossed over their own experience and, when asked, justified the conditions of apprenticeship, which they had since imposed on apprentices of their own.

13 For the discussion of this problem, see Alheit (1994: 17ff.).

14 The research logic of abduction, a term introduced and elaborated by Charles Saunders Peirce (1965), can include but reaches beyond deduction and induction, in exploring hypotheses about possible underlying patterns or structures of which the phenomena or data under consideration are manifestations. For a discussion of the work of Peirce, see Kloesel (1986) and Houser and Kloesel (1992). The 'documentary method of interpretation' by Mannheim treats 'an actual appearance as "the document of", as "pointing to", as "standing on behalf of" a presupposed underlying pattern' (Garfinkel 1967: 78). When asking in the course of data analysis, 'what is this a case of?' (Becker 1998), abductive theorising does not expect the data to fit already existing theories, but rather that the theoretical contexts that would adequately describe the rigorously analysed data can be discovered, or generated. Abductive research procedures are described in the writings on 'grounded theory' (Glaser and Strauss 1967; Strauss and Corbin 1990).

15 Oevermann et al. (1987: 446) states:

> [I]t must be taken into account that the interpretive methods of everyday life (which are) responsible for the achievement of economy and efficiency in action, themselves rest upon background assumptions. They express the spirit of the age and the ideology of a particular stage of social development. They are deep-seated and historically specific patterns of interpretations, and in principle open to criticism.

References

Alheit, P. (1994) *Taking the Knocks: Youth Unemployment and Biography*, London: Cassell.

Apitzsch, U. (1997) 'The Changing Role of Women in the Migration Process', in P.P. Armstrong, N. Miller and M. Zukas, *Crossing Borders Breaking Boundaries: Research in the Education of Adults*, London: University of London, Birkbeck College, pp.11–15.

—— (1999a) *Migration und Biographie: Zur Konstitution des Interkulturellen in den Bildungsgängen junger Erwachsener der 2. Einwanderergeneration*, Opladen: Westdeutscher Verlag (Habilitation thesis, University of Bremen 1990).

—— (ed.) (1999b) *Migration und Traditionsbildung*, Opladen/Wiesbaden: Westdeutscher Verlag.

Arbeitsgruppe Bielefelder Soziologen (eds) (1973) *Alltagswissen, Interaktion und gesellschaftliche Wirklichkeit*, 2 vols, Reinbek/Hamburg: rororo/ Opladen: Westdeutscher Verlag, 2nd edn, 1983.

Becker, H.S. (1998) *Tricks of the Trade: How to Think about Your Research While You're Doing It*, Chicago, IL and London: University of Chicago Press.

Bertaux, D. (ed.) (1981) *Biography and Society: The Life History Approach in the Social Sciences*, London: Sage.

—— (1996) 'A Response to Thierry Kochuyt's "Biographical and Empiricist Illusions: A Reply to Recent Criticisms"', *Newsletter of the ISA RC 38* 'Biography and Society', pp.2–6.

Breckner, R. (1994) 'Ich war immer froh ein Entwurzelter zu sein'. Aspekte biographischer Migrationsforschung in Ost-West-Perspektive, in B. Balla and W. Geier (eds), *Zu einer Soziologie des Postkommunismus: Kritik, Theorie, Methodologie*, Hamburg: Lit, pp.37–50.

Bude, H. (1985) 'Der Sozialforscher als Narrationsanimateur. Kritische Anmerkungen zu einer erzähltheoretischen Fundierung der interpretativen Sozialforschung', *Kölner Zeitschrift für Soziologie und Sozialpsychologie* 37(June): 327–36.

—— (1995) *Das Altern einer Generation. Die Jahrgänge 1938–1948*, Frankfurt/M: Suhrkamp.

Cicourel, A.V. (1964) *Method and Measurement in Sociology*, Glencoe, IL: Free Press.

Dausien, B. (1996) *Biographie und Geschlecht Zur biographischen Konstruktion sozialer Wirklichkeit in Frauenlebensgeschichten*, Bremen: Donat.

Fischer-Rosenthal, W. (1995) 'Schweigen-Rechtfertigen-Umarbeiten: Biographische Arbeit im Umgang mit deutschen Vergangenheiten', in W. Fischer-Rosenthal and P. Alheit, in co-operation with E.M. Hoerning (eds), *Biographien in Deutschland*, Opladen: Westdeutscher Verlag, pp.43–86.

—— (1999) 'Biographie und Leiblichkeit: Zur biographischen Arbeit und Artikulation des Körpers', in P.P. Alheit, B. Dausien, W. Fischer-Rosenthal, A. Hanses and A. Keil (eds), *Biographie und Leib*, Giessen: Psychosozial.

Garfinkel, H. (1967) *Studies in Ethnomethodology*, Englewood Cliffs, NJ: Prentice Hall.

Glaser, B. and Strauss, A. (1967) *The Discovery of Grounded Theory*, Chicago, IL: Aldine.

Habermas, J. (1967) *Zur Logik der Sozialwissenschaften (Philosophische Rundschau, suppl.5)*, Tübingen: Mohr.

—— (1981) *Theorie des kommunikativen Handelns*, 2 vols, Frankfurt/M: Suhrkamp.

Hanses, A. (1996) *Epilepsie als biographische Konstruktion: Eine Analyse von Erkrankungs-und Gesundungsprozessen anfallserkrankter Menschen anhand erzählter Lebensgeschichten*, Bremen: Donat.

Hildenbrand, B., Bohler, K.F., Jahn, W. and Schmitt, R. (1992) *Bauernfamilien im Modernisierungsprozeß*, Frankfurt/M: Campus.

Hoerning, E.M. and Corsten, M. (1995) *Institution und Biographie: Die Ordnung des Lebens*, Pfaffenweiler: Centaurus.

Houser, N. and Kloesel, C. (eds) (1992) *The Essential Peirce: Selected Philosophical Writings*, Bloomington and Indianapolis, IN: Indiana University Press.

Hughes, E.C. (1994) *On Work, Race, and the Sociological Imagination*, Chicago, IL: University of Chicago Press.

Inowlocki, L. (1993) 'Grandmothers, Mothers, and Daughters: Intergenerational Transmission in Displaced Families in Three Jewish Communities', in D. Bertaux and P. Thompson (eds), *Between Generations: Family Models, Myths, and Memories. International Yearbook of Oral History and Life Stories*, Vol. II, Oxford: Oxford University Press, pp.139–53.

—— (1997) 'Normalität als Kunstgriff: Zur Traditionsvermittlung jüdischer DP-Familien in Deutschland', in Fritz Bauer Institut (ed.), *Überlebt und unterwegs: Jüdische Displaced Persons im Nachkriegsdeutschland: Jahrbuch zur Geschichte und Wirkung des Holocaust*, Frankfurt/M: Campus, pp.267–88.

Jost, G. (1997) 'Strukturen und Muster berufsbiographischer Entwicklungen von Managern', *Zeitschrift für Sozialisationsforschung und Erziehungssoziologie* 17(3), 287–306.

Kloesel, C.J.W. (ed.) (1986) *Writings of Charles S.Peirce*, Vol. 4, Bloomington, IN: Indiana University Press

Kohli, M. (ed.) (1978) *Soziologie des Lebenslaufs*, Darmstadt/Neuwied: Luchterhand.

—— (1981) 'Biography: Account, Text, Method', in D. Bertaux (ed.), *Biography and Society: The Life History Approach in the Social Sciences*, London: Sage, pp.61–75.

Kohli, M. and Robert, G. (eds) (1984) *Biographie und soziale Wirklichkeit. Neue Beiträge und Forschungsperspektiven*, Stuttgart: Metzler.

Kupferberg, F. (1998) 'Transformations as Biographical Experience: Personal Destinies of East Berlin Graduates before and after Unification', *Acta Sociologica* 41(3): 243–67.

Lindesmith, A.R. (1965) *The Addict and the Law*, Bloomington, IN: Indiana University Press.

Oevermann, U. (1996a) 'Der Strukturwandel der Öffentlichkeit durch die Selbstinszenierungslogik des Fernsehens', in C. Honegger, J.M. Gabriel, R. Hirsig *et al.* (eds), *Gesellschaften im Umbau: Identitäten, Konflikte, Differenzen*, Zurich: Seismo, pp.197–228.

—— (1996b) 'Skizze einer revidierten Theorie professionalisierten Handelns', in A. Combe and W. Helsper, *Pädagogische Professionalität: Untersuchungen zum Typus professionellen Handelns*, Frankfurt/M: Suhrkamp, pp.70–182.

Oevermann, U. with Allert, T., Konau, E. and Krambeck, J. (1987) 'Structures of Meaning and Objective Hermeneutics', in *Modern German Sociology*, New York: Columbia Press, pp.436–47.

Osterland, M. (1983) 'Die Mythologisierung des Lebenslaufs. Zur Problematik des Erinnerns, in M. Baethge and W. Essbach (eds), *Entdeckungen im Alltäglichen: Hans Bahrdt: Festschrift zu seinem 65, Geburtstag*, Frankfurt/Main and New York: Campus, pp.279–90.

Park, R.E. and Burgess, E.W. (1924) *Introduction to the Science of Sociology*, Chicago, IL/London: University of Chicago Press, 2nd edn, 1969.

Peirce, C.S. (1965) *Collected Papers*, Vol. V, Cambridge, MA: Harvard University Press, pp.94–131.

Portelli, A. (1991) 'Uchronic Dreams: Working Class Memory and Possible Worlds', in *The Death of Luigi Trastulli and Other Stories: Form and Meaning in Oral History*, Albany, NY: State University of New York Press, pp.99–116.

Riemann, G. (1997) 'Beziehungsgeschichte, Kernprobleme und Arbeitsprozesse in der sozialpädagogischen Familienberatung: Eine arbeits-, biographie- und interaktionsanalytische Studie zu einem Handlungsfeld der sozialen Arbeit', Habilitation thesis, University of Magdeburg.

Riemann, G. and Schütze, F. (1987) 'Some Notes on a Student Research Workshop on "Biography Analysis, Interaction Analysis, and Analysis of Social Worlds"', *Newsletter No.8* of the ISA Research Committee 'Biography and Society', E.M. Hoerning and W. Fischer (eds), pp.54–70.

—— (1991) *'Trajectory' as a Basic Theoretical Concept for Analysing Suffering and Disorderly Social Processes: Essays in Honor of Anselm Strauss*, New York: Aldine de Gruyter, pp. 333–57.

Rosenthal, G. (1993) 'Reconstruction of Life Stories: Principles of Selection in Generating Stories for Narrative Biographical Interviews', in A. Lieblich and R.H. Josselson, *The Narrative Study of Lives*, Vol. I, pp.59–91

—— (1998) *The Holocaust in Three Generations: Families of Victims and Perpetrators of the Nazi Regime*, London: Cassell.

Schütz, A. (1962) *Collected Papers I: The Problem of Social Reality*, The Hague: Martinus Nijhoff.

Schütze, F. (1984) 'Kognitive Strukturen autobiographischen Stegreiferzählens', in M. Kohli and G. Robert (eds), *Biographie und soziale Wirklichkeit: Neue Beiträge und Forschungsperspektiven*, Stuttgart: Metzler, pp.78–117.

—— (1987) 'Symbolischer Interaktionismus', in U. Ammon, N. Dittmar and K.J. Mattheier (eds), *Sociolinguistics/Soziolinguistik: Ein internationales Handbuch zur Wissenschaft von Sprache und Gesellschaft*, New York/Berlin: de Gruyter, pp.520–53.

—— (1992) 'Pressure and Guilt: War Experiences of a Young German Soldier and their Biographical Implications, Part 1 and 2', *International Sociology* 7(2 and 3): 187–208, 347–67.

—— (1995) 'Verlaufskurven des Erleidens als Forschungsgegenstand der interpretativen Soziologie', in H.-H. Krüger and W. Marotzki (eds), *Erziehungswissenschaftliche Biographieforschung*, Opladen: Leske and Budrich, pp.116–57.

—— (1996) 'Organisationszwänge und hoheitsstaatliche Rahmenbedingungen im Sozialwesen: Ihre Auswirkungen auf die Paradoxien des professionellen Handelns', in A. Combe and W. Helsper, *Pädagogische Professionalität: Untersuchungen zum Typus professionellen Handelns*, Frankfurt/M: Suhrkamp, pp.183–275.

Strauss, A. (1959) *Mirrors and Masks: The Search for Identity*, Glencoe, IL: Free Press.

Strauss, A. and Corbin, J. (1990) *Basics of Qualitative Research: Grounded Theory Producers and Techniques*, Newbury Park, CA: Sage.

Völter, B. (1996) 'Die "Generation ohne Alternative". Generationstheoretische Überlegungen am Beispiel der nach dem Mauerbau geborenen DDR-Jugend', *Berliner Debatte Initial* 7/6: 107–18.

Wengraf, T. (1998) 'Representations of Interpreted Autobiographies in Contexts: General Concepts and Unique Cases', Paper presented at the ISA World Congress, Montreal, July.

Wohlrab-Sahr, M. (ed.) (1995) *Biographie und Religion*, Frankfurt/M: Campus.

3 Case histories of families and social processes

Enriching sociology

Daniel Bertaux and Catherine Delcroix

Introduction

A case history of a family, as we understand it, is made up of narrative accounts of persons belonging to several generations of the same 'family', i.e. kinship group. They will be asked by the researcher to talk about their own life history and experiences, but also about those of other family members as well, however sketchily, and to comment on their relations with these other members. Family documents may of course complete the database. The point however is not to focus on one family only, but on a number of them, all 'members' of a common 'social formation' – a society, a sub-society, a migration flow – within which their history has been embedded for the last generations.[1] One of the properties of case histories of families is indeed to function as small mirrors of general cultural and social patterns, of societal dynamics and change; and the idea is, by multiplying them, to grasp these patterns and their dynamics of reproduction and historical transformation.

We see, therefore, this method as a natural extension of the 'life stories approach' which we have used in research projects to study various social worlds (the artisanal bakery, immigrants in working-class suburbs) or various social situations (mixed marriages, divorced fathers losing contact with their children).

In this paper we wish to describe some of the properties of this method, which we have developed as we were using it for various research projects. We will focus on the specific sociological objects which it allows us to perceive, construct and study. Before turning to this, however, we would like to deal briefly with the teaching virtues of this method: for we know of no better method in conveying to students, through their concrete involvement in a small piece of research deeply meaningful to them, the spirit of sociology as its founding fathers understood it.

A teaching experiment

The method of family case histories was initially developed for teaching purposes. One of us, Bertaux, who had been developing the life story method, was teaching a course on social mobility at Quebec's Université Laval; in order to give his sixty students a first initiation into the spirit of research he asked each of them to pick up one family and study its recent history in the perspective of social reproduction and mobility.

As students began to work – most of them had chosen to study their own family – they asked for more directives on how to do it and what to focus on. This led Bertaux to define a 'standard' way of designing the frame of a family case history: you start with an Ego who is of student age; then go up two generations to the two couples of grandparents; then go down, including on the way every descendant and her/his spouse(s) within the frame. As a result not only Ego's father and mother but uncles and aunts (and their spouses), and not only Ego's siblings but her/his first degree cousins on both sides, are included in the picture (Bertaux 1995).[2]

Students were asked to collect the 'basic biographical (demographic) data' for each person included in the frame and to copy it on a genealogical graph. Besides gender, year of birth, place of birth, and level of education, the key piece of data, in the 'social mobility' or rather social reproduction perspective adopted, was of course the main occupation; the hope was that, by replacing names with occupations on a standard genealogical graph, one would make visible some lineages of occupations, some transmissions of trade from father to son and perhaps grandson or nephew.[3] They were also asked to choose one lineage, to reconstruct the history of its last three generations and to tell it in a twenty-page narrative essay.[4]

The exercise was supposed to sensitise students to an alternative, '*qualitative*', way of looking at social mobility; however, given the very large size of families (i.e. number of siblings) in traditional Quebec, students came back with wide graphs bearing a huge *quantity* of data. Although the graphs were only three generations deep most of them were very broad, one even numbering 220 persons! The 'stories' students collected about how the lives of their parents and relatives got shaped were often highly interesting, revealing as it were some of the social logics typical of French Canada's cultural model.

Taken together, these sixty family case histories mapped out many aspects of social-historical change as it had taken place in this region of the Quebec province for the past seventy years. In older generations one could find a vast majority of small farmers, and even one trapper (*coureur des bois*) having married the daughter of an Indian chief. In the next generation, farmers had mostly disappeared, being replaced by workers in the building trades, in industry and urban services, both in Quebec and in the north-east of the United States: family sizes got much smaller, married women who had a job were much more numerous. In the third generation the occupations in teaching, social work, health services were fast growing. But what was most fascinating were the details of this vast collective history: how social historical change had *actually* taken place, through which diverse, local, contingent mediations and initiatives, endeavours, dramas, victories, circumstances and happenstances – some happy, some tragic. Students and teacher shared a common enthusiasm for this new approach; and Bertaux came back to France keen to reflect upon the experience, repeating it, discovering the potentialities of the new method as he had done previously for life histories.

Now, more than ten years later, with such experiments repeated in several universities by both co-authors separately, with the experience learned from several research projects done in collaboration, the time has come to present the method as a well-tested, well-worked one.

From life histories to case histories of families

There is much in common, but also many differences between life stories and family stories.

The life history (or 'biography') is the case history of one person, where the person is the centre: their life story, their own narrative and evaluative account of their life and life experiences as told to an interviewer, puts them at the centre point of the picture. But few individuals live alone as isolated atoms; most live in households, clusters of persons connected to each other and moving together through time (Hareven 1982).[5] All of them become embedded in nets of strong, reciprocal, commitments and feelings; their actions, life decisions, life paths interact with each other; kinship, juridical, moral and other kinds of bonds relate them to each other. While granting that what counts most are not formal kinship ties but 'lived' ones, it remains that most people are connected most of their life with some 'significant others' by bonds of reciprocal dependence and moral solidarity. While individual life stories may glance only sideways at such relations, case histories of families put such bonds at the very centre of the picture and look at the development of such bonds over the *longue durée* – the long term – as they unfold and change through historical time.

Therefore the focus on a family rather than on an individual immediately sets within the field of observation, and at its very centre, not an individual but *relations*, which are at the same time interpersonal relations *and* socio-structural relationships. It is in this sense that we consider case histories of families sociologically richer than life histories.

What both forms have in common is the passage of time, and the unfolding of actions through time – that is, history. Hence the use of the term 'social historical' to refer to the nature of what is brought back by the case study. Both forms are also based mainly – but not necessarily exclusively – on stories collected through interviewing: for family case histories, the interviewees are asked to tell not only their own story but also what they know and may tell about the lifepaths of their kin, a task at which women prove regularly incomparably better than men. For a family case history, not everybody present in the 'window of observation' needs to be interviewed; three or four informants spread over three generations prove usually enough to provide an overall, cross-checked, picture.

A single life story, although it may make fascinating hearing and reading, although it may bring to the mind of the researcher many hypotheses about how this or that social world actually functions, needs to be supplemented by other life stories or by other kinds of materials in order to stand as sociologically relevant 'data'. Five life stories of individuals not connected to each other constitute five separated pieces, perhaps five gems but with no cumulative power unless they are taken from the same social world. But the life stories of five persons connected by close kinship ties, for instance a couple and their three grown-up children, bring more information than five separated life stories: they illuminate and reflect upon each other like the gems of a necklace. The reason is not only methodological: such *récits croisés* (Delcroix 1995), such linked lives, deal with one and the same cluster of persons and lives; one can see them unfold in parallel, and witness for instance how a given development in one impinges upon the other ones; how the elder generations attempt to shape the life courses of the younger one; or how relations of competition and complementarity between siblings contribute to orient their life paths.

With a nuclear family, one is confronted immediately with a relatively stabilised *system of interconnected actors*, a small organisation complete with goals, a stable division of labour, roles, norms and sanctions, with strategies turned either outwards or inwards, experiences being passed on, exchanged, imitated, rejected; with conflicts over values, beliefs, styles of conducts; with, therefore, internal dynamics.

We believe that each family (in the sense here of a household with at least one child) is not only a system of consumption or of living together, but also and perhaps primarily a unit of *production*, inasmuch as it is within it that, through a whole range of activities structured by the gender division of labour and summarised under the umbrella of 'domestic labour', the energies and energy-orientations of its members get produced and re-produced anew. The necessities of this kind of production – which we conceive as participating in what we call 'anthroponomic production', that is, the production of human beings themselves – make for the constrained and cyclic nature of daily family life (Bertaux 1994).

One of the most interesting features of such microsystems of 'production' in the widest sense (including the production of destinies) is the centrality of *gift* in their functioning: neither exchange, nor command and exploitation, but gift. All kinds of gifts, but the gift of life to begin with: a gift, from parent(s) to child, that by definition cannot be reciprocated as such to the donor(s), but which nevertheless *can* be reciprocated through the mediation of a third person, the child that a daughter or a son 'gives' to her/his own parents. Which is one more reason to include three generations in the picture.

But beyond such commonalities between families there are their differences, which make collecting case histories worth the effort: the infinite variety of patterns of relations, family settings and microcultures, histories and stories.[6] Thus a great variety, a great wealth of patterns is what one may expect, rather than uniformity; for the sociologist the task is then to make sociological sense of the data, either by comparing cases, or – preferably in a second phase – by focusing in depth on one singular case.

What is in a family case history?

Case histories of families bring forth materials which concern not only family life, and therefore not only family sociology, but also, for example, *gender relations* and how they have changed historically, through particular concrete actions of ordinary women; how practices of bringing up *children* vary within a given milieu, how they differ from one social milieu to another, and from one generation to another; how *migrations* take place, who has the nerve to go and check if the grass is greener elsewhere, how people manage to settle in a new environment; how *social encounters* end up sometimes in marriages; how parents try to help their children, how fortunes get accumulated or wasted, how destinies take shape – this is the traditional topic of '*social mobility*', but captured this time at the very root of the process; how various and multifaceted social games are played, especially the game of generalised competition; how political ideas begin to take shape within the family setting; and a host of other sociological issues. At a more abstract level they provide a great wealth of materials on *interaction*, *gift*, *identification* and the genesis of *identities*, and other key issues of general sociology.

One way to bring some order within the extraordinary wealth of possible topics is to refer to a simple framework. Anthropologists have shown that all kinship ties may be decomposed into a combination of three basic kinship relations: *union* (the relation between spouses), *filiation* (the relation between parents and children), and *germanity* (the relation between siblings).[7] But the question is, what are the *sociological meanings* of each of these three basic relations?

When, more than one century ago (1887), Tönnies put these three relations at the centre of his conception of *Gemeinschaft*, he described them, respectively, as carrying the elements of *social bond*, of (common) *blood*, and of (common) *spirit*. But this he did at a time when kinship relations were much more part and parcel of the structuring principles of society. Today, as the *Gesellschaft* has spread considerably over formerly *Gemeinschaft* territories, colonising them without however eliminating completely the previous forms, Tönnies' conceptions need to be revisited. Here is how we would redefine their sociological contents.

Sociologically speaking a *union* can be described, somewhat provoca-tively, as a joint venture by which two persons attempt to merge their inherited and self-accumulated 'capitals' and their subjective resources to build something new: a couple, that is a form that usually includes virtu-ally its transformation into a (nuclear) family. Mutual attraction, the desire to share their lives, love in a word, is of course what pulls the part-ners towards each other. However, each one comes with a specific set of values, tastes and cultural features, a specific habitus, a specific 'capital of biographical experiences', perhaps specific deeply ingrained projects conceived in the continuity of her/his own ancestral lineage and backed by its living members (i.e. her/his own parents and other kins). Thus tensions develop within each couple between forces of attraction and centrifugal forces: their ulterior dynamics can hardly be deduced or predicted, and case histories appear as the best way to get access to their description.

The term 'sociological dynamics' points to such issues as differential dynamics according to class;[8] processes leading to splitting and conse-quences for the children (divorce is not merely an event, but a process spread over years, beginning before and lasting after the event itself takes place); homogamy and heterogamy. In their processual study of mixed marriage, based on thirty case histories of mixed couples, Guyaux *et al.* (1992) have pointed out that, when partners come to the marriage carrying with them different religions, cultural models and/or nationalities – e.g. Belgian and Moroccan, Belgian and Italian, Belgian and Zaïrois – their couple constitutes one small point of contact between two wholes rubbing against each other as two giant tectonic plates would do; it func-tions as an experimental laboratory of interpersonal, but also intercultural and even international, communication. Their private conflicts may eventually involve nation-states if, when divorcing, both want to keep custody of the children; but conversely, it is also through the invisible everyday efforts – taking place in thousands of mixed couples – of mutually teaching to the other to understand, tolerate and respect alterity that intercultural communication really occurs. Learning the Other, which begins as a private experience and endeavour, generates new skills that many members of mixed couples subsequently use to find either a job or a role in volunteer activities: a good investment, a typical example of a *capital d'expérience biographique spécifique* (capital of a specific biographical experience).

The mixture of private and public, micro and macro, that characterises sociological issues about mixed couples may be found in many other kinds of families. It will be enough here to mention the families of traditional shopkeepers whose living comes from a 'family business'. In such couples the family relationships function as production relationships as well – not only couple relations but also relations to children, who often contribute their labour to the family business. In Taiwan, central Italy and many other regions throughout the world, the family business is a frequent, typical and dynamic entrepreneurial form. Case histories of such families allow us to understand not only family dynamics but also the economic and anthroponomic dynamics specific to a branch of industry, as in the case of the artisanal bakery in France (Bertaux and Bertaux-Wiame 1981). One of the most unexpected discoveries concerned the various ways young ambitious bakery workers moved from bachelorhood to marriage right at the same time that they moved into self-employment: coming to need a partner for their family business, they suddenly hurried from place to place to find a suitable one, secretly testing their dates on their labour skills, values and ambitions as they courted them.

The concrete pictures yielded by case histories of families may differ rather strikingly from common-sense assumptions about family life. For instance, when our colleague Jorge Gonzalez, at the Department of Communications at Colima University, organised the collection of one hundred case histories of families in Mexico's ten main cities, he was struck by the recurrent descriptions of situations whereby, in the 1950s and 1960s, a mother and housewife, in spite of her many children, was also – through informal activities – the main or sole family breadwinner. In the country which gave to the world the term *machismo* it appears that many a proud young man who had started a family and tried hard at first to become a good breadwinner, could not overcome his first failures and started to drift away from his role. In such families mothers had to invent ways to survive; as the Catholic Church insisted that they remain housewives no matter what, and as they had anyway several children to take care of, a frequent pattern of action was to transform the home into a workshop and enlist the labour of children to make goods – sweets, pastries, toys, dolls, paper flowers, etc. – which they would then sell in the streets. A woman whose kitchen window was on a busy street tore down part of the wall and began to successfully sell food to passers-by. Such cases shed a new light on the picture of 'family'.

The case histories of Russian families that Bertaux and a team of Russian sociologists collected in Moscow in the early 1990s revealed the frequency, during the 1940s and 1950s, of a particular type of household where the mother played the role of the hard-working breadwinner with very long hours while the grandmother, *babushka*, played the role of the mother, doing the shopping and taking care of the children. Many a husband was absent from home because he had been killed during the war, because he was detained, because he had been sent to work on one of those huge building sites in Siberia where it was impossible to raise children, because he had left home (especially in rural areas) in search of a better fate, or because he had been kicked out of his own home by his wife in view of his too frequent infidelities or drinking. The number of children – now grown-up men and women – who have been raised in Russia within such a form of family probably reaches millions; but, to our knowledge, the form itself, although familiar to ordinary folk, has not been studied as such by Soviet sociology.

These are only a few examples; they aim at giving a flavour of the extraordinary variety of forms that one discovers if one studies the 'social bond' of marriage through case histories of families, and especially case histories using narratives.

Filiation

We see the relation of filiation between parents and children as the core of the family phenomenon, whatever way one looks at it. Concerning time for instance, the birth (or adoption) of the first child not only leads to a restructuration of its use, but also introduces a wholly new 'arrow of time' leading virtually to a very distant future, way beyond the parents' death. Concerning anthroponomic processes, the 'production' (transformation) of children from mere flesh into fully socialised human beings mobilises immense energies and affects. Symbolically, children add meaning to the union itself (in those times and places where divorce was forbidden they even often provided, for couples that did not get along anymore, family life's only source of meaningfulness). Economically, the entire private wealth of a country is passed down from the proprietors to their children every thirty years or so – the entire private wealth of a nation: from the totality of the privately owned land and real estate to the sum total of enterprises, shares and bonds – and this generates a yearly flow of property right transfers whose magnitude is of the same order as the gross national product; however, rather than being organised by markets, it follows the channels of filiation.

This is enough to recall that the study of filiation should not be restricted to the narrow framework of family sociology. In this perspective Tönnies' conceptualisation of filiation as being about 'blood' appears particularly outdated.

Perhaps the most encompassing way of looking at it – although it is still bound to leave much out – is to conceive of the relationship of filiation as characterised by the parents' (and grandparents', and other kin's) efforts at passing on/down their own resources and values to their children. The *effort to transmit* is the key to deciphering what is taking place between parents and children.

Within sociology it is not family sociology but the badly named 'social mobility' research that has dealt most with this relation between two successive generations. It is badly named because it assumes that mobility is the rule and that its opposite, reproduction, is the exception; whereas in most societies it appears to be the contrary. Whatever the case, 'social mobility' research, proceeding exclusively with surveys, has been able to describe and quantify the anthroponomic ('human') flows between social origin and occupational destination; but these are only the end results of millions of very diverse processes having taken place within and outside families during half a lifetime. It is only by opening the 'black boxes' of family processes and getting the stories about how the life paths of their members got shaped that we may begin to draw a much richer and varied picture of 'social mobility' than the one yielded by survey research, and thereby enrich the field of social mobility and family research (Bertaux and Thompson 1997).[9]

Take for instance the issue of what happens to upper-class families which remain trapped in a country where a social revolution has been victorious, abolishing their former powers. This century has witnessed such revolutions in Mexico, Russia and China, in Cuba and Nicaragua, in Iran and in several other countries, not to mention the victorious wars of independence which kicked out the colonial powers in Vietnam, Congo, Algeria, Angola and many other countries; but – for obvious reasons – nowhere have serious studies been done about the fates of formerly ruling or well-established families. A recent study based on fifty case histories of 'families' picked at random in Moscow showed that, in eight of them, at least one branch of the genealogical tree went up to the pre-1917 upper class. The stories passed down, usually under condition of secrecy, to the descendants about how their parents had lived in post-revolutionary times showed how difficult it had been for them to help their children and grandchildren. Not only had they been dispossessed of most of their wealth (all that they could not hide) and of their former sources of income; but, especially after Stalin confiscated Soviet power, many adult men from former upper-class background were repressed, i.e. killed, imprisoned, deported, or deprived of any possibility of making a living. Their wives and daughters, most of whom had never worked before, had to find by themselves solutions to prevent their children – and themselves – from freezing and starving.

Bertaux's (1997b) study brought to light some of their strategies of resistance and adaptation, which were not always successful. One interesting point is that although they still commanded more 'capitals' (the name Bourdieu gives to objective or 'objectified' assets) than most families, they could hardly use them: to show that one had had an excellent education was dangerous; to be discovered as having hidden silverware or jewels from the Soviet State was more dangerous; and to have contacts with other members of the formerly ruling class could be lethal. Hence cultural capital, economic capital and social capital coming from the pre-revolutionary times had all changed their meaning to the opposite: they were not assets anymore, they had become dangerous handicaps.

This drastic inversion of sign, from positive to negative, may be interpreted as an effect of the *societal context*: family capitals are capitals or 'trumps' in the games of *generalised social competition* only insofar as the rules of such games are biased in favour of members of the ruling class; insofar as, for instance, the school system sifts and selects on the basis of that kind of knowledge which is acquired while growing up in the upper or middle class, insofar as credit for setting up one's business is granted in priority to those who already have property, and so on. As long as the same class is in power, such rules do not change; they become so much taken for granted, so much part and parcel of a fixed background, that they disappear from the perception of ordinary people and sociologists alike; it takes their brutal suppression to make them visible, in retrospect.

Generally speaking the literature on social mobility, perhaps because it stays too close to what is observable through surveys, is poor in concepts that could be used at family level. By contrast, although Bourdieu's 'reproduction' theory also claims its validity from surveys, his theoretical imagination (his ability to picture mentally what may be happening in families 'out there') has produced a number of useful concepts, such as the various forms of family 'capitals', that have been accepted by sociological communities worldwide. However Bourdieu and, even more, those who use his concepts uncritically, often seem to assume that such 'capitals' are handed down from one generation to the next as if they were mere things. This might be the case for the various forms of economic capital (depending of course on the laws about the transmission of property rights); but it is obviously not the case for two of the three forms of cultural capital that Bourdieu distinguishes, and neither is it for social capital.

Hence the issue of the varying degree of *transmissibility* of various forms of capitals. By extension, the same issue arises about values, traditions, religious beliefs, artistic and other kinds of skills, political orientations, cultural tastes, which more often than not parents attempt to pass on to their children so that 'something' of them – anything, provided there is something – survives: for all these the question is, *what is their degree of transmissibility?*

The answer to this question cannot be speculative. One needs series of case studies to study it, knowing that it will depend, among other things, on the cultural and socio-historical context. Some indepth case studies may also prove useful. Such might be the case in the study of a three-generation family business in southern France, which has discovered one hidden characteristic of small economic capital: that in some traditional contexts its real 'economic' value is made up of some immaterial (social) relations between the entrepreneur and a set of given customers – good-will – that can only be handed down if the son *himself* steps into the father's shoes; but at the same time, that – as Goethe pointed out long ago – the son may only 'own' the asset inherited from his father if he makes it his own by transforming it into something new, something of his own (Bertaux and Bertaux-Wiame 1997).[10]

Bourdieu's theory of family 'capitals' only takes into account parents' objective resources such as property assets and income, culture and connections. Other more 'personal' and definitely subjective resources may be used by parents, especially those deprived of any capitals, to build into their children self-confidence and other personality features, which may in turn prove very useful later on in their struggle for occupational achievement and status attainment. Numerous cases of economically poor but psychologically strong fathers, mothers and grandparents have been described in the (fictional) literature by writers, and in (non-fiction) autobiographies as well (for some striking examples see Roos 1987). In the Quebec 'founding experiment' mentioned in the first section, there was mention in one of the family case histories of a strong-willed woman living in the back country in the inter-war period, who would take her twelve children to the woods every single summer day to pick up blue-berries from dawn to night (they hated it, they would have preferred to play) and sell them on the local market in order to collect enough money to pay secondary school fees for the youngest ones. The five oldest brothers left school early and went to work, for the family needed their wages; but later on, when the youngest children got secondary diplomas and good jobs, the mother got them to finance retraining for their elder brothers. The methodological/theoretical point here is that survey research would have classified this mother as wholly deprived of any capitals, and the occupational success of her children as sociologically inexplicable. Perhaps she had no capitals to speak of, but she definitely had strong subjective resources!

We have been led to construct this concept of *subjective resources* in the course of a recent research project on 'working poor' families, mostly originating from Algeria, Morocco or Tunisia, who are living in a low-rent housing estate in Toulouse (Delcroix and Bertaux 1998): we felt the need to draw attention to the 'subjective resources' of such persons as we became so alerted to, and impressed by, the considerable efforts made by immigrant fathers and mothers, most of them illiterate, badly paid and with no middle-class connections – therefore deprived of any objective 'capitals' – to try to help their children reach some level of achievement at school and in the labour market in a very difficult context of discrimination against 'foreigners'. We had already heard many times of similar cases, for instance the 'blueberries grandmother' from Quebec, or the poor Finnish shoemaker who was able to give self-confidence to his daughter (Roos 1987); but it is only when we realised that the popularity of Bourdieu's theory of family capitals is unintendedly leading sociologists to conceive of members of the working classes as wholly deprived of *any* 'capitals' that we felt the need to create a new concept.

Many other examples could be given of the unlimited richness and complexity of the relationship of filiation in various social contexts and historical periods. One more issue however is whether the resources that parents attempt to pass on to their children are presented equally to all of them, whatever their gender or birth rank, or whether such offers are differentiated. This concerns the whole issue of 'sibship', i.e. the relations between siblings. Siblings who have been born from the same parents, within the same family, seem to have had initial access to the same range of resources and possibilities of development; how then does it happen that they more often than not take differing paths in life? This is a question we have to skip here; but it should be obvious that case histories of families provide a direct way to observe the phenomenon of siblings' differentiation of life courses.

So far we have looked at union and filiation, two of the three core kinship relationships, and mentioned the third, sibship. This is not the only way one may take a theoretically informed perspective on families. Let us now turn briefly to an alternative.

Families as microcosms

One way to look at families is to consider them as *microcosms*: small worlds, each one worth exploring, deserving description for its own 'sociographic' sake, but each one also capable of enclosing some sociological pearl – some vivid evidence of a given process whose awareness might illuminate thousands of other cases.

Probably the best approach here, the one yielding the richest harvest of facts and findings, is one inspired by the *anthropological* spirit, complemented by a *historical sensitivity to social change*. For it takes some degree of anthropological spirit to be able to look at a given household as a 'totality', a small world (microcosm) complete with its basis, structure(s) and superstructure whose specific patterns and internal consistency may be taken as objects of description and interpretation. And it takes some degree of historical spirit to complement the 'structural' look by a dynamic perspective at several generations, to identify the connections between overall social change and changes in families' patterns, and to realise that each 'anthropological' pattern is only a moment in historical time and social space.

As a point of departure it seems heuristically useful to conceive of households as small totalities made up of four main 'tiers':

1 material constraints and externally imposed rules;
2 patterns of behaviour corresponding to constraints;
3 internalised norms of behavior as mirroring but specifying external rules; and
4 value systems (specific to a given household) legitimising norms and routine practices, as well as projects embodying the household's members' aspirations to make their situation better or even to radically escape from it (Grootaers 1984).[11]

The point, of course, is not to refine this theoretical model by reflexive speculations, but to use it as a rough tool to be used in research projects for collecting data and analysing given cases: it is through fieldwork that the sociographic, and later on the sociological, work lives and blooms.

It is repeatedly fascinating to discover how indeed, in most cases, there are hidden connections between the *constraints* coming from work, housing, transportation, lack of means, and the moral commitments and the *patterns of conduct*, e.g. patterns of consumption and life styles, patterns of educating children, patterns of relating to neighbours, relatives and friends, and so on. The 'consistency' hypothesis, that there must be some coherence between constraints, conducts, internalised norms, and household ideology (i.e. its particular microsystem of beliefs, representations, values, and projects) gets regularly confirmed, but each time in new and interesting ways as actors specify which of the 'structural determinations' they do accept and internalise, which ones they fight against and try to overcome.

One might argue that this is too crude a model, still too 'materialist', not paying attention enough to the cultural level: after all, for example, skilled working-class families or schoolteachers' families may carry/- elaborate different microcultures according to their religion, political beliefs, family traditions, or tastes. One might also argue that if this rather deterministic model was to hold anyway, one would not need to include three generations in the research framework to 'deduce' its microculture.

But, to be precise, the answer to the first criticism is to include three generations in the picture: for it is only through knowledge about the previous generation(s) and what they passed on to their children, now adults and having formed their own household, that one may identify those roots of observable patterns which do not seem to stem from present-day constraints, but appear connected to inherited, moral/cultural/- ideological elements and past experiences. The anthroponomic perspective helps to see in which ways people's mentalities are the products of their experiences and in which ways they have been themselves 'produced'.

Let us draw an example from the 'Toulouse' research project which has been already presented. Its goal was to study how families cope with precarious conditions of life. As we have already mentioned, out of the thirty families whose case histories Delcroix collected in a low-rent housing estate, most were families of immigrants from the Maghreb. Practically all fathers had been workers in construction or industry, and many still were in these trades. During the fieldwork, Delcroix was struck by differences among households in their style of educating children. As an urban environment the housing project is rough, involving some dangers for the youths: confronted by these risks, some parents were keen on keeping their children within the flat whenever they were not at school; by contrast other parents allowed their children to participate in collective activities, cultural, sportive or otherwise, as organised by the school or local associations.

The first style of practice was referred to by Delcroix as *pratiques de fortin* (an educative style of 'closure'); the second one, as *pratiques de passage* ('open' style). This difference between family microcultures was first thought to derive from differences in the parents' value systems;

indeed the parents themselves related their values and conducts to their own childhood. However, when the households' budgets were studied closely and put in relation with educative styles, a striking correlation with income appeared: the lower the income, the more frequent the 'closed' style.

Families with the lowest incomes are the ones practising a thoroughly 'closed' style; for them the priorities are to pay the rent and to 'respect the rules' (of French society). All the other goals and expenses, and especially expenses for children's leisure activities, appear secondary and are actually sacrificed to the first two priorities. The children's freedom of movement is seen only from the point of view of the monetary costs it might involve if they break something, damage a piece of clothing, hurt themselves or – worse – somebody else.

Those families which allow their children more freedom (controlled freedom as it were) appear to have slightly higher levels of income per capita: although all parents have had the same type of poor childhoods back in the Maghreb the latter appear to have come to understand the necessity for, and desire of, their children to move to a more middle-class kind of social life, to participate more in the activities of their age group. It means also that they will be confronted by the risks and dangers of the neighbourhood, but in a controlled fashion, under the supervision of adults: so that they may learn to avoid them.

During the fieldwork, as awareness of differences between educative styles was emerging and patterns of interpretation were taking shape, Delcroix discussed the issue with some mothers and fathers; and it appeared that some of the households which were now practising the 'open' educative style had indeed practised the 'closed' one earlier on, when the family's income had been significantly lower.

This example vindicates the validity of the model presented earlier, where material constraints impinge strongly on patterns of conduct (here, educative practices), on internalised norms, and on ideologies (including values). It would seem however that there is no need to refer to the earlier (grandparents) generation to account for the observed educative behaviour. But parents educating in the 'closed' way have made clear in the interviews that, if they are able to stick to their educative practices, it is because they have inherited from their own childhood a specific world-view and internalised imperatives. They are actually using their own experiences of poverty to try and convey to their children the absolute necessity to hold tight even if it feels highly frustrating. Children however tend to compare their own situation not to the one of their parents when the latter were children – in which case they would feel very privileged – but to the one of their peers; a comparison which makes them feel definitely victims of strongly unfair deprivations.

Another example of the usefulness of a three-generation model is provided by a research project on the effects of social transfers on the level of living of families in Guadeloupe, an island in the French Antilles where there is much poverty (Attias-Donfut and Lapierre 1997). In brief, in this very interesting research project combining quantitative data and case histories, the researchers have been able to show that the recent governmental decision to give pensions to ageing housewives not only has made *their* lives much better, but that, by allowing them to stop working on odd 'survival' jobs and to take care of their grandchildren, it has given their own daughters the opportunity to take up jobs or to train for a skilled job, thus granting the grandchildren better opportunities too.

Conclusion

We began by presenting the method of family case histories as an extension of the life history method; what we hope to have conveyed during the course of this paper is that the word 'extension' may be understood in the widest sense, almost as if the life-history approach had been a seed and the family case-history approach the full-grown plant resulting from it.

It is plausible that most of the properties and uses of such an approach remain to be discovered. Among those we have already identified we have mentioned only a few; for instance we have not said much of the amazing ability of case histories of families to mirror societal change.

But above all, what we would like to underline is that this sociological approach encapsulates within itself, built into its very nature, openings towards the anthropological vision and the historical perspective. After so many decades during which sociological methods, in spite of C. Wright Mills' warnings and advice, resolutely turned their back to the spirit of the two sister disciplines of history and anthropology, it may be useful for sociology to replace, within some of its own instruments of empirical observation, channels of access to anthropological variety and to historical dynamics.

Notes

1   For a justification of the necessity of collecting a series of cases and of collecting them from within the same 'social world' or 'category of situation', before eventually moving to the indepth study of singular cases, see Bertaux 1997a (of which an English version is in preparation). Generally speaking, an empirical research project using comparative family case studies makes sense only if the field of observation is restricted to some specific part of 'society', the task being to describe 'how it works', what are the kinds of games played in it and what are the rules of such games. But the study will yield much richer results if it encompasses a historical dimension, showing the changes over

time and the dynamics of such changes. Specific working-class subcultures, for instance, are transient forms which follow industrial change but also express the capacities of resistance, adaptation and sometimes evasion of workers' communities. One way to give case studies some historical scope is to make them into case histories which means, for case studies of families, a historical depth of three generations.

2   The merits and drawbacks of this construction of a frame for the 'window of observation' is discussed in Bertaux (1995). A given person's formal kinship relationships form a trellis that extends indefinitely in the past but also 'laterally', to relatives of the first, second, third and nth degrees. For a family case history one needs to define what will be considered as the 'family' under scrutiny, i.e. the part of the kinship trellis that will be included within the window of observation. Two main approaches are possible: either to adapt the definition to each case, by restricting it to those kinship relations that have been and/or are practised, actually and concretely 'lived' – *non pas la parenté formelle, mais la parenté vécue* – or to put forward a standard definition, which is bound to rest on some arbitrary choices, and to make these choices according to the sociological perspective. It seems that the second one works better for the collection of a series of case histories of families, while the first is better adapted to the development of a single, indepth case history yielding a 'thick description' of a few lineages and their interactions through time.

3   Such phenomena appear indeed quite often on such 'social genealogy' graphs; in Quebec the frequency of lineages of carpenters was striking (in a country where many houses used to be built in wood a carpenter could build a whole house better than a mason). Some transmission of trades, or reconversions, are not obvious at first: such as for instance the case of blacksmiths who (or whose sons) became mechanics. The frequency of such a case may be explained not only by the proximity of the two trades (artisanal work on iron) but, more specifically, because horses whose shoes provided much of the blacksmith's workload, have been replaced by tractors which need maintenance and repair by village mechanics. This is only an example of the many 'occupational lineages' that may be found at ground level when one collects series of cases for comparative purposes.

4   In later experiments with groups of students in France and elsewhere, we have asked volunteers to present to the class the case history they have made; this makes for very vivid sessions. This kind of interactive teaching has been pushed further by Bertaux who asks his volunteer students to first draw a mute genealogical graph of their case history on the blackboard, then to begin by presenting one couple of grandparents (who they were, what they were doing, where, how, etc.), and stop: the teacher and the class have to try and guess who their children became, socially speaking. The student then gives the real answer (the teacher comments about why the guesses went wrong) and moves on to the presentation of the partners these children 'chose' when they grew up – and again, the class is asked to guess what happened to the children of these couples. Then the whole sequence is repeated for the other couple of Ego's grandparents. Every time this 'guesswork' has been tried, the level of participation of the class has been very high.

5   T. Hareven has used the metaphor of 'schools of fish' to express this fact.

6   One of us once wrote '*La Famille n'existe pas*': 'The Family does not exist', in the sense that there are types and classes of families, and within each one a

whole range of possibilities. No two families are exactly alike; therefore the meaning of 'the family' (singular) can only refer to the institution itself as a set of normative prescriptions, not to the numerous concrete forms that their combination with social classes, social milieux and a host of other 'variables' including individual ones, will take up. What we have in mind here is not only the contemporary variety of types of family arrangements: two-parents versus single-parent families, housewife versus dual career, etc. More radically, we believe that the similarity of roles ('every nuclear family is made of a father, a mother and children') is only superficial: sociologically speaking it does make a considerable difference whether a family's income comes from social assistance, from irregular hourly wages, from a stable job, from self-employment, or from property. The overall relationship between a household and society is bound to be very different across such typical cases, and as a consequence the relationships between family members should also take up quite different forms. But in order to observe such differences and grasp their full significance one needs to give them a chance to register on the instrument of observation.

7   Some add a fourth one, which is co-residence: it belongs to a slightly different order, but it becomes more and more relevant nowadays, in Western societies, with the growing number of reconstructed families.

8   As a small example one may assume that, all things being equal, the scarcity of a couple's monetary resources will make conflicts about their use a much more severe issue than in well-to-do couples; but what is really interesting is to see how couples in such tense situations actually deal with the tension, which problem-solving strategies they use to prevent escalation, and what kinds of backgrounds and contexts make for the success, or failure, of such strategies.

9   Besides a general introduction, Bertaux and Thompson (1997) is made up of ten chapters, each one describing the findings of some research project on intergenerational 'social mobility'. All the research projects have used life stories, usually as parts of case histories of families. The editors' intention is to show through concrete examples of research projects that survey research needs not be the only empirical method to study social mobility processes, and to demonstrate that case histories of families bring views and findings, hypotheses and sociological constructs, that could not be imagined and/or developed if the survey was the sole instrument of observation.

10 Bertaux and Bertaux-Wiame (1981) also show how the 'thick description' of a single case history may bring a host of hypotheses of general import about social phenomena, patterns and processes. It should be mentioned that knowledge previously acquired through a study of the artisanal bakery in France helped considerably to develop this single 'indepth' case history of a family business, by preparing the researchers to 'recognise' the general under the form of the particular, the universal under the guise of the singular. See Wengraf, this volume.

11 This is a modified version of Grootaers' conception.

References

Attias-Donfut, C. and Lapierre, N. (1997) *La famille providence: trois générations en Guadeloupe*, Paris: La Documentation Française.

Bertaux, D. (1994) 'The Anthroponomic Revolution: First Sketch of a Worldwide Process', *The Annals of the International Institute of Sociology* IV: 177–92.

—— (1995) 'Social Genealogies Commented on and Compared: an Instrument for Observing Social Mobility Processes in the "Longue Durée"', *Current Sociology* 43(2/3), special issue 'The Biographical Method', Autumn–Winter: 69–88.

—— (1997a) *Les récits de vie*, Paris: Nathan.

—— (1997b) 'Transmissions in Extreme Situations: Russian Families Expropriated by the October Revolution', in Bertaux and Thompson, 1997: 230–58.

Bertaux, D. and Bertaux-Wiame, I. (1981) 'The Artisanal Bakery in France: How it Lives and Why it Survives', in D. Bechhofer and B. Elliott (eds), *The Petite Bourgeoisie. Comparative Studies of the Uneasy Stratum*, London: Macmillan.

—— (1997) 'Heritage and its Lineage: A Case History of Transmission and Social Mobility over Five Generations', in Bertaux and Thompson, 1997: 62–97.

Bertaux, D. and Thompson, P. (eds) (1997) *Pathways to Social Class: A Qualitative Approach to Social Mobility*, Oxford: Clarendon Press.

Delcroix, D. (1995) 'Des "récits croisés" aux histoires de familles', *Current Sociology* 43(2/3), special issue 'The Biographical Method', Autumn–Winter: 61–7.

Delcroix, C. and Bertaux, D. (1998) *Enjeux prioritaires et types de conduite de familles populaires face à la précarité*, Research Report for the Caisse Nationale d'Allocations Familiales, Paris.

Grootaers, D. (1984) *Culture mosaïque. Approche sociologique des cultures populaires*, Bruxelles: Editions Vie Ouvrière.

Guyaux, A., Delcroix, C., Ramdane, A. and Rodriguez, E. (1992) *Double mixte, la rencontre de deux cultures dans le mariage*, Paris: L'Harmattan.

Hareven, T. (1982) *Family Time and Industrial Time*, Cambridge: Cambridge University Press.

Roos, J.P. (1987) 'From Farm to Office: Family, Self-Confidence and the New Middle Class', *Life Stories/Récits de vie* 3.

4 The vanishing point of resemblance

Comparative welfare as philosophical anthropology

Andrew Cooper

> Both in nature and in metaphor, identity is the vanishing point of resemblance.
>
> (Wallace Stevens)

In a helpful contribution to the meta-theoretical literature on comparative welfare Rebecca Van Voorhis reviews the development of theorising about welfare states, and revises previous 'three generations' models for this within a historical-evolutionary framework (Van Voorhis 1998). She cites the work of Kvist and Torfing (1996) according to whom the first generation of welfare state theory:

> emphasises the developmental similarity of welfare states i.e. convergence; the second era is distinguished by the importance placed on describing dissimilarity between welfare states, and the current epoch is dedicated to exploring the way pluralism has influenced the parameters of the welfare state.
>
> (1998: 191)

She herself argues for a model in which the first generation is characterised by 'grand theory', the second by empirical testing and elaboration of these theories, and the emerging third era by further empirical refinement inflected by concepts concerning globalisation and market requirements. Each phase, she argues, embodies a contest between functionalist and socio-political perspectives, with the former perhaps more inclined to emphasise similarity, and the latter differences.

In the present chapter I discuss a range of conceptual and methodological issues arising from a programme of comparative welfare study resting on very different assumptions and research methods than those deployed by traditional comparative social policy (Cooper *et al.* 1995; Hetherington *et al.* 1997). Nevertheless, over a seven year period, the analytical focus of this work underwent an evolution which bears striking similarities to both schemes outlined above, suggesting perhaps that there is a kind of deep structure to this form of inquiry, no matter what the point of methodological departure. The programme of study centred on comparative analyses of systems and practices in child protection work in various European countries, largely from the point of view of social work professionals who 'operate the systems' and 'implement' the practices. The methods we used to gather and analyse data are described below, but first I want to outline the evolution of comparative focus mentioned above.

- In the initial phase, comparison centred on two countries – France and England – and the discernment and understanding of similarities and differences in their professional practices, systems, state formations and cultures and ideologies as these bear upon the project of child protection work.
- The second phase enlarged the scope of study to several countries, but consolidated a focus on inter-country differences and a tendency towards a thesis of system incommensurability deriving from a functionalist account of the internal coherence of each system seen as the unique historical product of a range of interacting cultural, political, juridical and ideological variables.
- The third phase, inspired partly by a critique of the functionalist tendencies of the second, led to more analytic focus on intra-systemic differences and tensions, thus contextualising the 'legitimated' professional system of different countries more as the outcome of internal conflicts than as the product of a harmonious organic totality.
- The final phase embodies the search for possible deep structures, or invariants, within the variety of forms assumed by child protection systems in western European countries (Cooper and Hetherington 1999). If discovered, these will necessarily be at a high level of abstraction, but potentially useful as a 'generative grammar' for the articulation of principles of system stability within rapidly changing societies.

In outline, the methodology of the studies was as follows. In each of the two countries to be compared we assembled a group of social work practitioners responsible for child protection work. We had devised a four stage family case-study, neutral with respect to system factors in each country, involving escalating concerns about the safety and welfare of two children; at a first meeting of the group in each country, the practitioners were asked to complete individual questionnaires about their responses to each stage of the case-study. The questions were simple, but in the comparative context, proved telling – for example, 'What kinds of concepts would you use to help make sense of the situation at this stage?', 'What would a social worker do on the basis of this information?', 'What legal options do you think are available to you at this stage?' After completing the questionnaire, the groups undertook a video-recorded semi-structured discussion starting from the question 'As a group what plans would you now make at this last stage of the case?'

In preparation for a second meeting of the groups, we now dubbed the two video sound tracks into the language of the other country, and exchanged them; the groups reassembled, watched the discussion of their foreign colleagues, and then participated in an audio recorded discussion around the question 'What did you find different, similar, striking, surprising or puzzling in the responses of the other country's group?' A diagrammatic representation of the method is seen in Figure 4.1.

This chapter will not say much about either the results of the study or the methods of analysing detailed data. Rather, it will concern itself with the total character of the research enterprise, understood as a form of cultural anthropology. We had not anticipated that this would transpire to be its character, even though we set out with the explicit intention to investigate the cultural and ideological variables within which we took the practice behaviour of professionals to be embedded. However, we had not reckoned with quite how early in the research process we would encounter the influence of these factors.

Similarity, difference, comparability and equivalence – what are they?

Gregory Bateson wrote in *Mind and Nature* that: 'It takes at least two somethings to create a difference. To produce news of difference, i.e. *information*, there must be two entities (real or imagined) such that the difference between them can be immanent in their mutual relationship' (1980: 78). What does Bateson mean by the difference between two entities being 'immanent in their mutual relationship'? One answer is that, as well as being different, they must in some respect also be similar. A relation of 'no difference' is one of identity. A relation of absolute difference is that of incomparability, such that we have two incommensurable identities, or as Bateson says 'the sound of one hand clapping'. For there to be 'difference *between*' there must be a relation other than difference, which is similarity (Hetherington 1996).

The problem in cross-national comparative method is to find a relation of identity or sufficient similarity between the object of study in each country so that differences can be brought into a comparative relation. In

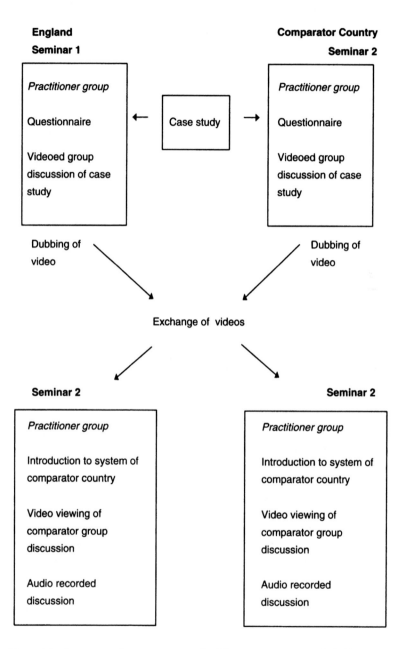

Figure 4.1 Structure of comparative methodology in cross-national child protection studies

our original study of France and England we had decided upon the use of a case study with accompanying questionnaires as a simple means of testing variations of response to an identical situation among practitioners in different child protection systems. However, this 'identical situation' proved more elusive than we had suspected. Precisely because of differences between systems, any individual case narrative from either country involves system-specific elements from early in its history, and ceases to be neutral with respect to both countries. We began by looking for a real case from either country which could be modified, but the necessary adjustments proved to be so great that the case became unrecognisable; we tried to design a fictional case study based on work in one country, but encountered similar problems, particularly once a case narrative involved legal factors, where differences between English and continental systems are great. Finally we collaborated with our French colleagues to design a fictional study describing the evolution of a 'case situation' which we believed to be neutral but recognisable to practitioners in both countries as one which would command their professional attention.

This exercise reveals a number of points of methodological importance. First, although we succeeded in isolating a 'core description' of professionally classifiable social behaviour in each country, it seemed that little, if anything, could be described as 'the practice of social work or child protection' independently of socio-legal context. Second, it was now clear that to undertake comparative research of the kind we were attempting, it was *first* necessary to understand the essential similarities and differences between the objects of comparison. There is much confusion, only partly semantic, between the concepts of equivalence (similarity or identity) and comparability. To clarify this, and render Bateson's arguments a little more transparent, we can think of matters as follows.

If I proposed a research study to compare zebras with personal computers, your first question would be 'What are you comparing about them?' You search for a relationship of similarity between the phenomena compared, which makes them worth comparing. If, on the other hand, I proposed a comparison of Citroën 2CV motor cars, you might ask for example, 'Ah, you mean between different models?' In the absence of other evidence you search for a relation of difference, such that the comparison is possible, let alone worthwhile. In one sense this is the self-evident basis of all social or scientific research. A conventional pharmaceutical trial proceeds by administering a new drug to a group of people with a particular condition, and administering something *different*, such as a placebo, to another group with the *same* illness, it then *compares* the outcome. However, in social research, which uses conventional survey or questionnaire methods, there is assumed to be no need to establish whether or not the research instrument makes the same sense for everyone to whom it is administered, because all subjects are taken to occupy a similar frame of linguistic and cultural reference. Data may be tested or controlled for evidence of variations among cultural, class or other group-ings, but variable findings are taken to be evidence of differences residing within the object of study, rather than evidence of ascription of different meanings by researchers on the one hand and research subjects on the other to the communications (questions, statements etc.) embodied in the instrument. Put more simply, different questions may have been asked and answered by subjects, than researchers believe have been asked and answered, if their respective interpretive frames of reference are different. Frequently this is not the case, simply because researchers have correctly assumed that they do occupy the same cultural and linguistic frames of reference as their research subjects. Under such circumstances *culture is an invisible or sleeping variable*, and does not disturb the validity of findings so long as they are not carried outside the cultural frame of reference within which the study was conducted.

Cross-national comparative research can make no such assumptions. Rather, as I propose to show, it works to disturb and awaken the sleeping variable of culture, and reveal it as a powerful shaping force potentially acting upon every level of data.

Beyond equivalence

Oyen (1990: 3–4) has asked the key question which I am broaching here:

> For most sociologists the very nature of sociological research is con-sidered comparative, and thinking in comparative terms is inherent in sociology.... One of the main questions is...whether comparisons across national boundaries represent a new or a different set of theo-retical, methodological and epistemological challenges. Or whether this kind of research can be treated as just another variant of the comparative problems already embedded in sociological research.

At first, it seemed as though our constructed case study acted as a 'bridge-head' between situations of difference, enabling satisfactory comparison by virtue of its function of 'equivalence'. When French and English social workers produced sometimes similar and sometimes different responses to the case study, they did so in relation to a case narrative which, brack-eting for the moment questions of translation between the two languages, we took to be 'the same' in the experience of participants of both nations. If this is a sustainable view, then the answer to Oyen must be that there is no methodological rupture: the case study is presumed to constitute a neutral 'object language' describing a neutral object, which allows comparison in the traditional and recognised sense. In retrospect, our first phase of theorising centred on an assumed-to-be-straightforward notion of describing and accounting for 'similarities and differences'. Yet even as we practised this, we found we were in the process of dismantling the assumptive basis of our thinking.

The structure of our methodology, wherein research participants were exposed to a kind of non-reflecting mirror in which the group discussion of the other country revealed radically different responses to their own, elicited a particular kind of reflexivity both in them, and in the research team. Thus, faced with evidence that French social workers appeared to have professional confidence in the Children's Judges who are responsible for children placed under statutory care and supervision orders, and that workers expected to have a continuing negotiative relationship with them, English workers typically asked 'How is this possible? What does it tell us about their system and practice assumptions?': however, they also asked 'What does it say about our own system and assumptions, that we do not expect or find we can have such relationships with English magistrates or judges?' In turn, French workers faced with corresponding evidence of English 'difference', asked themselves corresponding questions. Similarly, on discovering that French workers did not discuss gathering 'evidence' of possible child abuse in the course of their assessment of the family, while English practitioners had been heavily preoccupied with this as an aspect of their task, each was led to interrogate the meaning and implications of this for their conception of what constitutes 'child protection'.

The encounter with difference initiates a double interrogation of assumptions and meanings, simultaneously directed as it were at 'self' and 'other'. One significance of this turns on the disruption it creates to one's received idea of what 'culture' is. In the experience described, difference cannot be ascribed only as a property of the 'cultural other', since any interrogation of the assumptive world shaping the behaviour and organisation of the professional 'self', reveals the self as other to the other – as a construction or product of previously hidden but now revealed cultural contingencies, rather than an inevitable, natural or immutable datum of experience. If an anthropological attitude is predicated upon such a readiness to ask questions which provoke disturbance in taken-for-granted assumptions, by what means are these questions then answered, or at least pursued? Our experience has been that it is only by following a chain of questions and provisional answers, which yield more questions, that anything resembling satisfactory conclusions can be attained. Among our team, it was a basic discovery, although many have made it before, that

every datum in the social or cultural field is (or can be made to be) ultimately related to every other. However, while the project of inquiry may
be limitless, it is not internally undifferentiated. By interrogating
ourselves *about what kinds of questions we discovered ourselves asking in order
to produce plausible interpretations of particular data* about practice behaviour
and decision-making, an implicit analytical schema for the investigation
of cultural practices emerged.

Thus, while both French and English social workers asked and tried to
answer very similar kinds of questions in the course of their inquiries into
family situations, attention to the signifying context of these activities
revealed them to be divergent in extremely important respects. Thus, the
activity of 'making an assessment' in the different countries involved:

For English practitioners the gathering of *evidence* with a view to
constructing and *proving* a case in which legal *culpability* for abuse
may be a more or less central matter.

For French practitioners the gathering of *information* with a view to
achieving *understanding* so that the *suffering or predicament* of the
child can be a subject of decision.

Analysis of the questionnaire and discussion data revealed these as
coherent *languages of practice* in each country, comparable to the idea of a
professional discourse, or in Richard Rorty's (1989) phrase 'final vocabularies' through which specific universes of social practice are made and
sustained. Each element of the professional vocabulary of any country or
system is *internally related* to a network of others, and it is in the relation
of the particular unit to the wider signifying system that *internal coherence*
is discovered. Failure to take account of this relation will result in misin-
terpretations of meaning, action and value. A simple example suffices. To
an English social work practitioner or magistrate, the phrase 'Children's
Judge' will normally evoke a set of associations which include formality of
dress code, professional conduct in the context of a formal courtroom
setting, the exercise of powers of adjudication in adversarial cases, and so
on. All these associations and their logical relations are wrong, in the
sense, as I shall suggest in more detail later, that they are inapplicable in
France in the case of Children's Judges. The concept of 'judge' is logically
tied to other concepts which are in turn dependent upon higher order
ones. To paraphrase the philosopher Gilbert Ryle, the word 'judge' is
theory-impregnated (Winch 1970). But the 'theory' which situates the
concept is culture specific.

Thus, the meaning of practice behaviour, for practitioners as well as the children and parents who come to their attention, is shaped by, among other factors, legal context and tradition. French children's courts do not require 'evidence' to be produced before cases can be referred to the Children's Judge, and legally admissible evidence does not play a part in determining the process or outcome of proceedings in court. As institutions within each of the systems, French and English family or children's courts have very different aims and objectives, and equally divergent operational cultures. Comparatively, we have characterised these in a simple way:

England	France
Formal	Informal
Inaccessible	Accessible
Adversarial	Inquisitorial
Rights based	Welfare based
Adjudicative	Negotiative

To understand how or why, rather than simply *that* these institutions assume these divergent forms, entails reference to yet higher order categories of analysis. To take just one strand of the many required to account for all aspects of the above table of differences: the culture and structure of French children's courts appears to embody historically deeply rooted principles about the relationship between the family and the state, with origins at least as old as the revolution of 1789. The social contract between state and citizen embodied in the French constitution is explicitly cast in terms of reciprocal relations of obligation and duty, which French families expect to be honoured; thus the sense which many of our research participants had that French adults and children behaved as though they had a right to use the children's court in order to gain a hearing, and the right to be able to approach the Judge at any time for a consultation, while Judges expected that they should be accessible to being engaged in dispute and debate, appears to be a concrete institutional embodiment of a much wider set of political, cultural and historical currents which, taken together, constitute what we call 'culture'. A similar account of the political and historical production of English court culture is not hard to specify. The English concept of the residual state as set apart from the private domain of the family and civil society, into which it must not transgress unless there is transgression, typically calls for not a negotiation at its boundary, but a contest over the 'right' to intervene and seize authority within the Englishman's castle. Seen in this light, the much greater degree of professional anxiety carried by English social workers than by their French counterparts can be understood as the manifestation of a political task with which English social workers are charged – the maintenance of appropriate state-family boundaries (Cooper 1999).

All this seems to capture something which many social theorists have recognised, that culture is always both particular and general and local and global in its manifestations. As Richard Freeman notes in a recent and lucid review of the concept of culture in comparative study:

> For culture is made visible at the micro level: in organisations, in meetings, conferences, and consultations, in interactions between people. That is to say that cross national understandings of culture are predicated upon an unusually testing synthesis of macro and micro research.
>
> (Freeman and Rustin 1999: 9–20)

The nature of culture

> To repeat: don't think, but look!
>
> (Wittgenstein, *Philosophical Investigations*)

The direction of analysis sketched out above is schematised in Figure 4.2.

But this is a retrospective representation of a research experience which actually took the form of endless movement to and fro between micro, meso and macro levels of data, understanding and linkage. The confusion entailed by the disruption of 'taken-for-granted assumptions'

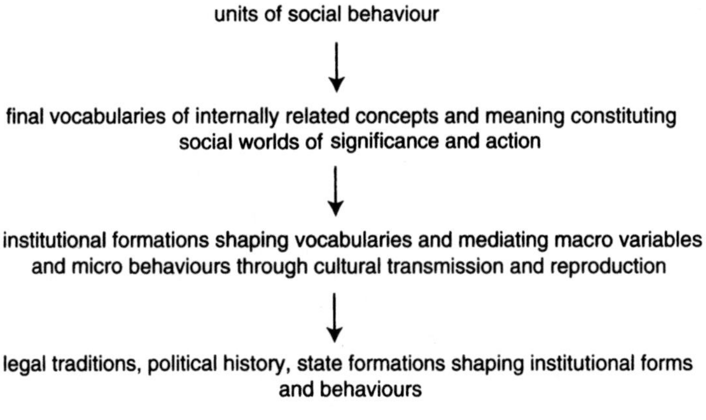

units of social behaviour

↓

final vocabularies of internally related concepts and meaning constituting social worlds of significance and action

↓

institutional formations shaping vocabularies and mediating macro variables and micro behaviours through cultural transmission and reproduction

↓

legal traditions, political history, state formations shaping institutional forms and behaviours

Figure 4.2 The logic of relationships between micro, meso and macro data sets in qualitative social research

was a continual and necessary process; continual because there actually is no end to the encounter with difference, necessary because without experiential openness to the impact of difference nothing new can be learned, and the act of sociological interpretation which produces the account of a complex phenomenon cannot occur.

The search for understanding of this kind, the experience of being 'lost in familiar places', appears necessarily to take the form of a search for coherence, and order. It was only later in the progress of this work that we came to question and reflect on this. For insofar as we were taken up with the task of rendering the unfamiliar familiar, the different assimilable, it seemed possible to discern how micro social behaviours in the professional field under study were actually in a circular and self-reproducing relationship with variables at all other levels. There are really two processes at work here. As Peter Winch (1970) and others have argued, one is concerned with 'learning the language' of another country in the sense of grasping the set of internal relations among meanings and behaviours so that an *understanding* of the way of (professional) life of that country becomes possible. This is the pursuit of *intelligibility* or *in vivo* symbolic coherence, the apprehension of a belief or knowledge system as a system. The other closely related but different process is the discernment of institutional relations within the same society. The advantage and the weakness of researching social relations through micro level study is that 'lived experience' reveals the interwoven character of phenomena which are often, and for some purposes usefully, kept theoretically separate. Institutional relations are not the same as symbolic ones, but it is clear that they cannot be understood in complete isolation one from the other.

Thus, as the following examples illustrate, institutional factors in the two countries concerned appeared to support the production and reproduction of symbolic relations, which in turn depended upon the stability and reproduction of institutional forms. There is no doubt that this formulation has a classically 'functionalist' character, but this may say something about a false polarity between 'consensus' and 'conflict' models in social theory, in that, arguably, no social formation is finally to be explained as the outcome only of social conflict and relations of domination, or only of consensus and relations of harmony. So, in France we discovered that the adoption of children is a rare event, apart from very young abandoned babies; adoption is legally much more difficult to effect than in England, and there is no effort or impetus to remove some minor but powerful judicial obstacles; we learned that ordinary French people find the idea of 'cutting the blood tie' unthinkable in a way which is not true in England where, while it may be an exceptional and unusual event, it is nevertheless culturally accepted as a positive solution in certain circumstances; the fact that children are therefore very infrequently permanently placed outside their 'birth families', seemed to partly explain why French practitioners conceptualised their work as directed towards the child-as-part-of-the-family even in circumstances where it seemed evident that the child was unlikely ever to resume a full and stable life within their family of origin; French workers took more risks in maintaining children in ostensibly 'unsafe' situations in their families than their English counterparts, but consistent with this directed their professional attention towards ameliorating 'whole family' relationships, deploying more 'qualitative' methods for assessing the balance between suffering, likely harm and the quality of relationships. By contrast, English practice was directed at securing the protection of individual children, outside the family of origin if necessary, and planned for their futures on the basis of their need for a 'permanent' place in *some* family, but not necessarily the family of origin; more 'quantitative' or objectivist measures of risk and harm to development were deployed, partly adapted to the forensic culture of the courts and the requirement to produce secure 'evidence'; in turn the law and the English courts were adapted to enabling the permanent separation of children and parents and their adoption or long-term placement within an alternative family. Thus there seemed to be a process of circular reinforcement among cultural values, professional practices and institutional provisions, specific to each nation (see Figure 4.3).

An analysis of this kind raises at least two sorts of question, the discussion of which will form the final part of this chapter. In the face of the discovery of the apparent uniqueness of the system of internal symbolic relations and institutional provisions which constitute the child protection system of different countries, which constitutes any particular 'event' or 'meaning' as context specific, we can ask:

- What now appear to be the theoretical conditions which researchers must establish in order to undertake the project of 'comparison'?
- What are the implications for the quantitative or scientific comparative study of similar phenomena in the two countries?

These questions, and their answers, are linked. Any 'system' of child welfare and the practices embedded within it are the product of a configuration of influences, determinations, and histories, which give rise to a unique phenomenon wherein the uniqueness is itself a product of the 'internal relations' among elements. Thus, a comparison of two such unique entities, or their elements, must occur within a framework which recognises their similarity, resemblance, or formal identity; otherwise as Bateson suggests, we can produce news of neither similarity nor

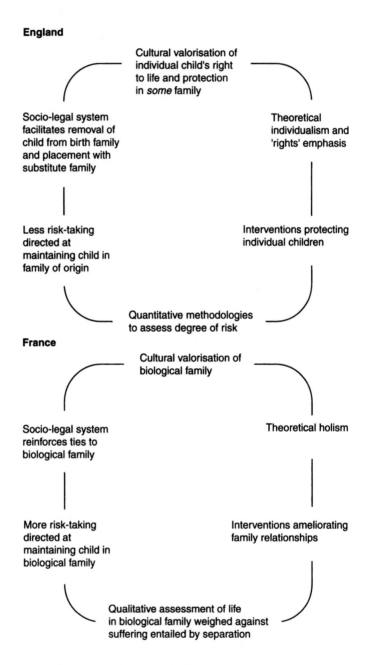

England

Cultural valorisation of
individual child's right
to life and protection
in *some* family

Socio-legal system
facilitates removal of
child from birth family
and placement with
substitute family

Theoretical
individualism and
'rights' emphasis

Less risk-taking
directed at
maintaining child in
family of origin

Interventions protecting
individual children

Quantitative methodologies
to assess degree of risk

France

Cultural valorisation of
biological family

Socio-legal system
reinforces ties to
biological family

Theoretical holism

More risk-taking
directed at
maintaining child in
biological family

Interventions ameliorating
family relationships

Qualitative assessment of life
in biological family weighed against
suffering entailed by separation

Figure 4.3   System reproduction in England and France

difference. The comparative project depends upon the explicit or inex-plicit assumption of certain higher order categories which denote similarities, and these may transpire to be of a very abstract character – so abstract that they may, in fact, appear banal. But their banality or other-wise is not the point here; their importance resides in the guarantee they provide of a logical foundation to the comparative enterprise, without which the slide into absolute methodological relativism or solipsism cannot be prevented.

In the particular case under discussion in this chapter, the higher order categories which we *discovered* as framing the joint comparative project were banal in some instances but not in others. We found we could agree that both French and English researchers were jointly engaged in the study of *systems of child protection* (which seemed banal, but true). We also concurred that the relationship between *the state, the family and the child* were key organising relationships in both countries, and this was a helpful discovery which later underpinned our ability to extend the research programme to other countries with a more confident expectation that we knew better where to direct our attention – for example at what happens at the *boundary* between the state and family life; we were led to realise that many, but not all, systems of child protection in Europe have identi-fied institutions which function to negotiate or mediate activity at this boundary. Nevertheless, it is essential to note once again that higher order categories of this kind, notwithstanding their abstract character, are still cultural, or at any rate socio-political phenomena. I once attended a large child protection conference in a north African country with strong histor-ical links to Europe, but many of the organising themes gathered under the heading of 'child protection' were not recognisable from a European standpoint – the provision of basic education for girls in a liberal Muslim society, irrigation schemes for rural desert communities to counter child-hood disease, as well as more familiar concerns about domestic violence, physical and sexual abuse.

I suggest that the situation described above may be elucidated with the help of Wittgenstein's notion of 'family resemblances'. In his later philo-sophical work, Wittgenstein abandoned the earlier project of a search for the single essence of language, and, relying more heavily on description and observation, concluded that there is no such thing. Rather, the evident similarities and differences among, for example, different kinds of game reveal a network of 'family resemblances' among them. Distantly related varieties of game may bear little resemblance to each other and much more resemblance to something adjacent which we would not clas-sify as a game at all. 'And the result of this examination is: we see a complicated network of similarities overlapping and criss-crossing:

sometimes overall similarities, sometimes similarities of detail' (Wittgenstein 1994: 49).

For Wittgenstein, neither similarity nor difference is a privileged category through which we can assert some underlying unity or logical ordering of relations among things.

> And we extend our concept…as in spinning a thread we twist fibre on fibre. And the strength of the thread does not reside in the fact that some one fibre runs through its whole length, but in the overlapping of many fibres. But if someone wished to say: 'There is something common to all these constructions – namely the disjunction of all their common properties' – I should reply: 'Now you are only playing with words. One might as well say: Something runs through the whole thread – namely the continuous overlapping of those fibres'.
>
> (1994: 49)

The further one travels in *cultural* space and time from one's own frame of reference, the more adjustment will be required to the categories which govern comparison; at certain junctures, it will seem as though a line has been crossed – no meaningful comparison can be undertaken, or in Wittgenstein's terms, to attempt comparison would be a transgression, a category mistake.

I will turn now to the second question posed above. How does the 'rediscovery of culture' as a ubiquitous feature of social welfare system and practices impact upon the traditional project of cross-national comparative survey research? This is a large question, and I will suggest just one line of thought in this respect. The arguments of this chapter suggest that *to compare 'outcomes' in welfare interventions across national boundaries without first researching and defining the norms of culture which shape the day-to-day intentions of welfare professionals and the equally significant everyday expectations of recipients or users, is no longer defensible.* The example given above of socio-legal assumptions with respect to adoption in France and England reveal that certain 'outcomes' available in one country are simply unavailable by definition in others; to some extent therefore, a kind of teleology must operate to alter professional actors' conceptions of apparently identical initial conditions in each country, so that the subsequent evolution of cases can only be understood or encountered by reference to the differentially available 'futures' represented by the available set of possible outcomes in cases of particular kinds. The availability or unavailability of such an outcome must act to alter practice behaviour across a whole range of potential decisions and subjective responses by both professionals and parents in child welfare cases.

In other words, the relationship between initial conditions, 'inputs', decisions and outcomes is not linear, but reflexive and processional. As Anthony Giddens (1984) has argued, any proper explanation of social life must refer to the 'knowledge' of social actors concerning the conditions of their own actions. This 'knowledge' need not be explicit, but can be tacit or 'practical', as indeed it will be with respect to the everyday taken for granted forms of life which constitute what we call 'culture'. Methodologically, the relationship which now emerges as really significant – between the scope for action and choice of individual social subjects and the cultural possibilities and constraints within which they think and act – is only now being fully explored empirically (see for example Chamberlayne and King 1996; Rustin 1997). But until the relationship between particular outcomes and reflexive understandings within particular complex cultural systems is better understood empirically *and* a method of comparing the effect of changing a single variable located in more than one such complex system is devised, comparative 'outcome' study is likely to produce more harm than good.

Until the 1990s most comparative child protection research was conducted among Anglophone countries, usually geographically distant but culturally adjacent, and this history itself entailed a process of cultural reinforcement of the cultural presuppositions governing the object of investigation. The encounter with continental European traditions of child welfare disturbs and disrupts this tendency to cultural convergence. I think that it is the experience of disturbance to one's professional assumptive world which largely accounts for a tendency in the first phases of comparative study, to search primarily for coherence in those unfamiliar societies or aspects of society with which comparison is being made. An account of inter-country similarities and differences depends in some measure on a conception of each as embodying a series of stable, meaningfully related characteristics which can be compared for similarity or difference. The identification of intra-systemic conflicts, contradictions or tensions introduces a further dimension of complexity, which can perhaps only be psychologically and theoretically accommodated against a backcloth of presumed coherence. But once discovered, Wittgenstein's methodological principles cannot relax their hold; the observable social world continually divides and unites, so that any unit of comparison may be found to be internally differentiated, so that these elements are brought into new relations of similarity and difference with phenomena in the comparator unit. In this sense his *Philosophical Investigations* foreshadows the later, more excitable, less ethically concerned, and often intellectually more shallow manifestations which we call postmodernism.

In the most recent phases of the programme of comparative study discussed in this chapter, we have begun to ask whether there might not be a kind of 'deep structure' to the diversity of child protection systems we have studied; not a deep structure which 'explains' them or generates them, or to which they can in any sense be reduced, but one to which they might plausibly each be understood as a socially creative response – a structure given by certain more or less irreducible *human* predicaments of late twentieth-century Western societies. Stated simply, the predicament can be translated into the question: what kinds of institutional and then legal responses do societies create when children are suffering harm at the hands of their parents or carers, and the latter resist or do not respond to proffered help, persuasion, or informal coercion? This triangle (see Figure 4.4) is a predicament for which all post-industrial societies have developed a response, but as our research has shown, an extremely diverse range of responses even among geographically proximate nations (Cooper and Hetherington 1999). This is not a discovery which I would wish to be harnessed to the project of 'harmonisation' in Europe or anywhere, but rather one which might serve as the basis for further creative diversification in pursuit of solutions to human problems in distinct cultures.

It is possible that the historical movement in the comparative theorisation of welfare states outlined at the start of this chapter is itself to be explained by history rather than a Hegelian movement of 'thought'. If the uncertainties (risks) engendered by globalisation in the second half of this century have been both a product of and a stimulus to accept more 'difference', then it may be that recent emphases on pluralist conceptions of

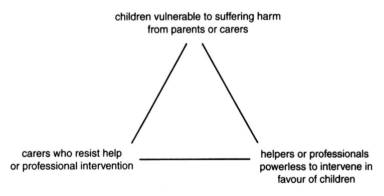

Figure 4.4 The core structure of relationships between children, carers and professionals in child protection work

welfare are simply consonant with this – our theories are produced by the times, as much as producing them. But the imperative that we embrace differences, and somehow negotiate the impact of this upon our increasingly fragile identities (sameness), is a call to fortify ourselves with certain capacities and skills, some of which this chapter has tried to delineate on the basis of researcher experience. Perhaps we are all cultural anthropologists now.

Acknowledgement

Many of these ideas were first originated and elaborated in discussions with research colleagues, but in particular Rachael Hetherington, who also discovered that Gregory Bateson had been there first.

References

Bateson, G. (1980) *Mind and Nature: A Necessary Unity*, London: Fontana.

Chamberlayne, P. and King, A. (1996) 'Biographical Approaches in Comparative Work: The "Cultures of Care" Project', in L. Hantrais and S. Mangen (eds), *Cross-National Research Methods in the Social Sciences*, London: Pinter.

Cooper, A. (1999) 'Anxiety and Child Protection Work in Two National Systems', in P. Chamberlayne, A. Cooper, R. Freeman and M. Rustin, *Welfare and Culture in Europe*, London: Jessica Kingsley Publishers.

Cooper, A. and Hetherington, R. (1999) 'Negotiation', in N. Parton and C. Wattam (eds), *Child Sexual Abuse: Listening to Children*, Chichester: John Wiley.

Cooper, A., Hetherington, R., Pitts, J., Baistow, K. and Spriggs, A. (1995) *Positive Child Protection: A View from Abroad*, Lyme Regis: Russell House Publishing.

Freeman, R. and Rustin, M. (1999) 'Introduction: Welfare, Culture and Europe', in P. Chamberlayne, A. Cooper, R. Freeman and M. Rustin, *Welfare and Culture in Europe*, London: Jessica Kingsley Publishers.

Giddens, A. 1984. *The Constitution of Society*, Cambridge: Polity.

Hetherington, R. (1996) 'The Educational Opportunities of Cross-National Comparison', *Social Work in Europe* 3(1): 26–30.

Hetherington, R., Cooper, A., Smith, P. and Wilford, G. (1997) *Protection Children: Messages from Europe*, Lyme Regis: Russell House Publishing.

Kvist, J. and Torfing, J. (1996) *Changing Welfare State Models*, CWR Working Paper 5, Centre for Welfare State Research: Copenhagen.

Oyen, E. (1990) *Comparative Methodology: Theory and Practice in International Social Research*, London: Sage.

Rorty, R. (1989) *Contingency, Irony and Solidarity*, Cambridge: Cambridge University Press.

Rustin, M. (1997) 'From Individual Life Histories to Sociological Understanding', in *SOSTRIS Working Paper 3*, Barking: University of East London, pp.112–19.

Van Voorhis, R. (1998) 'Three Generations of Comparative Welfare Theory: From Convergence to Convergence', *European Journal of Social Work* 1(2): 189–202.

Winch, P. (1970) 'The Idea of a Social Science', in B. Wilson (ed.), *Rationality*, Oxford: Blackwell, pp.1–17.

Wittgenstéin, L. (1994) 'Extracts from *Philosophical Investigations*', in A. Kenny (ed.), *The Wittgenstein Reader*, Oxford: Blackwell.

5   Biographical work and biographical structuring in present-day societies

Wolfram Fischer-Rosenthal

Introduction[1]

In the beginning was disillusionment. When sociology as an academic discipline took shape in Europe and America hardly more than a century ago, it was as a reaction to severe problems of early industrial society. Trust that enlightenment and science would bring about both technological and social progress for all had been eroded by the nineteenth century's severe economic, political and national antagonisms. Sociology tried to articulate the situation but did not provide practical solutions.[2] Instead, structural descriptions and theoretical explanations of a very abstract sort became a means of coping with a historical situation that had disappointed the projects of autonomy, freedom, equality and solidarity for all. The disappointment lay in the fact that a dialectical process of increased technical, cultural, and social *possibilities* had at the same time produced more *restrictions and dependencies*.

By the end of the last century, sociology had reinvented the question of social order in a structural and abstract manner. It used the old distinction of 'society' on the one hand and the 'interaction of individuals' on the other. But what was the unity of this structure, what kept both sides together? Society had become an abstract entity and the linking of individuals to it a difficult theoretical task. Where was society – among and in the interactions of individuals (Simmel), or in the 'structures' encompas-sing them (Durkheim)? Was social institutionalisation (*Vergesellschaftung*) the product of social action (Weber), and did institutions of modern society rely on such action, or were they systemically independent of it (Parsons)? In short, in attempts to answer the question 'How are co-operation and integration possible?', subject and object were: (a) identified as separate operational categories; and (b) perceived as *somehow* interwoven. Thus it was not possible to observe empirically the warp and woof of the fabric, nor to abandon the differentiating concepts themselves.

The general subject–object debate had been dealt with for three to four centuries since the late Renaissance in the guise of political philosophy (Hobbes), education (Rousseau), materialistic theories and practices of society (Marx), of helpless optimism (Comte) and academic reactions to the first shock of industrialisation (Durkheim, Weber, Simmel). The discussion continues today (among Luhmann, Habermas, Beck and Giddens, to name just a few). But contemporary reasoning about society and the individual tends to remain subject to the same old dualism.

In this paper I follow but disrupt such a subjectivity–objectivity discourse by using *biographical structuring* as an alternative conceptual tool.[3] The first part examines some core characteristics of modernity, focusing on the integration and disintegration of lives. This engenders the question of 'fixing' lives in the double sense of shaping and repairing. The second part introduces the central concept of 'biographical structuring'. The concluding part focuses on some consequences of using such concepts and perspectives for sociological research and practical support in the context of the helping professions. 'Social co-operation' is reintroduced and respecified as joint biographical structuring by professionals and clients, thus reviving the old hope of self-structuring *for the better*.

Disintegration of lives in functional differentiation?

The 'big bang' of classical modernity: the fission of the life world

Put simply, the beginning of 'classical' modernity was not the placing of the sun at the centre of the planetary system, but rather the placing of humans at the centre of our universe. Establishing the subject-centred vision that eventually prevailed in all areas of human activity liberated us from old obligations. Talk about subjectivity today is still in line with this early hope of freedom, though there is a question as to whether the 'right of the individual subject' is still as valid as it has been over the last four centuries. For complementary to the birth of subjectivity at the beginning of modern times has been the discovery, study and manipulation of the so-called objective world: this has gained such momentum that it seems to have overtaken the subject.

The subject/object distinction did not create symmetric spheres. Rather, subjectivity was preferred as the point for observing, and gaining knowledge about, the object world. However, in operating *vis-à-vis* its objects and constructing them, the ego or subject necessarily became the blind spot which, when not ignored, was at least a problem. Within the object world, no subject could be seen, only objects. For example, in medicine, only the body was there to be examined and treated. Focusing on the subject itself, as the 'object' of itself in idealistic philosophy or as 'mind' in psychology, was a reaction to the vanishing of subjectivity and the problem of how to integrate it in the objective, observable world. It seemed impossible to see both spheres at the same time. Whichever side one chose to focus on, the other side was missing, but not abolished. In the long run, the hairline fissure between subject and object which developed at the beginning of modernity opened into a large gap producing separate experts and expertises for both sides.

The success of medicine as a technique for dealing with the body in the style of natural sciences began with this opposition, producing neglect of the patient's psycho-social world and separating care for inner and for outer worlds.

The emphasis, on the eve of modernity, on rationality and on the individual as subject contributed to the formation of models of social order premised on the control and improvement of society (in the sense of *liberté, égalité, fraternité*, for example).

Both reason and the importance of 'the individual' – subject, citizen, actor, expert, professional, self – can be called guiding principles of classical modernity. Everything had to be accounted for in terms of rationality's means and ends. Its most prominent and effective institutions were the natural and life sciences, but law, economics and medicine followed as academic sisters in the same style. More rationality was equated with more control. In the second half of the twentieth century, the consequences of 'rational action' had produced ecological problems, growing poverty and unemployment on a global scale, dramatic changes of life worlds, the undermining of national regulation by 'global actors' – to name just a few major issues. Thus the extension of the principles of modernity to all sectors of society brought disastrous consequences. This development was so drastically felt that a break was posited and such terms as 'second modernity', 'reflexive modernity' (Ulrich Beck) or even 'post-modernity', stressing the non-rational character of the situation, were coined. The assumptions of modernity were found to raise two problems: first, order cannot be controlled sufficiently by rational action, and, second, order seems to be ambivalent in the first place: creating order means creating a corresponding chaos.[4]

With the complexity of choice, with the precariousness and ambivalence of order, the options for, and the central role of, the individual constantly gained in importance. By the same token, the former questions of how to be individualised *and* integrated became more difficult to answer.

From the very beginning of (classical) modernity, the development of the question of integration and disintegration is not accidental. Integration/

disintegration was the essential issue at the level of the individual and at that of society, as well as around their relation to one another. The issue was created by the distinction itself, cutting apart the pre-modern unity of a social order that did not separate society, the individual and the cosmological.

Functional differentiation

Using the sociological concept of differentiation[5] – which does not stand for 'progress' or 'social evolution' in the sense of 'an improvement of society' – we can distinguish different forms of differentiation (segmentation, centre–periphery, stratification, functional differentiation) (Luhmann 1997: 613, 595–865, esp. pp.707–76). Modern social development seems to have changed its *logic*: pre-modern *topological-spatial* differentiation has been replaced by *functional* differentiation (Luhmann 1980–95).

The diverse consequences can only be summarised here.

1   The change to *functional* differentiation entails the autonomisation and operational closing of subsystems in a society which develops organisations with *formal* membership definitions (Luhmann 1997: 42). Such areas include politics, law, economy, the production of academic and scientific knowledge, education, health care, art, the family, etc. By this process the individual and its interactions, as well as institutions and organisations, are 'constituted' in a way unknown to spatially organised societies.

2   The individual is no longer assigned to a single place (segment or stratum) in society, but is 'located' everywhere; this means that it is *de-located*, as many people's everyday experience confirms. The individual is functionally, i.e. *partially*, included in all subsystems. By the same token, he or she is excluded from these systems (except perhaps the family) as a person and as an integrated individual. Even if the system needs the individual, his or her absence does not terminate the system. This inclusion/exclusion pattern (Luhmann 1997: 131ff., 595–864) produces ambivalence. On the one hand the individual is increasingly important to society, because only the individual can transform possible choices into real ones. On the other hand, the 'individual' as an indivisible whole is endangered and expelled from institutionalised society. Functionally divided participation in many subsystems, at any given time as well as over a lifetime, is demanded and enforced. 'Fragmented selves', something Simmel discovered in urban Berlin as early as the turn of the century, or 'patchwork identities' (Keupp and Bilden 1989; Keupp 1994) may become the rule.

3   At the individual level, this amounts to the double question: how can *individual actors* develop and *orient themselves*, first as *self-integrated* persons, and second as *integrated members of society?*

4   At the level of social institutions and newly developing organisations, other questions arise: how can the functionally different social sub-systems at the same time: (a) *develop themselves* according to their own different, sometimes opposing, goals;[6] (b) *be functionally related* to each other, i.e. integrated at the macro level of society; and (c) *deal with individuals* as their personnel and/or clients? For institution-alised subsystems, individuals are uncontrollable, unreliable and costly. However, they are indispensable in maintaining inner dynamics of the institutions themselves, they react flexibly to changes in their environment, and they are necessary for innovation, growth and even the reproduction of the system. No institution or 'social structure' can reproduce itself without acting individuals.

5   The two separate spheres of *individual* and *society* – subject and object, citizen and state – are independent and yet must be related to each other. It is the self-describing semantics that produces the major theoretical and practical problem of modernity, namely to define their relations.

6   Social *institutionalisation* (*Vergesellschaftung*) and *individualisation* are both increasing; this produces *ambivalence* and *ambiguity*. More 'struc-ture and opportunities' seem automatically to entail *more risk of failure*, both for society and for individuals. *Integration* and *disintegration* are always simultaneously present at both individual and societal levels.

From the *perspective of society*, more powerful systems with increased capacity and complexity are harder to manage, and liable to risky outcomes. One strategy for minimising institutional responsibility seems to be *not* to take the individual – as personnel or client – into account. The 'costs' are increased disintegration, but this can often be 'externalised' as costs or tasks for other social systems, such as the health-care system, the political system, the family. Even individuals themselves may be burdened with the costs, and obliged to 'do' something 'to become integrated'.

From the *perspective of the individual*, the increased freedom from social and local bonds (mediated by money, in Simmel's analysis) brought with it the necessity of manifold choices. Thus the increased freedom in modern times is counterbalanced by the stress and strain of making such choices. Even if the means to choose (education, knowledge, money) are provided – and they are systematically *not* provided equally to all members of society – the process of choosing is hard work and may not produce the results desired by the individual. It may not automatically lead to continuous participation in any of the systems. Even participation on the level of national belonging is unsure: unemployment, loss of contact with the health-care system, or migration between societies, to name a few, have increasingly become hallmarks of present-day societies. The strain of combining all choices in a reliable structure becomes constant: the 'individual as institution' (Habermas 1988: 188). Is it possible for the individual to keep himself or herself 'together' under such conditions?

Functional differentiation entails the development of a more complex time pattern and time management. *Synchronising*, what can be done at the same time, as well as *sequentialising*, what can or must be done consecutively, becomes more and more important. With the increasing complexity of social activities to be co-ordinated and the multiplication of institutions with their own rhythms and their need for co-operation, a complex time-pattern is produced and forced upon everyone. Instruments and systems of measuring and co-ordinating time flourish. 'Being oriented' means to have some notion of what historical time, what epoch of society, one lives in. Temporal structures for routines and everyday life are often only implicitly 'known', becoming apparent only when they are disrupted.[7] Life-course patterns (childhood, youth, adulthood, old age; pre-work socialisation phase, working phase, post-occupational phase) are established culturally and through the occupational sphere, and function as a necessary co-ordinating system for orientation. In short, all social experiences and actions of individuals are linked to institutions and large subsystems by means of specific temporal orders.

Despite the assumption of a specious *disintegration of lives in the functional differentiation* of modernity, integration does seem to be possible, both on the individual and on the society level. The problems stated can be more or less managed in social reality. But how? This seems to be a riddle for sociology and its conceptual apparatus.

My thesis is as follows. During the process of functional differentiation and modernisation, the individual as well as the institutions developed new and more appropriate temporal orders, new networks for establishing meaning and co-operation, in which the individuals had new freedoms and new limits. To give a more general term to what has been named 'biographical work' (Strauss *et al.* 1985: 32, 132, 136–8), I call the specific *operation* with which I am concerned 'biographical structuring'.[8] The structures produced are called 'biography' (individual) and 'biographical patterns' (institutional).

Fixing lives by means of biographical structuring

How have both individual and society been dealing with *potentially* disin-

tegrating developments associated with modernity? How do they systemically try to prevent 'social entropy'?

Among other means, people as well as institutions in modern societies
have been dealing with the problem of complex social order by introducing
self-reflexive operations. One type of such self-reflection and self-description
that also uses temporal distinctions, and thus can structure the life-time of
individuals and define temporally differing engagements and participation
in institutions, is called 'biography'. Although the term reflects the
recent[9] cultural historical form of a written (auto)biography, biography is
originally produced in face-to-face oral communication. The term still
conveys the idea of a description produced by prior observation and self-
observation, thus structuring life before and after the event. The work of
orienting the temporal process of the individual's life and of social change
can be termed 'biographical work'. Biographical work is a practice that
has been developed in modern societies in order to solve some of the
main issues of integration and order. Biographical work is a way to orient
the individual and make him or her reliable for institutions in a historical
social situation when static personal definitions (such as status) or quasi-
natural phases of a life-cycle are not sufficient for this purpose. A biography
has to be both flexible and definite, integrating and open for new, unexpected situations and needs. Biographical work applies to both the
individual and the institution and is utilised by both.

Looking for a basic tool to deal with unexpected and ambiguous situations, to locate the individual and structure the world reliably, we first
come across the spoken language with its communicative and narrative
qualities. By means of communication we interpret what happens, pass on
to others what is important, fix experiences and build up knowledge.
Spoken language can recall and interpret past events, reorder them for
present purposes and even place them in a context of expected events or
planned action; spoken language is able to temporalise events, actions and
experiences and thus knit a multi-referential network in which the individual can orient himself or herself, i.e. be him- or herself and change as
well. The main form available to the person in command of a natural
language is the self-relational, self-expressive *narration*.[10] This is the
seminal competence that creates a more complex life-story. We may not
know who we are and what is happening to us, but if we are able to
narrate how we became who we are, then we can integrate ourselves,
because we can present ourselves as both consistent *and* contingent. Even
if I have gone through many contradictory phases in my life, the story
I can tell presents me as myself. We reconstruct our lives in a self-
relational attitude, *looking back* at what we have been through and lost
(such as a certain expected future), *looking forward* to what we aspire to,

putting it together for *present purposes*. This is an autopoietic process. In this process the relationship of the symbolic level – the story actually communicated – to the life really lived becomes an issue. Being truthful to our experiences, we cannot invent the life-story as pure fiction, but depend on our life history (which may be full of events that lead me to construct lies or impose certain readings and exclude others).[11] What I have been through, my life as I lived it, the communication with my fellow humans and its relevance, and last but not least my experiences with my body (Fischer-Rosenthal 1999a, 1999b, and, for the bodily experience of chronic illness, Fischer 1982): all this goes into my life story.

Is there empirical and historical evidence of this thesis?

At the level of the individual, the last two and a half centuries have seen an enormous expansion of written autobiographies covering all strata of society. Empirically, everyone is able to tell their life story, narrate a biography or parts of it in defined situations. In almost every type of communicative situation where we want or need to refer to the complex actions and experiences of a particular individual, biographical self-presentation may be required. Such situations range from hardly institutionalised occasional interactions between strangers (in a bar, in a train) to repeated narration in one's own social milieu (after dinner, during family celebrations), to highly formalised organisational settings (job interviews, visits to the doctor, testimony in court, political campaign speeches). Those who are in a strict sense not capable of biographically presenting themselves create interactional disturbances. Certain types of therapy are in essence provisions of professional support for constructing a reliable and liveable version of the life story, better fitted than previous versions to what the clients/patients have really lived as life history and to their present situation.[12] It is intended not only to change experiencing and behavioural patterns, but also to alleviate bodily symptoms. Any psycho-social therapy is professional biographical structuring.

All this can be explained sociologically by assuming that narrating one's life story (presenting the self in a biographical way) functions as a new means to cope with contingency. The 'mini-narrative' of oneself replaces those grand 'meta-narratives'[13] that were the previously pivotal ways of coping with a contingent world.

Given the precariousness of communication, presenting and creating oneself as a 'person' seems to be possible only by telling *how* one became what and who one is now. The individual as a dynamic system of plural sub-selves is realised in his or her *life stories* and not through a 'coerced identity'. Our position in the strata of society and our many functional relations to the major subsystems are less important for our own orientation and for others' perception of us than the narration of the story experienced, with its interpretive variance. Only my story seems to be able to transmit to others in good faith a clear enough idea of what to expect from me.

Not only individuals, but *organisations and social institutions* as well, have realised that the general social complexity and resulting tasks of organisational selection can be handled by the formalisation of membership and by requirements specific to different temporal phases. The formal regulation of admittance and 'processing', with regard to both personnel and clients, involves not just functional qualification, but also biographical checks. Individuals can be better expected to meet institutional demands if a temporally sensitive standardisation of such individuals is established. A 'career'[14] pattern – sometimes expanded to non-occupational strands of the biography – is made a prerequisite for membership status. This pre-shaping of biographical patterns happens on a small scale (e.g. in training for a specific occupation) in organisations. It accumulates on the large scale (e.g. the construction of familial life stages, the division of a lifetime into childhood, youth, adult occupational life, and post-occupational old age) over one or more functional subsystems of society (Kohli 1985). In the family, in education, in the occupational area and the economic sphere in general, and of course in the ordering agencies of law, politics and religion, biographical patterns are prescribed for individuals. Of course, this process of temporal differentiation also entails people losing options which they had before, simply by growing old and passing age markers (see, for example, Bornat *et al.* this volume). In general, we see an expanding network of temporally ordered positional and actional sequences, a network which is provided for the individual and which he or she has to go through in order to be a full member of society. Many of these sequences are also directly related to phases of the life-course.

As in the logic of institutionalisation, the very process of a developing plural biographical network in institutions feeds back, requiring a greater need for individual choices, thus reinforcing individualisation through the construction of biographical narratives.

Biographical structuring as a special practice and form of temporalisation allows both the individual and society to deal with more contingency, maintain complex social structures and balance more options. Biographical structuring thus is one way to connect individual and society in modernity.

To sum up:

1 Biographical structuring is *multi-relational*, it refers to and produces a network of events and options to be combined and continuously reinterpreted over a lifetime.
2 Biographical structuring is a time-sensitive, even more a *time-constituting and time-processing* process. This refers both to chronological,

irreversible sequential time (as in institutional careers) and to phenomenological time (as in autobiographical narrations) centred in
actual present time, filled with specific recollections and expectations.

3   Biographical structuring refers to an interpretive, open *process of
becoming.*

4   Biographical structuring is *dialogical and interactive.* The symbolic
network of self-orientation is constructed in a lifelong process of
communicating and sharing interpretations of what 'really' happened
and what to expect.

5   The researcher's biographical analysis mainly follows the same logic
as the biographical work of the 'biographer'. It is *hermeneutical and
reconstructive,* just as the biographical structuring itself – the
biographical narration – is *interpretive and constructive.*

6   Biography is related to the history and the capacities of the living,
animate body. Biographical communication entails the production of
meaning of ageing, sickness, social functions and parts of the body.

7   The concept of biography forestalls the individual–society split. It is a
structure operating in both spheres. Its manifestations of life history,
life story and institutional biographical patterns bridge the gap
between the theoretically induced 'inner' and 'outer' spheres.

Biography is a social structure provided by society, as it institutionalises
and organises the many types of timetables one has to go through in a lifetime and it is the individual's story *always in the process of being told,* which
he or she can and must tell.

Research and professional support

Biographical research

Biographical structuring is a general social phenomenon preceding the
'micro-macro' distinction in sociology (Fischer-Rosenthal 1990). The very
process of social differentiation in modernity calls for flexible reproduction and transformation of the person in relation to society. If the thesis of
'biographical structuring' as a means of creating and transcending consistency holds, then general sociological research on all levels of society can
be done as biographical research, stating how social order is achieved in
contemporary societies.

Once a Polish speciality, biographical research has developed greatly
since the times of Thomas and Znaniecki's *The Polish Peasant in Europe
and America,* the classical study on migration at the beginning of this

century (short edition: 1996; cf. Fischer-Rosenthal 1995d). Complementing a more quantitative strand of life-course research, recent biographical research makes extensive use of the narrations of individuals (for a concise history, see Fischer-Rosenthal 1995a; also Kohli 1981) in order to analyse social processes. A wide range of topics have been treated in order to study the biographical dimensions of social orientation in general. The meaning of historic change (Kohli 1986); the experience of institutional worlds, of living with chronic disease (Riemann 1987); the past and present meaning of large-scale disasters such as Germany under National Socialism (Rosenthal 1990), world wars (Schütze 1992; Rosenthal 1995b), or the Shoah (Rosenthal 1998); the recent reunification of Germany (Fischer-Rosenthal and Alheit 1995; Völter 1994) – these are just a few fields that have been analysed using biographies (and these few references are limited to German authors). Theory, methodology and methods have been refined (Fischer-Rosenthal and Rosenthal 1997a, 1997b).

As a research and diagnostic tool, the ability of biographical self-presentation in a narrative format is utilised to produce a narrative text as database. Additional sources (archives, written accounts of the same person, interviews of family members, etc.) may also be put into the body of material. However, the subsequent analytical task, the sociologist's reconstruction, cannot be another narrative. Rather, the goal is to discover the *generative structure* of certain selections.

The generative structures of the lived and experienced life history and of the self-presentation in the life-story interview, as well as their interdependence, are understood as principles that organise emergent events in the individual's life in order to enable him or her to achieve a consistent orientation. These generative structures can be discovered in a highly controlled hermeneutical process.

Finally, *types* of generative structure are formulated with respect to the specific research question and frame. The interviewing techniques as well as the whole process of reconstruction are quite elaborate (see Wengraf, this volume, for a more detailed sketch), but these remarks will have to suffice here (on interviewing and analysis, see Fischer-Rosenthal and Rosenthal 1997a: 412–21; 1997b: 139–57).

Going beyond the 'classical' focus of attention on the biography of the single individual, contemporary research concerns itself with the important question of the generational transmission of experiences (see Bertaux and Delcroix, this volume). Nothing is automatic in this interactive 'transfer' of knowledge and experience (Rosenthal 1997; Völter and Rosenthal 1997). There can be tendencies, and more or less legitimate reasons, to keep silent, *not* to convey what one saw, did or experienced.

The Germans in particular, in two wars of aggression and during the criminal Nazi system and during the socialist period of the GDR, produced a 'double burden of the past' which is now being studied in biographical research (Fischer-Rosenthal 1995b).

The collapse of the Central/East European socialist/communist states at the end of the 1980s is another very fruitful area for biographical research and incipient biographical research seems promising in these countries.

Professional support

Biographical structuring as an orienting practice has reached the helping professions. Therapy, social work, education in many institutions, secular and clerical counselling, supervision, organisational development, etc. all use biographical (re-)structuring and intervention. The internal conceptions differ from one profession to another, as does the degree of explicit consciousness that one is operating with *biographical* concepts. Somewhat programmatically, I shall conclude by sketching the uses and usefulness of structural biographical analysis in professional and expert contexts.

Given a cyclical process of continuous oscillation between the two functions of *analysis* and *interaction* with the client, two questions are obvious. What is the value of a biographical reconstruction as described above in professional support, and how can interactive interventions and unilateral expert reconstructions be practically established and linked?

Sociologically reconstructing the principles of an individual client's experience and presentation of his or her life on the basis of one or two biographical interviews and documents yields answers to two kinds of questions. One is, how is the behaviour and experience of this *individual*, especially when coping with and producing crises, brought about in the course of their life, and what crucial generative structures lie beneath the separate events/stories? The other type of question focuses on the *role of institutions* in these processes.

In most cases a professional expert has to deal with an elaborate 'history' of the client with different kinds of institutions (including their own) and the analysis has to discover what part institutions have played and play in shaping the client's trajectory – for better and for worse (Strauss *et al.* 1985: 8–39). Tracing the individual's and the institution's roles in shaping the trajectory not only demonstrates any positive potential, but also shows how any spiral of problems has developed and gained momentum.[15] The function of sociological reconstruction, identifying operating mechanisms, is identical with identifying *blind spots* of both the individual and the institutional actors. Making the blind spots visible to the actors themselves enhances their actional and experiential capabilities and reduces problems. For the client this means living better. For the professional, the self-critique and broadening of the institution's actional capacities not only applies to the individual immediately concerned, but potentially entails better support *for all clients*.

Taking a neutral position aside from the genuine interests of the client and of the expert, the sociological structural analysis of the biographical text – even if done by the expert himself or herself – can present the diverging interests of the two parties. The discovery of their respective blind spots, which are necessary elements of the actors' vantage points, brings the general paradox (Schütze 1996) of professional and client worlds into focus. More specifically, there is a distinction to be made between individual autonomy and social integration. The client identifies different problems from those seen by the expert, who is an agent of a social subsystem. The relationship between expert and client is asymmetric in regard to power, knowledge and autonomy. This tends to prevent the client from achieving greater autonomy, even though this is the explicit goal. Consequently, professional support systems very often produce the opposite of what they intend.

Focusing on these paradoxes in the concrete details of the case cannot make them vanish, but can make them less acute. The re-introduction of such knowledge in the interaction between expert and client cannot and should not dissolve the paradoxes, but, if they are known better, the range of action and co-operation between client and expert will be improved. The expert can thus avoid two common traps: he or she should identify neither with the client nor with the agency. Instead, the expert should develop a general professional knowledge and identity through skilled casework.

Today the critical point is not the level of structural biographical analysis as a unilateral expert method, but the practical re-introduction of the knowledge gained into the interactive process of the professional and the client. This problem cannot be solved by theoretical considerations but must be worked out practically, both in the training of professionals and in the actual communication between expert and client. It is not sufficient, and may even be harmful, for the professional simply to confront the client with the stark results of the biographical analysis. The insight into structures, both limiting and enabling ones, has to be transformed and respecified for a real communication and a process of guidance and support to take place. The pace has to be suited to the client's capacities and should allow for a slow restructuring of the client's biographical conceptions and narratives as well as for behavioural changes, including regressive movements, in the client's life.

Notes

1   Final responsibility for the editing of this version is taken by Tom Wengraf since, for technical reasons, it was not possible for the author to check the final manuscript.

2   Early this century the value judgement debate (*Werturteilsstreit*) in the continental social sciences was but one reflection of the tension between practical interests and 'pure' research. In Germany, the discourse reappeared in academic sociology: 1930s: between neo-positivism and critical theory; 1960s: the debate on positivism; 1970s till today: in the counterpoint between Luhmann's systems theory and Habermas' theory of communicative action.

3   Along this line of thought Luhmann has developed a non-actor-centred systemic view of society. Although relying in some aspects on his critique of sociology and on constructivist methodology, the author does not follow Luhmann's systemic approach.

4   Regarding the discourse on modernity and its derivations, cf. Beck 1992; Luhmann 1991; Beck *et al.* 1994; Bauman 1990.

5   Cf. classical: Simmel 1890; Durkheim 1893; Luhmann 1985.

6   E.g. making money in an economy, deciding right and wrong in law, deciding about truth in science, caring for health in medicine.

7   On the disruption of routines and lifetime patterns in chronic illness, cf. the author's study of terminal kidney disease and rheumatoid arthritis, Fischer 1982.

8   This is similar to Giddens' general notion of structuration, structure and the 'duality of structure' as medium and outcome of social practices, cf. Giddens 1984: 21–8.

9   There are only rare autobiographical documents out of pre-modern times, but we observe an abundance in the eighteenth and nineteenth centuries. Cf. Misch 1969; Pascal 1960; Niggl 1989; Fischer 1984: 478–82.

10   One crucial trigger for analysing stories in qualitative research in general and biographical research in particular was Labov and Waletzky 1966/1997; Bamberg (1997).

11   Rosenthal 1995a. In a critical appraisal of Gestalt theory and hermeneutics, Rosenthal has methodologically introduced and instrumentally refined the distinction and relation between *life story* and *life history*, the experienced and lived life, for empirical research; cf. also Rosenthal 1993.

12   This is also true of the ubiquitous forms of counselling in print and electronic media, ranging from serious to entertaining stage-management of giving biographically relevant advice: cf. Bergmann *et al.* 1998: 150f.

13   In this proposition I agree with and extend the thesis of the vanishing legitimising meta-narratives in the discourse of postmodernity: cf. Lyotard 1979, chaps 6–10.

14   In the eighteenth century the term originally referred to the double track of the carriage as it held its course.

15   On the negative role of helping institutions cf. Fischer-Rosenthal 1999b.

References

Bamberg, M. (ed.) (1997) 'Oral Versions of Personal Experience: Three Decades of Narrative Analysis', *Journal of Narrative and Life History* 7.

Bauman, Z. (1990) *Modernity and Ambivalence*, Cambridge: Polity Press.

Beck, U. (1992) *Risk Society*, London: Sage.

Beck, U., Giddens, A. and Lash, S. (1994) *Reflexive Modernisation*, Cambridge: Polity Press.

Beck-Gernsheim, E. (1994) 'Individualisierungstheorie: Veränderungen des Lebenslaufs in der Moderne', in H. Keupp (ed.), *Zugänge zum Subjekt*, Frankfurt: Suhrkamp.

Bergmann, J., Goll, M. and Wiltschek, S. (1998) 'Sinnorientierung durch Beratung?', in T. Luckmann (ed.), *Moral im Alltag*, Gütersloh: Verlag Bertelsmann Stiftung, pp.143–218.

Cooley, C.H. (1902) *Human Nature and the Social Order*, New York: Schocken, 1964.

Durkheim, É. (1893) *The Division of Labour in Society*, Basingstoke: Macmillan, 1984.

Fischer, W. (1982) 'Time and Chronic Illness: A Study on the Social Constitution of Temporality', Berkeley, Habilitation thesis, University of Bielefeld.

—— (1984) 'Biographische Methode', in H. Haft and H. Kordes (eds), *Methoden der Erziehungs- und Bildungsforschung*, Enzyklopädie Erziehungswissenschaft, Bd. 2, Stuttgart: Klett and Cotta, pp.478–82.

Fischer-Rosenthal, W. (1990) 'Diesseits von Mikro und Makro: Phänomenologische Soziologie im Vorfeld einer forschungspolitischen Differenz', *Österreichische Zeitschrift für Soziologie* 15: 21–34.

—— (1995a) 'Biographische Methode in der Soziologie', in Flick *et al.* (eds), *Handbuch qualitativer Sozialforschung*, 2nd edn, Munich: PVU, pp.253–6.

—— (1995b) 'Schweigen, Rechtfertigen, Umschreiben: Biographische Arbeit im Umgang mit deutschen Vergangenheiten', in W. Fischer-Rosenthal and P. Alheit op. cit., pp.43–86.

—— (1995c) 'The Problem with Identity: Biography as Solution to Some (Post)Modernist Dilemmas', in K. Davis, H.-J. Kuipers and H. Lutz (eds), *Identiteit en biografie*, Comenius (Utrecht), 151995 (H 3): 250–65.

—— (1995d) 'Znaniecki, F. and Thomas, W.I.: The Polish Peasant in Europe and America', in U. Flick, E.V. Kardorff, H. Keupp, L.V. Rosenstiel and S. Wolff (eds), *Handbuch Qualitative Sozialforschung*, 2nd edn, Munich: PVU, pp.115–18.

—— (1999a) 'Biographie und Leiblichkeit: Zur biographischen Arbeit und Artikulation des Körpers', in P. Alheit, B. Dausien, W. Fischer-Rosenthal, A. Hanses Keil (eds), *Biographie und Leib*, Giessen: Psychosozial-Verlag, pp.15–43.

—— (1999b) 'Der bandagierte Arm und die abgewürgte Wut: Zur Biographik eines Falles von Arbeitsunfähigkeit, Migration nach Deutschland und psychiatrischer Karriere', in U. Apitzsch (ed.), *Migration und Biographie*, Wiesbaden: Westdeutscher Verlag, pp.206–31.

—— (1999c) 'Melancholie der Identität und dezentrierte biographische Selbstbeschreibung', *BIOS. Zeitschrift für Biographieforschung und Oral History* 12, Heft 2.

Fischer-Rosenthal, W. and Alheit, P. (eds) (1995) *Biographien in Deutschland: Soziologische Rekonstruktionen gelebter Gesellschaftsgeschichte*, Opladen: Westdeutscher Verlag.

Fischer-Rosenthal, W. and Rosenthal, G. (1997a) 'Warum Biographieanalyse und wie man sie macht', *Zeitschrift für Sozialisationsforschung und Erziehungssoziologie* 17: 405–27.

—— (1997b) 'Narrationsanalyse biographischer Selbstpräsentationen', in R. Hitzler and A. Honer (eds), *Sozialwissenschaftliche Hermeneutik*, Opladen: Leske and Budrich, pp.133–64.

Giddens, A. (1984) *The Constitution of Society*, Cambridge: Polity Press.

Goffman, E. (1963) *Stigma: Notes on and Management of Spoiled Identity*, Englewood Cliffs, NJ: Prentice Hall.

Habermas, J. (1988) *Nachmetaphysisches Denken*, Frankfurt: Suhrkamp.

Hobbes, T. (1651) *Leviathan*, New York/London: Norton, 1997.

Keupp, H. (1994) *Zugänge zum Subjekt: Perspektiven einer reflexiven Sozialpsychologie*, Frankfurt: Suhrkamp.

Keupp, H. and Bilden, H. (eds) (1989) *Verunsicherungen: Das Subjekt im gesellschaftlichen Wandel*, Göttingen: Hogrefe.

Keupp, H. and Höfer, R. (1997) *Identitätsarbeit heute: Klassische und aktuelle Perspektiven der Identitätsforschung*, Frankfurt: Suhrkamp.

Kohli, M. (1981) 'Wie es zur "biographischen Methode" kam und was aus ihr geworden ist in', *Zeitschrift für Soziologie* 10: 273–93.

—— (1985) 'Die Institutionalisierung des Lebenslaufs: Historische Befunde und theoretische Argumente', *Kölner Zeitschrift für Soziologie und Sozialpsychologie* 37: 1–29.

—— (1986) 'Gesellschaftszeit und Lebenszeit: Der Lebenslauf im Strukturwandel der Moderne', in J. Berger (ed.), *Die Moderne – Kontinuitäten und Zäsuren?*, *Soziale Welt*, Sonderband 4: 183–208.

Labov, W. and Waletzky, J. (1966/1997) 'Narrative Analysis: Oral Versions of Personal Experience', *Journal of Narrative and Life History* 7: 3–38.

Luhmann, N. (1980–1995) *Gesellschaftsstruktur und Semantik: Studien zur Wissenssoziologie der modernen Gesellschaft*, 4 Vols, Frankfurt: Suhrkamp.

—— (ed.) (1985) *Soziale Differenzierung: Zur Geschichte einer Idee*, Opladen: Westdeutscher Verlag.

—— (1991) *Soziologie des Risikos*, Berlin: DeGruyter.

—— (1997) *Die Gesellschaft der Gesellschaft*, 2 vols, Frankfurt: Suhrkamp.

Lyotard, J.-F. (1979) *La condition postmoderne*, Paris: Éditions de Minuit.

Misch, G. (1969) *Geschichte der Autobiographie. Bd. IV/2: Von der Renaissance bis zu den biographischen Hauptwerken des 18 und 19. Jahrhunderts*, Frankfurt: Schulte-Bulmke.

Niggl, G. (ed.) (1989) *Die Autobiographie: Zu Form und Geschichte einer literarischen Gattung*, Darmstadt: Wissenschaftliche Buchgesellschaft.

Pascal, R. (1960) *Design and Truth in Autobiography*, London: Garland, 1985.

Platta, H. (1998) *Identitäts-Ideen*, Giessen: Psychosozial-Verlag.

Riemann, G. (1987) *Das Fremdwerden der eigenen Biographie*, Munich: Fink.

Rosenthal, G. (1990) 'Als der Krieg kam, hatte ich mit Hitler nichts mehr zu tun': Zur Gegenwärtigkeit des 'Dritten Reiches', in *Biographien*, Opladen: Leske and Budrich.

—— (1993) 'Reconstruction of Life Stories: Principles of Selection in Generating Stories for Narrative Biographical Interview', in *The Narrative Study of Lives*, New Delhi/London: Sage, pp.59–91.

—— (1995a) *Erlebte und erzählte Lebensgeschichte: Gestalt und Struktur biographischer Selbstbeschreibungen*, Frankfurt: Campus.

—— (1995b) 'Vom Krieg erzählen, von den Verbrechen schweigen', in H. Heer and K. Naumann (eds), *Vernichtungskrieg: Verbrechen der Wehrmacht 1941–1944*, Hamburg: Hamburger Edition HIS, pp.651–64.

—— (1997) 'Zur interaktionellen Konstitution von Generationen: Generationenabfolgen in Familien von 1890–1970 in Deutschland', in J. Mansel, G. Rosenthal and A. Tölke (eds), *Generationen-Beziehungen, Austausch und Tradierung*, Opladen: Westdeutscher Verlag, pp.57–73.

—— (ed.) (1998) *The Holocaust in Three-Generation Families*, London: Cassell.

Schütze, F. (1992) 'Pressure and Guilt: War Experiences of a Young German Soldier and their Biographical Implications', *International Sociology* 7: 187–208, 347–68.

—— (1996) 'Organisationszwänge und hoheitsstaatliche Rahmenbedingungen im Sozialwesen: Ihre Auswirkungen auf die Paradoxien des professionellen Handelns', in A. Combe and W. Helsper (eds), *Pädagogische Professionalität*, Frankfurt: Suhrkamp, pp.183–275.

Simmel, G. (1890) *Über Sociale Differenzierung*, Leipzig: Duncker and Humblot.

Strauss, A.L., Fagerhaugh, S., Suczek, B. and Wiener, C. (1985) *Social Organization of Medical Work*, Chicago, IL: University of Chicago Press.

Thomas, W.I. and Znaniecki, F. (1918) *The Polish Peasant in Europe and America*, E. Zaretsky (ed), Urbana, IL: University of Illinois, 1996.

Völter, B. (1994) '"Ich bin diesen Feind nicht losgeworden", Verschärfter "Identitätsdruck" als Handlungsproblem ostdeutscher junger Erwachsener vor und nach der Wende', *Österreichische Zeitschrift für Geschichtswissenschaften* 5: 547–66.

Völter, B. and Rosenthal, G. (1997) 'Trois générations allemandes: Nationalsocialisme et holocauste au travers des récits de vie', *Documents: Revue des questions allemandes* 3: 26–37.

6 Clinical hermeneutics

From the ontology of self to a case example

Anthony Hazzard

Introduction

As a science of interpretation and philosophy of understanding, hermeneutics is implicated whenever human communication takes place. Originally developed for the purpose of interpreting ancient and classical texts, hermeneutic thinking has in more recent times become adapted to the needs of the human and social sciences. This paper sets out the principal perspectives within the hermeneutic movement with reference to the work of Dilthey, Gadamer, Habermas and Ricoeur. Possible justifications for the applicability of hermeneutic philosophy to the clinical encounter are then explored and the application of hermeneutic approaches is illustrated by means of a brief vignette taken from general practice. The vignette records a genuine consultation, taken at random. General practice was chosen here because the consultations are brief, but clinical hermeneutics might equally well be illustrated by nursing, physiotherapy, speech therapy, psychology, or any clinical context.

Clinical hermeneutics remains a tentative notion. Although Dilthey's hermeneutics proposes a model of interpretation which is not so far from some aspects of established clinical practice, post-Heideggerian hermeneutics sets itself up as an ontology, asserting that hermeneutical structures support the very foundations of experience and the human world. According to Heidegger, they actually constitute being: human being is fundamentally hermeneutic (1962: 62). The arguments for this foundation, even when Gadamer has managed to show their application to the human sciences, may only be extended towards the clinical context with some agility.

The implications of the development of hermeneutics for the human sciences have been considered by philosophers from Vico to Ricoeur and beyond. To some extent, clinical practice has to take account of models of human and social science as well as of the natural sciences that properly inform biomedical explanation. The natural sciences are able to derive adequately coherent justification from conventional assumptions about objective evidence, and to assume fundamental grounding in elemental physics (where, incidentally, it is not to be found); but what of the human sciences and those aspects of clinical practice that conform to their model?

Might not hermeneutics, as philosophy and methodology of interpretation, be capable of offering a framework of justification for the value as data of clinical 'texts', and might hermeneutics not also provide a reliable instrument for the critique of propositions, conclusions and interpretations concerning the clinical encounter? Certainly, the hermeneutic method of Dilthey fits quite well with the conventional model of the clinical relationship, with its striving towards 'empathy', but the analyses of Heidegger and subsequent hermeneutists have necessitated far more tortuous examination of the structures of human understanding.

Having worked as both general practitioner and psychologist, and recognised the 'human science' character of much of the work, I found myself echoing the disquiet of Dilthey, who proposes that human science should have its own philosophy, and Gadamer, who worries about the tendency of technological thinking to encompass every issue. Concerning the clinical encounter in its communicational mode, it seemed to me that the disciplines of philology, history, literary criticism and aesthetics offers more suitable models than natural science. Any number of human sciences could be added to the list, all of whose disciplines are concerned with the interpretation of their subject matter. Any discipline whose subject matter presents itself for interpretation can expect to find justification and critique for its frameworks of analysis from the philosophy of interpretation, namely hermeneutics.

Hermeneutic views of subjectivity in relation to the clinical encounter

Medicine is familiar with the notion of the 'history' but clinical history-taking is hardly designed to deliver the patient's unique biographical narrative. Instead, it is designed to accommodate an ahistorical, pre-structured taxonomy of disease. A medical history is designed to overlook the unique and eventual, while emphasising the typical, the repeatable and the predictable. For such a history the interpretation of biographical text serves to objectify the target self as if she or he were a naturally occurring object. For medicine, the event in historical time is fitted to a set of rules previously assembled through the observation of events in great numbers. The event becomes an item of quantity within a predictable pattern and loses its historical uniqueness. This is appropriate when confined to a natural disease process, but natural science objectifies the patient and takes for granted the neutral subjectivity of the observer. In critical response to the kind of assumptions made by scientism when applied universally, hermeneutic philosophy has used the model of inter-pretation to explore the aims and modes of inquiry of human science.

Just over a hundred years ago, the epistemological universality of natural science was questioned by the hermeneutic philosopher Wilhelm Dilthey. Dilthey argued that the objects of the human sciences could not be investigated from the point of view of natural science because they were not natural objects. Rather, they were mind-created objects consti-tuting a mind-created world (Dilthey 1976: 195). Dilthey saw that the human sciences had never achieved a firm philosophical grounding since the demise of theocentric metaphysics. He proposed that the appropriate methodology for a human science was not empirical observation but interpretation, and that its goal should not be explanation, but under-standing (Dilthey 1989: 8, 7–91, 439–40).

According to Dilthey, the fundamental data for knowledge are lived experiences, or what he called 'facts of consciousness' whose analysis is the proper task of the human sciences. Dilthey does not restrict these 'facts' to the Kantian assembly of concepts structured from perception, representation and thought, but insists upon including the 'whole of human nature as revealed in experience', with its emotional and conative constituents. He says that human nature cannot be the timeless object of a rigid epistemology, but is the product of historical development (1989: 50–1). Its epistemology therefore needs to be historical. A science of understanding with an historical epistemology, making use of interpreta-tive methods, leads Dilthey to examine the ancient practice of hermeneutics. For Dilthey, all human communication results in some form of textual objectification that can be used as data for interpretation towards an understanding of the subjective consciousness that created it.

Dilthey recognises the historical and contextual quality of humanly intelligible communication. Any text is shaped by its historical context. Temporality – the ever-widening gap between text and interpreter – constitutes a growing source of misunderstanding. It is the task of inter-pretive human sciences to overcome misunderstanding by skilled hermeneutics and to open the way towards understanding of the author's intentions; even, to improve upon the author's own self-understanding (1976: 226). For the human sciences, Dilthey's hermeneutics confers the status of data for understanding upon whatever is unique and historically particular about a patient's, a client's or a research subject's narrative.

Dilthey's hermeneutic methodology intends that the self of the interpreter should become as neutral and transparent as possible, in the same way as the self of the observer in natural science. Dilthey recommends the 'transposition' of the being of the interpreter into the historical context of textual creation (1976: 226). The event of textual creation is recognised as historical, so a sophisticated hermeneutic methodology is required to grasp the context of a created work to be used as data for understanding. On the other hand the act of interpretation tries to be timeless, with interpreting consciousness remaining neutral and privileged, as with natural science.

The conventional view of the clinical encounter models the self as a circumscribed entity as if with a boundary and contents. This applies to the self both of the interpreting clinician and that of the patient whose expressions are interpreted. This conventional view fits with hermeneutic method as explicated and elaborated by Dilthey. Just as Dilthey's textual interpreter seeks approximation to the inner experiences of an author through the study of created expressions and of the context within which they were created, so the clinician strives to gain an approximation to the experiences of the patient, through a study of their expressions and of the context within which they were created.

In Dilthey's view, the lived experience that is familiar to the interpreting subject supplies a reliable model for understanding the inner experiences of others (1976: 226–31).

As method, Dilthey's hermeneutic model strives for objectivity in a parallel way to natural science, even though he seeks understanding rather than explanation. By contrast, Heidegger's phenomenological disclosure of human being as integral with its world relegates all notions of objectivity, and subjectivity too, to the status of derivative consequences of artificial separation, or 'distanciation'. Dilthey's hermeneutics of understanding through interpretation was reversed by Heidegger. For Heidegger, the 'disclosure' of our being-in-the-world as both thrown into the world and as reaching – 'projected' – understandingly towards our own possibilities, established understanding as a primordial aspect of our being. For hermeneutics this delivers the consequence that understanding can no longer be regarded as a mere human activity among others, but is actually a part of what we are: understanding as being. Subjectivity has to lose its status as 'container' of knowledge, or as the privileged, separate position from which to observe the world. Subjectivity and self become derivative interpretations of the disclosure of human being as understanding (Heidegger 1962: 188–95).

After Heidegger's establishment of understanding as a fundamental and primordial aspect of human being – something we are rather than something we achieve through interpretation – and after his disclosure of human being as continuous with its world rather than as encapsulated subjectivity over against an objective world, the conventional distinctions of subject/object, interpreter/author and clinician/patient must dissolve, and with them the conventional notion of the subject as assumed by Dilthey. The relation of human being to the world, the discourse and the text becomes one of immediate belonging and primordial understanding. Any subsequent definition of subjectivity or objectivity is necessarily derivative, regional and pragmatic. Interpretation becomes a development and articulation of understanding. First we understand our world, then we reflect, and only on reflection do we become subjective: individual consciousness situated over against an objective world.

Heidegger was not concerned with the implications of his radical redisposition of hermeneutics for the actual practice of interpretation. It was left to his pupil, Hans-Georg Gadamer, to explore the structures of understanding that are primordial for the practice of interpretation, working from the examples of aesthetics and history, and also to examine the status of language as fundamental to the human world.

Gadamer considers that Kant's account of aesthetic judgement excessively emphasises the primacy of the reflective self (Gadamer 1975: 42–81). According to Gadamer, Kant's conclusions imply the presence of a subjectivity, or judging self, that stands over against the art object. In Gadamer's view, this distanciated self, or what he calls aesthetic consciousness, is an abstracted derivative of the primordial understanding to which the artwork already belongs (1975: 81; 1976: 4–5).

A work of art is already understood within the event of re-presentation towards interpretive recognition of something as something already understood. The event of re-presentation requires a mode of belonging between artwork and interpretation that Gadamer characterises as 'play'. Interpreting consciousness gives itself over to the to and fro movement of the playful event. Aesthetic self-consciousness cannot therefore occupy either an original or a fixed position, but is a derivative interpretation of the flow and movement of the play. Each event of playful dialogue entails a development/interpretation of artwork and of self, but also the 'true' work of art possesses the power to re-present a coherent, enduring structure that can maintain a continuous truth-claim (1975: 101–34). Similarly, events of dialogue that re-present a lasting truth-claim are the mode of being of hermeneutic consciousness that is revealed to itself through the interpretation of its belonging in the dialogue. So selfhood rediscovers itself in dialogue with the tragic and the beautiful (1975: 133).

For Gadamer, the encounter with historical text discloses the historical situatedness, not only of the text, but also of the interpreting consciousness. Whereas Dilthey sees historical distance between self and text as an obstacle to understanding, Gadamer regards interpreting consciousness and text as belonging to each other and interwoven with the intervening traditions that join them across historical temporality. Gadamer sees interpreting consciousness and text as each situated within a historical horizon constituted by the tradition within which it finds itself; or, in Heideggerian terms, into which it is 'thrown'. Interpreting consciousness is formed, or 'effected' by its history, and the history of its tradition. Gadamer calls it 'historically-effected consciousness' (1975: 291–307).

When we are taking the position of interpreting consciousness, we should reflect upon our own historical effectedness and the inevitability of our starting from a position of prejudice, otherwise the effect takes place 'behind our back'. Such self-awareness can, however, only be partial, as our effectedness is an aspect of being, and being is 'never fully manifest' (1976: 38; 1975: 301–2).

As for language, according to Gadamer it is only thanks to language that we have a world at all. All structures of understanding, effective history, tradition, etc. are constituted in language, which is always already ahead of our reasoning. Being and its world are language, and also, inevitably, the derivative interpretation we know as selfhood. Gadamer discloses the world as language, being as understanding and subjectivity as interpretation (1976: 59–68).

Using artwork and historical text as examples, Gadamer makes use of the same kind of examination that Heidegger adopted and developed from the phenomenology of Husserl, but he also makes use of the rich resources of classical, humanistic, historical and etymological tradition. He uses his evidence to reveal the subjectivity of the aesthetic or historical interpreter – the distanced, aesthetic or historical form of consciousness – as derivative. Primordially, he argues, the interpreter and the artwork, the interpreter and the text, mutually belong in dialogue as the horizons of their respective traditions take part in a process of 'blending'. The beautiful work did not begin as an 'aesthetic' object, nor did the text begin as 'history' but each arose from within its tradition. Likewise, the interpreter's outlook arises inescapably from her or his tradition.

Gadamer's philosophical hermeneutics has profound implications for the clinical encounter, which from his point of view may be regarded as a mutual blending and belonging of the patient's and clinician's contextual horizons in dialogue, rather than an interpretation of objective data aiming at an understanding of subjective experience. The clinician who has undertaken the task of interpretation needs to be aware of the effectedness of their own consciousness, by the historical tradition to which they belong – an effectedness which no amount of self-reflection can entirely disclose. Understanding takes place from within a tradition and horizon that shapes the clinician's consciousness: a tradition within which they find themselves situated. There is no chance of neutral approximation to the consciousness of the patient. 'We understand in a different way' says Gadamer, referring to the tradition of the other, 'if we understand at all' (1975: 297). It must be remembered that Heidegger's immediate, fundamental understanding, which is part of our being, is inescapably also part of our own tradition. It is possible, however, in accordance with Gadamer's thinking, for the horizon of an interpreter to blend with the horizon of a text in mutual belonging and mutual questioning. Perhaps it is possible for the clinical dialogue to be afforded textual status and therefore achieve the same kind of belonging.

Habermas, representing critical theory, sees Gadamer's rehabilitation of tradition and prejudice as threatening to the fundamental human interest of emancipation, and as a likely source of false consciousness (Habermas 1980: 181–209). Habermas is critical of Gadamer's apparent surrender of self-reflective consciousness to the determining power of tradition (Habermas 1980: 204–9), but even for Habermas, the human subject does not seem to be a 'natural' entity, whose reality can be assumed (Habermas 1987: 355–60). All such assumptions, for Habermas, are derivative of the human interests they serve. The state of consciousness to which Habermas would urge us to aspire is constituted in the participation within emancipated, rational discourse, free from all threat and free from the distortion that tradition is likely to impose.

Habermas' enemy is false consciousness, determined by unreflective submission to ideological interests (Habermas 1987: 208–13) and it has to be admitted that history, including the history of his own nation, lends great support to his argument. He takes a particular interest in psychoanalysis as a promising vehicle for emancipation from false consciousness, comparable with the critique of ideology. His position is primarily an ethical one, so for him the clinical dialogue would be part of a discourse whose value depends upon the extent to which it contributes to the emancipation of the participants from false consciousness (Habermas 1980: 190–203).

While a student at the Sorbonne in the 1930s, Paul Ricoeur became influenced by the work of Marcel, who shared Husserl's views on the intentionality of consciousness and was interested in the participatory structure of being. Later, while a prisoner of war, Ricoeur was allowed the opportunity to study the works of Husserl, Heidegger and Jaspers. After the war he became an authority on Husserl and phenomenology and developed an interest in the problem of subjectivity (Ricoeur 1981: 2). It is Ricoeur's aim to deflect Gadamer's philosophical hermeneutics and Habermas' critical theory from the direct opposition which would reduce them to a pair of conflicting ideologies. Ricoeur argues for a dialectical rather than an oppositional relationship between concepts such as belonging and critical distance, understanding and explanation, truth and method (Ricoeur 1981: 63–100). As well as unifying the hermeneutic movement, Ricoeur has worked definitively on the nature of textuality. It is likely that the viability of clinical hermeneutics as a notion depends not only upon a unified hermeneutics, but also upon meeting Ricoeur's exigencies about what constitutes a text.

Following Frege's distinction between the sense and the reference of a statement, Ricoeur sees discourse as a dialectic between the sense conveyed by structure and the reference indicated by context (Ricoeur 1981: 140). In spoken discourse the reference is ostensive and bound to the event. Once fixed in writing, however, the text is released from ostensive reference but still says something about something. The 'about something' now constitutes the reference of the text. The 'about something' is the reference, matter, or what Ricoeur calls the 'world of the text' which the text projects in front of itself, and which interpreting consciousness encounters in a relationship of belonging. This is in contrast to Dilthey's quest for the creative consciousness behind the text: however, interpretation of sense and structure still takes place in a methodical and explanatory mode. In contrast to Gadamer, and in agreement with Habermas, this requires some critical distance, but at the same time interpreting consciousness belongingly 'appropriates' to itself the world of the text.

By 'appropriation' Ricoeur means that in the present reading the reader makes the reference and meaning of the text their own, so that the meaning, reference, or world of the text belongs to the present reader. Appropriation of the written text takes the place of the answer in dialogue and constitutes the completion of an event of interpretation (Ricoeur 1981: 185).

Ricoeur argues that only the permanent and ostensive-context-free nature of written text, or a speech act or social action meaningful enough to leave a trace on time, permits enough freedom from ostensive reference to be capable of projecting a possible world open to appropriation. Structured sense, cultural horizon, narrative sequence and transmitted meaning offer to us as interpreting consciousnesses our own self-understandings, whose central meanings are 'brought to language and articulated by literature' (Ricoeur 1981: 143). The world of the work that unfolds in front of the text is appropriated by belonging consciousness, whose understanding becomes: 'to understand oneself in front of the text. By appropriation and open-ness to the text, an enlarged self is received'. The self, says Ricoeur, 'is constituted by the matter of the text' (Ricoeur

1981: 144). So subjectivity, for Ricoeur, is textual: a dialectic of structure and possible world.

Ricoeur's dialectical approach makes room for the disclosure of self as methodical, distanced consciousness, open to both understanding and explanation, but also as a projective process of interpretation and development of the understanding that is being. Ricoeur allows for the critical distance demanded by Habermas, but does not reify rational self-consciousness. Subjectivity is reconstituted as a project, as narrative, as meaningful, textual discourse, and as the appropriation of possible worlds.

Ricoeur is concerned to reconcile the apparently conflicting views of Gadamer and Habermas into a productive dialectic. In his view historical situatedness and an emancipatory project should not be mutually exclusive. Tradition and hope, history and aspiration, biography and ambition nourish and develop each other (Ricoeur 1981: 63–100). Also, there must be room for critical distance as well as belonging (Ricoeur 1981: 131–44); for methodical appraisal of the sense of the discourse, as well as for the event of understanding. Mutual belonging of clinician and 'text' in the clinical dialogue has to be balanced by rational and methodical work on the making of sense.

Ricoeur is concerned with the nature of textuality. He bases his model of understanding upon the encounter with written text, and not all discourse is worthy to be regarded as textual. Ricoeur's view is that to be regarded as text, a discourse must not simply take place, but must be a kind of enduringly meaningful action (1981: 197–221), in the same way as a speech act, that can leave its mark on time (1981: 205). It must sustain an enduring meaning, comparable to the way a text becomes freed from circumstantial reference by the work of writing down.

It is necessary for the viability of clinical hermeneutics to ask if the clinical encounter is comparable in this way. It might make such a claim, as it constitutes the making sense of a discourse of suffering, and its articulation into memorable and enduringly effective interpretation, as well as a blending of the alien horizons that support consciousness and evoke subjectivity. It has always been the case that when human consciousness encounters an alien tradition it achieves an enriched awareness of itself. History is full of such examples, from Herodotus to the postmodern.

Ricoeur agrees with Gadamer about the mutual belonging of interpretive consciousness and the world of the text (Ricoeur 1981: 182–93). In the encounter with the text, both text and consciousness are developed. Subjectivity becomes dissolved and receives itself again, both changed and sustained in the encounter of belonging (Ricoeur 1981: 142–4). It is well known that a great text possesses the power to shape self-consciousness not only of individual subjectivity, but of whole societies.

On the other hand, at each encounter, the text is recovered in a different, developed way, that both reflects and reforms interpreting subjectivity. To return to the patient, perhaps it could be said that the patient's expression, whether narrative, plaint, elegy or lyric, has the character of textual discourse, with a structure that allows methodical interpretation and critical distance. Also the discourse projects a possible world to which the clinician, in the event of interpretation, finds herself/himself belonging, and so finds herself/himself disclosed.

So what light do the hermeneutical versions of subjectivity throw upon the clinical encounter? It is still possible to make pragmatic use of Dilthey's methodology involving the encounter of conventional, encapsulated subjectivities, in order to re-experience an author's intentions or a patient's inner experience. Dilthey's version of subjectivity is essentially the Cartesian Cogito, adopted by Kant as container for conceptual understanding and accepted as conventional by cognitive theorists thereafter. Despite the most faithful use of Dilthey's methodology the experience of the other is actually inaccessible. The patient's inner world can only ever be speculatively and metaphorically interpreted.

Gadamer challenges us with the necessity of reflecting upon the historicality of our own subjective experience and upon the inaccessibility of at least some of this historicality to conscious reflection. Subjectivity is derivative and neutrality is impossible. The clinician belongs understandingly to the clinical dialogue before they acquire the derivative status of self in possession of clinical consciousness.

With Habermas, we are suspicious of our false consciousness and the traditional assumptions that encourage it. We strive to free our clinical discourse from the influence of ideology by vigilant critique.

Finally, with the aid of Ricoeur, method, critique and belonging can be assembled in the service of clinical understanding. Critical distance is permitted, but through openness to the world of the clinical text, which may consist of a patient's expressions or the clinical dialogue as a whole, interpreting subjectivity becomes both de-reified and reconstituted in the encounter. Ricoeur's dialectical subjectivity is defined, located and fulfilled in relation to its text. Critical distance confers the sense, and belonging discloses the sensation of self. The regional text of the clinical encounter sustains the provisional subjectivities of doctor, nurse, therapist and patient. It must be remembered that any audience or reader who interprets or contemplates a clinical encounter, in progress or in record, also participates in the discourse. This means you!

A clinical example, with hermeneutic interpretation

A teenage schoolgirl comes to my evening surgery. She complains of a sore throat, blocked nose and a little post-nasal discharge for the past few days. She is accompanied by her father. I remember that the girl was born a year after the sudden death of a sibling.

I begin to wonder what it must be like to grow up in a family that has suffered the sudden death of a child. I try to imagine the relationship with anxious parents that must have constituted the patient's early experience. I consider the family's social and economic background and the level of the parents' education. I bring to mind my own encounters with the parents.

I use my own inner experience as a guide in interpreting the patient's expressions towards an understanding of the patient's inner experience. I consider the patient's social and historical context so that I can make allowances for it and so achieve sufficient objective neutrality in my interpretation. This kind of hermeneutic method, which corresponds to the kind of interpretation proposed by Dilthey, demands the acceptance of the self as a given entity. For the practice and results of such method, Dilthey's hermeneutic analysis can provide adequate justification and critique, but I want to go further.

I consider the sources of my own subjectivity and consciousness, which I no longer take for granted. I am quite elderly and of medium economic status. My education was conventional, with a heavy bias towards the natural sciences. I have long experience in the observation of pain, suffering and death. I recognise that my consciousness is shaped (effected) by my history, and by the history of the cultural tradition of which I am a part. I cannot be fully aware of these effects and their operation, so I accept that my subjectivity is provisional and historical.

The patient says: 'I told them I needed to see you urgently, but I am probably being silly. I was just worried when my throat started hurting; I was sure something bad was happening'.

If understanding is primordial to the self, it is clear that no neutral subjectivity can be achieved from which to gain access to the inner experience of the patient. I can, however, achieve openness to the matter of the patient's text. I experience an immediate and pre-reflective belonging and understanding of the textual material. The limiting horizon of my own tradition-shaped consciousness blends with the horizon of the text, which extends my understanding. As understanding is part of being, my being and selfhood are changed. From a position of primordial understanding I am able to make interpretations and to explicate my understanding.

Gadamer's philosophical hermeneutics necessitates the recognition of the interpreter's historicality and gives an ontological basis for the structures of understanding.

Nevertheless, turning away from the immediacy of primordial understanding, I want to achieve a critical distance from the patient's expressions. I notice that the patient is more anxious than her symptoms justify. Perhaps the patient has unconscious anxieties that are responsible for a degree of false consciousness. Perhaps false consciousness is maintained by the family's ideology of fear. Looking beyond surface expression for sources of false consciousness is consistent with Habermas' proposal of a depth hermeneutics deriving from critical theory. Is there something that the patient would say if the father were not present? What is the father's contribution to the encounter?

I am poised between my need to keep a critical distance and the aspect of my being that belongs understandingly to the patient's material. Ricoeur provides a dialectical justification for this position. Critical distance is necessary if sense is to be made of a set of expressions that can count as a text. Expressions are textual if they achieve freedom from the arbitrary context and occasion of their expression. Clinical responsibility and effectiveness demand that what is said is clearly preserved from the fleeting, referential circumstances of the saying. This is, however, not incompatible with a belonging and appropriation of the world of the patient's text.

The text opens up a world in front of itself in which the interpreter immediately belongs. Ricoeur calls it 'the mode of being unfolded in front of the text' (1981: 93), which subverts and delivers back the interpreter's subjectivity. Openness to the mode of being unfolding before the text brings about a shift of the clinician's selfhood: a moment of being-as-understanding that is as disclosive of truth for the clinical encounter as are the conceptualising achievements of critical distance.

Patient: I get so worried. Sometimes I think I can't breathe and I want to open the windows.

Doctor: Yes, isn't it strange that a silly sore throat can sometimes make our bodies seem so unsafe, almost like being shut in with something frightening?

The doctor uses openness to the world of the text to extend understanding, but achieves enough distance to work out a conceptual interpretation and try to frame it in language that will both convey understanding and provide reassurance.

Patient: That's right. How did you know? (*Sits silently for a while. Everyone is silent. Then.*) I'm sure I don't need antibiotics.
Doctor: You are right. Your sore throat is most likely caused by a virus. Antibiotics would not help, but it is easy to get worried. You were right to come along and let me look at you. I hope you will soon feel safe and well.
Father: Better safe than sorry. Would you look at my throat now?

This vignette is intended to illustrate how hermeneutic philosophy of human science might help to justify the value of clinical text as data and truth. The patient's text projects a world in which understanding finds that it belongs. Selfhood is dislocated, then retrieved as something new. At the same time, sufficient critical distance is achieved to preserve the textuality of the encounter, to form concepts and reflect upon meanings. I am left with an aggregate of concepts, from which I maintain enough critical distance to contemplate the sense, but more immediately I am left with my belonging to the world of her text, and a difference in myself. I, male, old, middle class, steeped in medical culture; she, adolescent, 'working class', shop worker, peer-group member: to a degree my tradition-bound consciousness and her text belong to a blended horizon.

Very occasionally a patient will produce a spontaneously written document for the attention of the clinician. More often the biographical data of clinical research emerge as dialogue, which may be fixed by the researcher into some form of enduring record. The structure of the text will range from narrative to expressive – epic to lyric. The world of the text may be tentative, or overwhelming in its power to engage in a relationship of belonging.

That observation changes the observed is nowadays axiomatic. Hermeneutic philosophy of human science makes the demand that the interpreter should also understand the provisional nature of their own subjectivity. Not only is interpreting consciousness historically effected, but consciousness is actually casuistic – textually effected: the text in hand is part of effective history. How often do we begin the reading of a poem with a certain sense of self, only to acquire another in the course of the encounter? On the other hand, critical distance and the making of sense remains essential for competent hermeneutic practice. This, then, is the dialectical structure that challenges inquiry into clinical encounter from the standpoint of hermeneutics.

References

Bleicher, J. (ed.) (1980) *Contemporary Hermeneutics*, London: Routledge.

Dilthey, W. (1976) *Selected Writings*, ed. and trans. H.P. Rickman, Cambridge: Cambridge University Press.

—— (1989) *Selected Works*, ed. and trans. R.A. Makkreel and F. Rodl, Princeton, NJ: Princeton University Press.

Gadamer, H.-G. (1975) *Truth and Method*, London: Sheed and Ward.

—— (1976) *Philosophical Hermeneutics*, trans. D.E. Linge, Berkeley, CA: University of California.

Habermas, J. (1980) 'The Hermeneutic Claim to Universality', in J. Bleicher (ed.), *Contemporary Hermeneutics*, London: Routledge.

—— (1987) *Knowledge and Human Interests*, Oxford: Polity Press.

Heidegger, M. (1962) *Being and Time*, Oxford: Blackwell.

Ricoeur, P. (1981) *Hermeneutics and the Human Sciences*, ed. and trans. J.B. Thompson, Cambridge: Cambridge University Press.

7 Uncovering the general from within the particular

From contingencies to typologies in the understanding of cases[1]

Tom Wengraf

Introduction

This chapter addresses two questions concerned with interpreting biographical interviews in the social sciences. The first question has to do with the limits of 'staying with the interview text' and I argue that we need to be more explicit about how we always – except for limited technical purposes – go beyond the text in order to interpret it. The second has to do with the way that analysing the interview text of one case can already generate considerable – but normally neglected – resources for understanding other cases, for typologising, and for elaborating general models.

Much of the motivation behind oral history and feminist research in Britain and elsewhere for interview work with ordinary people has been to give such people their own voice, after having been kept 'hidden from history' or allowed into social research only if 'spoken for' by others. Simplifying, one might say that *the function of the researcher is held to be to give voice and the printed page* to those who require mediation to get their voices into the public arena. At most, the words spoken might be minimally edited, to eliminate repetition and to facilitate reading. Replacing the words of the speaker by the interpretation of a researcher was, though, counter to the ethos of the operation. The work of Studs Terkel (1975) might be considered as a classic example, and indeed he refers to himself as 'compiling' the book in question. However, in the chapters of this book, as in other social science research publications using biographic materials, there is a considerable amount of interpretation involved in the reporting of most of the work. Together with contemporary oral historians (Perks and Thomson 1998), I argue that, in order to understand the voice of the Other as fully as possible, we must explicitly go beyond simple recycling of the verbatim text, and even beyond sophisticated formal text-analysis. The social science researcher's professional comparative knowledge and universal concepts make such a 'going beyond the text' by way of the social science researcher's imagination (Mills 1959) inevitable; questions of context and of subjectivity necessarily arise and should be formally addressed and researched. I discuss this in the first part of the chapter and put forward a 'diamond' model to contextualise the practice of text-analysis.

Having taught qualitative interviewing for a number of years, I have found that students have a considerable difficulty in moving from the study of the single case to that of comparing and contrasting multiple cases, developing typologies and generalising. More recently, I have been involved in the SOSTRIS (1998a, 1998b, 1999b) cross-cultural comparative research across seven European societies, using narrative interviews analysed according to the biographic interpretive method (BIM) associated with Gabriele Rosenthal and Wolfram Fischer-Rosenthal (Rosenthal 1998: 2–7 and references; Breckner 1998). This has made me realise how a grounded-theorising method of work on a particular case, as practised within BIM, provides considerable – if frequently unused – resources of generality and typification with which to work on other cases, resources that I argue ought to be inspected *before* one starts to search 'in the literature' for pre-existing concepts and typologies into which the 'case' might be squashed. I highlight these resources and the desirability of using them in the second part of the chapter.

In the third part of the chapter, I discuss the way that real and imagined different historical contingencies are a good ground for formulating types and typologies between the 'particular' and the 'general'. Finally, I suggest an eight-fold typology of typologies used and usable in biographical analysis.

Understanding the told story

Biographic narrative interviews are constructed around enabling the interviewee to provide an uninterrupted narrative of their own life (Wengraf 1998). They are asked to 'tell their story in their own way, beginning wherever they like, for as long as they like'. This initial narrative – which can last ten minutes or three hours – is their told story. Treated as text, it is the pivotal focus of analysis, supplemented by material developed by further questioning which starts only when the initial narration is brought to an end by the interviewee.

If the task is to understand this initial narration, the told story, how is 'understanding' to be achieved? I find an idea of Scheff (1997) helpful in this respect. He argues that understanding is accomplished through the process of social and societal *contextualisation*: by relating, in Spinoza's words, 'the smallest parts to the largest wholes':

> No matter how exhaustive the analysis of a text, the determination of meaning will be incomplete and therefore partially subjective without referring to relevant historical and biographical knowledge.... Verbatim excerpts from discourse, one might argue, are *microcosms*, they contain within them, brief as they may be, intimations of the participants' origins in and relations to the institutions of the host society.
>
> (Scheff 1997: 30, 48)

Scheff argues for the widest possible version of 'context': he provides us (1997: 54) with a 'part/whole' ladder for the analysis of interview material. The 'macro' end of the ladder is startling, but, for some arguments that one might wish to make, he convincingly argues that it may have to be brought into explicit consideration:

- Single words and gestures.
- Sentences.
- Exchanges.
- Conversations.
- Relationship of the two parties.
- Life histories of the two parties.
- All relationships of their type.
- The structure of the host society: all relationships.
- The history and future of the host civilisation.
- The history and destiny of the human species.

He continues:

> Practical intelligence in the lifeworld appears to involve abduction, that is, the rapid, effortless shuttling up and down this ladder.... All levels are implied in the actual understanding and practice of discourse. The process is awkward to describe in explicit language, but it takes place constantly, effortlessly, and instantaneously in discourse.
>
> (Scheff 1997: 54–5, 58)

This seems very useful. It is worth noting that 'all relationships of their type' in Scheff's ladder would include all other cases that might be relevant to be compared with, and so help us to understand, the focal-case of any particular piece of biographical research. It is also worth noting that his last three 'levels' include cross-cultural and cross-time comparison as essential components in the understanding even of one particular single-moment, single-time, case.

Extending Scheff, it should be noted that we bring with us to the work of analysis – and can also construct – *alternative* 'part/whole ladders' of conceptual framework and theorisation. Just to illustrate, Freud might provide one theory (paradigm), Marx or Weber another, for the illumination of the same interview text. Relating Scheff's argument to that of Kuhn (1962), different disciplines or collections of disciplines can be defined in part by their different conceptualisation of part/whole ladders and their different procedures for relevant data-collection and data-interpretation.[2] We cannot evade our specific inheritances and our training, and they are valuable cultural capital when properly used, but we can avoid giving them a false ontological inevitability which blocks any critical self-review. As interdisciplinary and cross-cultural research teams know (Cooper, this volume) but as Scheff does not sufficiently emphasise, there is more than one (conceptualised and proceduralised) ladder to choose from!

The historical dimension

The *historical dimension* should also be stressed. It is a component of Scheff's ladder but perhaps an understated one. There is still a tendency for sociology and some other social sciences to deal in relatively unhistorical pictures of the present, leaving the discipline of history to research and describe the past. In order to understand the present perspective and situation of an individual interviewee, we need to know as much as possible about his or her personal and interpersonal history, and to locate that personal and interpersonal history within the history of contexts. Such a knowledge of the real history of the person and contexts enables us to understand – rather than just recycle – personal stories:

> Given the precariousness of communication, presenting and creating oneself as a 'person' seems to be possible only by telling *how* one became what and who one is now. I can only understand myself and communicate myself in a narration if I conceive myself as someone who is constantly changing and yet still me, i.e. as an integrated person, including my biographical transformations and contradictions. The individual as a dynamic system of plural sub-selves is realised in his or her *life stories*.
>
> (Fischer-Rosenthal, this volume)

This emphasises the told story, but Fischer-Rosenthal elsewhere stresses the need to explore *relevant documentation* for life stories being interpreted: a good example would be the attempt to document the war record of ex-Nazis suspected of attempting in their told stories to obfuscate that record (Rosenthal 1998: 249–63). Without knowledge of the evolving history of Nazi and post-Nazi Germany, the significance of any stories told cannot be properly understood. Such a researched knowledge of history *and* context, not least of evolving history *of* context, is necessary to understand anybody's story, including our own (see e.g. Friedlander 1998).

Scheff's insistence upon the importance of *context* and of *history*, deliberately taken very broadly, is a major reason why understanding biographic materials cannot stop at the recycling of the text.[3] A second question that he does not foreground but is of extreme importance is that of *the researcher's theory of the interviewing subject(s)*.

One defended subject: two defended subjectivities

Hollway and Jefferson, this volume, argue convincingly that how we interpret interview material depends on our theory of the individual subject, and that much social science research analysis implies a self-knowledgeable and potentially transparent self. Against this implicit model, they argue for a psychoanalytically informed model of subjectivity as being always engaged in unconscious defences against anxiety. Such a model entails the assumption that the interviewee is always 'motivated not to know' certain things about themselves and always produces 'self-defensive' biographical accounts, told stories, which avoid such knowledge.

I would only add that, in an interview, there are two anxious defended subjects, not one.[4] In the interview, *the researcher also* must be assumed to be at least potentially 'motivated to not know' certain things that would be upsetting for him or her, and thus subtly or obviously influencing the production of some or all of the text of the interview. In addition, the researcher's anxieties do not vanish after the end of the interview. They may even be exacerbated. Defence and anxiety are features of the researcher-position right through data-analysis and into writing-up and publication. The operation of such anxiety in the stages of analysis and interpretation cannot be avoided, but its shape and implications need to be detected and combatted.[5]

This is best done by using a panel of analysts. The value of a panel of analysts and of peer review lies in part in the capacity of different researchers to have anxieties that are different from those of each other and from that of the interviewee. Well handled, the material that the *interviewer* is 'motivated not to understand' or 'motivated to understand only in a certain way' may be better understood through the discussion among peers in the interview-analysis panel. The more intercultural and cross-cultural the panel, the more 'sleeping assumptions' (Cooper, this volume) of any given researcher are likely to be disturbed and raised to consciousness, thereby often forcing a clarification and a rectification of the researcher's theory of subjectivity.

The lived life and the told story

To go beyond the defended discourse of the told story of any informant, we must be able to put that self-presentation in the context of other knowledge. To illustrate the way that biographical research develops such knowledge even from within interview material, we can consider the explicit procedure of one research tradition. Several of the studies in this volume (Jones and Rupp, Chamberlayne and Spanò, King, Schiebel) were developed on the basis of narrative interviews structured and panel-analysed according to the 'biographic-interpretive method' referred to as BIM.

The BIM methodology rests upon the sharp distinction, within the material of the interview, between the data of the lived life and the structure of the told story. These are separately analysed, and afterwards the results of the two analyses of the separate materials are brought together.

1   The *lived life* is composed of the uncontroversial hard biographical data[6] that can be abstracted from the interview material and any other helpful source. This is seen as a long chronological sequence of the 'objective' historical facts about the person's life, the life-events as they happened, independently of whether or how they are referred to in the interview.
2   The *told story* is the way that the person presents him or herself – both in their initial narrative and in their answers to specific questions – by selecting certain events in their life (and omitting others) and by handling them in a certain way (and not in another).

'Understanding' the 'told story' in BIM involves the researcher interpreting that told story in the context of knowledge about the other elements on Scheff's part/whole ladder, including the lived life. The story that is told in the interview text – typically but not always in the form of a biographic narration – must be understood in terms of the history of the lived life that it is about and out of which it springs. This requires a theory of the relation of told stories to the historically evolving and conditioned subjectivity that tells them. Consequently an account of the narrating subjectivity relating a told story at a given moment needs to be placed within the history of the lived life and the historical contextualisations required by Scheff's ladder of smallest parts–largest wholes. Much biographical-interpretive work does not, of course, go anything like as far as Scheff's 'maximalist' model would recommend: for example, not every case-study has to 'place' a particular case within the history of the human species! However, Scheff would argue that, to the extent to which such work is not done, there is at least a potential failure in objective under-standing. To complement that, I would argue that the more explicit and subject to rectification are the presumptions about past and future histor-ical reality, about the contemporary world picture made and assumed within the interpretation, the more 'objective' the analysis is likely to be.

The limits of recycling or decontextually analysing the told story/interview text

Without a contextualisation of the 'told story' by the lived life and other Scheff elements, the analyst can do little more than recycle *the story as told* in a more naive or more sophisticated form. I shall use the concept of 'formal-textualism'[7] to refer to any tendency of research that attempts to avoid going beyond the limits of the text. I have already mentioned the journalistic attempt to stay with the (lightly edited) words of the inter-viewee, and merely recycle them for the reader (as in the work of Studs Terkel). A similar attempt to stay within the text characterises some prac-tices of contemporary discourse analysis. However, I would argue that, in its applied uses, even discourse analysis tends to have to confront ques-tions of context and subjectivity.

For example, in Corinne Squire's insightful and stimulating chapter in this volume which gets very close to a solely textual analysis, she is obliged to assume a model of subjective reality and one of objective reality in order to make some of the points that she wishes to make about the texts as 'mediated speech'.[8]

She presumes a model of subjectivity in relation to text-delivery in at least two places. First, when she argues that 'To live with HIV is to live with abjection insistently and repetitively; interviewees' story genres provided a way both to register abjection, and to continue around it', she makes an assertion about the subjective experience of 'living with HIV' and discusses the 'registering' (or not) of such abjection. A language of subjectivity and psychic states is clearly and necessarily being used. Second, although she argues that one should not 'treat language as a more or less transparent route to subjectivity', her general argument does include a passage with a different implication:

In order to examine narrative language and its effects on subjectivity, the study focused on narrative *genre*, a category that foregrounds specific structures of language. Such genres also provide a fairly concrete way of looking at the relationships between subjectivity and the cultural sphere, since they are articulated in both.

How are 'effects on subjectivity' to be assessed if no independent route to subjectivity is identified? For that matter, how are the effects of subjectivity on language to be assessed, either? Knowledge of subjectivity has crept in by the back door, after having been, more or less, dismissed from the front! The moment one wishes to make inferences from the text to the subjectivity of the individual producing the text – even that of living with abjection – one is obliged to presume or to build a model of individual subjectivity and a model of the possible modes of text-production that such a subjectivity might engage in.

Squire's goal is to 'treat the stories really *as* stories, as expressions of cultural genres, not just as unmediated speech'. I agree that the 'subjectivity' cannot be simply read as 'given' by the stories, but argue that stories are not just 'mediated speech' but that also 'genre-mediated speech' itself mediates experience, for example, the experience of 'living with HIV' that she has asserted is an experience of 'living with abjection'.

In addition, the text-analysis also presumes a model of historical-social objective context. Squire's account of John's account of his phone calls and of his coming-out narrative (pp.203–4) involves her treating and evaluating the accounts as 'realistic' in a way that 'pure' formal discourse analysis would avoid. Squire says that she knows that John would not be allowed to do some of the things that real doctors can do. Common understandings of medical power and the power of laymen are assumed between Squire and the reader. Knowledge of the external real is presumed and used to interpret the significance of the text.

The strength of her argument depends in part upon the assumptions about subjectivity and the knowledge of external context which support the very valuable insights she wishes to convey about genre and its mediating function. The point I am making here is Scheff's point, namely that, if we wish to 'understand' the text,[9] it is very hard to sustain a consistent refusal to use knowledge about subjectivity or about contextual reality and actual history.

The 'diamond model': four components in relation

My argument so far is that the implicit model of all biographical research and the explicit methodology of BIM contrasts *the history of the lived life*

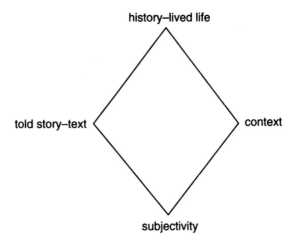

Figure 7.1   The four implicit components of biographical research: diamond
model

and the *text of the told story*. I have added two further items: Scheff's
general argument about understanding requiring a knowledge of *historical
and comparative context*, and Hollway and Jefferson's stress on the significance of *the researcher's general model of (text-producing) subjectivity* within
an *intersubjective interview*.

Better understanding of a given text requires considerable knowledge
about contexts, history and subjectivity, as well as knowledge about texts.
These four components are represented in Figure 7.1 above.

Understanding of biographic interview material, and particularly of
narrative, requires us to be conscious of these four *implicit components*, and
of the way we think they interact. Our image of these four components
and how they interact governs the way that the particular interview text
is read and understood by the researcher.

Resources for typification and generalisation *within* single-case research

Both novice and seasoned researchers find it difficult to determine the
procedures necessary for comparing cases, and, though there is considerable literature on the analysis of interview interaction and the analysis of
each case taken separately, there is much less on the still mysterious
processes of comparative interpretation (Wolcott 1994; Wengraf 1998).

I argue, however, that it is, luckily, impossible to produce a report on a
particular case – or to read such a report – without implicitly comparing

other possible and actual cases and without certain universal concepts for describing and understanding cases being more or less strongly implied by the text and by the act of reading.

If this can be shown, then there is no *logical jump or discontinuity* involved in moving from single-case to multiple-case analysis. Neither is there a particular difficulty in moving from the particularities of a single case to general concepts suitable for comparative work and for generalisation, since some general concepts were already employed to evoke and make sense of the particular case.

The biographic-interpretive method (BIM) of analysing biographic narrative interviews renders explicit what is implicit in other less elaborate and formalised approaches to analysis. I am arguing that this can usefully be formulated as a procedure. The aspect I am particularly concerned with is the use in biographical researching of the general procedure of grounded theorising, as developed originally by Glaser and Strauss (1967). A name which they gave to the practice I wish to highlight here is that of the 'constant comparative method'. This involves two stages: first, the multiplication of hypotheses around any given datum until the imagination and knowledge of the researchers is exhausted; second, the consideration as to whether the next datum being examined enables any of the previous hypotheses to be eliminated. Strauss (1987) gives useful examples of this process of the multiplication of hypotheses and the subsequent attempt to consider which have been falsified[10] and Bertaux (this volume) in a footnote evokes the application of this 'guessing game' in a classroom situation.

In BIM, this two-stage procedure is applied twice: to the sequence of events in the lived life, and to the sequence of narrative expression within the interview text.

While the events of the lived life form a natural chronological sequence, the principles of *sequentialising the told story*, the interview text as 'emitted', are less obvious. There are two main dimensions of sequentialising the told story: *themes raised* and the *text-sorts* in terms of which themes or parts of them are treated. We cannot go into detail here, but in general, the process is described by G. Rosenthal (1998).

> In analysing their biographical self-presentations, or life-stories, what we are aiming to achieve is an analysis of the biographer's present perspective. We interpret in what form, i.e. at what point of the text, they speak about certain parts of their lives, and we reconstruct the mechanisms behind the themes they choose to talk about and the experiences they choose to tell. We assume that it is by no means coincidental and insignificant when biographers *argue* about one

phase of their lives, but *narrate* another at great length, and then give only a brief *report* of yet another part of their lives or *describe* the circumstances of their lives in detail.

(Rosenthal 1998: 4–5)

The life-sequentialisation and the text-sequentialisation are 'processed' by interpretive panels of co-researchers quite separately but according to the same principle. The common principle is described by Breckner as follows:

The starting point is an empirical phenomenon [in our case an event or a segment of text] which is to be explained by a general rule formulated as an hypothesis. The core of the abductive program is to construct alternative hypotheses to explain a given empirical datum. The analyst is invited to think about all possible hypotheses, each of which could be regarded as sufficient to explain the empirical phenomenon.... A prediction is made about what later data are likely to follow if the general rule embodied in that hypothesis about datum D were true.

(Breckner 1998: 93, modified)

As each new datum in the series is examined (*the next event in the life* or *the next theme or text-sort change in the told story*), then there is a search back to see which of the hypotheses previously put forward – 'later occurrence' or 'following' hypotheses – can be *falsified* by this new datum. This having been done, there is then a search back to see which surviving hypotheses have been *strengthened* by this new datum. This having been done, then further new hypotheses are developed around the significance of the new datum, together with predictions – new 'later occurrence hypotheses' or 'following hypotheses' – about what will occur later in the series were such new hypotheses to turn out to be correct. And so on, to the end of the series.[11]

A record of such a grounded theory procedure as applied to a sequence of biographical data can be found in Breckner 1998; and, as applied to sequences of text data, in Schiebel and in Jones and Rupp in this volume.

The question of formalising the development of such 'later occurrences' might be represented by a diagram. The task of multiplying hypothetical possibilities for the individual biographical datum is precisely that of inventing any and all possibilities that the social and cultural knowledge of the panel can come up with. They are creatively proliferated; not systematically organised. They might look like Figure 7.2.

At each datum-point, a number of (dotted line) hypotheses are developed. The subsequent datum either suggests that one of these were correct

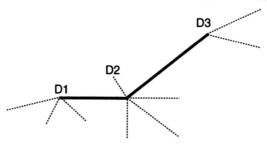

Figure 7.2   Later occurrences diagram at point D3

or that a new one needs to be retrospectively constructed.... and that the hypotheses which remain unsupported or even refuted by later occurrences remain as unrealised possibilities of life-events or text-sequences in the particular case being studied. Realised (confirmed) hypotheses are represented by a solid line; unrealised (unconfirmed or refuted) ones remain as dotted lines.[12]

Multiplying contingencies for cases, multiplying types for typologies

How does this procedure for multiplying contingencies for a particular case support the development of types and typologies? I shall show below that comparative questions and comparative knowledge are inherent in our understanding of a given case as expressed in a case report. I shall show that, in the very description of particular cases, general concepts are also involved.

In Table 7.1, I have taken an extract from a case report on an East German, 'Sophie', reported upon by Astrid Segert and Irene Zierke (see also their chapter, this volume) and have attempted to show some of the implicit comparative questions that can arise when reading it and some of the universal concepts in terms of which the description of the single case is couched.

1   The first column contains the propositions of the case report.
2   The second has to do with comparative questions that prod one to think 'What might have happened to Sophie – or to someone in some respects like Sophie – if...?'.
3   The third column identifies organising general concepts more or less strongly implied in the case report discourse, general concepts which are necessarily available for describing all other cases.

Table 7.1   Implicit comparisons and universal concepts in Sophie's case report

Case report	Comparative questions to help think about the focal, and possibly other, cases	Some organising universal societal concepts implied in the case report extract
Born at the beginning of the 1950s, she is twice married and has a son.	Cohort experience of current 50-year-olds in East Germany; twice-married, why? and what are the implications of having a son? (of what age?)	Birth Marriage Children
She comes from a vicar's family who experienced the political repression of both the Fascist and the GDR period.	What about vicars' families who do not have that experience? What is the significance of having that experience? What about those who have the experience of repression but come from non-vicar's families? What happened in that part of Germany during the Fascist period? What happened during the GDR period? What is meant by repression in the two contexts?	Family of origin – types of families Father's? occupation Periods of history Types of society Repression and its absence – political and other repressions
Belonging to a politically marginalised church, the family lived in modest circumstances.	What is the significance of 'non-modest circumstances'? Were there vicar's families who lived in better/in worse circumstances? What might be the different effects?	Churches Organisations – marginalised or not Circumstances – better than, or worse than, modest
They preserved their high education standards, cultural values and close social connections to like-minded others.	In a different location or situation, or even in the same one, similar families might not have been able to achieve such 'preservation', or at least not all of them. Implications of different patterns of non-preservation?	Family culture preserved or not Education standards – high/medium/low Cultural values – variable Social connections to like-minded and other than like-minded – close/distant

To some of the comparative questions, the researcher-writer or the reader may have definite and well-grounded answers. Particularly if he or she does not yet know much about East Germany and its history, the chances are that other answers may be tentative, and that to many of the questions one can only respond – like any researcher in a new field at the beginning of a research project – 'I must find out more'. Also implicit in the case-description are universal concepts being applied. There are presumed theories of child and personal development, of family/non-family relations, of types of society and types of family and societal regime operating: how well grounded are they? Again, research may be needed.

In considering Table 7.1, you may wish to refer back to the 'later occurrences diagram', Figure 7.2.

I wish to stress here that, when we suggest possible 'later particular occurrences' in the case of a particular individual, we are very close to suggesting possible *later types of occurrence* in a *typology of classes of individuals*.[13]

For example, taking an imaginary case, 'Raymond', we suggest that the biographical datum of a divorce from Mary might be followed by an affair with Suzie or by an intensification of an old friendship with Clement. This is very close to suggesting a generalisation that, for some men, the breakdown of a marital relationship may be followed by the development of a new sexual relationship or by the development of an old non-sexual relationship. The 'later occurrences diagram' of branching possibilities is the same: the difference is that the names on the branches are 'abstract' rather than 'proper' names.

The closeness between multiplying *particular alternatives for particular people* and multiplying *typical alternatives for typical people* might be even greater. It may be that it was our general sense that came first; that we applied a general set of typical possibilities and probabilities to the particular case of Raymond, a general sense or set derived from experience, stereotypes, fictional works (see Rustin, this volume) and our social science imagination, of what a certain type of person is likely to do in particular types of situation. Perhaps previously existing typifications in our heads produced the prediction of possible alternative 'later occurrences' for the particular case?

If the actual sequence of agents and actions in this new particular lifeworld requires us to rethink our pre-existing sense of personal and historical possibilities and probabilities, then new cases are interesting to the extent that they force our previous mental models[14] into consciousness and then force us to revise and improve them.

My argument is that we already have a complex, many-branching, usually not very coherent, tacit typology of agents and actions and situations in our heads *before* we start to make sense of a new particular case, and we use those typifications to make sense of the new particular case by applying it to the unique particular life-world of the particular person, their *idioverse*.[15] This tacit, usually not very coherent typology, like the organising universal concepts implied in particular case descriptions, these mental models, are implicit resources available for subsequent explicit comparison between cases.

If we take the case of Sophie, she comes from a vicar's family who experienced the political repression of both the Fascist and the GDR period in East Germany. Our speculations about what possible 'shapings of the biographic life experience' might be true for Sophie might include predictions that repression would demoralise the family of origin and turn her into a cynical opportunist. In terms of the 'later occurrences diagram', this might be a dotted line hypothesis. The last cited item in the extract from the case report indicates that this hypothesis was *not* born out in Sophie's case: the family preserved their high education standards, cultural values and close social connections to like-minded others. *Refuted for Sophie, this hypothesis remains as a potential line of development for cases other than Sophie's* that might have been analysed already or might be considered later on. Every later occurrence hypothesis suggests a 'type of outcome' that might not be true in the case under consideration but might be true of some other case. Alternative 'particular later occurrences' suggest types of occurrence in an implicit typology that can be made explicit and thus function as a first resource for *explicit* comparative understanding.

In the first part of this chapter, I argued that there is a connection between the implicit four components involved in the understanding of any particular biographical case – the history of the lived life and the text of the told story, the evolving context and the inferred subjectivity of the interviewee – and that these often implicit components – together with the subjectivity of the researcher – are best made explicit. In the second part of this chapter, I argued two points, both exemplified in the Sophie example. The first was that the practice of imagining different 'later occurrences' within the lifecourse of the particular biographical individual was closely connected to the researchers' stock of known and imagined (types of) events, actions, situating contexts and outcomes, depended on that (typological) stock and might well contribute towards enriching it. The second point was that the researchers could move up the spectrum of generality–specificity from their account of a particular case, uncovering the general concepts necessarily implied by their particular case description, and turning later occurrence statements (with proper names and dates in them) to statements of types of possibility (without proper names and dates).

In the following section of this chapter, I will bring together the arguments of the first two sections, and then end with a discussion of the types of typologies.

Differences/typologies between the particular and the general

Typologies – implicit or explicit – lie between the general and the particular: they can be regarded as the formalisation of real and imagined historical difference. I would argue that one can think more clearly if no hard epistemological line is drawn between descriptions of difference and typologies of difference, since none is justified. However, in any particular research process the typologies will be seen in different ways.

- Seen from 'above', from the point of view of the general and abstract orienting concepts, ideal types or typologies[16] function as *specifications of the general concepts* in their movement towards the particular.
- However, from the point of view of the particular case descriptions, such ideal types or typologies function as *generalisations from particular cases* in the movement of thought towards greater generality. Most qualitative researchers into biographic materials tend to develop their sense of differences within lives and between cases from the ground *upwards*; we turn knowledge of concrete particulars into implicit typologies into explicit ones, and then attempt to clarify the general concepts that – as I showed with the Sophie example, above – were inherent at the previous levels.

How can we summarise the relation between the particular and the general, and the relation between multiple possible occurrences and multiple possible types?

Spradley distinguishes (1979: 210) six levels of proposition that can be found in an ethnographic text. I use a reduced version of this to suggest the importance of levels of abstraction (see Table 7.2).

Presenting the 'diamond' model of the four necessary components of biographical research (p.148 above), I argued that, even if only one

Table 7.2   Modified Spradley three-level model: differentiating concepts between the general and the particular

Level
1 Universal concepts for all societies
2 Differentiating concepts
3 Specific concepts for specific cases

component was the focus of the research effort, all the other three were implicit and should be consciously attended to. At the level of case description, each of the components needed to be addressed and related to each other: history – lived life; told-story, the text; subjectivity; and context, *all of one particular person*. The model of a particular case involves: (a) describing each of the four components; and (b) relating them to each other in the way that they are specified for that person, at that time, producing that story, from their lived life in that context in that epoch. Each of the four components needs to be described *separately* in individually particular ways ('thick description', Geertz 1973). In addition, how they are supposed to have *interacted* to produce the biography in the particular case must also be described in the same way. Such a '4-components interacting' particular description operates at the level of concrete particulars with Spradley level-3 statements. This is summarised in Figure 7.3.

However, inherent in any *particular description* are *general models* of each component and their relationships. To make a particular statement about Sophie's subjectivity in telling the story, we *have to have had* a general model of 'subjectivities in general and their possible relations to the other three components'; to give a particular account of evolution of the societal-historical context of Germany from, say, 1939 to 1998, we *have to have had* a general model of 'societal-historical contexts and their possible relations to the other three components', etc.

Such implicit or explicit '4-components interacting' general models of subjectivity, text, context, history are Spradley level-1 models; the third column of the Sophie-diagram indicated a list of some of these.

My argument is that to describe any or all of the four components that are to be found interacting in any *particular* historical case (Spradley level 3), the researcher is obliged to be using implicit *general* models at or closer to Spradley level 1. *Without general concepts/models* of subjectivity, of context, of lived lives, of told stories, and of the possible interaction of such components, *no accounts of particular instances* could be generated. This homology is shown in Figure 7.4.

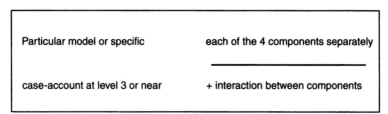

Particular model or specific	each of the 4 components separately
case-account at level 3 or near	+ interaction between components

Figure 7.3　The four components at case-description level (Spradley level 3)

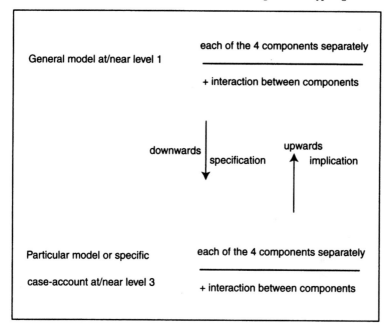

Figure 7.4 The four interacting components at two Spradley levels (1 and 3)

The model needs to be enriched still further. Returning to the middle zone of my modified version of Spradley above, between the general and the particular lie multiple indications of difference: there are contingent statements close to level 3 and relatively formalised typologies close to level 1. In this intermediate zone, too, the four components – lived life, told story, context, subjectivity – and their relations remain mutually implied to some extent or explicitly spelled out. As I have argued earlier, the description of multiple possible contingencies (as in the later occurrence hypothesising) is directly related to implied multiple typologising. Statements of 'type' differences are higher in the level of abstraction than statement of 'occurrence' or contingency differences, as is suggested by Figure 7.5 on the next page.

Summarising, my argument has been, first, that the four components of the diamond model are *horizontally implicated* with each other at each level. Second, that any account of any and all of the components at the level of case description involves a model of the most general sort: consequently, there is a line of *vertical mutual implication*, as well. Third, that there is no hard epistemological line but rather a spectrum between level 1 (universal) and level 3 (specific particularity).

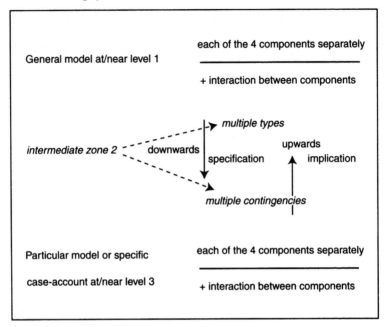

Figure 7.5   The four interacting components at three Spradley levels

I wish to address one further point, before considering types of typologies. The resources of conceptualised knowledge with which the multiple contingencies of later occurrences were developed in the analysis of sequences of life and sequences of text in a single case imply resources of generality and of typification that need to be made explicit and thus liable to correction and improvement. Such resources of generality and typification as operating in the analysis of one/the first case have the great advantage that they are part of the 'system of relevancy and thinking' of the researcher doing the work of case-description at level 3.

However confused and incoherent the cultural common sense (Gramsci 1957: 58–9; 1971: 323–5) of the researcher may be from which these resources have been taken, emerging from his or her own individual and professional biography, the selection and utilisation of such resources of generality and typification by the researcher in his or her case-description means that they are the raw materials from which *that researcher* can best develop a clearer and more coherent set of interlocking general models and particular descriptions. The stages, the necessity and difficulty of that iterative struggle are brought out in this volume by Cooper. Just as the uninterrupted narrative interview enables the 'system of relevancy' of the *interviewee* to be expressed and understood, so the multiple later-occurrence arguments and descriptions of the researcher enable the *researcher's* '*systems of relevancy*' to be expressed and improved.

I would argue that, after doing the case-descriptions and before looking to the indefinitely large field of social research literature, the typologies and typifications implicit in the researcher's multiplication of contingencies, and the generalities implicit in all his or her particular case-accounts produced, need *first* to be attended to. They must be made adequate and the general and the particular models must be made reasonably coherent, both horizontally and vertically.[17]

Once a reasonable stab at creating such a coherent and explicit set of such general and particular models has been made, on the basis of the resources internal to the particular case(s) studied and the concerns and system of relevancy of the researcher, *then*, *but only then*, the more explicit search for existing particular typologies and existing general models in social science research literature will invigorate rather than crush the now reasonably well-developed comparative apparatus of the researcher.

Types of typologies

If typologies either determine or exist virtually within real or imagined contingent historical differences, and if they depend upon and feed general concepts at Spradley level 1, can we develop a typology of typologies? Layder (1998) has argued strongly and persuasively for the need to develop typologies and distinguishes between typologies of action (behaviour) and typologies of system (structure), stressing the danger of restricting research to typologies of action:

> *Action or behavioural typologies* restrict themselves largely to the depiction of lifeworld elements of society concerning subjective meaning, lived experience, motivations, attitudes and so on. The importance of *system or structural typologies* is that they concern themselves with depicting the settings and contexts of behaviour and thus provide the necessary requirements for more inclusive and powerful explanations of social life.... It is also crucial to emphasise the important role that structural or system typologies may play in research; otherwise, their influence on the behaviour or people in question will be vague and partial, or treated as an implicit, inchoate backdrop to the analysis....
>
> (Layder 1998: 74–5)

Given that those drawn to biographical interview-based research are likely to be spontaneously oriented towards action-alternatives or subjectivity-alternatives, Scheff and Layard's insistence on the importance of *context-alternatives* is salutary. The socio-biographical work developed in SOSTRIS develops our 'sense of context' (SOSTRIS 1998a, 1998b, 1999a, 1999b; Chamberlayne and Spano, Rustin, this volume) and these lay the ground – as I have argued above – for richer typologies of context.

Three more distinctions perhaps need to be made to enrich Layder's model, an alternative to the 'diamond' model presented earlier.

First, since our concern here is with biographic research in the social sciences, I think it important to distinguish the level of the biological 'individual'. Obviously, it would be possible to treat the individual subject as a particular type of 'system' contextualising the text, but for convenience I think it useful to distinguish the individual actor, or 'subjectivity' from other features of context.

Second, in addition to this important distinction, I think it necessary to add another, that between relatively *synchronic* typologies – where the typology is of different actions or systems treated in an ahistorical fashion – and relatively *diachronic* typologies – where the typology is of the historical development of a sequence of actions (like a history of community, family, or individual actions) or of the historical development of a system or structure of greater or lesser scope.[18]

Third, it is perhaps important to identify the 'told story' text – or even the whole of the interview text – as a distinct object for theorising.

The net effect of these distinctions is to yield the following table:

Table 7.3   Textual, individual, action and system typologies – eight-fold table

That which can be typologised (*theorised*)	*The temporal dimension of the typology* (*theory*)	
	Synchronic at a given 'moment'	*Diachronic* over a sequence of 'moments'
(Interview) Textual	I	V
Individual – subjectivity	II	VI
Action – behavioural	III	VII
System – structural	IV	VIII

My argument about biographising would be that particular accounts, typologies and general models of a synchronic nature (column 1) should always serve and lead towards accounts, typologies, and generalities of a diachronic nature (column 2).

Conclusion

I have tried to show that, in order to understand an interview text, one has to do, but go beyond, an analysis of the text itself. Naive or sophisticated recycling does not produce understanding. I have put forward a diamond model of the four interacting components of understanding.

I have tried to show that within particular accounts of real and imagined historical differences of action, context and so forth, there exist virtual types, typologies and orienting concepts (Layder), which are resources for understanding the particular cases and all other cases: these are generated in the dialogue between the interviewee's self-expression and the researcher's frame of reference.

In conclusion, I have suggested two different formulations of the (usually implicit) 'general models' that are to be found in the (usually explicit) models of the particular. One is based on the 'diamond' model at the different levels of abstraction suggested by Spradley; the other, the eight-fold typology of typologies, is based on Layard.

Notes

1 I am indebted to Joanna Bornat, Prue Chamberlayne, Jeff Evans, Amal Treacher, Lisa Blackwell and Margaret Lipscomb for their comments on earlier drafts.
2 What we, like Scheff, tend to take as the natural empirically given concrete realities are probably better seen as a mixture of universal human assumptions and constraints as mediated through historico-cultural assumptions and constraints of a specific general and disciplinary culture at a specific time within a civilisation and a (natural language) socio-linguistic community.
3 See Wengraf 1999 for a further discussion of this point.
4 'In every consulting room, there ought to be two rather frightened people; the patient and the psychoanalyst. If they are not, one wonders why they are bothering to find out what everyone knows' (Bion 1974: 13, cited in Casement 1985: 4).
5 Schiebel (this volume) identifies a collusion in not-knowing between herself and an older German man, and ascribes this to a specifically German culturally prescribed 'defensiveness in communication'. However, if we accept a model of subjectivity with the Hollway and Jefferson's defended self and Cooper's assumption (both, this volume) of sleeping and normally invisible cultural assumptions, then all communication in all cultures will involve defensiveness in communication.
6 If there is or could be a controversy, then the postulated 'datum' is not 'hard enough', and is left out!

7   Hollway and Jefferson (this volume) refer to this as 'inter-textualism'.
8   I am indebted to Corinne Squire for clarification on this point.
9   So would be a refusal to use any new knowledge gained from 'formal-textual' analysis to add to our knowledge and understanding of the other three components.
10 The history of the 'grounded theory movement' cannot be considered here. See Strauss and Corbin (1994) for a disguised polemic from one (dominant) side; Glaser (1992) for an overt polemic from the (not so dominant) other.
11 In SOSTRIS Working Paper 2 there is an example of such hypothesis generation and hypothesis falsification/validation in respect of the biographical data of Tony on pp.94–6, and in respect of the analysis of the sequentialisation as the expression of a thematic field on pp.99–102.
12 This model is clearly a simplification. In actual practice, towards the start of the process a large number of hypotheses are generated and relatively few are refuted; towards the end of the process, there are a larger number of refutations and a smaller number of new hypotheses. Our concern in this chapter is the multiplication of imagined later occurrences.
13 The same is true in relation to texts, societal contexts, told stories, subjectivities. The reader may wish to pursue this argument which I have not space to develop here.
14 See Senge (1990: ch. 10) for a formal discussion of mental models.
15 A parallel argument holds true about imagining different ways – at each point in the text (sequence) a different topic/treatment might be chosen by the speaker, and what implications might be drawn from such patterns of recurrent choices. There is not space to develop this discussion of 'later occurrences' in the flow of interviewee speech.
16 We cannot here explore the distinction between 'collections of types' and 'typologies'. See Max Weber (1949) and Gerth and Mills (1948: 59–61) for discussion. The orientation to delivering understanding of particular historical cases is suggested by Weber's assertion that 'the goal of ideal-typical concept-construction is always to make clearly explicit not the class or average character but rather the unique individual character' (Weber 1949: 101, cited Mommsen 1974: 10).
17 The need for such coherence is well brought out by Mason (1996: Ch. 1).
18 This model reduces the four components of the earlier diamond model to three, by eliminating 'the historical' as a separate category and adding the potentiality of a historical dimension to each of the other three components.

References

Bion, W.R. (1974) Brazilian Lectures 1, Rio de Janeiro: Imago Editora.
Breckner, B. (1998) 'The Biographical-Interpretive Method – Principles and Procedures', see SOSTRIS Working Paper no. 3: 91–104.
Casement, P. (1985) On Learning from the Patient, London: Tavistock.
Friedlander, P. (1998) 'Theory, Method and Oral History', in R. Perks and A. Thomson (eds), The Oral History Reader, London: Routledge.
Geertz, C. (1973) The Interpretation of Cultures, New York: Basic Books.
Gerth, H. and Mills, C.W. (1948) From Max Weber: Essays in Sociology, London: Routledge and Kegan Paul.

Glaser, B. (1992) *Basics of Grounded Theory Analysis*, California: Sociology Press.
Glaser, B. and Strauss, A. (1967) *The Discovery of Grounded Theory*, Chicago, IL: Aldine Publishing.
Gramsci, A. (1957) *The Modern Prince and Other Writings*, London: Lawrence and Wishart.
—— (1971) *Selections from the Prison Notebooks*, London: Lawrence and Wishart.
Kuhn, T. (1962) *The Structure of Scientific Revolutions*, Chicago, IL: University of Chicago.
Layder, D. (1998) *Sociological Practice: Linking Theory and Social Research*, London: Sage.
Mason, J. (1996) *Qualitative Researching*, London: Sage.
Mills, C.W. (1959) *The Sociological Imagination*, Oxford: Oxford University Press.
Mommsen, W. (1974) *The Age of Bureaucracy: Perspectives on the Political Sociology of Max Weber*, Oxford: Basil Blackwell.
Perks, R. and Thomson, A. (eds) (1998) *The Oral History Reader*, London: Routledge.
Polkinghorne, D. (1995) 'Narrative Configuration in Qualitative Analysis', in J.A. Hatch and R. Wisniewski (ed.), *Life History and Narrative*, London: Falmer Press.
—— (1996) 'Use of Biography in the Development of Applicable Knowledge', *Ageing and Society* 16(6): 721–45.
Rosenthal, G. (1993) 'Reconstruction of Life Stories: Principles of Selection in Generating Stories for Narrative Biographical Interviews', in R. Josselson and A. Lieblich (eds), *The Narrative Study of Lives*, vol. 1, London: Sage.
—— (1998) *The Holocaust in Three Generations: Families of Victims and Perpetrators of the Nazi Regime*, London: Cassell.
Scheff, T. (1997) *Emotions, the Social Bond and Human Reality: Part/Whole Analysis*, Cambridge: Cambridge University Press.
Senge, P.M. (1990) *The Fifth Discipline: the Art and Practice of the Learning Organisation*, New York: Doubleday.
SOSTRIS (1998a) *SOSTRIS Working Paper 2: Case Study Materials – the Early Retired*, Centre for Biography in Social Policy, University of East London.
—— (1998b) *SOSTRIS Working Paper 3: Case Study Materials – Lone Parents*, Centre for Biography in Social Policy, University of East London.
—— (1999a) *SOSTRIS Working Paper 4: Case Study Materials – Ethnic Minorities*, Centre for Biography in Social Policy, University of East London.
—— (1999b) *SOSTRIS Working Paper 6: Case Study Materials – Ex-Traditional Workers*, Centre for Biography in Social Policy, University of East London
Spradley, J.P. (1979) *The Ethnographic Interview*, New York: Holt, Rhinehart and Winston.
Strauss, A. (1987) *Qualitative Analysis for Social Scientists*, Cambridge: Cambridge University Press.
Strauss, A. and Corbin, J. (1994) 'Grounded Theory Methodology: an Overview', in N. Denzin and Y. Lincoln (eds), *Handbook of Qualitative Research*, California: Sage Publications.

Terkel, S. (1975) *Working: People Talk About What They Do All Day and About How They Feel About What They Do*, London: Wildwood House.

Weber, M. (1949) 'Objectivity in Social Science and Social Policy', *The Methodology of the Social Sciences*, New York: Free Press.

Wengraf, T. (1998) 'Representations of Interpreted Biographies in Contexts: General Concepts and Unique Cases', paper read at the International Sociological Association, Montreal, July.

—— (1999) 'Contextualising Subjectivity in the Exploration and Presentation of Cases in Biographic Narrative Research', in SOSTRIS 1999b.

Wolcott, H.F. (1994) *Transforming Qualitative Data: Description, Analysis and Interpretation*, London: Sage.

Part 2

Examples of biographical methods in use

8 Biography, anxiety and the experience of locality

Wendy Hollway and Tony Jefferson

Introducing the anxious defended subject of biography

It is fashionable nowadays for sociologists to argue the importance of biography for an understanding of social identity. Implicit in such a shift of attention is an idea about the limitations of demographic factors like class, gender, race, age, to encapsulate fully the diversity of individuals' lived experience; either because the demographic factors are too reductively broad to do so; or because the social is now hopelessly fragmented; or because such a structural approach effectively denies appropriate individuality and agency to subjects. Biography is to post-structuralism what demography is to structuralism; and, in a certain sense, we are all post-structuralists now. But, such a shift brings in its wake a set of new problems, all of which stem from the 64,000 dollar question of who or what is the post-structuralist (or biographical) subject? If subjects are more than the sum of demographic factors, in what sense can a biographical approach produce less reductive, more 'real' subjects?

For many academic biographers intertextuality rules: all biography is interpretive, discursive reconstruction; a speculative attempt to impose an orderliness, a shape, on a life which is essentially irrecoverable, and thus, strictly speaking, unknowable. Liz Stanley draws on the work of Merton to make the point 'that reality is not "single"' (that is, it can be 'known' in various ways), that 'there are no *sociological* means of systematically adjudicating between these knowledges' produced by the multiplicity of 'reality', and that, consequently, the textual nature of autobiography needs to be recognised. She therefore wants to see (auto)biography as 'a topic for investigation in its own right, and not as a *resource* to tell us about something lying outside the text itself' (1993: 42–3). For 'intertextuals', then, the search for the 'real' biographical subject beyond the textual traces of a life is illusory: deconstructing and reconstructing such traces is all that is possible. For all the strengths of such an approach, we are not satisfied with its bleak conclusion. Nor can we rest content with the related position that we are all now fragmented, de-centred, multiple selves, that is, 'postmodern' subjects.

While Stanley may be right to suggest that sociology is not up to the task of 'systematically adjudicating between these knowledges', she overlooks the possibility that other knowledge than sociology may be necessary to make sense of the biographical subject. In particular, by positing a psychoanalytic subject, we believe it is possible not only to work with a theory of the subject that is not reducible to discourse, but also one that, to a greater or lesser extent, posits a coherent, agentic 'I'.

There are many approaches to the subject which could be called psychoanalytic; for example the libidinous, drive-based subject of Freud, or the Lacanian subject who is inevitably alienated from an early fantasy of coherence by its positioning in language. Our subject is based on the psychoanalytic proposition that anxiety is inherent in the human condition and that people's actions, lives and relations with others are centrally influenced by the unconscious defences which we all deploy to cope with anxiety. While anxiety is a psychological characteristic, it is not reducible to psychology: anxiety and the defences which it precipitates are complex and mediated responses to events in the real world, both present and past.

There is a rich vein of empirical (clinically based) psychoanalytic writing, readily classifiable as biographically based research, which contributes to theorising inter/subjectivity and its relation to the 'real' world. Our work draws particularly on the British neo- or post-Kleinian tradition which shares with all psychoanalysis the premise of a dynamic unconscious but emphasises intersubjective unconscious defences against anxiety. It is this theorisation of anxiety which we found useful in our case-study analyses.

According to Klein (1988a, 1988b), the state of early infancy is one dominated by anxiety precipitated by complete dependency. Outside of a conception of time, the infant experiences polarised emotions of 'bad' and 'good', without mitigation; for example, it is incapable of anticipating the satisfaction of a feed when it is feeling the frustration of hunger. The relation with the object develops, along with the infant's capacity to recognise the breast, and later the (m)other, as a whole object containing both the capacity to fulfil and frustrate. However, the bad and good will still be kept mentally separate for defensive purposes, in order to protect the good from the bad.

This polarisation and splitting of objects is the basis for what Klein terms the 'paranoid-schizoid' position; a position to which we may all resort in the face of self-threatening occurrences, because it permits us to believe in a good object, on which we can rely, uncontaminated by 'bad' threats which have been split off and located elsewhere. Klein contrasts the paranoid-schizoid position with the depressive position which involves the acknowledgement, when faced with lived reality, that good and bad are contained in the same object, for example the mother who both fulfils and frustrates. This is a hard position to sustain in the face of external or internal threats to the self, when the good needs to be preserved – at the cost of reality if necessary.

We all move between these positions, variably in relation to different areas of our lives, but different people may be characterised by a predominance of one or the other as typical responses. For Klein, to the extent that coherence of self is achieved (not a once-for-all achievement), this is enabled by the depressive position, that is, by the acknowledgement of good and bad in the same object; in the other and in the self. The two are simultaneous achievements and, in this crucial sense, the self is relational, since parts are moved unconsciously from outside (in the other) to inside (the self) and vice versa.

Mediations and producing subjects

Armed with this conception of an anxious, defended, biographical subject, we believe we can move beyond both text and multiplicity. Nonetheless, the postmodern insight that subjectivity is discursively *produced*, and is not some inner essence, is a reminder for all producers of biography that the biographical 'I' is always the product of a set of mediations. We need briefly to address three of these, namely, theoretical assumptions about the subject, conventions for representing the self, and the research relationship. We need also to point to the methodological implications that follow from them.

Probably the most ubiquitous *theoretical assumption* about the subject in biographical research, as in qualitative social science more generally, is that research subjects are knowledgeable agents, willing and able to 'tell it like it is'; subjects who are always somehow closer to the truth of their self-hood than the researcher can ever be. The best interviewers within this tradition are presumed to be the best because they manage to facilitate the emergence of their interviewees' own, authentic voices. Our assumption of anxious defended subjects presupposes the opposite, namely that subjects are motivated *not* to know certain aspects of themselves and that they *produce* biographical accounts which avoid such knowledge.

Since all biographical accounts, however produced, draw on *conventions* for representing the self, this constitutes a second form of mediation. Depending on the interview method, these conventions will have different effects on the biographical subject which is produced. Typically, this manifests in the research pair searching for meanings, consistency, and a sense of closure, among disparate data and apparently discrete stories: searching for a single, unifying thread, a 'grand' narrative uniting the many accounts peppering the biography. But what if, as with our psycho-analytical subject, contradiction and apparent lack of reason are the baseline assumptions out of which meaning has to be produced by inter-pretive, analytical work? This alters both the analytical strategy, what is taken to be significant in accounts, *and* the biographical subjects so produced.

Awareness of the *research relationship*, our third mediation, usually amounts to asking how can researchers, from their different and often more powerful positions, produce knowledge about their different, usually less powerful and less educated, research subjects. In extreme versions, transcending such social differences is thought to be impossible. Thus, it needs women to investigate women's experiences, black people to capture the experiences of black people, and so on. This prescription derives directly from a sociological analysis of structural sources of power which reads off specific relationships, and the plays of power therein, from the social identities of the participants. However, deploying the idea of a defended subject, other issues become apparent, which usually get over-looked, about the means by which someone understands another and the veracity of that understanding.

The clinical psychoanalytic literature abounds with such discussions (for example, Aron 1996). This alternative perspective should affect the entire research process, starting from the expectations preceding the first encounter, continuing throughout the production and analysis of data, and including the process of writing up. For example, the sort of questions asked in the biographical interview, both those prepared in advance and those arising out of the research interaction, are replete with meanings which cue the other's responses in ways that are profoundly influential and yet not subject to much conscious control. It was our experience that when an interviewee felt recognised by the way the following question was phrased in response to what s/he had just said, an emotional, intersub-jective event was in train which therefore shapes the subsequent course of the interview.

This view is a long way from seeing interview questions as neutral tools for securing information. The semi-structured interview, probably the method of choice for most academic biographers, makes no distinctions between narrative questions which invite subjects to tell stories and 'explanatory' ones which invite subjects to explain why they did what they did. We have been struck by how often social science researchers ask their interviewees what amounts to the same question that their research is posing (for example, to women managers in organisations 'why do you think you have not broken through the glass ceiling?'). The researcher is likely, by so doing, to reproduce subjects who position themselves in just those discourses which the researcher is deploying.

In our experience, asking narrative questions (eliciting stories of actual events, avoiding why questions) produces dramatically different data which can illuminate the search for the biographical subject. This seems to be because the stories people tell contain traces of their defences, and hence clues to their biographical meaning, whereas explanatory questions invite merely conventional discursive justifications (Hollway and Jefferson 1997).

In the production of data, the common assumption is that the analysand is a separate, independent entity who produces data for the analyst to make sense of. Our assumption, in contrast, is that the biographical 'I', as with our psychoanalytic subject, is a dynamic, intersubjective product of the relationship. In our view, this relationship is also present in data analysis, even though the interviewee is usually no longer on the physical scene. Certainly our interviewees maintained a powerful presence in our lives during intensive phases of working with their transcripts.

Using our theorisation of unconscious intersubjective defences against anxiety, then, provides us with certain methodological axioms for doing biography. We largely followed these in producing our biographical case studies (although the principles of intersubjectivity were only emerging for us during the field work and we are aware of how much further these implications need to be taken). In summary form, these axioms are:

- The research strategy has to be such as to get behind subjects' defences. In practice we found that what we called the free association narrative interviewing method,[1] where we attempted to elicit relevant narratives of real world events, produced the kinds of accounts that assisted this strategy significantly.
- While defended subjects are (variably) knowledgeable about the events of their lives, they cannot be assumed to be the best judge of their meaning.
- Biographical meanings are the product of theoretically informed, interpretive readings of the stories that subjects tell which will need to be read symptomatically for their full meaning to be produced.
- The data to be analysed are never free of their intersubjective provenance.

Two case studies: demography, biography and anxiety

In this chapter we have chosen to compare the cases of two women, Kelly and Joyce, from among thirty-seven people whom we interviewed in the course of our research on the fear of crime.[2] We selected these two because they were strikingly similar on sociological dimensions. They were thirty-four and thirty-six respectively, were brought up on neighbouring streets on the high-crime estate where they both lived. Each came from a large family, nine and eight siblings respectively. Each was absent from the estate when first married (for eight and ten years respectively), moved back subsequently and bought their house from the council. Each has family close by. Each has four children and is separated from the father(s) of their children, though Kelly is remarried. Each has a part-time, unskilled, typically gendered job.

Given these demographic similarities between Kelly and Joyce as sociological subjects, we were interested in exploring and explaining how two such similar women, with not dissimilar histories of criminal victimisation, expressed such differences in their fear of crime (Kelly, highly fearful and Joyce, relatively unafraid). Our biographical search for the meanings of risk, fear and crime for Kelly and Joyce led to the discovery of their remarkably different relationships to the estate on which they both lived. In other words, although their sociological location – past and present – was almost identical, their psychological locatedness was strikingly different. We could not have discovered this without the use of a biographical method.

Kelly: a pen portrait[3]

Kelly is a woman who has lived nearly all her life on a high-crime estate, but whose most direct experience of victimisation on the estate[4] is the theft of her husband's van. This immediately serves to problematise any simple relationship between her risk and her high fear; the more so since this victimisation experience occurred when she was ensconced in the respectable area of the estate, where she feels safer from the risk of criminal victimisation. This distinction between different parts of the estate is central to Kelly's fearful concern with crime. Although she takes a range of precautions, for example not walking back from garaging the car after dark (and never without her huge dog) and locking the car from the inside when driving, these become extreme when she goes to her brother's, just down the road on the rough part of the estate; the area she calls 'little Belfast'. There she 'pips' rather than get out of the car, even in broad daylight.

Kelly was born on the high-crime council estate where we conducted our interviews; the youngest of a family of nine, though since the family took in her sister's illegitimate child, she had, in effect, a younger brother (nephew) whom she was obliged to look after, something she profoundly resented. At twelve, her father died, after which 'there were no one there to love me'. At eighteen, she got married 'to get away' and only returned to the estate eight years later. In the meantime she'd had one child with her husband, left him for a man with whom she was 'besotted', who became increasingly violent over the course of three pregnancies (one a miscarriage resulting from his violence). It got to the point where she feared that the children 'wouldn't 'ave a mum' (that he would kill her). After being hospitalised and deciding to press charges, which subsequently put her partner in prison, she returned – 'a complete wreck', her weight down to a dangerous six stone – with her three children, including two who were illegitimate and mixed-race, to the same road where she'd grown up, close to her mother and a brother where she was 'born and bred'. Her return with two mixed-race children, born out of wedlock, left her traumatised, ashamed and anxious: 'I used to think everybody were looking at me and talking about me…that's more paranoid than…being unsafe'.

Over the course of the next two years, her feelings about the estate were transformed. At first 'I really, really loved the estate' but this changed to a horror of the 'nightmare' of crime. The crime 'never 'appened to me' but was 'all around me'. By the time she moved, the estate had changed from being her family 'territory' to a place where 'I don't fit in their territory'; 'them' being people she'd known all her life, but whose changes were evidence to her of the estate's decline into violence and drug use. During this time she met the man whom she subsequently married. Their now mutual dislike of the estate was catered for when they moved into, and subsequently bought, a house half a mile away in what is widely regarded as the respectable part of the estate. Aged thirty-four, she has now lived there for five years. She speaks of her present location as off the estate, though it is geographically central. Her contrast between the two locations is between 'paradise' and 'little Belfast', despite the fact that she was never a victim of crime prior to her move, but only since.

Kelly: anxiety, respectability and fear of crime

Kelly's fear of shame dates back to her adolescent fear of sexuality and getting pregnant.[5] This was linked to her mother's similar fear, which, in her mother's case, was linked to her lifelong unmarried state and the illegitimate pregnancies of her two older daughters (Kelly's older sisters). Kelly's shame did not disappear, as it rationally might have done, after her white wedding supposedly secured her own and her mother's respectability.

It was probably compounded by the physical and emotional abuse she suffered from her violent partner.

The most salient clue to Kelly's fearful investment in discourses of local crime comes from her determination – in direct contrast to local use and geography – to describe herself as living off the estate. We picked up this clue by paying attention to our initial confusion (it was one of the first things she said when we knocked on her door) rather than pursuing logic and consistency. By asking what emotional or identity purpose this served, by immersing ourselves in her position via her stories, and by deploying a theoretical framework emphasising the centrality of defences against anxiety, we could make sense of what might have been rejected as nonsense. We could then make links to her biography more generally.

The effect of positioning herself as off the estate is to situate crime somewhere else (albeit only half a mile away), in 'little Belfast', thus preserving her crime-free 'paradise'. The polarisation of meaning in these two terms suggests a paranoid-schizoid splitting of bad (little Belfast) and good (paradise). This serves the purpose of locating the good – safety, security and respectability for her self and her family – where she now lives. As predicted within Kleinian theory, there is a cost to her relation with reality, namely her refusal to acknowledge that her current location is also 'on' the estate. Many others alluded to the distinction between rough and respectable parts of the estate, though none but her used the 'little Belfast'/'paradise' metaphor, nor referred to her part being off the estate altogether.

However, Kelly moved between this paranoid-schizoid position and a more reality-based one, for example, when she said 'I'm sure, from estate, it'll eventually work its way down'. Thus she not only takes extreme precautions 'there', as we saw when visiting her brother, she also worries about crime where she lives, pointing anxiously to a neighbouring house where a 'problem family' might be moving in, leaving her house open to risk. Nonetheless, there is something puzzling about this anxiety, since she does not believe she is at risk of burglary, given her large dog and ever-alert neighbours. Instead we can posit that her concern with 'problem families' is less to do with the risk of delinquent children, and the accompanying threat of burglary, and more to do with the threat to her recently achieved respectability ('I've been a problem family'). Her fear of crime might therefore have more to do with the respectable distance it puts between her and those she was brought up with who have not moved (including her brother), than a likely place to put her anxieties for her own and her family's safety.

An endorsement of this reading may be found in her understanding of anxiety. When asked about times when she'd felt anxious, she interpreted this to mean 'can't wait' (keen or impatient). She answered 'what, to get away?...I were anxious to move off estate...very, very, anxious'. (This is an example of the importance of not imposing ones own meaning on the interviewee. Her association here gave us a further valuable clue to her identity and desires.) Now she is off (in her terms): 'I'm anxious to get on. I'm wanting more and more and more. And I think it's because I've got more and more and I want more and more'. Later she states that she lives for the future, imagining in detail her children with established careers and herself with grandchildren: 'it's nice to 'ave thoughts like that'.

This future-driven anxiety, which is effectively insatiable (the more she has the more she wants) symptomatically reveals its anxious source, as it defensively reinterprets the question towards a more benign rendering of anxiety (keen, impatient). What this insatiable desire for a rosy future suggests is a terror of the past, a driven desire to escape: from a big, rough family, which robbed her of a childhood (spent looking after an illegitimate nephew); from her mother's shame (despite her attempts to avoid her sisters' fate); from the unrespectability of bearing two, mixed-race, illegitimate children to an abusive man, whom she feared she could never stop loving. All this fear of the past is lodged with the estate (though it does not all rightfully belong there): 'If I'd have stayed on estate, I'd 'ave been in a worse state...and probably still a one-parent family'.

Though she has managed only to move half a mile from her past (and even less from her mother, who lives just around the corner and criticises her constantly), she needs to have made it 'off estate'; out of the rough, into 'paradise'. This motivated, unrealistic reading of her present situation is assisted by her present husband's strong identification with respectability for them both: '[he] used to like – I suppose brain wash me into like, – saying "it's a right estate...what's a nice girl like you doing on estate"'. Once we took note of Kelly's shame of her past, we could make good sense of her particular form of investment in fear of crime, her strong commitment to respectability, especially to being 'a proper family' and her idiosyncratic relationship to locality.

Joyce: a pen portrait

Joyce, aged thirty-six, was born on an adjoining road to Kelly, one of eight siblings. Now, after ten years off the estate starting when she got married (similar to Kelly's eight year absence), she lives, with her four children, in her original family home (on the rough end of the estate, in the centre of what Kelly calls 'little Belfast'), which, like Kelly, she has bought from the council. A sister lives close by.

Her husband left three years ago and, although her brother is living with her temporarily and she has a 'friend' (boyfriend) who sometimes stays, she has become accustomed to being on her own in the house, all the more so since the children spend a proportion of their time with their father. Like Kelly, her history of criminal victimisation is low: the lawn mower and two children's bikes were taken from her garden shed (which she had forgotten to lock up). Unlike Kelly, she is not fearful: 'I don't think I've been unsafe…[or] felt unsafe'. Like Kelly, being identified with the estate raises some questions in terms of respectability, but her response to these is quite different: 'I'm gonna show everybody that good does come off this estate'. So, despite her worries about crime, drugs and her children getting in with 'riff-raff', her own and her children's respectability does not depend on putting a distance between herself and the estate. In the middle of boarded-up windows and stolen scrap metal on front gardens, her house and garden are immaculate, her children well behaved.

Evidence suggests that Joyce's sense of safety – which is by no means invulnerable – derives from her knowledge of the families on the estate. She illustrates how she actively cultivates this feeling of familiarity when she says, of the first times when she was left on her own (when she turned down her sister's suggestion of going round there to stay the night):

> I weren't frightened about being on [my]…own. Everybody used to go 'ome at night from pub, early hours of morning…. I knew all the voices, 'good night', in fact it could be quite a game for me, 'cos I could tell you who voice were.

She attempts to keep her local knowledge up to date by getting to know new children as they come on to the estate. One young boy whom she caught picking flowers out of her garden was invited to a barbecue there soon after. She knows who is doing the thieving and, in one striking case, continued to support a young man after his imprisonment; a young man whom she'd helped as a child because of the deprivation of his own family circumstances. In this respect she behaves like her mother did when Joyce was young.

Joyce: anxiety, local identity and fear of crime

Joyce believed that her safety from crime depended on the fact that she and her large family were local and known and the local criminal ethic was that you don't steal from those like yourself. This principle, however, appeared to be under threat from young local drug addicts. She knows this because drugs is the reason for her local nephew having 'gone off the rails'. Joyce's direct evidence that the local ethic might no longer protect her was the theft from her garden shed. She wished that the thief had been a non-local because she was disturbed by the threat a local posed to her safety and its basis in her local identity:

> When I were robbed, I was 'urt...I just thought, right the rotten bastards...I knew that me shed were robbed by someone round 'ere,[6]...it'd 'ave been better for me if the person that robbed me would 'ave been one of the newcomers.

On the other hand, she continues to think of the criminals who might be a threat in the neighbourhood as local, because in this way their threat to her is minimised: 'Even your...burglars what we 'ave round 'ere...they're big softies, honestly... Two of biggest thieves round 'ere...they used to be in my year at school... When me 'usband left...they were smashing'. In her case, these local connections protect Joyce from constructing a dangerous 'criminal other', which could provide a receptacle for her fears. However, she does not identify with the criminals, since she has worked hard for what she has got: 'to know that the person that robbed me...knew that to pay for them two bikes...besides my job, I worked at a...factory for three months'.

So far, then, there is a fair bit of evidence that Joyce's estimation of risk is quite realistic, neither denying the problem nor amplifying it: 'there's always been crime, but it's never been as bad as what it is now... I've never honestly 'eard of anybody round 'ere being mugged... I don't think it's as bad as what people make it out to be'. We interpreted this as a fairly balanced view of the reality of local crime, and thus indicative of the depressive position being accessible to Joyce in this arena. There are threats to her identity involved in facing this reality, however, as Kleinian theory would predict: 'I don't want to...know about [drugs]...I just don't like to think of it in area'. Since this is her greatest fear for her own children (it has happened to her sister's son), it is threatening to contemplate. Further evidence of Joyce's moves between a depressive and a paranoid-schizoid position came in response to the question 'Is there anything you're frightened of?' She replies:

> I know this is awful to say it, but blacks in area frighten me. Not that I'm frightened of 'em as such, 'cos when I went to school we'd got lots of coloureds in our class. But they do frighten me... I don't know why they frighten me because probably they're...nice people.

She then goes on to give an example of a 'smashing' neighbour of hers who is black. In this sequence, she starts by splitting off characteristics to be feared in generalised black others and then immediately engages with the reality of the familiar and safe black neighbour. In a similar move – equivalent to the one we witnessed in Kelly – Joyce identifies 'lone parent families' as spoiling the estate and then qualifies this by pointing out her own status and asserting that it's not about being a single mother, but about how you bring your children up.

If all this makes Joyce's risk/fear calculations relatively realistic, there is nonetheless a factor which mediates her relationship to local crime: that of her identification as a local. In Kelly's case, we saw how the rejection of that identity – as not respectable – amplified her fear of crime, at the same time as splitting it off into another place. Joyce, by contrast, is determined to hold on to the possibility of being local *and* being respectable, despite the tension posed by rising crime and drug use on the estate and her fears for its effects on her children. As a result, she has a tendency to downplay (but not to deny) local crime and to emphasise her local identity, which is based on a happy childhood and, until her husband left, a trouble-free life. Identifying closely with her mother, she is committed to stemming the downward slide of a locality which represents the most cherished aspects of her self, including her dead parents. To this end, she takes risks by challenging and reporting young criminals, something which many do not do, for fear of reprisals. When threatened by one boy in this way, her robust response was: 'You piece of shit... You think you bother me?...I've lived round 'ere years. Take more than you to frighten me luv'. Her respectability does not stop her talking rough. She thereby ensures that she is not cast as 'them', rather than 'us', by local criminal youths. Her stability and relative freedom from anxiety partly account for her low fear of crime, but this stability is premised on a local identity which has the effect of mediating her relation to local crime in a direction which emphasises the unthreatening, familiar identities of local criminals who have principles.

Conclusion

In summary, the similarity of Kelly and Joyce's demographic profiles are incapable of uncovering the crucial differences which lead to their contrasting relations to fear of crime; differences which include not simply levels of anxiety but the paranoid-schizoid or depressive forms they habitually take. Expressions of their anxiety come out in their different relations to localness: Kelly rejects the estate in search of respectability, while Joyce embraces it in the hope of preserving the security of a local identity. Their respective fear of crime is a part of these wider differences in meanings concerning their relation to the high-crime estate, meanings which do not reflect the demographic similarity of their past and present location.

Finally, we should remind readers that these meanings were produced out of a particular methodological strategy informed by a particular set of theoretical ideas about subjectivity: a strategy and set of ideas premised on the centrality of defences against anxiety as a helpful method of researching biographies. Our attention to the production of meaning out of textual data is a reminder of the importance of discourse in rendering lives meaningful; but our commitment to the notion of a defended, psychoanalytic subject with which to interrogate our data provides us with an analytic means to arbitrate between possible alternative interpretations and thus take us beyond the sterility of intertextuality. While the stories do not speak for themselves, we hope that the way that we have produced our interviewees' voices feels not only true to their lives but, in so doing, testifies to some important truths of our chosen approach.

Notes

1 Details of our research method and examples of the workings of the narrative format are discussed in Hollway and Jefferson (2000).
2 'Gender Difference, Anxiety and the Fear of Crime', grant no L2102522018, was funded by the ESRC. WH interviewed both women, twice each. Between the interviews and subsequently, we worked as a pair, utilising the difference in perspective of 'insider' (interviewer) and 'outsider'. In some respects, this reflects the clinical model of analysand, analyst and supervisor.
3 Our approach to data analysis was to immerse ourselves in the whole transcripts, summarise them on a sheet whose categories derived from our research questions, and then write a 'pen portrait'. These are exemplified here, but edited for reasons of space. The two sections for each person distinguish between mainly descriptive and more interpretive treatments, albeit both framed in relation to prior research questions.
4 Our criterion that victimisation had to be estate-based eliminated her horrendous experience of partner violence from this particular reckoning.
5 For an extended analysis of respect/ability and anxiety in Kelly and two other family members, see Hollway and Jefferson (1999).
6 She was right: in three days, she was told who it was, along with an offer of the goods back.

References

Aron, L. (1996) *The Meeting of Minds: Mutuality in Psychoanalysis*, London and Hillsdale, NJ: Analytic Press.
Hollway, W. and Jefferson, T. (1997) 'Eliciting Narrative Through the In-depth Interview', *Qualitative Inquiry* 3(1): 53–70.

180   *Wendy Hollway and Tony Jefferson*

—— (1999) 'Gender, Generation, Anxiety and the Reproduction of Culture', in R. Josselson and A. Lieblich (eds) *The Narrative Study of Lives* 6: 107–39, Thousand Oaks, CA.: Sage.

—— (2000) *Doing Qualitative Research Differently: Free Association, Narrative and the Interview Method*, London: Sage.

Klein, M. (1988a) *Love, Guilt and Reparation and Other Works 1921–1945*, London: Virago.

—— (1988b) *Envy and Gratitude and Other Works 1946–1963*, London: Virago.

Rosenthal, G. (1993) 'Reconstruction of life stories: principles of selection in generating stories for narrative biographical interviews', in R. Josselson and A. Lieblich (eds), *The Narrative Study of Lives* 1: 59–91, Thousand Oaks, CA: Sage.

Stanley, L. (1993) 'On Auto/Biography in Sociology', *Sociology* 27(1): 41–52.

9 Texts in a changing context
Reconstructing lives in East Germany

Molly Andrews

> It is important to ask the question, who wants whom to remember what, and why? Whose version of the past is recorded and preserved.... To understand the workings of the social memory it may be worth investigating the social organization of forgetting, the rules of exclusion, suppression or repression, and the question of who wants whom to forget what, and why.
>
> (Burke 1989: 107–8)

The decade following Eastern Europe's revolutionary changes has been widely characterised by an uncritical enthusiasm for 'the rediscovery of memory' of those who lived under state socialism (Brossat *et al.* 1990: 7). But representations of the past which emerge in the present are precisely that, representations, with the stamp of the present upon them. Members of societies in acute social change are not only (and perhaps not even) experiencing a liberation of their memory; they are scrambling to construct new and acceptable identities for themselves, ones which will be compatible with the changed world in which they now live. The stories which they tell about themselves and their pasts are connected to this struggle to form a new identity. Thus their pasts are also products of the present, and just as certain memories are being selected as component parts of the constructed past, so are other memories excluded.

In the first half of 1992, I was in Berlin collecting life stories from women and men who had been leaders in the citizens' movements which spearheaded the revolutionary changes of East Germany in 1989.[1] I arrived only weeks after the Stasi files had been opened to the public, and the general atmosphere in those grey winter months was of a very raw society. Conversations about identity were commonplace – where to get one, how to lose one, how to find one which had been lost. East German Wolfgang Herzberg, the country's first oral historian, told me that identity had become 'a fashionable word'. People of East Germany, he said, have 'lost their old identity, which has always been a bit unstable. Now they are looking for a new identity'. Bertaux (1992) refers to the 'struggle for reconstructing the past' as involving an 'overturning [of] both a collective and an individual identity, and historical consciousness' (p.206). Major social changes had occurred in East Germany between the opening of the Berlin Wall in 1989 and when I collected my data in 1992; what I witnessed in the months I spent there was a revolution of memory and identity.

Ruth Reinecke is an actress at the Maxim Gorki Repertoire Theatre in Berlin, and was one of the organisers of the 4 November demonstration in Alexanderplatz, which precipitated the opening of the wall five days later. She describes that time in her life as 'difficult to analyse, because the events took place so rapidly, one was chasing the next. Not only the events in the street, but the events inside the self'. As the Berlin Wall was opened, Reinecke was immediately aware that this would have vast implications, not only for the political situation in the GDR,[2] but for her very personal sense of self.

> When the wall was opened, suddenly another world existed, which I did not know, which I would have to live in, whether I wanted it or not. There was of course a great curiosity to explore the world, this still exists. On the other hand I had the fear somehow whether I would be capable of making this new world...my own.... Maybe there was also some fear that I could not stay anymore the same person I had been so far.

By 1992, many East Germans had come to feel inferior to their Western neighbours. At this time, the postcards for sale on what were once East German streets had messages such as 'Greetings from the new states' while showing cartoons of old dinosaurs eating each other. In old East German factories, workers received instruction on how to 'cleanse' their language of its socialist residue – an attempt to bring the very mode of communication in line with Western standardisation. East German author Christa Wolf vividly conjures up a different, and more paralysing, loss of language which the revolutionary changes produced in her, a sensation she likens to 'a bush growing in [her] throat' (1997: 152). Wolf describes 'the manner and the speed with which everything connected with the GDR was liquidated, considered suspect' and views herself and her fellow citizens as being 'housed in a barracks under quarantine, infected with Stasi virus' (1997: 241).

André Brie, Deputy Chairperson of the Party of Democratic Socialism (the remake of the old Communist Party), believes that East Germans are 'forced into the West German identity' whereas he 'would have preferred to come to a new identity.... I think millions of East Germans are living at the moment as if they have no past'. This is why, he explains, many East Germans 'are now orienting again towards a national identity'. Barbel Bohley, who has been labelled 'the mother of the revolution' and 'the Joan of Arc of the movement', shares Brie's assessment. She explains 'some people do not want to profess their identity, they feel second class citizens compared to the West Germans, so they say they are German'. One example of this is that of a twenty-two-year-old 'punkfrau' from the GDR who was interviewed six months after having moved to West Germany. 'Why did you leave the GDR' she was asked. 'The GDR? Never heard of it' (Naimark 1992: 87).

Barbel Bohley bristles when I ask her if there has been 'a shift in the general consciousness of what it means to be East German'.

> I think that there is an East German identity, and there are those that accept it and those that reject it. But it does exist. And even this rejection is a way of distancing oneself from it, of saying 'farewell'. We have lived here for forty years, and you cannot deny that. One can say ten times one is German,[3] but Germany did not exist. There was the Federal Republic and there was the GDR and this formed the West Germans[4] and the East Germans.

According to this explanation, the young punkfrau, quoted above, is merely trying to say 'farewell' both to a country, and to a self, that are no longer. But the strategy she employs is not a very constructive one. In denying the existence of her country, she effectively deprives herself of a past. Why does she construct this amnesia? Hers is a conscious forgetting, an attempt to erase that which was. She will construct a new past for herself which is better-suited to this new present.

In contrast, some East Germans find refuge in holding on to an East German identity. For them, their national identity has become 'a symbol of defiance hurled at the West Germans; "eine Trotzidentitat", an identity of defiance', as Jens Reich, one of the fathers of East German revolution, put it (LeGloannec 1994: 142). This is often accompanied by *DDR-Nostalgie* 'a nostalgia for a rose-tinted view of the good old days...rooted partly in a sense of anomie' (Fulbrook 1994: 224). Paradoxically, both the denial, or 'forgetting' of the past, and the romanticisation, or 'misremembering' of the past, serve similar functions: they are the means by which individuals try to accommodate profound external changes into their psychic reality.

Ruth Reinecke comments on the distinction between normal forgetting, which, as discussed earlier, is and by necessity must be part of our daily life, and that which is enforced.

> The human being is organising for him or herself a natural system of forgetting, pushing things away. They will continue doing it. This is one thing. But if I want to forget, to push things aside in a deliberate manner, in the end I am destroying myself.

The critical element here seems to be that of volition. Desire to forget is itself a significant indicator that the memory in question will linger in some form, and suppression of it will come only at a cost to the essential self.

The young punkfrau is not alone in her attempt to submerge herself in a new identity, achieved by passing through a tunnel of historical amnesia. She and others like her will try to rewrite the past in order to meet the needs of the present. Although it is virtually inevitable that social and individual identity will be recast as a response to acute political change, there are greater motivations for some groups of people to actively change their past than for others. In the case of East Germany at the time of my interviews, many tried to portray themselves as having been part of the (minuscule) resistance movement under the old system. In a conversation with East German sociologist Marianne Schulz, she summarised this phenomenon; she explained that of the East German population of 16 million, there were then 16 million resistance fighters, as well as 16 million victims. The incentive to portray oneself as having been part of the opposition, and/or a victim of the system was very powerful: it was the most highly valued past in the new Germany. Christa Wolf comments on this phenomenon:

> I have the impression that many former GDR citizens, experiencing a new alienation and finding that if they are candid with others their openness is used against them, are employing this experience as a pretext to avoid any critical self-questioning and are even revising their life histories. I am sometimes amazed to hear normal, well-adjusted acquaintances of mine reveal what brave resistance fighters they have been all along. I know how hard it is to work yourself out of feelings of injury, hurt, helpless rage, depression, and paralyzing guilt and soberly to confront the events or phases in your life when you would prefer to have been braver, more intelligent, more honest.
> (1997: 301)

In this environment, those who actually were part of the underground citizens' movement[5] – and there were very few of them – could tell their stories and not be ashamed. They were the heroes that we in the West wanted to love. This very small sector of the population most probably experienced the highest degree of consistency between their pre- and post-revolutionary selves. What they were formerly jailed for, later brought them praise. But most citizens of East Germany were neither resistance fighters nor employees of the Stasi;[6] most people passively acquiesced with a system which they regarded with varying degrees of criticism. They were neither heroic nor demonic. But if individuals cannot tell stories about their past, they either remain silent or create a new past. East Germans have done both.

The new blank spaces

Although there seems to be a consensus among oral historians that 'East Germany's harsh political structures had led to a general speechlessness: to a popular memory full of blank spaces' (Thompson 1990: 20), in fact the changes of 1989 have produced another kind of 'speechlessness'. Ruth Reinecke describes the new blank spaces, particularly acute among older East Germans who dedicated their lives to the building of the GDR:

> I believe that this older generation is the one which was punished most.... To see now that these forty years were 'in vain' that they haven't brought anything...and the idea of socialist equality could not be applied in practice, this is a bitter experience.... [They] are very bitter now, and they will be silent for the rest of their years. Their youth, their thoughts, their creativity has been invested in a life which is now nothing.

Although this speechlessness is perhaps most pronounced with the older, founding generation of East Germany, it is not limited to them. Many people who lived under state socialism found themselves, in the wake of its demise, in search of a new past.

There has been a very concerted effort among portions of the East German population to come to terms with their past; first to search out (inwardly) and document what actually happened, and then to try to understand it. However, this effort has been hampered by the judgmental atmosphere in which the work has been carried out.

> East Germans – especially the intellectuals among them – commonly argue that the West first muscled in politically and economically, and now it is trying to rob the East Germans of their history, to tell those

who lived through it how it *really* was.... Seeking to bolster an embattled sense of self, many have thus insisted, 'This is our history, let us process it on our own'.

(Torpey 1992: 6)

Christa Wolf writes: 'there is nothing more important than...self-critical analysis.... It is made inexpressibly more difficult by attacks from ignorant or malevolent victors' (1997: 62). Von Plato (1993) found that there existed among his East German interviewees a certain consensus: 'Only East Germans have a realistic understanding of conditions in the GDR; only East Germans can judge East Germans' (p.41). But East Germans have had great difficulty in meeting this challenge of processing their history on their own, precisely because of the political dimensions of such a project. People cannot speak openly about a past that they know they will be damned for. Werner Fischer, one of the most prominent of the human rights activists in East Germany, was the person appointed to dissolve the Stasi. In the immediate post-revolution period, he and others worked very hard to create an atmosphere in which those who co-operated with the Stasi could come forward, in an effort to set in motion the necessary healing process for the whole country. At the time of our interview, his hopes had not been realised; in the two years that he had occupied his position, he had grown less tolerant of collaborators, not because of what they did before 1989, but because of what they failed to do after 1989.

> Unfortunately, what I had expected from people did not happen, that they come clean about their actions. Of course, they can only do so if they are without fear. And the atmosphere was, and still is today, not very conducive for that to happen. I think that this is tragic not only for their personal future development but for the inner peace of the country. In human terms, I find this reprehensible.

Very few among the Stasi employees and informers chose to speak openly about what they had done; rather, most waited with silent hope that their collaboration would go undetected. Fischer characterised this hope as 'a delusion', adding 'If they have to be unmasked bit by bit on the basis of the Stasi files, then any reasonable understanding ceases'.

Fisher elaborated on his view of how and where a more fruitful 'working through the past' could in fact take place:

> in the immediate environment, at work, at home, among friends or within the church, one must discuss the events of the last forty years,

what part a person played in it.... Then one listens to his story, analyses why somebody does it, has done it, has worked as an unofficial collaborator. And only then, when somebody has told his story, one begins to understand. This is the only way it can be done.

But this necessary openness proved to be very hard to create in an environment scrutinised by the rest of the world's judgemental gaze. One former Stasi employee whom I interviewed, Jorg Seidel, expressed a strong reaction against what he perceived as the pressure to rewrite one's past. He and two of his colleagues created a group which they originally had called 'Ministry for State Security [STASI] Working Through the Past Group' whose name they very quickly changed to 'Insiders of the Activity of the Intelligence Service of the former GDR'. Seidel explained why they changed the title of their group:

> I do not want to apologise for the activities of the MfS which have taken place in the society.... I don't call into question [my past], I am supporting what I have done.... I reject that I should now bear the guilt of everything which has happened because I say you can't write history anew, and you can neither work it through. You should really stand by history and you should give an evaluation of history.

In renaming the group, Seidel and his Stasi colleagues exhibited a determination to resist the pressure to 'rewrite history anew' as they saw it. There were other MfS employees who adopted very different strategies, who saw themselves more as victims than victimisers. Most of the informal collaborators of the Stasi tried to keep their former intelligence activities secret, fearing – with some justification – how they would be regarded and treated if their pasts became known.

However, the Stasi employees and informers represent only the most extreme cases of those persons who tried to hide their past after 1989.[7] The pressure which was exerted upon East Germans, and which they exerted upon themselves, to fabricate an identity, existed with lesser intensity across the whole population. The problem of rendering East German life histories has two central components. First, as I have discussed, the political climate has changed, and is still changing, to such a degree that what constitutes the memorable – at both the collective and individual level – is itself in acute transformation. One can reasonably suggest then that the stories that people tell, even, and perhaps most importantly, to themselves about themselves and their past, have been and continue to be in dramatic flux.

But there is another part of this dynamic which is important to address.

Since 1989, when citizens of the former GDR have been asked to render their life histories, it has been to an 'outside' audience, people who, however well intentioned, have only a very limited possibility of understanding that which they are told. Ironically, while East Germany has been flooded with Western sociologists and oral historians,[8] enthusiastically documenting the lives which once were, their East German colleagues have lost their jobs.[9] Eastern institutions have been effectively closed down, and West German agencies do not wish to fund East German academics to do this sort of work, reasoning that they cannot be objective about a situation in which they themselves lived and breathed. But among East Germans there is a real concern that their stories cannot be understood by people who never experienced the conditions which characterised their lives; moreover, they argue, the past cannot be analysed through the spectacles of the present. Von Plato states that there is 'a wide consensus [among East Germans]...that only the people of the former GDR can judge the conditions and the quality of life in the GDR, and the decisions and the political commitment of its citizens – not the West Germans' (1993: 73).

At the time of our interview, East German human rights activist Bärbel Bohley was deeply cynical about the one-sided nature of the communication which characterised much of the dialogue between those from the East and those from the West after 1989. In a piqued moment towards the end of our interview, she exclaimed 'the people in the West have not yet comprehended that the wall is gone...an empire has collapsed. It has not fully penetrated people's awareness what this really means'. It is not only people from Central Europe who must regroup the way they think about the world and themselves, but everyone.[10]

> If you come here and ask me questions for two and half hours, that is meaningless. It is really I who should put the questions. I mean somebody from the West, somebody from the East...it should be more like a discussion. People from the West come and want to understand, but they do not want to understand themselves. They only ask us.

Ostow describes the history of biographical research in Germany, which has:

> its roots in the early postwar years when Germans were systematically 'interviewed' by their occupiers. Through testimony and the narration of biography, individual Germans created accounts of politics and the details of daily life under Hitler. These biographies – part denunciation and part confession, part fabrication and part exorcism

– literally reformed the lives of the subjects and effected their personal metamorphoses from 'Nazis' to citizens of the 'democratic' or the 'socialist' Germany.

(1993: 1–2)

Plus ça change, plus c'est la même chose.

When people who are neither heroes nor villains in the current construction of the East German past tell their stories to an outside audience, their words are often interpreted through a meaning-making lens which is not their own. When East Europeans speak the unspeakable – i.e. the details of their non-heroic lives – their stories are rejected. Western academics often emerge from their projects in Central Europe totally baffled; when they do not hear what they think they should hear, they offer the explanation that their respondents cannot verbalise their true thoughts. In time, it is likely that the stories do change, not because respondents feel that finally they are able to speak of a past which really did happen, but rather because they have found ways of narrating their life stories for popular consumption and approval.

The oral history project carried out by Lutz Niethammer, exploring working-class experience in the GDR, gives evidence of some of the problems discussed above. One aspect of this research was to examine the memory of 17 June 1953,[11] in the lives of those who were old enough to have lived through it. The initial interviews were conducted in 1987. Not surprisingly, the only people who claim to have been at a site of political turmoil, and who spoke quite openly about their experiences on that day, were members of the Socialist Unity Party (SED); they, of course, had been good socialists, had stood by the government, and had nothing to be ashamed of. But where were those thousands of workers who demonstrated on that fateful day? Was there really no one around who had participated in the strike, and could remember doing so? Interestingly, Niethammer's work is not a testament to straightforward governmental repression (though surely that existed in East Germany as well). For though his interviews were conducted in a still-communist East Germany (and interviewees might have been understandably fearful of repercussions for actions done nearly forty years before), when he attempted to re-interview participants after the changes of 1989, the majority of respondents declined. Niethammer comments 'Even though people might now recollect their experience more freely than before, the impact of collective on individual memory is just as important now as before, but different, and most people were reluctant to show us both sides' (1992: 69).

That is to say, his interviewees not only told him their particular story in the way they did because social conditions required that they did so,

but moreover, those very social conditions were manifest not only externally but also internally. They had lived in an environment which
favoured one version of the past so strongly (and accordingly, one must
assume, influenced them to reconstruct their own pasts in such a way as to
be in accordance with that version) that even after that environment had
been radically altered, and indeed a different version of the tale was now
in vogue, they did not choose to re-amend their narrative. Long after the
Communist Party had ceased to exercise any significant political power, it
continued to wield an influence on the way in which individuals structured the stories of their lives. And why wouldn't it? They had lived for
forty years with certain social markers lending organisation to their mental
and physical beings; far quicker to destroy the gigantic statues of Lenin
and Marx than to dismantle their influence on the collective memory of
the population. When Niethammer asked participants if they would like
to be re-interviewed, what he was implicitly asking was if they had
changed their story – yet. There seems to be an underlying assumption
that the story would at some point change; with the removal of external
pressures, they would be able tell what had really happened. But he himself is guilty of applying another kind of pressure, that to rewrite the story,
according to principles which he believes should prevail. Niethammer
explains that 'most people were reluctant to show us both sides'; while
that is one explanation, it is not the only one. Most people do not
consciously manipulate their own memory. It is indeed possible that they
were also reluctant to show their own selves 'both sides'. The transition, if
it does happen, is bound to be more subtle, and a person might well avoid
a situation in which they are confronted with, or indeed asked to produce,
two starkly contrasting renditions of the same story, both as told by
him/herself, about him/herself. Moreover, this particular date, 17 June
1953, has been the centre-piece of such varying 'commemorative narratives' (Torpey 1993: 20) it is not so surprising that the memory of the
actual day is now, as Niethammer describes, opaque and fragmented.

Von Plato, who is part of the same research team as Niethammer, states
that their research shows evidence of respondents trying 'to change their
biographies in the light of the new circumstances after 1945 – a process
which has also been evident since the "Wende" of 1989' (Von Plato 1993:
38). But it seems that interviewees have failed to alter their biographies in
the ways in which their researchers think that they should. Von Plato
comments that 'the same melodies [of retrospective reconstruction of the
past] are sung in the East, and are as little understood, as in 1945' (p.38).
By whom, exactly, are these 'melodies' not understood? Presumably the
stories offered by the respondents connect through an internal system of

meaning-making; if this system is not discerned by the researchers, that is not to say it does not exist.

Dorothee Wierling, a third member of the West German research team conducting oral histories in East Germany, offers evidence of the gap of understanding between Western researchers and their Eastern subjects. She describes an interview with Rudolf Kamp, Communist Party Secretary, in which Kamp is detailing for his audience the 'rules of the game'. Wierling comments:

> To the Westerner listening to him, these rules may appear to be boring, confusing, or unrealistic. Yet, Kamp understands something about this and presents them indefatigably; defends and explicates them. Lovingly, he unfolds the system of 'socialist competition' – with its code numbers, funds, premiums, and commissions – … spreading them out before his audience of uncomprehending Westerners for over half an hour.
>
> (Wierling 1992: 78)

Wierling observes the very real difference between speaker and listener, but she does not address the important question of what this difference might imply for her research. There is never any evidence that she tries to understand from what point of view the comments of her interviewee might be anything other than 'boring, confusing, or unrealistic'. Indeed, she later states 'It was my intention in the second interview, to lure Kamp from his inflexible defensive position' (p.79). Clearly, the story he wants to tell is not the story his researcher wants to hear. Perhaps next time he will be a more accommodating interviewee.

As a society undergoes acute social and political upheaval, members of the community are presented with a challenge of rearranging their own identities, a challenge of recasting their pasts in a way that makes sense from the perspective of the present. Given that there are multiple versions of the past created and recreated by individuals and groups who stand in very different relations to dominant power structures, the researcher must develop a conscientious sensitivity to the question of precisely whose past they are recording. Often the life experience of an interviewee is evaluated not on its own terms, but rather according to how it compares to the researcher's previously held expectations. These expectations must be reassessed, but in order for this to happen, they must first be acknowledged. Central Europeans do not need Western cassette players to liberate their memory. What they want, and need, and are trying to create for themselves, is space to talk about their lives, both past and present, in the way that they perceive them.

Conclusion

A decade after the 'revolutions' of Eastern Europe, former Soviet bloc countries are in the midst of rethinking, re-evaluating, and ultimately recreating their pasts. However, as biography precedes history, the individuals of these societies must first make the transition in their identities from the old regime to the markedly altered present. Who were they then, who are they now, and who do they now perceive themselves as having been then? These are the very probing questions which, through force of circumstance, many Eastern Europeans are now asking themselves, questions which are also relevant to the lives of people the world over. Hard questions demand hard answers, but unfortunately not everyone is in a position to reflect upon, and respond honestly to them. It is not a matter of whether or not they will remember their past, but rather which past they will remember, and which past they will feel at liberty to voice. The relationship between the forgotten and the unspoken is a fragile one. Those of us who cheer the 'rediscovery of memory' in these post-communist times must be mindful not to assist in the replacement of one form of speechlessness with another.

Acknowledgement

I would like to acknowledge the assistance of the Max Planck Institut in Berlin and the Global Security Programme at the University of Cambridge in making the research possible.

Notes

1   Unless otherwise indicated, all quotations are from the data which I collected in 1992.
2   East Berlin First Party Secretary Schabowski's statement on 9 November 1989, announcing immediate free travel rights for all citizens later proved to be the death knell of East Germany. Historian Timothy Garton Ash describes the effect of this event:

> the opening of the Berlin Wall on 9 November, and subsequently of the whole inter-German frontier, changed the terms of the revolution completely. Before 9 November, the issue had been how this state – the German Democratic Republic – should be governed. The people were reclaiming their so-called people's state.... After 9 November, the issue was whether this state should continue to exist at all.
>
> (Ash 1990: 69)

On 24 November, Egon Krenz proclaimed the elimination of the leading role of the SED (Socialist Unity Party), and by 3 December, the Central

Committee and the Politburo collectively resigned. The following March, the first and only free elections were held in East Germany in which the pro-Western Christian Democratic Union received 40.9 per cent of the vote. On 3 October 1990, unification between the two Germanys became formalised. Writing in 1994, German historian Jurgen Kocka observes: 'Germany has changed more in the last four years than it has in the last four decades' (1994: 173).

3   One of the questions I asked in my interviews was 'When you are asked where are you from, what do you say?'. Virtually everyone I interviewed paused over their response, but gave some form of the answer 'the GDR' – in the present tense, with comments such as 'throughout my life I will remain a citizen of the GDR'. This question provoked a strong response from Jens Reich, one of the most prominent leaders of the citizens' movement:

> I am from the GDR. I've lived in the GDR, I was brought up in the GDR. I've no misgivings of any sort in saying it. I never use the word *ehemalig* [former, as in 'the former GDR'].... I find it ridiculous. The GDR is a fact, an historical fact. You don't say the *ehemalig* German Reich; it [simply] doesn't exist any longer.... This emphasis on *ehemalig* and on the disassociation of yourself from it...is a sign of psychic instability in those people [who use this word]'.

Later in the interview, Reich elaborates further on this point:

> I've no inner drive to deny the GDR...[which] has proven its right of historical existence in '89. By our own activity we freed ourselves and made it a decent society, for some weeks and some months. We did it at least, so...without any feeling of shame you can say '[I am from the] GDR'.

4   Unification has also caused West Germans to review the meaning of their national identity. Fulbrook writes 'It is not so much the visible boundaries as the invisible ones – those defining citizenship and immigration, who is welcome and who must be kept out – that West Germans are now being required to rethink' (1994: 212).

5   For a discussion of the composition of East Germany's internal opposition, see John Torpey's *Intellectuals, Socialism, and Dissent: The East German Opposition and its Legacy* (1995).

6   Although statistics vary, approximately 85,000 people were officially employed by the Stasi, with an additional two million estimated as informal collaborators.

7   Von Plato refers to a 'community of hiders' (1993: 75) which has developed as a consequence of these circumstances, not dissimilar to that which could be observed in post-war Germany.

8   Ostow states that 'by early 1992, there was reason to suspect that citizens of the former German Democratic Republic had become the world's most interviewed population' (Ostow 1993: 1). Elsewhere she refers to the 'carnival of interviewing and biographical publications' which followed the revolutionary changes of 1989, stating that 'Being interviewed played a part in the reconstruction of the self that informed every GDR citizen's *Wende* (or

turnaround); in the West this was called "transition to democracy"' (1993: 3–4).

9   Jurgen Kocka gives one example of this. Writing in 1994, he states 'Of the twenty-nine professors of sociology in East German universities today, only four come from the East' (1994: 183).

10   For a very thoughtful elaboration of this argument, see Zygmunt Bauman's 'Living Without an Alternative' in which he states that 'the current western form of life…[has] only adulators and imitators' and 'has practically de-legitimized all alternatives to itself' (1992a: 183). The implications of this are vast. 'The world without an alternative', he argues, 'needs self-criticism as a condition of survival and decency' (pp.185–6).

11   Before 1989, 17 June 1953 stood out in East German history as the single largest citizen uprising against the government. For two and a half days, workers throughout the country demonstrated. Ultimately, the Red Amy came in, and order was imposed. Indeed, during the height of the demonstrations in the autumn of 1989, Honecker is said to have asked one of his aides 'Is this another '53?'

References

Ash, T.G. (1990) *We the People: The Revolution of 1989*, London: Granta Books.

Bauman, Z. (1992) *Intimations of Postmodernity*, London: Routledge.

—— (1992a) 'Living Without an Alternative', *Reflections on Postmodernity*, London: Routledge.

Bertaux, D. (1992) Book review of Brossat *et al.* 1990, in Passerini 1992.

Brossat, A., Combe, S., Potel, J.-Y. and Szurek, J.C. (eds) (1990) *A L'Est la memoire retrouvée*, Paris: Editions La Decouverte.

Burke, P. (1989) 'History as Social Memory', in T. Butler (ed.), *Memory: History, Culture and the Mind*, Oxford: Blackwell.

Fulbrook, M. (1994) 'Aspects of Society and Identity in the New Germany', *Daedalus* 123(1): 211–34.

Kocka, J. (1994) 'Crisis of Unification: How Germany Changes', *Daedalus* 123(1): 173–92.

LeGloannec, A.-M. (1994) 'On German Identity', *Daedalus* 123(1): 129–48.

Maier, C. (1997) *Dissolution: The Crisis of Communism and the End of East Germany*, Princeton, NJ: Princeton University Press.

Naimark, N. (1992) '"Ich will hier raus": Emigration and the Collapse of the German Democratic Republic', in I. Banac (ed.), *Eastern Europe in Revolution*, Ithaca, NY: Cornell University Press, pp.72–95.

Niethammer, L. (1992) 'Where Were You on 17 June? A Niche in Memory' in Passerini 1992.

Ostow, R. (1993) 'Restructuring Our Lives: National Unification and German Biographies', *Oral History Review* 21(2), Winter: 1–8.

Passerini, L. (ed.) (1992) *Memory and Totalitarianism*, Oxford: Oxford University Press.

Thompson, P. (1990) 'News from Abroad: Europe', *Oral History* 18(1), Spring: 18–20.

Torpey, J. (1992) 'German Intellectuals and Politics After Unification: Some Aspects of "Working Through" the East German Past', Unpublished Paper presented to DAAD Interdisciplinary Summer Seminar in German Studies. University of California, Berkeley.

—— (1993) 'The Abortive Revolution Continues: East German Civil Rights Activists Since Unification', Unpublished Paper presented to Center for European Studies, Harvard University.

—— (1995) *Intellectuals, Socialism, and Dissent: the East German Opposition and its Legacy*, Minneapolis, MN: University of Minnesota Press.

Von Plato, A. (1993) 'An Unfamiliar Germany: Some Remarks on the Past and Present Relationship between East and West Germans', *Oral History* 21(1): 35–42.

Wierling, D. (1992) 'A German Generation of Reconstruction: The Children of the Weimar Republic in the GDR', in Passerini 1992.

Wolf, C. (1997) *Parting from Phantoms: Selected Writings, 1990–1994*, Chicago, IL: University of Chicago Press.

10 Situated selves, the coming-out genre and equivalent citizenship in narratives of HIV[1]

Corinne Squire

Introduction

Organisations and activities that have arisen around HIV in the over-developed world are often presented as exemplars of new political forms. Accounts of these forms vary from Philip Kayal's (1993) description of gay men's health crisis as a gay politics reconstituted around healing; through images of the angry queer activism of ACT UP (the AIDS Coalition To Unleash Power) as the emblem of a postmodern representational citizenship and ethics (Aronowitz 1995; Butler 1993; Crimp and Ralston 1990; Saalfield and Navarro 1991; Weeks 1995); to Michael Callen's and the People with AIDS Coalition's (Navarre 1988) picture of grass-roots self-representation and self-help transgressing social categories and intent on survival.

Each of these accounts assumes individuals with identities strongly determined by HIV – via their sexuality, their politics or their HIV positivity – united in communities of shared ethics and action. It has however been pointed out that notions of community current around HIV need careful qualification. Stuart Marshall (1991) emphasises the shortcomings of such a useful imaginary identification when the AIDS 'community' is really many communities that 'differ in their needs, their priorities, their agendas and their strategies' (1991: 88). HIV is clearly not the sole or even the most important determinant of identity, as Ines Rieder and Patricia Ruppelt (1989) indicate when they discuss the functional marginality of HIV to many infected women's lives. Even if an HIV identity or community exists, its political implications are not transparent. It can be articulated as sadness, anger or hope, resistance or affirmation (Marshall 1991; Nunokawa 1991; Watney 1991; Yingling 1991). In representations, it can confront us through naturalism, metaphor or what Simon Watney calls 'a long, sustained, deliberate derangement of... common sense' (1991: 190). Finally, recent advances in treatment, through the use of protease inhibitors in combination with other drugs, have given rise to popular images of HIV not just as a chronic but almost as a curable condition. At the same time, the drugs' side effects, their ineffectiveness with some patients, problems of increasing toxicity, resistance and noncompliance, and their simple unavailability to most people infected with HIV globally, mean that HIV remains an inescapable element in the subjectivities of those who are infected or affected.

The uncertainties of HIV identity and community also raise more general questions about the unity of the self and the viability of community. In the field of HIV, these questions are intensified by the epidemic's breaching of physical, social and psychic barriers, its heavily allegorical character, and rapid developments in the condition and our understanding of it, all of which serve as dramatic instances of the limits of comprehension and symbolisation (Yingling 1991).[2] We might then see the stories told by people living with HIV, on which this chapter focuses, as responses to an exemplary 'fateful moment' – diagnosis with a virus that leads, eventually, to death – around which identity must be reshaped. The stories would thus act as models of the difficult but hopeful fluidity of the 'self' in the fragmented 'late' modern period that Anthony Giddens (1991, 1992) has described. More modestly, we might, like many writers on HIV and other narratives (Reissman 1993; Schwartzberg 1993; Seale 1995) view the stories as routes towards a creative and in the circumstances somewhat heroic negotiation of subjective meaning.

I was disinclined to adopt these frameworks. Although their apparent focus is on 'stories', they often de-emphasise language's own structures, treat language as a more or less transparent route to subjectivity and neglect subjectivity's own imbrication in language. Instead, this chapter concentrates on the narrative *genres* of stories, on their particular patterns of plot and theme (Todorov 1990; see also Squire 1994). This focus was supported by the specific stories that emerged in this study. Interviewees' narratives did not seem to fit with accounts of first-person narratives as self-reconstructions that are valuable for lived identity and community, and that are indicative of the social and political moment. Instead, I shall argue, the 'self', where it appeared in interviewees' stories, was an occasional, situated resistance, supported by, in particular, the 'coming out' narrative genre, which was used to articulate coming to terms with HIV rather than sexuality.

The characteristic absences and contradictions in this genre, and in other genres that were present in the interviews alongside it, allowed the interviewees' narratives to reject as well as accept HIV 'identity' and 'community'. Through infelicitous, out-of-genre moments in the stories, interviewees could articulate other, sometimes more important, identifications.

They could also express HIV's abjection, its continual hints at the horrific otherness of illness, sexuality, pleasure and death. The psychoanalyst Julia Kristeva has described abjection as the repugnance and shame that overcome us at the crossing of borders, 'the in-between, the ambiguous, the composite'. In abjection, borders between, for instance, life and death come into our world as something like objects – or ab-jects (Kristeva 1982). To live with HIV is to live with abjection in a particularly insistent and repetitive way; interviewees' story genres provided a way both to register abjection, and to continue around it.

Finally, the chapter examines how interviewees' narratives indicate not just the instabilities and the situated nature of HIV 'identities' but also of the HIV 'communities' which are deduced from these identities. For the interviewees produced stories of HIV citizenship, rather than community: stories of qualified, limited associations of mutual interest. Moreover, this citizenship was often configured unconventionally, transnationally across nations, or within nations, around neighbourhoods or specific, politicised aspects of HIV, as much as around nation itself.

Thus the stories produced in the study seemed a useful antidote both to attempts to turn HIV into an exemplar of grand-theoretical conceptions of contemporary modernity, and to more modest but related attempts to 'read' HIV stories as stories of self-development. Instead, these interviewees' stories indicate repeatedly the value of considering the *particular* meanings of a phenomenon like HIV, and of treating the stories really *as* stories, which involves considering them as expressions of cultural genres, not just as unmediated speech.

Procedure

The chapter derives from an interview study of thirty-four people infected or affected by HIV, who used HIV support groups for HIV positive people, and for workers, carers and volunteers in the HIV field. Interviewees heard about the study through voluntary AIDS service organisations' (ASOs') noticeboards, newsletters, announcements at groups, and word of mouth.

Twenty of the original thirty-one interviewees were women, eleven of the fourteen male interviewees self-identified as gay, five of the black interviewees were of African and two of Caribbean origin, and seven other interviewees were not originally British nationals. Interviewees spanned a wide range of class backgrounds, and ranged in age from early twenties to sixties. Twenty-two were HIV positive, twelve HIV negative or of unknown HIV status. The HIV positive men had more experience of HIV-related illness than the HIV positive women.

Each person was interviewed for between forty-five minutes and two hours. Seventeen people were reinterviewed after three–four months, and two years on, twenty of the original group of thirty-one were interviewed again – five had died, four had moved abroad or were untraceable without breaching confidentiality, and two had ceased involvement with HIV support at the time of their earlier interviews. A group of three – one HIV negative white gay man, one HIV positive black heterosexual man and one HIV positive black heterosexual woman – were interviewed in 1997–8 for the first time, to help restore the sample's numbers. Future interviews at three-yearly intervals are planned.

The study asked interviewees to talk about their experiences and expectations of HIV support groups and other forms of social support. In the course of this account, interviewees almost inevitably delimited the place of HIV in their lives, and their degree of closeness to others infected or affected by HIV. One interviewee indeed described the study to another prospective participant as about people's 'relationship' to HIV. I did not ask people to talk about this relationship generally, because the project's first concern was indeed with support, particularly support groups. Moreover, by asking about support rather than 'experiences of' HIV, I wanted to avoid entraining interviewees into autobiography, a form whose cultural salience makes its telling a highly significant act, subject to variable but strong conventions. People infected/affected by HIV also have some more specific autobiographical conventions available to them: the medical story of risk behaviour, symptoms, diagnosis and subsequent health and illness (told, alongside others, in first-person accounts like Oscar Moore's book *PWA* 1996); the living-with-HIV story that moves from being owned by to owning the virus (Schwartzberg 1993); the volunteer or activist story that progresses from fear and despair, through anger, to satisfaction, even epiphany (Saalfield and Navarro 1991; Watney 1991). In this study, people were asked to speak in the first person. They might therefore find themselves telling, or might set out to tell, autobiographical *stories*; but they were not required to produce autobiography. I wanted to let people deploy a variety of speech forms, and to be able to distance themselves from autobiography, a form derived from the nineteenth-century Euro-American literary autobiography that aims to 'speak most fully the complex expression of complex individuals in complex societies' (Marcus 1987: 93). I wanted talk that would likely – though not necessarily – be less rehearsed than such autobiography, and that would probably be less directed at seamlessness, homogeneity and a particular kind of subjective truth.

Selves, strategies and stories

The study adopted a fairly general criterion for narrative: temporal or causal sequencing. This criterion was preferred to more precise criteria (Labov 1972) on the grounds that such temporal and causal sequences are treated in everyday speech as stories and that adopting stricter grounds, while producing a clearer, perhaps less trivial, 'narrative' category would mean omitting many of the interviews' narrative elements. This study's definition of 'narrative' is thus broader than that in some narrative sociology, but narrower than in studies that refer in an unqualified way to 'stories'.

Using this definition, much of the interview talk took a narrative, predominantly temporally sequenced, form. Sometimes these narratives had first-person singular or plural subjects, clear 'I's or 'we's denoting identity or community. At other times, the narratives' relationship to HIV was less direct, focusing on a group to which the speaker belonged like 'long-term survivors', or invoking a generalised, inclusive 'you'. Multiple narratives occurred in each interview, and narrative lines were usually discontinuous, repetitive and incomplete. People returned to stories they had started or told earlier, sometimes spontaneously, sometimes after an interviewer's comment or question.

Interviewees produced some stories that fitted with the accounts in much psychotherapeutic and sociological writing of HIV as life-changing and life-shaping, sometimes even a condition that emblematises the reflexive reconstruction of the self under late modernity (Crossley 1997; Heaphy 1996; Herek 1990; King 1995; O'Brien 1992; Remien and Rabkin 1995; Seale 1995; Schwartzberg 1993). HIV-positive interviewees described the identities that took them over after diagnosis as fabricated out of stigma, but progressing towards acceptance, even affirmation, of their condition, and towards an enhanced awareness of what is important in life. They charted a move from stigmatised ex-communication, towards finding community with other people affected or infected by HIV. Such HIV identities and communities crossed over differences in gender, sexuality, health status – even, sometimes, HIV status. They supported people in their depression as well as their optimism; they were also said to offer them possibilities of transcendence, ways to act and think that had not been open to them before. Several interviewees of all HIV statuses on this account described HIV as a turning point or opportunity, albeit one they wished hadn't happened. At the same time, many narratives in this study seemed to put in question notions of HIV identity and community, or to disregard them. For instance, interviewees often did not progress between interviews in their narrated relation to HIV, or they moved 'backward' from anger to guilt, from acceptance to deep depression – regressions that were not associated in any simple way with health, work or relationship problems. Sometimes there were discontinuities that made it sound like a different person was speaking from interview to interview. Karl, for instance (all interviewees' names have been changed), an HIV-positive gay man who initially described his relationships as happy but brief periods when 'I parade my fucks', two years later was sharing a flat with his lover, and devoted the interview to a story, marginal in the previous interview, of physical, psychic and spiritual balance and growth.

All interviews included narratives of disengaging from HIV, describing a need to get away from it, whether well or ill. Many HIV-positive narrators also raised the significance of other aspects of life – drug addiction, spirituality – over HIV, either explicitly, or implicitly, by concentrating on work, relationships or legal or medical issues and mentioning HIV incidentally or not at all. The narratives also described identities and communities of sexuality, gender, national origin, or economic, health or survival status, for instance, that limited the significance of HIV identity and community. Newly diagnosed people were said by everyone to be different from other HIV-positive people, still weighted down with fears about survival and disclosure. Long-term survivors thought only others in the same position would understand their survivor guilt. People who were well found it dangerous to identify with people who were ill; 'I'm sorry for them', Morag, an asymptomatic HIV-positive white woman said, 'but I'm also very sorry for myself, I don't like to be reminded'. In the last set of interviews, people who were doing well on combination therapies felt, with mingled relief and guilt, that they were marked out from people who had decided not to take them or who could not tolerate them, from friends who had died just before the drugs became available, and from HIV-positive relatives in other countries where the drugs were not available. One woman said she had more in common with other HIV-negative women from her national and educational background than with, for instance, an HIV-positive woman who was a refugee from the Ugandan civil war. Another said unemployment and poverty, not HIV, defined the community of ill-health for her.

Psychotherapeutic and sociological accounts do not suggest that complete, continuous or unrevised engagement with HIV status is adaptive, and they agree that denial or 'minimising' can be helpful (Crossley 1997; King 1995; Herek 1990; O'Brien 1992; Odets 1995; Schwartzenberg 1993). They also accept that when, as was often the case with HIV, 'dying' happened suddenly, without opportunities for planning or heroism or when, as now, it is long drawn out and characterised by wellness for many years, it may profitably be hidden from and evaded, rather than reflectively engaged with. But the accounts nevertheless assert that some discernible engagement with HIV's meaning for identity, community and their potentially imminent ends is needed for psychological and social wellbeing. Despite their contradictions and omissions, these interviews could be read as evidence of such engagement. The stories could be argued to take cognisance of the complex relations between subject positions simply by articulating them, and thus revealing and enacting an agentic subjectivity that is psychically valuable even if unconscious.

Psychotherapeutically grounded accounts of HIV and identity often understand clients' stories in this way, stressing how people are moving, even if unconsciously, towards integration and acceptance (Herek and Greene 1995). But such accounts differ in two important ways from the research I am presenting here. First, they are necessarily and rightly concerned with therapeutic efficacy. Hence they search out and encourage narratives of progress among their clients: narratives where you can hear people describing their subjectivities in increasingly affirmative and reflexive or, at the very least, more and more complex ways. Of course people's descriptions of themselves may show this progression in research interviews, especially if, as here, interviews were repeated, and were often lengthy. Indeed, many interviewees in this study called attention to the interviews' therapeutic or cathartic properties, to the value of 'talking things through'. Perhaps, too, the longitudinal nature of the research imposed a demand to progress narratively from session to session, However, beyond this, the research did not seek progressive, developmental descriptions of identity, or emphasise them in its analysis. I think it would be hard to find criteria for identifying many such descriptions in the interviews, unless you made the rather strong assumption that the descriptions are present, albeit unconsciously.

That brings me to the second distinction between this study and therapeutically based work. The clinical studies emerge, broadly speaking, from conventions of psychoanalytic theory and practice. These conventions are not in play in a research interview, or the analysis of it. Many of the sociological studies that claim HIV stories as exemplars of identity under modernity do use psychoanalytic concepts, in a metaphorical way we might call 'psychoanalystic' rather than 'psychoanalytic'. I was not completely opposed to using psychoanalysis metaphorically, since psychoanalytic claims to theoretical and therapeutic purity are weak and since many of the most interesting and rejuvenating deployments of psychoanalysis, like those of Judith Butler (1993), are precisely of this form. But to claim to find HIV 'identities' or 'selves' being struggled with or negotiated in a consistent but unconscious way in these interviews, would require a careful formulation and justification of the interpretive procedure – the kind, indeed, that one finds in Butler's work, however contested it is – that didn't seem possible or appropriate in the context of these interviews. To make a leap to the unconscious without such a formulation is to indulge in interpretive arrogance and unwarranted therapeutism, and to use academic authority to claim a vicarious psychoanalytic authority.

Perhaps the interviewees in this study whose narratives engaged little with HIV community and identity were too disempowered by poverty, isolation, the onrush of illness, or the individual and social constraints surrounding HIV (Heaphy 1996: 158–9) to make such an engagement. It could be argued, however, that all subjectivities are produced within constraints, though some subjectivities are more powerful and some constraints more obvious than others (Foucault 1977; Rose 1989). Moreover different constraints will generate various forms of subjectivity that are lived out against and in relation to each other, rather than in pursuit of a general, unified 'self'. In this study the interviewees produced some narratives of 'identity' and 'community' that supported this argument: stories of the 'self' that directly opposed the intense metaphorising and professionalised objectification conventionally attached to the 'person with HIV'. I shall call these *strategic narratives* of the 'self'.

One example is John's account in his first interview, of how he, a white, gay, HIV-positive man in his thirties, brokered an active, egalitarian identity in his relationships with medical professionals and institutions, and thus became part of an inclusive HIV-related medical community. At one point, John took on the voice of a medical professional in this narrative (see Potter and Wetherell 1987, for transcription conventions):

John: I think that's the sort, that's the sort of support I, I personally need medical support. I suppose being a fairly medically minded person who, and I can sort of, you know I read everything, I mean the doctor says, 'Oh god', you know, 'you know far more than I do because you have time to read all the relevant journals and everything that comes out', you know, 'you tell me which trials are working and which one isn't and where it's happening' and all that sort of thing, so I quite, I get quite a lot of support from that.

Later, again speaking in both his and a professional voice, John acted out a typical telephone conversation with his GP surgery at the onset of one of his frequent infections:

John: Hello, it's John [second name] here.
GP Surgery: Yes John, I'll put you through straight away. Do you need something urgent? Do you, do you know what it is that you need?

John: Yes, I need some amoxycillin, I think I've got another respiratory
    infection. A hold er you know, um.
GP Surgery: You'll want it today won't you?
John: If I can have it within the hour.
GP Surgery: What dose do you want?

In his third interview, on a combination therapy regime that had much
improved his health, but still intensely concerned about how long this
health would last, John described himself working in the hospital HIV ward
and clinic as a kind of volunteer paramedic and counsellor. He showed
people round, he listened, he provided information about medical and
service issues he was familiar with: he was part of the team. His negotiation of
an expert-patient identity had, he said, made him rethink himself as
someone who could have been a medical professional (Giddens 1991: 143).

John's narrative of an empowering medical identity and community did
not seem part of a more general articulation of a self or selves, consistently
referenced and drawn together by reflexive consideration. Rather, the
narrative's particularity and containment suggested a specific, discursively
produced and resistant 'self', who is knowledgeable and effective in a
well-defined domain. If John's body had become his 'project', then that
project was less a self-actualising choice (Shilling 1992: 4) than a highly
determined intervention in a particular medical regime of fatal illness and
its probably temporary remission. John's story of his medical masquerade
was less life politics, an expansion and transformation of politics to take in
identity (Giddens 1991: 9), than a narrative transformation of identity
into politics. It annexed a degree of medical authority in a situation where
the narrator could easily have had very little; even the spectacular
reprieve offered by the new drugs depended on John attending a hospital
with access to them and being seen regularly by a consultant who judged
the drugs were medically effective. Where readers of implicitly political
performances of identity like John's make a mistake is, as Cindy Patton
(1995: 241) says, in assuming that inalienable rights follow from the
performances. John's narrative of breaking or being given the codes of
HIV-related medical knowledge and institutions, right down to the
numerical codes that open the clinic and ward doors, may indeed have
been regularly enacted, and endorsed by the professionals concerned.
Even then, John would be unlikely to have a voice in important decisions
– about, for instance, cutting services in the light of the new drugs'
success, or about who should get the drugs, and when. John will be heard
only faintly, still as a 'patient', at this level of medical power, unless he
undertakes a more dramatic and collective reformulation of patient identity as for instance ACT UP did.

Narrative genre

Following on from this, we might want to argue that the interviewees' talk should be understood as discursively produced – shaped and constrained, that is, by powerful institutions and knowledges like those of medicine. Discourse did not, though, seem a wholly adequate category with which to approach this material. There is, for a start, considerable uncertainty about what discourse is (Parker 1992). If we adopt a simple notion of discourse as a repertoire of representation, the strength of that repertoire is difficult to judge unless, for instance, we simply count the number of times an interviewee mentions 'viral load' or 'disability living allowance', a quantification that seems inadequate to the complexity of interviewees' stories. If we allow a higher-level notion of discourse as a means of exercising and reproducing power, then we may start comparing boluses of decontextualised text from different sources (Labov and Fanshel 1977: 30), on the reifying assumption that unified discursive entities underlie these segments. In addition, the notion of 'discourse' can, despite its apparent concern with language, subsume language into subjectivity. Pieces of discursive language are often then treated as guides to a level of experience that is assumed to be 'deeper', and are also assumed, as in other content-directed analyses, to be susceptible to more or less unproblematic interpretation (Squire 1995).

I wanted to pay attention to large, narrative elements of language within the interviews, that would be split up by an analysis of cross-textual discourses. But 'narrative' alone is a category that again often serves, paradoxically, to de-emphasise language. We all think we know what stories are. Psychologies of narrative frequently declare subjectivity to be structured like stories and built up by story-telling, thus suggesting that stories have a single, universal pattern, and that there is a synergy between that pattern and psychic life (Sarbin 1986; Van Langenhove and Harre 1993: 93) so that stories serve psychological ends. This account renders specific properties of narrative language insignificant. And so, in order to examine narrative language and its effects on subjectivity, the study focused on narrative *genre*, a category that foregrounds specific structures of language. Such genres also provide a fairly concrete way of looking at the relationships between subjectivity and the cultural sphere, since one would expect them to be articulated in both (Squire 1994).

The most obvious genre on display in the interviews was the coming out narrative, a largely Western, twentieth-century form of autobiography that chronicles the process of coming to terms with a lesbian or gay sexual identity. Parallels exist between literary and research accounts (Cass 1983–4; Sedgewick 1990; Troiden 1979). Several writers have suggested experiential or discursive resemblances to the process of learning to live with HIV (O'Brien 1992; Patton 1990: 9–10). There are also analogies with Kenneth Plummer's more general account of the sexual story-telling genre. The five phases Plummer notes are those of imagining, articulating and then inventing identities, creating social worlds and finally, 'creating a culture of public problems' (Plummer 1996: 35). A further phase noted by many researchers (Burke 1995) is one of accepting and then to some extent disengaging from the marked, 'lesbian' or 'gay' identity category.

This genre could be said to structure the overall narratives presented in initial interviews, which charted the trajectory through stigma, community and acceptance described earlier. Sub-sections of the genre also shaped smaller self-contained narrative segments within the interviews. John for instance described how he revealed his diagnosis, in what he said later was 'almost a carbon copy' process to coming out:

John: ...you're very careful about who you tell, you can't untell....
Initially I mean for years I, I think only two people knew, that was my partner and, and I suppose one of my closest friends [name], er, and, because I was scared by (what), even people I know who were perfectly alright, I thought 'well, I don't know how they are going to react to this,' but I find now as people are better educated...I have been able to tell one or two straight friends, and fortunately they reacted in just the way I would have hoped they would...and we've just carried on as normal and it's very rarely mentioned, but of course those people were sort of hand picked by me.... Probably hearing comments that they've made about HIV, and me getting feedback before, particularly knowing I'm gay and I'm affected by it...out of sort of close friends I've told, I've had an even better relationship with them, with them knowing, than before, because I feel I can be open with them.

Women and heterosexual men also used this genre. It may be that it is generally a culturally contagious genre but many interviewees' initial experiences of talking about HIV in a predominantly male gay context also seemed to contribute to this genre transmission.

Of course the genre took various forms within the interviews. Sometimes, too, it was interleaved with other genres; such as a kind of conversion narrative, as Cornell West (1990) might describe it, often derived from twelve-step programmes, or New Age religiosity, or both, or with a more therapeutic genre of 'remembering, repeating and working through'. The genre could also be seen, as in Plummer's (1996) own account, as part of a much broader narrative category that takes in other sexual disclosure narratives – stories about menstruation, sexual abuse and coming to feminist self-consciousness for example as well as about coming out as gay. Moreover, the genre has formal connections with for instance coming-of-age novels and perhaps the novel form generally. I would argue though that a coming-out narrative is not just one aspect of a general representational democratisation of intimacy. Rather, as a genre of stigma it is particularly helpful as a resource – and not just for gay men – for the articulation of aspects of living with HIV. Moreover, since homosexuality is the model, the coming-out genre queers HIV narratives even more than HIV queers them by itself (Patton 1993) and thus conducts a kind of continual 'regaying' of HIV, against politicians' and policymakers' tendency to make HIV 'everyone's' – and thus no one's – problem (King 1997).

Abjection

'Coming out' about your sexuality is not of course the same as 'coming out' about your potentially impending death. The coming-out genre does not articulate death – except obliquely, as the shadow of homosexuality, the horror against which the closet door is shut (Bersani 1989; Sedgewick 1990). Other cultural forms, film and writing, have developed AIDS narratives that address death by deploying a form of elegy (Miller 1993). In these interviews, mortality was sometimes subsumed into the narratives as something, like gayness, to accept and live with. Alternately it operated in the narratives as a moment of non-negotiable horror, fateful in a full and unrecoverable sense: a gaping abjection, to use Kristeva's (1982) term. Karl for instance, in his second interview gave a long and consistent account of long-term survival as a matter of physical and spiritual balance and growth, the moral responsibility for which rested with the individual. The narrative broke, though, when he remarked that 'some people just suddenly go'. Then, without elaboration, he went back to his coherent narrative within which people never 'just go', they give up or treat themselves badly, and nothing is a shock, everything can be explained. John's interviews contained some similar moments of potentially annihilatory horror, extrusions from the main narrative. Describing his stonewalling of nosy neighbours, he says, 'I often dream of just blurting it out…"I've been pensioned off, I'm too ill to work, *I've got AIDS love*", you know I mean I never would do that…'.

These moments of abjection did not derail the narratives; the narratives continued around them, probing at the edges of abjection. John's moment of narrative transgression was bracketed on both sides by his reasoned account of accepting, disclosing and withholding his HIV status.

In another interview, Ben, a white heterosexual man with AIDS, frequently fell into silence or incoherence and produced a story which was explicitly about depression, but which continued, despite these difficulties of speech. Perhaps it was the coming out genre, with its own unavoidable uncertainties about what lesbian and gay 'identity' and 'community' are, and what being 'out' really means, which, translated into the field of HIV, allowed interviewees to face abjection without being erased by it. Kristeva has also described how in some modern literature subject and object 'push each other away, confront each other, collapse and start again', tracing, not excluding or trying to repair abjection (1982: 18). Some narratives in this study seemed to be engaged in the same project.

Citizenship and HIV

Across these narratives, the interviews produced subjects with identities and communities determined by, but also independent of, HIV, using story genres, particularly the coming-out genre, that both accept HIV and express its ultimate unacceptability. Identity is not simply illusory as Marcus (1987) suggests. It is necessary for narratives, and also for living, and notions of community inevitably attach to it. But you do not always need the same identities, the same communities, or the same strength of either. Just as HIV 'identity' is not stable and continuous, so HIV 'community' is also variable and contingent. The 'identities' and 'communities' described in these interviews come closer, perhaps, to the equivalent subject positions and to the citizenship that in Chantal Mouffe's (1993) work they constitute, than to identity and community as they are conventionally conceived.

Stuart Marshall (1991) suggested that people with AIDS might want to tell stories of alliance rather than belonging, of loose and transient links that may develop into lasting associations, or weaken, or attenuate to breaking point, leaving them to turn to other aspects of their lives. Interviewees in this study did, indeed, tell stories of such multiple and flexible forms of citizenship. One participant, for instance, structured his initial interview in the study around a description of HIV 'community' as a form of contingent neighbourliness. Chris, a white, HIV-positive man, told the story of starting a local self-help group, made up of infected people of both genders and all national backgrounds and sexual orientations. He made the starting point for his crusade the experience of meeting an African woman whose only support on leaving hospital had been a once-daily visit from a district nurse, and contrasted this paucity with his own supportive partner and friends. Then, playing on the theme song of the TV show, *Neighbours*, he envisaged the local group as one of

'neighbours who might become friends'. This neighbourliness was pragmatic, contingent and limited. It depended on equivalence, not idealised
identity. Emphasising these qualifications, Chris discussed his own difficulties with understanding the concerns of drug users and recent migrants
from Africa, and said he himself felt more at home in groups of HIV-
positive gay men.

Some writers have given more ambitious accounts of HIV's relation to
citizenship. Stanley Aronowitz has described the activist citizenship
supported by ACT UP, within but against the state, 'ultra-democratic' in
its decision-making ideals rather than relying on traditions of leadership,
developing a new style of politics that pays attention to representation,
and that works by significatory terrorism, signifying disrespect (1995: 365,
368). Jeffrey Weeks sees similar forms operating in commemorations like
the memorial AIDS Quilt, and more generally in a range of postwar social
movements that try to combine emancipatory politics and a liberal rights
agenda (1995: 118). Acting up about AIDS, though, is not the same as
living with HIV. This life can depend on a highly conventional legal
concept of citizenship (Spivak 1996). Helana, who obtained British citizenship between the second and third interviews, described being thereby
relieved of the possibility of returning to Eastern Europe, with its few
treatment options, and of the uncertainty of her child's future after her
death: with her new passport she could really 'live' with HIV, which
includes living with the possibility of death. The citizenships emerging
from narratives of HIV thus assert 'equivalence' in a range of contexts
from the customary – legal citizenship in the nation – to the subversive –
activist citizenship, and the citizenship of neighbours and friends.

Similarly, the intimate citizenship Plummer describes, which can
'extend notions of rights and responsibilities' (1996: 46), and the sexual
citizenship within 'a new democratic imaginary' pictured by Weeks (1995:
14) are possibilities with at best equivalent value for people within the
field of HIV. For every John, describing HIV disclosure in the politically
and subjectively effective coming-out genre, there is an interviewee like
Sally. In her first interview Sally, who is white, heterosexual and HIV
positive, characterised her story as that of a search for a good HIV-positive
man who would be a father to her son, unlike her own father who drank.
This blended-family AIDS romance, only barely ironic, was drawn to a
close in her second interview two years later, which she started with the
words, 'Well, I got married recently'. She and her husband help each
other deal with HIV; they are on the same treatment, go to the same
hospital, use the same support services. He is 'more of a father' than her
son's real father; he is a strong, mature man she loves. He is also a black
African migrant applying for political refugee status, but he did not marry

her for her passport since he loves her, and she is in any case a national of another European country. He is not keen to go there, but 'in a way he doesn't really have much choice' she says, laughing uneasily, 'it's, it's like they would send you back to (his country) or you come to (my country) so (laughs), it sounds terrible really but (laughs) I know he loves me anyway I know, I know he (*sic*) not like that, because of that'.

A narrative that intercalates the feminine romance genre with the politics of gender, race and migration like this is very distant from the new citizenships of the person that Plummer and Weeks imagine and John explicates, but it is an eloquent example of the transmutation of a traditional narrative genre under the exigencies of HIV. Moreover, because of HIV, Sally's narrative of sexual citizenship has like John's to address an unspeakable abjection. The narrative genres that achieve this are different, the place of the subject in them also differs, but the narratives are made equivalent, similarly plural and open, by this demand.

The stories in this study continually disprove suppositions that they exemplify a late-modern social or emotional *zeitgeist*, through their reiteration of highly specific HIV selves, genres and citizenships. This reiteration calls attention to the requirement for theories that are particular to HIV. It suggests, too, that other phenomena-less 'exotic', less stigmatised – whose particularity is less pronounced – may also be somewhat imperfectly contained within the theoretical 'community' of late modernity. At the same time, these narratives seem to me a helpful rhetorical and ethical model for stories of 'identity' and 'community' beyond those produced in the HIV context. It is through reading them as culturally 'genred' texts, rather than simply as authentic expressions of the self, that this rhetorical and ethical usefulness becomes apparent.

Acknowledgements

I am grateful to Joanna Bornat for her insightful editorial work on this chapter, to suggestions made by Prue Chamberlayne, Mike Rustin and Tom Wengraf, and to participants in the Subjectivity Revisited Conference (University of East London, London, May 1997) for their comments. I would like to thank Victoria Clarke for her research assistance and the Nuffield Foundation for supporting the research.

Notes

1   Portions of this chapter have appeared, in a different and extended form, in Squire 1999.
2   While in the overdeveloped world the transformation of HIV from fatal into chronic illness is widely heralded, the new treatments' long-term effectiveness

and side-effects are unknown, infection itself remains ineradicable, treatment in the developing world is almost unaffected and new infections are still on the rise. In these circumstances, Treichler's (1988) significatory epidemic has changed but not abated.

References

Aronowitz, S. (1995) 'Against the Liberal State: ACT-UP and the Politics of Pleasure', in L. Nicholson and S. Seidman (eds), *Social Postmodernism: Beyond Identity*, Cambridge: Cambridge University Press, pp.357–83.

Bersani, L (1989) 'Is the Rectum a Grave?', in D. Crimp (ed.), *AIDS: Cultural Analysis/Cultural Activism*, Cambridge, MA: MIT Press, pp.197–222.

Burke, M. (1995) 'Gay Police Officers', *The Psychologist*, London: British Psychological Society.

Butler, J. (1993) *Body Matters*, New York: Routledge.

Cass, V. (1983–4) 'Homosexual Identity: a Concept in Need of a Definition', *Journal of Homosexuality* 9: 105–26.

Crimp, D. and Ralston, A. (1990) *AIDS Demo/Graphics*, Seattle, WA: Bay Press.

Crossley, M. (1997) ' "Survivors" and "Victims": Long-term HIV Positive Individuals and the Ethos of Self-empowerment', *Social Science and Medicine* 45(12): 1863–73.

Foucault, M. (1977) *Discipline and Punish*, London: Allen Lane.

Giddens, A. (1991) *Modernity and Self-Identity*, Cambridge: Polity.

—— (1992) *Transformations of Intimacy*, Cambridge: Polity.

Heaphy, B. (1996) 'Medicalisation and Identity Formation: Identity and Strategy in the Context of AIDS and HIV', in J. Weeks and J. Holland (eds), *Sexual Cultures: Communities, Values and Intimacy*, London: Macmillan, pp.139–60.

Herek, G. (1990) 'Illness, Stigma and AIDS', in P. Costa and G. VandenBos (eds), *Psychological Aspects of Serious Illness*, Washington, DC: American Psychological Association, pp.107–49.

Herek, G. and Greene, B. (1995) *AIDS, Identity and Community*, London: Sage.

Kayal, P. (1993) *Bearing Witness*, New York: Westview Press.

King, E. (1997) 'HIV prevention and the new virology', in J. Oppenheimer and H. Reckitt (eds) *Acting on AIDS: Sex, Drugs and Politics*, London: Serpent's Tail, pp.11–33.

King, N. (1995) 'HIV and the Gay Male Community: One Clinician's Reflections Over the Years', in G. Herek and B. Greene (eds), *AIDS, Identity and Community*, New York: Sage, pp.1–18.

Kristeva, J. (1982) *Powers of Horror*, New York: Columbia University Press.

Labov, W. (1972) *Language in the Inner City: Studies in the Black English Vernacular*, Oxford: Blackwell.

Labov, W. and Fanshel, D. (1977) *Therapeutic Discourse*, New York: Academic Press.

Marcus, L. (1987) ' "Enough about You, Let's Talk about Me": Recent Autobiographical Writing', *New Formations* 1(Spring): 77–94.

Marshall, S. (1991) 'The Contemporary Political Use of Gay History: The Third Reich', in Bad Object-Choices (ed.), *How Do I Look? Queer Film and Video*, Seattle, WA: Bay Press, pp.65–89.

Miller, D. (1993) 'Dante on Fire Island: Reinventing Heaven in the AIDS Elergy', in T. Murphy and S. Poirier (eds), *Writing AIDS*, New York: Columbia University Press, pp.265–305.

Moore, O. (1996) *PWA: Looking AIDS In The Face*, London: Pan.

Mouffe, C. (ed.) (1993) *Dimensions of Radical Democracy*, London: Verso.

Navarre, M. (1988) 'Fighting the Victim Label', in D. Crimp (ed.), *AIDS: Cultural Analysis/Cultural Activism*, Boston, MA: MIT Press, pp. 143–6.

Nunokawa, J. (1991) '"All the Sad Young Men": AIDS and the Work of Mourning', in D. Fuss (ed.), *Inside/Out*, New York: Routledge, pp.311–23.

O'Brien, M. (1992) *Living with HIV: Experiments in Courage*, Westport, CT: Auburn House.

Odets, W. (1995) *In The Shadow of The Epidemic*, Durham, NC: Duke University Press.

Parker, I. (1992) *Discourse Dynamics*, London: Routledge.

Patton, C. (1990) *Inventing AIDS*, London: Routledge.

—— (1993) '"With Champagne and Roses": Women at Risk From/In AIDS Discourse', in C. Squire (ed.), *Women and AIDS: Psychological Issues*, London: Sage, pp.165–87.

—— (1995) 'Refiguring Social Space', in L. Nicholson and S. Seidman (eds), *Social Postmodernism: Beyond Identity*, Cambridge: Cambridge University Press.

Plummer, K. (1996) 'Intimate Citizenship and the Culture of Sexual Storytelling', in J. Weeks and J. Holland (eds), *Sexual Cultures: Communities, Values and Intimacy*, London: Macmillan. 34–52.

Potter, J. and Wetherall, M. (1987) *Discourse in Social Psychology*, London: Sage.

Reissman, C. (1993) *Narrative Analysis*, London: Sage.

Remien, R. and Rabkin, R. (1995) 'Long-term Survival with AIDS and the Role of Community', in G. Herek and B. Greene (eds), *AIDS, Identity and Community*, New York: Sage, pp.169–86.

Rieder, I and Ruppelt, O. (1989) *Matters of Life and Death: Women Speak about AIDS*, London: Virago.

Rose, N. (1989) *Governing The Soul*, London: Routledge.

Saalfield, C. and Navarro, R. (1991) 'Shocking Pink Praxis: Race and Gender on the ACT UP Frontlines', in D. Fuss (ed.), *Inside/Out*, New York: Routledge, pp.341–72.

Sarbin, T. (ed.) (1986) *Narrative Psychology*, New York: Praeger.

Schwartzberg, S. (1993) 'Struggling for Meaning: How HIV Positive Gay Men Make Sense of AIDS', *Professional Psychology: Research and Practice* 24: 483–90.

Seale, C. (1995) 'Heroic death', *Sociology* 29: 587–613.

Sedgewick, E. (1990) *The Epistemology of the Closet*, London: Harvester Wheatsheaf.

Shilling, C. (1992) *The Body and Social Theory*, London: Sage.

Spivak, G. (1996) 'Diasporas Old and New: Women in the Transnational World', *Textual Practice* 10(2): 245–69.

Squire, C. (1994) 'Safety, Danger and the Movies: Women's and Men's Narratives of Aggression', *Feminism and Psychology* 4: 547–70.

—— (1995) 'Pragmatism, Extravagance and Discourse Analysis', in S. Wilkinson and C. Kitzinger (eds), *Feminism and Discourse Analysis*, London: Sage, pp.145–64.

—— (1999) 'Neighbours Who Might Become Friends: Selves, Genres and Citizenship in Narratives of HIV', *The Sociological Quarterly* February 40(1): 109–37.

Todorov, T. (1990) *Genres In Discourse*, Cambridge: Cambridge University Press.

Treichler, P. (1988) 'AIDS, Homophobia and Biomedical Discourse: An Epidemic of Signification', in D. Crimp (ed.), *AIDS: Cultural Analysis/Cultural Activism*, Cambridge, MA: MIT Press, pp.31–70.

Troiden, R. (1979) 'Becoming Homosexual: A Model of Gay Identity Acquisition', *Psychiatry* 42: 362–73.

Van Langenhove, L. and Harre, R. (1993) 'Positioning and Autobiography: Telling your Life', in N. Coupland and J. Nussbaum (eds), *Discourse and Lifespan Identity*, London: Sage, pp.81–100.

Watney, S. (1991) 'Representing AIDS', in T. Boffin and S. Gupta (eds), *Ecstatic Antibodies*, London: River's Oram Press, pp.165–92.

Weeks, J. (1995) *Invented Moralities: Sexual Values in the Age of Uncertainty*, London: Polity Press.

West, C. (1990) *The American Evasion of Philosophy*, Basingstoke: Macmillan.

Yingling, T. (1991) 'AIDS in America: Postmodern Governance, Identity and Experience', in D. Fuss (ed.), *Inside/Out*, New York: Routledge, pp.291–310.

11 Extreme right attitudes in the biographies of West German youth

Martina Schiebel

What attraction do the groups and the ways of thinking of far-right extremism hold for young people? What social, familial and biographical factors bring about the formation and dissolution of that attraction and of a career with the far right? How does this political affiliation get embedded in a young person's biography? And what effects does it have on his or her presentation of that biography? These questions are central to this chapter, which is based on the research I carried out between 1989 and 1991 in West Germany, involving youths, currently and formerly, on the far right (Michel and Schiebel 1989; Schiebel 1991, 1992).

In what follows I will first examine some contextual conditions, and then, on the basis of two contrasting case histories, describe the biographical processes involved in moving in and out of far-right involvement. This permits the examination of some of the strategies with which young people confront their biographical past.

From everyday racism to far-right extremism

Hostility towards foreigners, and acceptance and use of nationalistic and racist stereotypes, did not just appear in Germany with the recent pogrom-like acts of violence against asylum seekers, nor with the electoral success of far-right parties in East Germany either. They were already part of a spectrum of political discourse, of a societal pattern of meanings (*Deutungsmuster*). Examples can be found in debates over changes in fundamental legal rights to asylum, and over rights to citizenship, as well as in stereotyping of migrants in everyday talk. Since such ethnocentric denigration is liable to legal sanctions, as is any discriminatory treatment between Germans and immigrants, then we must talk of 'institutionalised racism' (Osterkamp 1997). Even though the dividing line between racism and the extreme far right is sometimes blurred, nevertheless the extreme far right – unlike mere racism – promotes violence as an acceptable way of tackling political or social conflict (Heitmeyer 1987). Following Dudek and Jaschke (1984) I prefer to define right extremism as a 'problem of political culture'.

Alongside structural conditions of ethnocentrism, the general accommodation to the Nazi period specifically contributes to the re-awakening of racist and far-right attitudes. It is not just a question of *conscious* denial, the playing down or glorification of the 'Third Reich' and its crimes, which can be found among ideologues of the far right. More decisive from the point of view of reproducing such an outlook is the widespread tendency to maintain silence in the face of such events and experiences, or at least to resort to the collective slogan: 'It's time to finish with all that'. Such attitudes indicate a failure to come to terms with the past and contribute to a definition of reality which yields the far right increasing support.

Our biographical analyses of actual witnesses to the Nazi period show[1] a variety of strategies, which the individuals we interviewed use to come to terms with their past. For example, one woman, who was born in 1915, de-politicises the whole period of her life until 1945. A man, also born in 1915, limits the phenomenon of Nazism to the war years, which he characterises as non-political. In this way he can discount politics from his military career in the Wehrmacht. Walter Langenbach, born in 1914, was witness to Nazi crimes in the former Yugoslavia. He does not specify his actual conduct, the extent to which he personally participated,[2] but he is still haunted by his memories and sense of guilt. A decisive feature of Langenbach's understanding of his past, is his perception of events in his life as imposed by external forces. With this biographical strategy he can avoid the question of his own role in Nazi crimes, even though he cannot escape his memories, nightmares and sense of guilt (Schiebel 1990).

It would go beyond the brief of this chapter, and take us too far from our purpose to examine in detail the strategies of normalisation and reparation in individual cases. The three cases already briefly cited should suffice here, to give the reader an idea of the different possibilities which witnesses of that period have found for coming to terms with the burden of their memories and experiences, and with their needs for justification. Our studies showed that each biographical strategy is shaped decisively by a de-politicisation of the Nazi past.

But it is not only the witnesses who themselves experienced the Nazi period and the war, and who were thus confronted with the gross inhumanity of Nazi politics, who have to go to some lengths to present their history as non-political and to obscure their life experiences. Gabriele Rosenthal (1992) shows graphically how a defensive stance with regard to Nazi crimes has become institutionalised, and how this in turn has led to a social pact of silence and the collective myth of 'unwitting accomplices (*Mitläufer*)', which has been passed on to the next generation. The children and grandchildren of witnesses to the 'Third Reich' have learned both to internalise this defensive stance, and to observe the taboo. It follows from Rosenthal that the prescribed defensiveness in communication is constantly reproduced in social interaction, and not only in everyday family conversation. How such a defensive screen is erected (Bar-On 1988) is illustrated in the above mentioned interview with Walter Langenbach.

The various contemporary attempts at explaining the emergence, since the mid-1970s, of the extreme right, with its peculiarly youthful activism, make reference to the economic crisis and associated youth unemployment, as well as the loss of a sense of direction and meaning (Heitmeyer 1987). It is clear that social crises, anxieties about the future, and insecurity about how to cope, can have consequences for shifting biographical perspectives – indeed such breaks in continuity spur on reflection and finding a theme for one's biography. Nevertheless such a widespread and ahistorical perspective on the extreme right is, in my opinion, problematic on two grounds.

On the first count the far right factions in the 1970s and 1980s in West Germany were not just spontaneous outbreaks, or a particularly contemporary phenomenon, but must be understood as a historical product of the German Federal Republic. The current movement is linked not just organisationally and in terms of membership, with comparable groupings over the last decades, but with their anachronistic, nationalistic ideas of social Darwinism, and with militaristic symbols and stances.[3] Furthermore neither the outbreaks of violence against asylum seekers nor the electoral successes of extreme right parties in East Germany are devoid of history. In the German Democratic Republic (GDR), in spite of, or maybe even because of the State-imposed anti-fascism, there was an increasing incidence of assaults against foreigners. At first the government tried to silence the media, but by the 1980s the phenomenon became impossible to deny (Hartmann 1991). The perpetrators were mainly groups of skinheads, who became politicised during the 1980s and 'whose members increasingly identified themselves with the images and goals of the extreme right' (Korfes 1995: 285).

Second, it seems to me to be inadvisable, when carrying out sociological analysis of any contemporary phenomena, including that of extreme right youth, to leave out of the account the particular nature of the way the present is shaped by the past in Germany (Fischer-Rosenthal 1995: 59), in both East and West. This can have its effect on the biographical constructions of young extreme right followers.

These dimensions furnish the primary basis of research on biographical reconstruction. My biographically focused interviews examined the life-historical accumulation of experience including individual, familial, generational and historical developments.

The case of Rolf Strunz[4]

The interview took place in 1990 with Rolf Strunz, at that time twenty-two years old, in his own home. He had ended his associations with the extreme right three or four years before.

Rolf Strunz was born in 1962 in a small town in West Germany, as the second child in the family. His sister is five years his senior. His father was working at that time as a metal worker in a small firm and was an active member of the German Social-Democratic Party (SPD). Up to Rolf's seventh year his mother was a housewife. When he looks back on his early childhood he recalls a sense of wellbeing and security connected above all with his mother. His father was seldom at home. He was either at his regular work, moonlighting, since the family's financial situation was tight, or pursuing his political interests. Thus the family suffered not only financial problems but frequent disputes between the parents, which grew in intensity until they separated 1982.

With his parents' separation the thirteen-year-old Rolf entered a crisis which would be of biographical significance. When his mother went off to live with her new partner in another town he stayed with his father, even though he was not close enough to him to talk about his problems. From the current perspective he tries, in the interview, to present this as a rational decision. The analysis indicated however that Rolf stayed with his father because he was jealous of his mother's new partner. In this situation Rolf felt himself abandoned, disappointed and not understood by his mother, or by his teachers, to whom he attributes indifference towards himself. His almost only positive family experience consists in the long talks he had with his grandmother, who told him about her experiences during the Nazi period. The thirteen-year-old Rolf didn't get a very clear picture of the Nazi past from his grandmother's accounts, these being quite ambiguous, oscillating between her repudiation of and enthusiasm for the regime:

N: But she had other contradictions (3) the big-wigs of the NSDAP (1) she *really* hated them, and the same with the SA types who, for example, were around her area (1) on the *other hand* there was one who (1) during bombing raid, she told me, was allowed in their *bunker* with them, in her *bunker*

```
I:                                          hm
N:                                                    you couldn't (1) there was always
      this contradiction you know (2)
I:                                          hm
N:                                                    on the one hand what wasn't true, and
      then comes something else⁵
```

Rolf Strunz is not sure to what extent his grandmother influenced him, but he suspects that her stories confirmed his attitudes. So, as he reported in the interview, he was 'naturally pleased' if his grandmother made some negative comment about Jewish faith or origins. Although at this point he did not yet see himself as of the extreme right, he did begin, at the age of thirteen, to interest himself in politics and history.

On changing schools at fifteen his interest in German history and the politics of the extreme right intensified. From 'openly accessible' history books about the 'Third Reich' and the Second World War he formed the impression 'that it must have been a great time'. He stressed, during the interview, that he had acquired a sound knowledge of the German past. This historical expertise gave him, and two school-friends, enormous self-confidence.

The teacher had tried, without success, to 'talk him out' of his political ideas. Similarly unsuccessful were his father's efforts. The latter was not in a position to convince him with sound arguments or perhaps did not really take him seriously, but was rather worried about what other people might think. This perceived concern with appearances angered Rolf so much that, whether for the sake of rebellion or to attract attention, he adopted even more extreme positions.

He now felt reinforced by the recognition of his contemporaries. He was chosen as the spokesman for the extreme right in school, and could speak with pride and awe about the war injuries of his grandfather on his mother's side. At the same time he was ashamed of the trade union and social-democratic membership of his grandfather on his father's side. He leafleted for extreme right organisations with his friends and contacted various extremist groups. From his present perspective he judges these contacts to have been 'horrible', though his detailed stories showed that the rhetorical skills of one group at least had aroused his enthusiasm. The fact that Rolf did not actually join up was partly to be explained by his fear of retaliation from his father, on whom he was financially dependent. However he emphasises that he would have joined a party if social and political popularity and acceptance of extreme right groups had been as strong then as they are today.

The former ideological ideas that Rolf Strunz describes in response to probes in the interview, show clearly how the borderlines between 'the world views of the extreme right' and the racist, chauvinistic attitudes which were discussed earlier are very fluid. His former views about foreigners, encapsulated in the slogan 'German jobs for Germans', are broadly in accord with those held by the Nazis, and are shared by many (West) Germans, a connection he made himself during the interview.

From the age of eighteen Rolf spent his free time in a local church youth centre in which social workers were also involved. There began his slow re-orientation. He was listened to and taken seriously, and his opinions countered with sounder arguments than his teachers and father had been, up to that point, able to muster. From the analysis of the interview it is clear that Rolf found a new sense of security in the youth centre, which up until then he had lacked. By the age of nineteen he had completed this biographical transition.

So how does Rolf handle his problematic biographical past? At the time of the interview he was trying to 'repair' his actions by doing what he could to oppose those kinds of movements, since he fears he may have influenced a number of people to turn to an ideology of the extreme right. Those four years of support for the extreme right which require legitimating are played down now against the background of his present perspective with its successful political re-orientation. This re-interpretation of the past works as a remedial strategy for his life history (*lebensgeschichtliche Reparaturstrategie*), so long as he is in a position to construct some kind of biographical continuity and see himself as 'never having really been on the extreme right'.

The organised extreme right

As already noted, the spectrum of extreme right factions in the Federal Republic appeared in the mid-1970s with new forms of militancy, an open adoption of Nazi symbols, the justification and glorification of the 'Third Reich', as well as a changed membership structure mainly based on a youth following. The main feature of these 'political action groups' was their determination to attract public attention and to exploit the potential for, but as yet not organised, youthful protest. Participation in the parliamentary or democratic process was, for the most part, decisively rejected.

With the fall of the Berlin Wall the West German neo-Nazi groups saw a great opportunity for recruitment in the (former) GDR and made contact with groups there. During this period they provided extreme right organisations in East Germany with informational material, literature, uniforms, badges, cassettes and technical equipment, and set up courses and shared contacts with Western European groups, so that they could furnish 'movement stewards', who could offer an ideological framework of interpretation. In fact the politically organised right-wing extremism in West Germany did not manage subsequently to integrate organisationally the whole milieu of violent extreme right elements in East Germany, but there remains a close link. 'The common basis resides in images of the enemy, fragments of right ideology, and an emphasis on direct action, that in contrast to left groups, is not against institutions and social structures, but rather pitted against targeted vulnerable groups' (Bergmann and Erb 1994: 87).

Ingo Förster, another case of a youth on the extreme right, which I shall present shortly, was involved first for several years with the German National-Democratic Party (NPD) – a nationalistic right-wing party – then got into a West German 'action group'. In such groups the ideological components were often downplayed in favour of 'activism'. Collective and provocative demonstrations and the like served to strengthen the comradeship and solidarity of the group, and arrests were often consciously planned, or at least accepted, in order to promote this closer within-group solidarity. Dudek and Jaschke (1984) speak, in this connection, of 'negative integration'.

The effects which these mechanisms can have on the biographies of young supporters is illustrated by the case analysis of Ingo Förster. Here the accumulation of experiences in the life story are not to the fore. In this presentation, rather than focusing on the structuring of experiences in the life story, I emphasise the telling of that life story, that is, his biographical self-presentation (Michel and Schiebel 1989; Schiebel 1992).

The case of Ingo Förster

At the time of the interview Ingo Förster was twenty-four and had been for some years a member of an extreme right group. The group's chairman had chosen him as an interviewee for us,[6] and the interview took place in their centre with another member present.

After a short discussion about the research question, in which he was irritated that we were interested in his personal life experiences, Ingo agreed to 'tell' his story. He started with some basic facts of an institutional character (his date of birth, year of starting school, etc.) and then embarked on a report of his school years in which problems and conflicts with Turkish school pupils were prominent. From his current perspective he did not consider these skirmishes to have been politically motivated – there were no grounds for thinking that.

What needs interpreting here[7] is why his biographical presentation begins with his experiences of Turkish schoolmates. It raises the question of what function this theme has at this point in the interview for the biography and in what thematic field it belongs.[8] One can go on to ask why Ingo begins his life story without even a mention of his parents or siblings. There seemed to be a noticeable glossing over of his entire child-hood and family life, which occurred again in the interview when one of the researchers asked about his family. Though the question regarding his evaluation of his school and family was not strictly in a narrative form,[9] I would like to quote it, together with the ensuing sequence, in support of the interpretation:

I1: So perhaps your family wasn't all that important? You've talked about school, and schoolmates
N: What formed me, I thought it was about that
I1: Yes, what was important to you personally
N: That I've become like I am, what I am, I mean you've been looking out for the neo-Nazi theme that it describes me, although that's another thing
I1: Yes but the first thing's your life story
N: Oh, I see, mm
I1: So that's the main point
N: my family, I should, my family[10]
I2: Yes, what was important in your life
N: Yes, naturally it's important, my family

If we look at the course of the interview up to that point, various possibili-ties for interpretation are suggested by this passage, together with a range of associated hypotheses concerning how the interview will proceed. Was Ingo assuming that we were simply interested in his political career, and gearing his selection of experiences to fit this assumption? In that case he would direct his account towards our supposed interest, which might not coincide with his own. This would involve a separation between 'politics' and 'family life', and if the extreme right career were to be recounted without any elements of family biography, a lack of connection between the two themes could be supposed. In this case, the interviewer's reminder that the issue is his life story and what is important to him personally may well set in motion a lengthy biographical narrative. A further interpreta-tion is that, rather than being directed to what he imagined to be relevant to us, his account actually corresponded with his own interest in portraying those specific experiences which came into the thematic field of 'neo-Nazism'. That would not contradict the previously mentioned separation between the two areas of life. It could mean that while Ingo allowed himself to present his extreme right career to outsiders, he viewed all the other biographical strands (*biographische Stränge*) as too 'private' or even problematic to want to, or be able to, relate to strangers, especially those with a com-pletely different political orientation to his own.

A detailed and fully explicated demonstration of the sequential layering of interview text would go beyond the brief of this contribution. But the analysis shows that what is suggested in the quoted section of text is revealed throughout the interview, and makes up the structure of the case: Ingo saw the interview as an occasion for representing the extreme right group. With this 'we' presentation he tried to highlight political content and to show his own involvement as politically motivated. He wanted to make clear that purely political reasons and grievances underlay his commitment to and the founding of the party. However, the analysis shows that there were serious sources of conflict in his family (his parents separated when he was five), and with his friends, which led him to find in the group a sense of belonging that he otherwise lacked.

In the interview Ingo is caught in the dilemma of both having to represent the group to the outside world and also not wanting to discuss problems. Nevertheless, or perhaps precisely because of this, he understood every inquiry on our part into his story as an inquiry into his problems. He avoided the danger of producing something which might contradict his intended presentation by not allowing himself into the narrative flow of recall in an extended biographical story (*biographische Großerzählung*), but restricting himself to argumentation.

Ingo's expectation of the interview was that it would be a political discussion. The mention of 'life story' alerted him to difficulties, given that the period before his extreme right involvement was on the one hand problematic, and on the other too 'private' to be a topic for discussion. It is not certain whether Ingo has excluded the period of his life before his political involvement from his biography completely. But it is likely not only that his contacts outside the circles of the extreme right will decrease, but that his non-political life history experiences will lose relevance for his biographical construction.

It is surprising that Ingo was careful in the interview to present his entry into the extreme right movement as politically motivated, even though he could articulate neither his motives nor his grounds for this political involvement:

> I can't I can't answer the question of why I=have (1) say=who it's=simple anyway NOW I'M in it I 'stick to it' (2) even though (4) I'm not angry about (2) 'that I think and feel like this and (1) so act' even=though it's not always easy (4) 'it's=not=always=easy' (1) 'and

sometimes even' (1) not only not easy but /bloody difficult ((faltering voice, sounds tearful))[11]

This extract shows up two aspects. First his expression 'anyway now I'm in it...' does not have the very convincing ring one might expect from a youth of the extreme right. However, the idea that his joining the group came less from political conviction than from the need for a feeling of community experienced at the group level makes this fragment comprehensible. Only during membership did the biographer internalise the ideological commitment to the party, by which he is currently bound – and here we arrive at the second point – and from which he cannot turn back: as he revealed later in the interview, his secret dream is to become actively involved with Robin Wood (an environmental organisation) or Greenpeace, but he lacks confidence to contact these organisations because he fears that he is already known as a supporter of the extreme right.

Discussion

The biographical accumulation of experiences occurs at the 'junction between lived life-history and lived societal-history' (Fischer-Rosenthal 1995: 44), between individual projects and institutional scripts. Youths of the extreme right similarly developed their political orientation within such a tension. Both Ingo Förster and Rolf Strunz grew up during the 1970s and 1980s in West Germany. Their horizons of experience included official discourse and political events concerning protests over nuclear power, nuclear disarmament, debates over right to asylum and hostility towards foreigners, and public discussions over the presence of the Nazi past or the slogan 'it's time for an end to all that'. Thus, against this social political background, within their particular life-world conjunctures, institutional settings and social milieus they were confronted with a range of contrasting opinions, ideas and themes, as well as expectations and norms.

At this point I would like to recall the questions posed at the beginning of this chapter: What is the source of attraction for youths of right-wing groups and patterns of meaning? What social, familial and life-history events contribute to the stabilisation and de-stabilisation of such orientations and careers?

These two case studies show that experiences of insecurity in the parental home (due to parental separation) or in relationships with friends led to an emotional instability, and caused these two youths to seek a sense of community, security and self-affirmation outside familial circles. Hopf *et al.* (1995) are right to point out that, on the basis of their research into the relationship between socialisation and orientation to the extreme right in young men, it is not only such serious biographical turning-points, as for example the close experience of parental separation, that influences the development of certain tendencies in behaviour.

Hopf *et al.* have shown in their work the association between a style of upbringing which is based on understanding and affective attention, and the internalisation of moral principles in their research subjects. Besides the importance of relational experiences in the family they stress the importance of the way such experiences are coped with. None of the right-wing youths in their sample showed a 'securely autonomous' reflective response to their relational experiences in the family. Instead they demonstrated 'defensive trivialising', in which they denied the significance of family life, or else had little distance from such experiences, were still 'embroiled' in them and either angry or still suffering (Hopf *et al.* 1995: 107f.). There is a parallel here with my own findings: while Ingo Förster is anxious to blot out his experiences in family biography and any problems connected with it, Rolf Strunz appears to still suffer a sense of rejection by his mother, and of not being taken seriously by his father. Furthermore, Lena Inowlocki's biographical analysis of extreme right youth indicates, as does mine, that a three-generational perspective in family biography is needed for purposes of reconstructing the establishment (*Tradierung*) within families of values and societal patterns of meaning, the institutionalising of taboos and repression of themes.

Rolf Strunz experienced recognition first from his contemporaries as school spokesman for the extreme right and thus, together with two sympathetic school-friends, gained attention from grown-ups in authority (teachers as well as his father). And similarly for Ingo Förster, solidarity with his comrades of the extreme right and commonly experienced 'actions' had an integrating effect. He simultaneously puts up barriers against those who think differently, an opposition which has the function of establishing his identity and strengthening his self-definition as a member of the extreme right. As a consequence, the boundary-testing which is associated with puberty and finds expression in opposition to authorities and institutions, or the State (as for example in the former GDR (Korfes 1995)), or simply against those who think differently, can strengthen an orientation towards the extreme right, to the extent that such challenges receive no support (from significant others, such as parents, teachers or social workers), or are not taken seriously in their wider implications.

From his grandmother's stories of her ambivalent and altogether undigested experiences of National Socialism, Rolf Strunz concluded that

German history must have been 'fascinating'. Only through the intensive efforts of social workers could this image lose its grip. On the other hand the case of Ingo Förster brings out the way in which the extreme right movements take advantage of the problems and insecurities of young people in their recruitment strategies. Furthermore his biographical self-presentation shows that, within the world of the extreme right, one encounters not just the effects of political socialisation, but also influences on the biographical constructions of young people. This tendency appears strikingly in the work of Lena Inowlocki (1988, 1992) which is concerned with young people in extreme right movements. She shows how in the course of their membership, their knowledge and experience of Nazism becomes so extensively integrated into their biographical construction, and there transformed and absorbed, that their 'own life' almost disappears, or is re-written. If these movements could not call upon a 'social repertoire of historical justification' (Inowlocki 1988: 49) in the recall of the Nazi period, or connect with the increasing hostility towards foreigners in the public, everyday and political domains, their ideologies and opportunities for interpreting social reality would be less attractive to young people.

This is also the conclusion of Thomas Rausch (1999) in his study of the patterns of social understanding among East German youth, whose extreme right orientation and patterns of behaviour are part of everyday experience. Rausch's case studies show clearly that such youths are continually confronted with extreme right attitudes in their leisure environments (youth clubs, discos, neighbourhoods), indeed are immersed in an extreme right subculture, to which there is little leisure time alternative. The State-sponsored anti-fascism in the GDR appears not to have made young people resistant to racist and extreme right ideas (Rausch 1999). Moreover, besides drawing on racist stereotypes and folkloristic symbols, East German right extremists play on elements of 'GDR nostalgia', or the commonly felt anxiety about economic insecurity, thus seeing themselves as representatives of a silent majority.

In order to address the rising militancy of extreme right groups and the increasing openness to their interpretations of reality, it is insufficient to focus just on youths. It seems to me that within social policy a family biography approach is more apposite. My research findings have helped in sharpening my awareness that discussion – and life-history-based forms of interaction which are also historically informed – can set in motion a process of biographical reflection which can lead to change and reorientation in a life history. Bans and punishments, by contrast, intensify self-stigmatisation, leading to stronger identification with the rhetoric of extreme right groups and to closer organisational ties.

Notes

1   This study was carried out as a student research project at the University of Bielefeld, supervised by Gabriele Rosenthal and published in 1990.

2   His possible complicity in Nazi crimes could not be assessed within the framework of the analysis, because we 'missed' his references to those experiences in the first interview. The combination of his obliqueness and our 'deafness' illustrates the institutionalised phenomenon, which crosses generations, that can be described as a 'collective defence' (see the following section of this chapter). Regarding other parts of his life story Walter Langenbach was an eager interviewee.

3   Neither the (re)organisation of the extreme right in the Federal Republic after 1945 nor the associated basic values and political outlook of each grouping can be reported here. For further elaboration see Dudek and Jaschke (1984) and Schiebel (1991).

4   The names of interviewees were changed for anonymity purposes.

5   Bracketed numbers give pauses in seconds. Italics denote emphasis. Indentation portrays the sequence of utterances.

6   Ingo Förster was interviewed by Sybille Michel and me.

7   The method I adopted in the reconstruction of the case can be referred to in Rosenthal (1995).

8   A thematic field consists of the construction of cross-references in which the themes are built up in relation to each other. This approach was developed by Wofram Fischer in his work on thematic field analysis; clearly illustrated in a sample case in Fischer-Rosenthal (1996), and has contributed to my own use of the procedures of sequential analysis (see note 7).

9   Narrative questions ask for the re-telling of actual experiences, rather than for opinions.

10 Ingo interjects while the first interviewer (I1) is still speaking.

11 See note 5. An equal sign denotes rapidity, inverted comma a quiet voice, capitals loudness, double brackets the transcriber's comments.

References

Bar-On, D. (1988) 'Did the Holocaust Perpetrators Feel Guilty in Retrospect?', in D. Bar-On, F. Beiner and M. Brusten (eds), *Der Holocaust. Familiale und gesellschaftliche Folgen*, Wuppertal: Universitätsdruckerei, pp.11–32.

Bergmann, J. (1976) 'Richtlinien und Symbole für die Anfertigung von Transkriptionen', Konstanz: unv. Ms., unpublished paper.

Bergmann, W. and Erb, R. (1994) 'Eine soziale Bewegung von rechts? Entwicklung und Vernetzung einer rechten Szene in den neuen Bundesländern', *Forschungsjournal Neue Soziale Bewegungen (NSB)* 2: 80–98.

Dudek, P. and Jaschke, H.G. (1984) *Entstehung und Entwicklung des Rechtsextremismus in der Bundesrepublik. Zur Tradition einer besonderen politischen Kultur*, 2 vols, Opladen: Westdeutscher Verlag.

Fischer-Rosenthal, W. (1995) 'Schweigen – Rechtfertigen – Umschreiben. Biographische Arbeit im Umgang mit deutschen Vergangenheiten', in P. Alheit and W. Fischer-Rosenthal (eds), *Biographien in Deutschland. Soziolo-*

gische Rekonstruktionen gelebter Gesellschaftsgeschichte, Opladen: Westdeutscher Verlag, pp.43–86.

—— (1996) 'Strukturale Analyse biographischer Texte', in E. Brähler and C. Adler (eds), *Quantitative Einzelfallanalysen und qualitative Verfahren*, Gießen: Psychosozial Verlag, pp.147–208.

Hartmann, M. (1991) 'Ausländer in Ostdeutschland', *Deutschland Archiv* 24(11): 1137–40.

Heitmeyer, W. (1987) *Rechtsextremistische Orientierungen bei Jugendlichen: empirische Ergebnisse und Erklärungsmuster einer Untersuchung zur politischen Sozialisation*, Weinheim, München: Juventa-Verlag.

Hopf, C., Rieker, C., Sanden-Marcus, M. and Schmidt, C. (1995) *Familie und Rechtsextremismus: Familiale Sozialisation und rechtsextreme Orientierungen junger Männer*, Weinheim: Juventa.

Inowlocki, I. (1988) 'Ein schlagendes Argument: Geschichtliche Rechtfertigung und biographische Konstruktion von Jugendlichen in rechtsextremistischen Gruppen', *BIOS Zeitschrift für Biographieforschung und Oral History* 2: 49–58.

—— (1992) 'Zum Mitgliedschaftsprozeß Jugendlicher in rechtsextremistischer Gruppen: Ergebnisse einer interpretativ-qualitativen Untersuchung', *Psychosozial* 15(3): 54–65.

Korfes, G. (1995) 'Biographien rechtsextremer Jugendlicher in der DDR', in P. Alheit and W. Fischer-Rosenthal (eds), *Biographien in Deutschland. Soziologische Rekonstruktionen gelebter Gesellschaftsgeschichte*, Opladen: Westdeutscher Verlag, pp.284–94.

Michel, S. and Schiebel, M. (1989) 'Lebensgeschichten von rechtsextremen Jugendlichen', in G. Rosenthal (ed.), *Wie erzählen Menschen ihre Lebensgeschichte? Hermeneutische Fallrekonstruktion distinkter Typen*, University of Bielefeld: Faculty of Sociology, unpublished research report, pp.212–33.

Osterkamp, U. (1997) 'Institutioneller Rassismus. Problematik und Perspektiven', in P. Mecheril and T. Teo (eds), *Psychologie und Rassismus*, Reinbek: Rowohlt.

Rausch, T. (1999) *Zwischen Selbstverwirklichungsstreben und Rassismus. Soziale Deutungsmuster ostdeutscher Jugendlicher*, Opladen: Leske und Budrich.

Rosenthal, G. (ed.) (1990) *'Als der Krieg kam, hatte ich mit Hitler nichts mehr zu tun': Zur Gegenwärtigkeit des 'Dritten Reiches' in Biographien*, Opladen: Leske und Budrich.

—— (1992) 'Kollektives Schweigen zu den Nazi-Verbrechen: Bedingungen der Institutionalisierung einer Abwehrhaltung', *Psychosozial* 15(3): 22–33.

—— (1995) *Erlebte und erzählte Lebensgeschichte: Gestalt und Struktur biographischer Selbstbeschreibungen*, Frankfurt a.M.: Campus.

Schiebel, M. (1990) 'Walter Langenbach: "Und dann ging´s los, das großes Morden"', in G. Rosenthal (ed.), *'Als der Krieg kam, hatte ich mit Hitler nichts mehr zu tun': Zur Gegenwärtigkeit des 'Dritten Reiches' in Biographien*, Opladen: Leske und Budrich, pp.165–92.

—— (1991) 'Rechtsextreme Deutungsmuster: Genese und Wandlung in Biographiekonstruktionen: Fallstudie eines ehemals rechtsextremen Jugendlichen', University of Bielefeld: Faculty of Sociology, unpublished diploma thesis.

—— (1992) 'Biographische Selbstdarstellungen rechtsextremer und ehemals rechtsextremer Jugendlicher', *Psychosozial* 15(3): 66–77.

12 The metamorphosis of *habitus* among East Germans

Astrid Segert and Irene Zierke

For a long time discussion in German social scientific research has been dominated by doubts about the capacity of East Germans to act with independence, flexibility and competence across a variety of social domains. They have been routinely categorised by a negative image of the grey 'Ossi' (Easterner), who could not cope with conflict or the need for flexibility. East Germans were expected to recognise the advantages of the normal West German outlook and quickly adopt them into daily life. In contrast to this one-sided view, in our research we wanted to show that the uniform 'East German' does not exist. To this end we oriented our research towards conceptualisations of 'uncompleted moder-nisation' (Glaessner 1995) and 'multi-layered experience' (Schütz and Luckmann 1991).

The first concept takes as its starting point that partial political changes in the German Democratic Republic (GDR), mainly during the 1970s, were accompanied by increasing social differentiation. Political constraints blocked such differentiation from developing in full. However from the 1970s onwards there was an expression of an increasing and unsatisfied need for personal freedom, for an undamaged environment, for better consumer goods as well as for possibilities for shaping public opinion. The concept of 'multi-layered experience' argues that daily behaviour patterns are rooted in individual and social experiences which are influenced but not caused by structural factors. That is why the process of comparing old and new experiences reveals a change in patterns of daily behaviour. That means that, for the East Germans, tendencies towards individualisation since the 1970s (including during the transition period) have been held in check not only by external structures but also by positive experiences of social relationships. Individualisation has not undermined social ties but become combined with them. This East German tendency continues today.

From these ideas we developed two questions:

1   Can a variety of milieus also be distinguished in East Germany?
2   Which specifically East German patterns are being used by members of different milieus to manage their integration into the new Germany, and how are such patterns changing in this process?

We carried out, between 1990 and 1997, three empirical studies on East German attitudes and patterns of behaviour during the transition period.[1]

When we started to plan our empirical study we were confronted with the problem of choosing a methodology. Given that we were critical of the widespread notion that the East German way of life must fall into line as fast as possible with the model set by West Germans, we did not want to add another standardised opinion survey to the existing stock. Rather we decided quite consciously to keep our research perspective open through the use of qualitative methods (Soeffner 1984).

Bearing in mind the limitations of the quantitative perspective of research within the frame of 'catching up with modernity' (Zapf 1993), and in order to uncover a picture of more differentiated social change in East Germany, we opted for hermeneutic analysis and comparison of biographical material from interviews. In this we depended on the methodological work of Niethammer *et al.* (1991), Oevermann *et al.* (1979) and Vester *et al.* (1993).

From a sociological viewpoint qualitative research methods are particularly relevant because they can offer a more precise analysis of the connections between structural change and attitude change. Quantitative research produces statements regarding dimensions of clear changes which are already completed, but cannot tell us much about the causes of unclear and ongoing changes. In other words, qualitative research methods are of great importance in the study of processes of social transformation. They can reveal the subjective basis for lasting social change in the patterns of perception and behaviour of particular social groups. Patterns of activity can be approached through the concept of 'habitus' and 'milieu'. These concepts help to define the principles according to which particular groups of individuals bestow meaning on objects and actions, the criteria people use for setting reciprocal boundaries. It is through this 'habitus' that people develop their life-styles (Bourdieu 1989), evolve symbols which designate others as insiders or outsiders, and create their special 'places' and rituals to feel at home. From this a social milieu emerges, based on integration and boundaries (Hradil 1987; Vester *et al.* 1993).[2]

This was our theoretical premise for analysing what resources and barriers GDR people from different milieus encountered while adapting to the continuing upheavals. It is generally recognised by sociologists that social milieus are relatively stable formations. The individual cannot easily change his or her milieu, since that would require shifts in structural and habitual assumptions. We were interested in the degrees of latitude available in the different milieus for changing 'habitus', and in the different ways people could integrate themselves into the new social field.

As a basis for this milieu-oriented research we adopted the research categories of the SINUS Institute in Heidelberg concerning the structure of East and West German milieus. Using both qualitative and quantitative measures, SINUS (1990/91) identified nine distinct social milieus in East Germany (see Figure 12.1 below and, in detail, Becker *et al.* 1992).

The *bourgeois-humanistic* milieu combines elements of traditional bourgeois attitudes with Protestant virtues. It has been a long-lasting and resistant milieu, not extinguished and only somewhat modified during the GDR period.

The *rational-technical* milieu is dominated by a faith in science and in the application of reason to the conduct of life. In the course of the economic changes consequent on the political changeover, this milieu was and is likely to expand.

For members of the *status- and career-oriented* milieu, professional and social promotion are important. The system changes suited their particular purposes and in recent years they have moved into corresponding social positions. With the exception of the GDR political elite, this group's upward professional mobility is assured.

Striving for security and a life ruled by convention are characteristic of the *petit-bourgeois-materialistic* milieu.

In the *traditional deeply-rooted worker and farmer* milieu the characteristics of the good life are simplicity and intact social relationships. With the decline in the industrial and agricultural sectors this milieu has undergone a considerable contraction.

The *non-traditional worker* milieu prioritises material security, even though both their labour market situation and their social background have become less favourable.

In the *left-wing intellectual/alternative milieu* concern for green issues in the face of global onslaught predominates. This milieu was extremely influential in the 1989/90 peaceful revolution in the GDR. Its members regard themselves as having played a key role in the social upheavals, and at that time took responsibility for the emerging shape of the society.

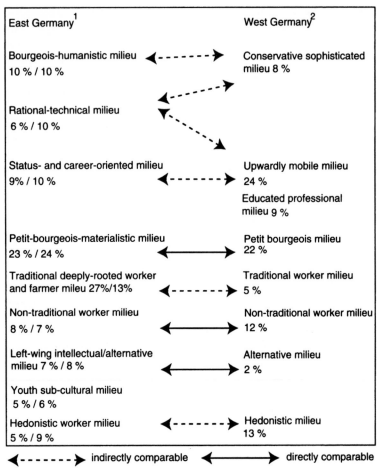

Figure 12.1   Social milieus in East and West Germany

Source: Becker *et al.* 1992

For members of the *youth subcultural* milieu a fun culture and the distinctiveness of the individual life-style are foremost. This milieu provides its members with a kind of 'transitional space' in which they can move during a particular period of their lives.

In the *hedonistic worker* milieu members seek a 'good life', often realised in leisure pursuits. These were the younger employees in the GDR. Ironically it has been this group that has contributed to the collapse of GDR society, though less by their political actions within the country than by their mass exodus into West Germany.

These milieus, which all existed at the beginning of the transformation process, have developed in different ways over the last five years, and continue to show clear differences in modes of living. One can pick out the commonalities with and differences from West German structures and see parallel developments with respect to the *petit bourgeois, non-traditional working class* and the *alternatives.* However, given the background of differently configured life-styles, different conditions of development in the two societies, and different sets of expectations, the East German *bourgeois-humanistic, rational-technical, status- and career-oriented* and *hedonistic worker* milieus are more distinct than their titles might suggest. This expresses itself in the distinct features of particular milieus and in their size (Becker *et al.* 1992).

In GDR society traditional modes of life predominated. In particular the *traditional working-class and farm worker* milieu, which in the GDR enjoyed conditions of life and work similar to each other, were much larger than in West Germany. Earlier in the life of the GDR the modern milieus were less widespread, due to the political and social constraints, but after the structural changes following 1989 they expanded, while worker milieus contracted. Those milieus whose members have distanced themselves from the dominant culture, whether 'old' or 'new', but whose demands on life are largely met within the new society, have remained at a relatively constant level.

Although these developments imply an approximation to the West German pattern of milieus, different outlooks are still to be found in East Germany even after unification, and may possibly be significant for the future. This arises because some elements in attitudes in particular milieus appear relatively enduring, changing more slowly than expected.

To examine such patterns of persistence and change we relied above all on biographical interviews, as a source of depictions of life stories, socialisation, the social realm itself, images of self and other, as well as of networks in various social milieus. The foremost discussion motif was intergenerational social and life domains. A standardised questionnaire provided the basic biographical and social data of the respondents. The several hours of interview texts were transcribed and then analysed in group sessions (Oevermann *et al.* 1979), in order to establish some basic features of the 'habitus' of particular cases and follow up their development (Schweigel *et al.* 1994). The analysed case studies were then compared with those of the parental generation, to highlight changing trends between generations.

In this chapter we follow up the phenomena of changes in 'habitus' in examples from the selected East German milieus. First we focus on the two major working-class milieus (*traditional* and *non-traditional working class*) which have been forced into change by contemporary processes: the two young East German workers, Bernd and Carlotta, show different metamorphoses in worker habitus. Second we focus on the context of the middle-class movements occupied predominantly by the *left-wing intellectual/alternative* milieus, which were so clearly implicated in the various forms of renewal subsequent to the social collapse. The case of Christa demonstrates patterns of habitus which are characteristic for this milieu. Space does not allow us to elaborate further differentiations within particular milieus, which we have developed in our research. Müller *et al.* (1996) detail the characteristics of other East German milieus, using the categories of the SINUS Institute.

We start with patterns of persistence and change within the habitus of workers during the transition period, showing their roots in GDR experience. In contrast to the situation in the Federal Republic, GDR workers were peculiarly courted on ideological grounds as the 'ruling class', even though only those members of the SED-leadership[3] born before the war really originated in this milieu. Children of the GDR working class either remained working class or became qualified in technical professions. The maintenance of political allegiance from this working class became an overriding aim of the GDR regime. This included, for example, a wages policy in which workers were highly paid in comparison with white-collar employees and academics, and in the workplace supply of goods, services and cultural benefits. The bigger the workplace the better the chance of buying bananas or a new car. In contrast to the Federal Republic nearly all workers were members of the General Trade Union, as indeed were all those who were employed. The union played almost no role in the struggle for higher wages, but was concerned with the distribution of social advantages like cheap holidays or nursery school places. By focusing on conditions peculiar to that milieu and the achievement of solidarity within it, the State further promoted the non-political nature of their everyday attitudes. Thus was the solidarity of the working class officially sponsored by the State. Workplace collectives maintained a cultural and social life in a way virtually unknown in the Federal Republic (Segert 1995).

With German unification all these features disappeared. Many firms were closed down, along with their kindergartens and holiday homes. East German workers lost not only their work place but its central function for communication and help. So their loss was two-fold: loss of their status as a privileged social class, and a disproportionate insecurity which followed in the wake of industrial dismantling.

East German workers' initial reaction was one of shock. However, the majority managed quite quickly to mobilise whatever specific resources they still had in their milieu. But our interviews showed that ways of dealing with completely changed prospects differed between generations. Faced with unemployment and enforced early retirement, older workers, men and women, withdrew into their familial and neighbourhood circles. From the safety of these vantage points they could stay faithful to their old patterns of value and activity. Many of them have access to a garden which they use as a space for sociability with other members of that milieu. The middle generation has linked such retreats with various forms of professional mobility. Many commute between workplace and home, or change to a different branch of their firm, or change the firm itself. Many female workers of the middle generation were perfectly happy to take the opportunity to retrain, even if this extended their period of unemployment. Our case studies among young adults show more marked changes in habitus, however, with different degrees and different directions of change. That means that the metamorphosis of the East German worker habitus is based particularly in the younger generation and that the emerging differentiation of milieus was impelled primarily by this group. Our two cases illustrate these tendencies.

We begin with Bernd whose story exemplifies a specific form of metamorphosis of worker habitus from traditional to hedonistic, and which is now in motion again. He represents the case of someone whose attitudes had developed through dependence on figures of authority. Bernd was thirty years old in the year of the changeover (1990), unmarried and without children. He was brought up by his grandmother, who rewarded him with sweets and praise when he complied with her rules. Thus he was brought up on the one hand strictly, while on the other hand he was freed from all household chores and personal decision-making, first by his grandmother and later his mother. Bernd learned early to leave all decisions to trusted authorities.

Following his parents' advice, and in order to prove himself, he decided to go in for the demanding occupation of machine tool-maker. However the difficult economic situation in the GDR meant that he found himself insufficiently challenged in this work. He therefore decided with a group of colleagues to move to the largest metalwork firm in the town, which, because of its strategic importance for GDR industry, was particularly privileged in terms of wages and social benefits. General distortions in the wage structure meant that despite doing unskilled work he now earned more than in his qualified job. The emotional significance of his life now shifted from recognition as a specialised and experienced worker to the free time he enjoyed with like-minded young workers within the hedonistic worker milieu. With them he enjoyed his relatively good earnings and access to the GDR consumer market. He acquired a sought-after Trabant (car), for which people usually had to wait ten years. His resources and availability to help friends and neighbours gained him respect.

In 1991 when rumours grew that the big plant was about to be closed, he, led by his friends, switched to a smaller, newer plant making car trailers. Here the status of his work sank to that of unskilled work. Unemployment, which he avoided, would entail an even further loss of social status. His income was higher than that of someone unemployed, but much less than that of his leisure-time friends, who had continued in skilled work. But his comparatively low wages meant that he experienced the newly unified Germany as threatening. Nearly all his friends had cars now, and his main fear of being unemployed and unable to keep up with his friends continued to grow. Thus he is still inwardly searching for a social foothold to prevent both his social decline and his loss of meaning in life. Maybe, with the help of his friends, he will be able to change his employment situation again. He will not manage it alone, for throughout his life he has depended on the decisions of other people.

This example helps us to see how a habitual pattern of social dependence, in this case dependence on authorities in the immediate milieu, is learned through socialisation in the family of origin. It was reinforced through his life experience in GDR society, and by the substitution of a leisure-time orientation for the unsatisfied needs for a challenging professional career. Thus there grew up in the GDR a milieu of a particular working-class nature which was oriented to consumerism and a hedonistic life-style, while the corresponding milieu in the Federal Republic was made up of the offspring of the middle classes. Admittedly the GDR offered very limited consumer opportunities; nevertheless a way was opened up for young workers in their after-work associations, to liberate themselves from the work-oriented restrictions of their own families of origin and those of socialist society in general. As Bernd's example illustrates, after 1990 this typical GDR habitus was then mobilised to set aside the risk associated with unemployment and social decline in favour of acting out freely their adopted hedonism. Ties with his milieu proved to be an important source of security for Bernd in a context of high unemployment. They compensated for his individual weaknesses in a restrictive social context, and without them his downward mobility would have been certain.

The case of Carlotta illustrates a different form of the *metamorphosis of worker habitus*. She was twenty at the time of the changeover and a qualified lathe-operator. Carlotta tells the story of her childhood as a continuing experience of disadvantage relative to her brothers, who were allowed more personal freedom and expected to contribute much less than her in household chores. She wanted to be a hairdresser as a teenager, but, like many children of the traditional working class, she had to train for a job in which she had no interest, one her parents thought was right. The collective support and sociability during the apprenticeship and early days of work were the only good things about her work that she remembers. She used the changeover to leave the close environment of her family. She took herself off to the city and within a relatively short time had two children by two different partners, but was unable to find work. Dissatisfied with the isolation of being a housewife, she returned after a few years to her home town with her second partner and children, and tried to find work. She managed to get one year in a job creation scheme (ABM – *Arbeitsbeschaffungsmassnahmen*). Still she was determined that even a good offer would not draw her back to her old work. She was looking for a job which would satisfy her desire for some kind of aesthetic expression, as in hairdressing or something similar, and her need to be in contact through work with like-minded others. She decided to abandon her ABM and to work as a saleswoman on her partner's market stall. She sells clothes and, in spite of it being unregulated and with long hours, she is happy with her job. But she suffers the double burden of being a mother who works, together with the high risk of a small, uncertain income. Nevertheless she is prepared to meet these risks and she would never live apart from her children. They are as much part of her life as her demand for a self-determined job. She can deal with this double burden because she can count on the help of her own family who often take care of the children. Without this help from her milieu of origin she could not continue.

Carlotta's habitus is one of constant and precarious searching. She changes partners, moves twice, and takes on and breaks off the ABM. Unlike Bernd, she changes activities fast. People in this group will apply for work outside their profession and take on casual work. They move around different regions for work, or else they take advantage of the freedom from employment which social benefits and the support of friends and family permit them. Often they travel a lot. Impervious to risk, they explore the possibilities of the personal latitude permitted them by the new social conditions. They do not have precise ideas about ways of realising new biographical possibilities; characteristically their ideas about and demands on life are diffuse, though clustered around some particular reference point. The search is for a sense of self-determination and with it a loosening of previously taken-for-granted authority. Instability and asymmetry in relationships is typical of this type. These are people who easily use the help of others in their search for self-development, but have no sense of reciprocal obligation.

The two forms of metamorphosis of workers' habitus which have been sketched out here have their roots in GDR experience and are functional in overcoming the social structural changes. In each case the habitus has changed in particular ways while also having an impact on the social situation of its protagonists.

In contrast to the *traditional worker* milieu as the milieu of origin of Bernd and Carlotta, the *left-wing intellectual/alternatives* already existed during the GDR period. Many such persons were critics of the system, opposing it politically, and there emerged, particularly during the 1970s and 1980s, various ways of life at odds with dominant traditional values and behaviour. Compared to other groups, members of this milieu were less concerned with material security and with professional engagement in the existing structure, and more with new kinds of political engagement. In close circles of family and friends they discussed how global conflicts could be limited. They took up the obvious problems of GDR society: ecology, international peace and the education of future generations. But the possibilities for such mutual exchanges, let alone common activities, were extremely restricted. They sought protection in the Evangelical churches, which offered a space for practical and intellectual alternatives, and, with artistic works, posters and small demonstrations, they drew attention to their ideas. In this way they opposed norms of public behaviour and were repeatedly banished to positions of marginality.

In a range of political attitudes and life practices these 'critical' GDR citizens are similar to those who form the basis of the alternative milieu in West Germany. However, the East German system was much more restrictive in allowing attempts at individual and social alternatives to established life forms and structures. Since even distancing oneself from official views was regarded as threatening to the existing system, social critics were already being discredited in the mid-1980s. Their professional work, for example, was either blocked or under surveillance. Nevertheless many continued to search for workable solutions to conflictual situations in the GDR. Activity in the political domain, which was conducted in their free time, and which created alliances and oppositions among themselves, was the starting point for their engagement.

From the specific standpoint of the East German alternatives, we tackled the question of the biographical backgrounds of members of these small social milieus and of the origins of their vitality. For a more precise characterisation of their outlook and its typical origins, we adopted the method of the two-generation interview. A comparison between the respondents and their parents revealed commonalities in attitude as well as their transformation over the two generations. It revealed that the GDR alternative milieu emerged particularly from the *bourgeois/humanistic* and *petit-bourgeois-materialistic* settings. The bourgeois-humanistic parents had kept up their erstwhile middle-class intellectual ways of life during the GDR period under complex conditions. They had tried to secure their professional positions as doctors, scientists and artists and to adapt their social and cultural values to changing conditions. The children carried on and further adapted the familial culture.

East German alternatives also came from lower middle-class families who could be classified as committed to modernisation. The churches played a particular role in cementing their cultural values. The parents had experienced a severe uprooting in all regions of life in the postwar period. The children were caught in a conflict between home and school. With their families they experienced the emotional rejection of the system during the 1960s and 1970s, but they also had to engage on a daily basis with State policies. This promoted the development of independence, so that they became not just independent but also able to handle conflict and to be creative. The outcome of this tension was the emergence in the 1980s of a subculture born out of the GDR system. With their considerable cultural capital in the personal domain, their value system promoted self-development and conflict management. The left-wing intellectual/alternatives concerned themselves with those social political issues implicated in demands for social justice. Not wanting to depend on others or compromise their single-minded views on life, they entered into conflicts with members of the official order.

These experiences of exclusion ended in 1989/90. The demands and actions of the left-wing intellectual/alternatives resonated within a range of groups in the population. Because of their outlook and relatively autonomous life-styles the left-wing intellectuals/alternatives experienced the social collapse of 1989/90 differently from workers, since it offered them the chance to pursue their philosophies of life in new ways. And the new social structures offered scope for different approaches.

A prototype for the fundamental habitual pattern in this milieu is Christa. She was born in the mid-1950s and has worked since the end of the 1970s in church-sponsored social work. She has been married twice and has three children. From childhood Christa has frequently had to make biographical decisions without the material and cultural support of her parents, and her personal needs developed in a conflictual way. In her family she experienced the gap between their socialisation practices and official policy. She developed behaviour patterns to resolve the resulting conflict situations mostly by herself. The limited support is explained by the social insecurity of her parents. Her mother, due to the attitudes of her own family during the 1930s and 1940s and the war, had been unable to realise her own professional ambitions. And because of her membership of the BDM[4] she experienced considerable personal and social loss as well as social exclusion later. Because of her life experiences her mother often told Christa and the other children: '*don't let yourselves be used, as we were used*'. The close emotional ties within the family and the demands of church and community supported this aim. Nevertheless, Christa did not always look to the family for protection, because her father's authoritarian and rigid style was unhelpful to her. Her parents aspired to a high level of education for her, but in terms of relevant knowledge their resources were of limited value and she was largely on her own.

In a gradual process of self-definition, Christa outgrew the cultural limitations of her family, but the path was by no means straightforward. She rapidly dropped out of a number of professional training courses, because they were unlikely to satisfy her social needs. She wanted something that could match her personal and educational background. The arena for this she found eventually in a church, which protected her political and educational commitment. She worked in an evangelical kindergarten as a helper, and later qualified as a head. She got involved in the 1980s in the Evangelical Peace Groups in her town, even though this entailed various pressures and trouble. In these arenas she made small steps towards change.

The social collapse of 1989/90 brought new professional horizons. Christa was now free to gain further qualifications and during this period took on a church-sponsored position of counsellor for people with life crises. Like others of the same outlook, with her interest in social work, she has been prepared to accept a rather precarious work situation. Her priorities are self-respect and the wellbeing of others, rather than establishing a social position. Because of her political engagement she was nominated in 1990 as a deputy for *Neues Forum*.[5] She dropped this role after the first electoral term, on the grounds that she found the scope to shape things too narrow. Now she fulfils her social interests in work in voluntary associations, where she also finds new friendships and networks. What she has found problematic has been the disappearance of the 'GDR' as an oppositional target, together with a range of political issues and the possibilities for collectivity. She also finds the new political structures restrictive.

This independent approach to the changed social relationships indicates that autonomous ways of life could be established in GDR times. In the new circumstances such patterns of attitude and behaviour lack a workable basis for profound metamorphosis. Members of these milieus continue to express their differences openly, but as if still in opposition to a restrictive world-view and global conflict. Their approach therefore remains confined within its initial social networks.

Our analysis of this case, from a medium-sized town, illustrates autonomous ways in which East German alternatives may orient their lives. The internal tendencies towards differentiation are accompanied by a stabilisation of these minority milieus. This can be explained by the way they are able to combine their socially critical perspectives with social engagement for others.

The results presented here illustrate how qualitative measures are able to capture social change. They allow the tracing of varying phases of development, distinguish stages in the establishing of subjective meaning, and highlight the significance of a creative rejection of particular potential changes in habitus and milieu. Even from this sketchy empirical material we can see that processes of change are not simply brought into being under the pressure of such dominant social structures as market, democracy or the rule of law. Rather change in social meaning follows its own logic (Segert, 1998), and reacts back on changes in macro-structures. There are two insights gained from our research which in conclusion we should bring together.

1   Even radical social collapse does not unleash fundamentally new biographical strategies or ways of living. Rather change begins in action patterns, which are connected with continuities. On the one hand empirical analysis shows how attitudes within different groups are 'passed on' (Bertaux *et al.* 1991). On the other hand there is an interplay between patterns of action and actual social conditions, producing change in the next generation through structural changes within the social arena itself. The new generation constructs novel coping strategies, in which patterns which have been passed on are modified and extended. Prior themes from the family of origin and its milieu thus remain recognisable. They will certainly be modified, but they can be traced back in a 'habitus family tree' (Müller 1990: 58).

2   Changes in social context, which are related to the biographical background in precise ways, can only be processed individually. Within the course of their lives people accumulate a treasure trove of experiences, which under changed conditions are re-evoked as a basis for confronting the demands and crises of everyday life. To that extent it is not critical life events themselves which are the immediate catalysts for change. What is decisive is the biography on which they impact (Vollbrecht 1993). For the people of East Germany an 'entire scaffolding of normal routines, trusted assumptions and certainties has collapsed, whose intrinsically equivocal nature nevertheless provided a basis for stabilised everyday habits' (Thomas 1991: 105).

From these reflections it will be clear that in both primary and secondary socialisation specific modes of thought become modified over the biographical life-cycle, both by action requirements and through experience. The research we have presented here indicates a largely buried GDR culture of thought and action in the everyday life of many East Germans that remains significant even for the coming generation.

Notes

1 In the GDR there was virtually no biographical research. The exceptions were a few historians of cultural history who approached the subject via oral history, as well as writers and film makers. Lutz Niethammer put together numerous biographical interviews in the book *Die volkseigene Erfahrung* [The People's Own Experience] (1991). A corresponding literary example would be Maxi Wanders' accounts of talks with women in *Guten Morgen, Du Schöne* [Good Morning, Lovely]. There was also the documentary film *Winter ade* [Farewell Winter] by Helke Misselwitz.
2 While 'habitus' identifies basic features of practical action, 'milieu' focuses on forms of interaction which generate social integration or exclusion. 'Lifestyle', by contrast, is restricted to aesthetic forms of expression.
3 SED – Sozialistische Einheitspartei Deutschland – The Socialist Unity Party of Germany.
4 The German Girls Union (Bund Deutscher Mädchen) was one of the Nazi youth organisations.
5 The Neue Forum (New Forum) was founded in Autumn 1989 as a civic movement with the goal of political renewal in the GDR.

References

Becker, U., Becker, H. and Ruhland, W. (1992) *Zwischen Angst und Aufbruch: Das Lebensgefühl der Deutschen in Ost und West nach der Wiedervereinigung*, Düsseldorf: ECON Verlag.
Bertaux, D. and Bertaux-Wiame, I. (1991) 'Was du ererbt von deinen Vätern', *BIOS* 1: 13–40.
Bourdieu, P. (1989) *Die feinen Unterschiede: Kritik der gesellschaftlichen Urteilskraft*, Frankfurt/M: Suhrkamp-Verlag.
Glaessner, G.-J. (1995) *Kommunismus-Totalitarismis-Demokratie*, Frankfurt/M: Westdeutscher Verlag.
Hradil, S. (1987) *Sozialstrukturanalyse in einer fortgeschrittenen Gesellschaft*, Opladen: Leske u. Budrich.
Müller, D. (1990) 'Zur Rekonstruktion von "Habitus-Stammbäumen" und Habitus-Metamorphosen der neuen sozialen Milieus', *Forschungsjournal Neue Soziale Bewegungen* 3: 57–65.
Müller, D., Hofmann, M. and Rink, D. (1996) *Diachrone Analysen von Lebensweisen in den neuen Bundesländern: Zum historischen und transformationsbedingten Wanderl der sozialen Milieus in Ostdeutschland*, Hannover und Leipzig: Expertise.

Niethammer, L., Plato, A. and Wierling, D. (1991) *Die volkseigene Erfahrung: Eine Archäologie des Lebens in der Industrieprovinz der DDR*, Berlin: Rowohlt.

Oevermann, U., Allert, T., Konau, E. and Krambeck, J. (1979) 'Die Methodologie der objektiven Hermeneutik', in H.-G. Soeffner, *Interpretative Verfahren in den Sozial- und Textwissenschaften*, Stuttgart: Deutsche Verlags-Anstalt.

Schütz, A. and Luckmann, T. (1991) *Strukturen der Lebenswelt*, vol. 1., Frankfurt/M: Suhrkamp.

Schweigel, K., Segert, A. and Zierke, I. (1994) 'Ostdeutsche Lebensgeschichten', *Mitteilungen aus der kulturwissenschaftlichen Forschung 34*, Humboldt-Universität Berlin, pp.192–398.

Segert, A. (1995) 'Das Traditionelle Arbeitermilieu in Brandenburg: Systematische Prägungen und regionale Spezifika', in M. Vester, M. Hofmann and I. Zierke (eds), *Soziale Milieus in Ostdeutschland*, Köln: BUND-Verlag, pp.298–329.

—— (1998) 'Problematik Normalization: Eastern German Workers Eight Years After Unification', *German Politics and Society* 16(3): 105–24.

Segert, A. and Zierke, I. (1997) *Sozialstruktur und Milieuerfahrungen: Empirische und theoretische Aspekte des alltagskulturellen Wandels in Ostdeutschland*, Opladen: Westdeutscher Verlag.

Soeffner, H.-G. (1984) 'Hermeneutik–Zur Genese einer wissenschaftlichen Einstellung durch die Praxis der Auslegung', in H.-G. Soeffner (ed.), *Beiträge zu einer Soziologie der Interaktion*, Frankfurt/New York: Campus, pp.9–52.

Thomas, M. (1991) 'Husserl und Schütz in der gegenwärtigen Diskussion zur Sozialstruktur', *BISS public* 3, pp.101–20.

Vester, M., Oertzen, P., Geiling, H., Hermann, T. and Müller, D. (1993) *Soziale Milieus im gesellschaftlichen Strukturwandel: Zwischen Integration und Ausgrenzung*, Köln: BUND-Verlag.

Vester, M., Hofmann, M. and Zierke, I. (eds) (1995) *Soziale Milieus in Ostdeutschland*, Köln: BUND-Verlag.

Vollbrecht, R. (1993) *Ost-West-Widersprüche*, Opladen: Leske and Budrich.

Zapf, W. (1993) 'Die DDR 1989/1990-Zusammenbruch einer Sozialstruktur?', in H. Joas and M. Kohli, *Der Zusammenbruch der DDR*, Frankfurt: Suhrkamp, pp.29–48.

13 Researching the implications of family change for older people

The contribution of a life-history approach

Joanna Bornat, Brian Dimmock, David Jones and Sheila Peace

> You know, I come from a very steady background. I was evacuated for three and a half years.[1]

> I'm the product of a divorced family. But I didn't see as it affected me all that much, because I was in my teens. To me, divorce affects younger children more, their stability. They've got to have two – there's got to be a balance you know. There's got to be a balance. There's got to be a good and an evil to make a whole.[2]

In this paper we explore the implications of interviewing around a topic which is embedded in personal experience while also being the property of public debate. Our research began in 1994, the International Year of the Family.[3] Since then it seems that in the UK family life has never been out of the headlines. During the period of our fieldwork the public was entertained by debates such as *Who Killed the Family?* (BBC2, 31 October 1995), threatened by the spectre of the rise of the lone parent family (*Independent on Sunday*, 14 November 1995) and told that divorce is good for women (*Guardian*, 8 July 1995) but that it 'blights children's lives' (*Guardian*, 3 April 1995). At this time the most prominent family in the land was adding no less than two separations, a divorce and a remarriage to the statistics of family change.

Anxiety about the future of family life has been fuelled by reference to statistics which describe the ageing of the population and the rate of family change through divorce and separation. By the mid-1990s the proportion of the population over the age of sixty-five had reached 15.1 per cent while four in every ten marriages in England and Wales were expected to end in divorce (HMSO 1994; Haskey 1996).

An ageing population, together with evidence of high rates of divorce, separation and cohabitation, suggests a possibility that the nature of inter-generational relationships within families might show signs of change. Structurally, two conflicting outcomes are broadly predicted. There is the scenario of postmodern optimism with a shift away from the restrictive confines of normative roles and a move towards more equitable family relationships (Stacey 1990: 16). Then there is the nightmare scenario which foretells moral decline and social fragmentation where the most vulnerable in society, older people especially, come off worst in an indi-vidualistic struggle for survival (Giddens 1991: 176–7). Within a UK context, neither of these scenarios has been exposed to investigation in specific relation to the position of older people. While there has been extensive research on the effects of divorce on dependent children, step-family life and the crisis of the divorcing couple (see, for example, Burgoyne and Clark 1984; Gorrell Barnes *et al.* 1998; Rodgers and Pryor 1998) there has been little investigation into the implications of family change for older adult members in terms of kinship behaviour and adult relationships.

A central focus of our research was the way family members talk about and make use of past experience of family break-up and reconstitution and how this relates to their current understanding of change in their own family life. Through interviewing we rapidly became aware that our respondents were working with understandings and explanations of family change in their own histories while at the same time adopting a variety of strategies in their negotiation of the public discourse surrounding this topic. The two opening quotations illustrate these processes, each is an example of defence against negative experiences and the negative cast of social policy discourse in relation to disruptions to family life. By focusing on the different meanings employed by the older people we interviewed we identify the extent to which the experience of family change is accom-modated in everyday life and also the continuing investment which older family members make in the continuity of family relationships and their continuing involvement in their children's lives.

In this chapter we provide examples of ways in which the dissonance and disjunction of family change is accommodated in the narratives of our older respondents by focusing on three themes: the counterposed negotia-tion of personal morality with public discourse; the preservation of narrative coherence; and the search for personal integrity. These three themes, as we go on to explain, draw on wider theoretical frameworks in relation to identity maintenance in late life under conditions of post-modernity. Each is illustrative of individual agency in the maintenance of identity and meaning through strategies which include the incorporation of elements of public discourse into personal accounts, the narrative management of biographically disruptive events and a focus on balance and integrity while being confronted by the actions of immediate family members and the shifting structures and moralities of wider society. In each case, we suggest, biography is not only a means by which people explain change, it is also a support and a resource when change presents challenges to identity in late life. First, however, we outline our research methods.

Research methods

We set out to interview people from different income groups and across a wide age range who had experience of 'family change'. Our aim was to identify a sample of people who, while they might have experience of family reconstitution had not necessarily defined themselves in terms such as 'stepfamily' or 'broken family'. This meant that we chose not to obtain our sample by contacting organisations such as Stepfamily (Batchelor *et al.* 1994) or Relate (providing marriage guidance). For the same reason we chose not to advertise for volunteers since this again might involve a significant risk of bias, perhaps attracting people with a particular point of view or motive. We identified three socially contrasting electoral wards, within the town of Luton,[4] by referring to census data. Our sample was drawn from responses to an initial screening questionnaire as well as through community networking. These were followed up and eventually a total of sixty interviews was completed.[5] Though our ultimate interest lies in investigating how older people's lives are being affected, or will be affected, we have not focused exclusively on older people. In fact our interviews span three generations, though, with the exception of four people, these were not from the same families.

Our approach to life-history interviewing was, inevitably, affected by our own backgrounds (Okely 1992) in sociology, social gerontology, psychoanalysis, geography and oral history. Consequently our understanding of what is meant by life history borrows from more than one tradition or practice in biographical interview methods.

In adopting a life-history approach to interviewing we aimed to elicit an account from interviewees which was retrospective but which highlighted topics which we had identified as likely to be significant: caring, inter-generational relationships and transfers of family wealth. In identifying topics at the outset, were we in danger of shaping the accounts, or predetermining 'the selective principles guiding the narrator's choice of stories to be related in the interview' (Rosenthal 1993: 65)? The conviction that we were not doing so stems from our understanding of the meaning of the life-history interview as seen from the perspective of the interviewee. For us, a key concept is agency. People bring their own agendas and interests to the interview, consequently interviewer topics may well be reinterpreted, managed or straightforwardly resisted by the interviewee (Bornat 1993; Jones 1998). Accounts from interviewees are few and far between (Borland 1991; Echevarria-Howe 1995; Rickard 1998), nevertheless, those available to us demonstrate how their perceptions and perspectives shape and determine the direction of an interview. Focusing on three topic areas within a life history or biographical framework provided both the interviewer and the interviewee with opportunities to situate examples of, and issues stemming from, questions raised in relation, for example, to care, grandchildren and inheritance. Indeed in their responses it soon became clear that these were areas which interested our respondents and to which they freely alluded.

Coupled with agency is the assumption that a narrated life history is as significant for the meanings it conveys as for the events described (Portelli 1991: 50). A sociological understanding of meaning is not simply the recognition of the validity of the subjectivity of the interviewee, but more a recognition that interaction with the social and public world implies active renegotiation and reconfiguration (Gubrium and Holstein 1995: 212) particularly in relation to life events (Schütze 1992; Chamberlayne and King 1997). Grele, an oral historian, suggests this implies an understanding that interviewees:

> are capable of complex cultural formulations, that they can interpret their own pasts, that they can look at themselves and us critically. It also assumes that they can and do use history, and that they can use it to actively involve themselves in the cultural dialogue in a fully participatory manner. People become not simply objects of study but part of the community of discourse.
>
> (Grele 1991: 271–2)[6]

An additional characteristic of the life-history interview which we identify is its interrogative character (Bornat 1994). It is the product of a method shaped by the rules, conventions and opportunities of questions and answers. Not only does this suggest a wider purpose than a simple conversational exchange, it means that what is written down as a story under one set of conditions may come out quite differently if told in an interview. So, for example, where an oral account may be lively and responsive, with fresh insights provoked through questioning, a written account of the same events may be pallid, formalised, complying with literary conventions and consequently less personalised (Bohman 1986; Portelli 1991: 279; Bornat 1994: 23).

Finally, and as significant, is an understanding of the life history as an account told in relation to a life stage. Taking a perspective which borrows from Erikson *et al.* (1986) it would seem appropriate to anticipate age-related differences in narrative forms at different ages. To what extent such differences are generalisable, or culturally or cohort relative, is not yet well understood (Gergen and Gergen 1987; Coleman *et al.* 1993). We do, however, assume the need for a perspective which is sensitive to the effect of age on life-history narrative forms.

By configuring a perspective of the life history as a product of agency, imbued with meaning and being interrogative and age-related we inevitably brought a particular set of interpretive strategies to the accounts we were given of family change. In analysing the data we were aware of the strategies which interviewees were adopting in their talk of family change and identified the three already mentioned which are the focus of this chapter: personal morality versus public discourse, narrative coherence and integrity. Taking each in turn we select a life history from our sample of sixty interviews. The three people whose interviews we have chosen are all drawn from the 'old' generation of interviewees. These we distinguished from the 'young' and 'middle' generations on the basis of their having children and grandchildren but no living parents. In age, they were all over sixty at the time of interview.

Personal morality versus public discourse

Although, as we have already pointed out, family change or 'breakdown' is a major item on the agendas of public debates, it quickly became clear to us that personal experience of these events was not always so freely communicated. There was, for example, no ready acceptance of the term 'step'. For some people this clearly had pejorative meanings and many talked about step-relationships without reference to the word 'step' at all. The lack of a well-understood and stigma-free language to describe post-divorce or successive families creates many difficulties when giving an account of events. Plummer characterises the telling of sexual stories in terms of 'generic processes' moving the story-teller from an inner world where only they are the audience, to a public world where the private story becomes part of 'a public domain' (Plummer 1995: 126). At a point in this development, the storyteller identifies appropriate 'social worlds' (p.128) where a story may or may not be told. A significant factor in this process is the adoption of a language or discourse which enables what is personal, or inner, to be expressed and understood by an outer world.

The experience of family change is an aspect of life where public accounts are on offer for private interpretation and use. Several of our interviewees used the opportunity of an interview to explore an experience of family change in a semi-private social context. Others who were also seeking ways to explain events over the past sixty or more years, seemed to be actively trying out ideas and theories as they told their life history to an interviewer. Gubrium and Holstein suggest that in this way the boundary between the public and the private is constantly being breached and discuss the 'elasticity of privacy' (1995: 209) as people increasingly use a public language to give meaning to their private lives. They argue for an 'interpretive practice' (1995: 218) to tease out this relationship between the public and the private.

Someone who had several stories of family change to relate was Molly Lowe. At the time of her interview she was sixty-eight, living in sheltered accommodation, and still wife to the man she had met at the end of the Second World War. They had married when she was nineteen. Her parents had separated when she was sixteen, her father moving back to his widowed mother's house with his new partner. She was attached to both her parents and has strong views on the effects of divorce on young children. She feels her sister was badly affected. She kept in touch with her father who continued to provide for his ex-wife and their younger daughter, Molly's sister, until he died. At this point, her mother and this younger sister moved in with Molly, her husband and their eight children. Her mother helped with the children and married again, briefly and for financial reasons, eventually dying in residential care. One of Molly's daughters has divorced, another is a widow and her son has married a divorced woman. Molly and her husband now live in sheltered housing. All but one of their children and most of their twenty-one grandchildren live in the Luton area.

In describing the divorce which ended her daughter's marriage Molly uses practical and matter-of-fact language, tracing the sequence of events in an unemotional way, yet conveying the strength of family support. Molly Lowe and her husband helped their daughter financially, as did their other children. A constant expression she uses is of someone 'coming into the family'. Thus, her daughter's new partner 'came into the family', as did her own mother after her father died. When she talks about her own experience as a child she adopts a more formal, almost professional language. As the middle of three daughters she was 'attention-seeking' and 'I wouldn't conform. I think that's the word. I wouldn't conform'. Her widowed daughter recovered from 'the trauma' of her husband's fatal motor accident, but later went for counselling when her two daughters were about to leave home because 'She'd got to let them go. And she couldn't'. But, 'she's not had the stability of a family unit'.

She comes over as someone who is deeply committed to a traditional marriage and invokes her own particular model, of a 'balance' between 'a good and an evil' in the marriage partnership, 'one to comfort and one to punish'. She feels that their eight children are learning from the positive experience of their parents' partnership. She was able to cope with her own parents' separation and divorce because she was already seventeen and involved in the Land Army but also, from her own account, because she dealt with it by physically attacking her father's new partner and then continuing to stay in contact with both her parents. Though she 'accepted' that he had left, 'I never let him forget I was around' and 'basically he admired me for taking a stance against it'. To be even-handed, she emphasises: 'I was supportive to Mum'. Ideals of family closeness and even-handedness come through as important to her, in accounting for her own past and her own and her children's relationships.

Although she draws on her own biography to present her personal philosophy of the survival of a marriage partnership, public accounts do impinge when she introduces the role of 'shame'. Her younger sister was 'shamed' by her father's infidelity while she was protected because 'I was into my own way of life' by then. She contrasts the 'shame' of divorce with the 'pride' in marriage and, again in describing something which she disapproves of, a more public, formal, language takes over as she explains that shame follows because of loss of 'social status.... I don't know where it comes from. Perhaps Queen Victoria'. She speculates that 'women's lib might, one day, get rid of all that – that shame'. Public agency might change what she cannot see a way to changing: 'I'm too set in my ways, now, to change' and though she concedes that 'we were kept down years ago, were kept down, definitely' she distinguishes between women as a generation and her own personal experience: 'thank God, I've never considered I've been kept down'. The public account fits other people's experience, but not her own.

In narrating her own experience of family change, Molly Lowe, draws on a more public, almost therapised, discourse with references to conformity, letting go, shame and history interwoven with a more private language which she uses to describe her personal concept of partnership in marriage. It seems as if the public language describes the issues which she appears to find unacceptable, while the ideals she espouses are accounted for in words and philosophy she makes her own with her references to 'balance' and 'good and evil'. In his work with parents of children born with congenital impairments, Baruch draws a similar distinction between private and professional languages. In so doing he suggests the interesting possibility that the manipulation of such differences in parents' language enables both a display of 'moral adequacy' and assertion of control in an unfamiliar and disturbing situation (Baruch 1981).

Molly Lowe is typical of our older interviewees in the way she combines a public language with personal and more private explanations. In this way life histories which tell of divorce and separation accommodate these changes with the aid of a personal morality which patterns the experience and gives it an internal consistency. At the same time her recourse to elements of a more public discourse suggests that she is able to dispel any tendency towards incongruity or disempowerment when faced with the norms and trends of a wider society.

Narrative coherence

In searching for ways to characterise the disruptive effect to self-identity of positive HIV diagnosis, Carricaburu and Pierret (1995) discuss Bury's use of the term 'legitimation' to describe 'the individual's attempt to maintain a sense of personal integrity, and reduce the threat to social status, in the face of radically altered circumstances' (p.70). They conclude by rejecting the more publicly oriented concept of 'legitimation', favouring instead the more internally focused phrase 'biographical work' as used by Corbin and Strauss (cited p.70 Carricabura and Pierret and see Fischer-Rosenthal this volume). The strategies which people adopt when coping with the implications of unexpected and sometimes inexplicable change in themselves are in many ways similar to those adopted by some of our older interviewees when explaining the disruptive effects of family change. In analysing the interview transcripts we were interested to identify how they manage to describe these discontinuities. While 'biographical work' describes a general tendency to draw on past life experience to maintain a sense of self-identity, in the actual telling of stories of unexpected and sometimes inexplicable change they are attempting something which is perhaps more exact in its dimensions: a storyline which has narrative coherence.

Keith Gardener at the time of interview was sixty-seven, living alone and separated from his wife who, with his two children, had become a Jehovah's Witness. Brought up in North London, he was the youngest of four children. His father was in the music business and he recalls home, where his grandfather also lived, as a place where there was music and home entertainment. He married at the age of twenty-eight, having met his wife while he was working at a holiday camp where she was a waitress. She was twenty, was from what he described as a 'broken home' and had lived in care as a child. He was employed initially as a musician and then as a technician. They had two children, a son and a daughter. He describes his wife as being depressed after the second child was born and increasingly alone as he played in bands several nights a week after work to supplement his earnings. This, he says, made her susceptible to the intensive persuasion of the Jehovah's Witnesses. After a number of years she left him taking the children with her, yet the couple seemingly retained a platonic affection for each other. Latterly they have become yet more amicable because, as he explains: 'we're beginning to talk more now, because there's not this anger in her'. His children visit him and he is a grandfather now that his daughter is married with a child.

Although Keith Gardener describes the separation as a process which developed over a number of years, the situation he now finds himself in is not one that he had either anticipated or adjusted to:

> It wasn't a family thing any more...we never managed to sit down at the table.... You know the whole thing had gone fwuff, you know. And of course, I've always said to them that the best time I ever had at home was Sunday, sitting round the table, chatting about things – the idea of my Dad talking about politics and all that...and I can remember listening and talking.... And you get a good idea of what you're you know – what life's about, don't you, when you're young.... You can hear your Mum saying that Mrs so-and-so's got into trouble up the road and that. And you think, oh well, that's a bit – I have to watch that when I – you know, it's all important, isn't it really? But she took the whole concept of that out really.

Although he can't be reconciled to what has happened, he is able to maintain narrative coherence by adopting various strategies. There is, for example, a feeling of inevitability in the way he tells his story. He describes his wife as someone who, by nature and origin, was vulnerable even before her post-natal depression. As a woman, she is 'poetical' and 'hairy fairy' (*sic*) unlike men who are 'more practical and rational'. Then there are her origins. She 'had a broken childhood...she was brought up in an institution.... She was separated from her brother' and the people at the holiday camp where they met: 'are people that haven't got on too well at home, say'. In contrast he describes his own background as 'steady' and they were 'a happy family...close family', though in the next breath he mentions being evacuated for three years during the Second World War. When it came to the break, however, he says he was unable to call on either side of the family for help. His side didn't want to get involved and neither did his wife's stepmother, despite her Christian convictions.

He finds a way to accommodate the events leading to the separation and afterwards by maintaining distance between his own and his wife's world views. He talks significantly of the way he has never accepted his wife's faith:

It's not a rational – you know, you either believe in the magical things, or you don't. Personally I'm just a humanist you know. I know that there's laws, and there's the commandments, as they're called, but they were really laws written by wise men.

He describes her belief as something which came to 'alienate our marriage'. There were no Christmases and, because 'they confiscate all birthdays', he's not even sure exactly when his children were born. Finally, though he felt angry and 'undermined' in his own home, he says he 'couldn't put a stop to it…. Because I would have lost her and the children. I mean, you can't – you can't do it, can you? So I stayed on…'. In the end he says his wife left, moving into her own flat with the help of her co-religionists. Despite the 'alienation' he backs away from the implications of a confrontation because of the threat to the continuity in relationships with his family. He says his friends thought he should have taken a firmer line, he says he couldn't:

How can you fight that sort of passive – with the weight of all that organisation? You can't. Because you're only going to make it worse, inasmuch as you're going to be a warrior aren't you really? Either a verbal warrior or a warrior. And I just couldn't do nothing about it. And I felt bloody helpless – that's why it alienated me.

Neither of them has ever taken another partner. Though he has two lady friends who call, 'they're only mothering me…I mean there's no sexual thing in it or nothing like that'.

The account he presents is one which is emotional both in its telling and in content, it is also one which, late in life, he is able to live with because he is able to retain narrative coherence in telling his story, sustaining an identity as open-minded and family focused despite the apparent challenges from his wife. By invoking inevitability and distance, he manages potentially biographically disruptive events. And he uses his own life history and humanistic beliefs in a cohering narrative strategy which is inclusive of his wife while rejecting her beliefs and actions.

Integrity

While narrative coherence is perhaps an issue of presentation of self, a search for integrity may be perceived as linked to an inner need. Among our accounts were some from people who were clearly looking for ways to achieve what Erikson *et al.* refer to as 'integrity': the search for 'balance' as opposed to 'despair' (1986: 37) in the final stage of life. An impending

sense of finitude prompts a need to find resolution and arrive at a personally acceptable account or version of a life. Though Erikson's theory of life
stages has been criticised for being strongly conformist in its explanation
of the development of identity (Sugarman 1986: 93–4), his highlighting
of unavoidable existential issues which are to be faced in late life is of
some significance. Other commentators place this psychological task at an
earlier phase of life, middle age (Jacques 1965; Levinson *et al.* 1978).
Their focus on middle age may be because, as Biggs suggests (1998), in
psychoanalysis old age tends to be a neglected category for interpretation.
In contrast, Erikson, and others who have followed his broad schema,
extends the reach of analysis to include old as well as young.

Coleman and his colleagues, in research into self-esteem in late old
age, suggest the possibility that beyond Erikson's seventh stage of integrity
there may be an eighth stage of acceptance, a 'transcendence of history' in
which narrating a past life is less important than living day-to-day
(Coleman *et al.* 1993: 191). Although without comparable tools for
measurement we are not in a position to argue for or against the position
which Coleman takes, there were several among our older informants who
were keen to reflect and engage with the way their family structures were
changing as younger members repartnered or chose alternatives to marriage
as an institution. At the same time they also spoke of issues connected
with mortality and reflected on past life events.

For some it was the incomprehension of death; an older man, for
example, described having to face the death of his second, much younger,
wife. Looking back was a solace:

> I think the only thing that is wrong about life now. I miss having
> something to look forward to. I don't seem to have anything to look
> forward to, you know. That's a bit sad I think. But you can only sort
> of look back.[7]

Rituals connected with death could be important. Tending a grave, or
making plans for burial or cremation were mentioned by several people. One
woman, as young as fifty, had plans for her ashes to be taken to Ireland and
placed in her mother's and father's grave. She expected her daughter to do
the same.[8] A Muslim man wanted to be 'buried properly in a Muslim way'
and pictured his children coming by on Sundays with a few flowers.[9]

The urge to resolve differences through death and to arrive at a feeling
of integrity, in the sense of an honest account as much as a weighed up
balance to a life, comes through in Paula Loudon's life history.

Paula Loudon was seventy-two at the time of her interview and
widowed. She divorced her first husband in 1975. He had become 'moody'

following a brain haemorrhage and had also begun an affair. They had two children. She wanted to emigrate to Canada but was turned down. She married a widower, from abroad, who did not have children and was happy with him for twelve years until he died in 1993. She has lived alone since then. She worked, from the time her children started school, for twenty-six years at the same company. She feels she is relatively well off, has a house in Spain and has travelled abroad several times. She kept an amicable relationship with her first husband, who did not remarry after they divorced, until he died. She was one of seven children who were all 'no trouble' and who she now describes as 'very close'. Both her children are married and her daughter has two children.

Given that she had offered to be interviewed about her experience of family change it is not altogether surprising that her account focuses on her adult life and in particular her two marriages. Unlike others interviewed she uses very little of her own, or even her children's, early history, as a source of reference. It seems as if her childhood years are an experience apart. There are perhaps no debts owing, there is no unfinished business to tidy up. In contrast, the deaths of her two husbands raised issues for her which, characteristically it seems, she managed to resolve with what she describes as appropriate ritual and behaviour.

Her first husband died as she was about to go on holiday to Canada. They'd kept in touch since their divorce, occasionally having a drink and dancing together at British Legion (an organisation of former members of the armed forces) nights. He never remarried though he did have 'a lady friend' in his last couple of years. Hearing that he'd had a heart attack she visited him in the local hospital with their son. She says he was pleased to see her and held her hand because, 'I think when you're very ill...to me you know all these bad times go out...and you know you think of all the good times then.... I could imagine how he was feeling...'. A night or so later she went back to see him and he 'was back to his old self', full of accusations about the hospital and his new partner. His behaviour helped her to complete the break, 'I said, Well I was off'. He died two weeks later while she was away. As she describes it she had managed to say goodbye to both the versions of the man she had been married to. In telling the story she then moves on quickly to a description of her second husband's looks and English accent.

She describes *his* death in some detail, again the impression is given that she managed what was an unexpected event blamelessly. She was reassured by the doctors that she had done all that was possible, saying, in a revealing slip of the tongue, 'it was just the one consolation I've got'. Her search for a balanced and fair outcome was achieved in the arrangements she made for his burial:

And actually I had him put in with his first wife, because we used to – you know, go and put some flowers up the crematorium. And he'd got a lovely picture of her. And he'd got, you know 'till we meet again' on it. And I think deep down that was really where he always wanted to be. Although as I said, we did have a very, very good relationship. And, so and I just had him put there with her.

Paula Loudon's account is of course unique but the careful description of the two deaths and of her manner of dealing with these is not so untypical. She appears anxious to give a good impression to her hearer and to portray herself as someone whose life is well managed, in which right decisions prevail. Again, this is not surprising, however it does suggest that a life history may need to be listened to, and analysed, in the light of an understanding of the life stage. Do we need to take into consideration that the story of her first husband's death might have been told differently in the period immediately afterwards, or during the lifetime of her second husband? In telling her story to a stranger was she indulging in moral self-justification? We may not know the answer to these questions but what is evident, if we compare her account with that of others at the same life stage, is an emphasis on integrity, resolution and a settling of accounts.

Conclusion

We have identified three themes: personal morality versus public discourse, narrative coherence and integrity in the narratives of people interviewed in relation to research into stepfamilies and older people. In doing this our aim has been to highlight the ways in which recourse to episodes in a life history may be used by older interviewees to make sense of their own lives, their childrens and the times they are living through. These were experiences which many older people interviewed associated with shame and personal failure, in their different roles as married partners and as parents. At the time we were interviewing family life, and divorce in particular, were subjects for daily media speculation and opinion shaping. Many of the narratives illustrate the ways in which older people were finding ways to account for their personal feelings and experience of family change in relation to these public debates.

Awareness of the ways in which the language of narratives combine personal moralities and public discourse highlights the active integration of broader social change with more private and personal preferences and moralities. The disruption of family change may challenge an individual's concept of self and the meanings attributed to core relationships. The maintenance of narrative coherence helps to sustain those meanings.

Finally, we considered the ways in which the life histories which older people narrate may also play a part in organising meaning about the end of life itself, with accounts of endings being managed without threat to their own integrity or others who have been significant to them.

Eliciting life histories is a key method in researching family change. However, to be useful as research data, these biographies need to be heard and understood as the product of context and as accounts to be viewed from a number of perspectives. These include their recognition as a profoundly social act linking personal meanings to broader social change as well as their role in providing insight into the active individual management of those personal meanings in late life. In all they remain an unquestionably rich source of evidence about family life over the generations.

Notes

1   Ken Gardener, aged sixty-seven, separated from his wife and children who are Jehovah's Witnesses.

2   Molly Lowe, born 1927, parents split up when she was sixteen, mother subsequently remarried in late life for financial reasons; eight children, one divorced, one widowed. Lives with her husband in sheltered accommodation.

3   The project was one of seventeen funded by the Economic and Social Research Council under the programme 'Population and Household Change'. A more detailed description of the project and its research methods appears in Bornat *et al.* 'Stepfamilies and Older People: Evaluating the Implications of Family Change for an Ageing Population', *Ageing and Society*, 1999.

4   Luton is an industrial town in South East England. In the nineteenth century the principal industry, straw hat making, was dependent on a predominantly female labour force. From the 1920s and particularly in the postwar years it experienced a rapid growth in population as the new industries of the motor trade drew in large numbers of male workers and their families from all over the British Isles and New Commonwealth countries. It has been subjected to some considerable sociological study, principally in relation to the thesis of embourgeoisement of the working class in *The Affluent Worker* (Goldthorpe *et al.* 1969) and subsequent volumes.

5   A more detailed account of the research methods is included in Bornat *et al.* (1996).

6   A similar variability is also, of course, a characteristic of the interviewer. Thanks to Tom Wengraf for this reminder.

7   Richard Lathwaite aged seventy-four. Married twice, both wives died. Second wife divorced with children. He has one child from his first marriage and three stepchildren, nine step-grandchildren and two grandchildren.

8   Alice Lumb, aged fifty; pregnant and married at twenty-one but left her husband after two weeks; she divorced her second husband while he was in

prison for fraud. She has a daughter and a son from each partner. She lives
with her current partner but won't remarry.
9   Mr Patel aged seventy-five has lived in Britain since he was a young man. His
first wife was English. He married her in 1943. She died and their son was
adopted by her parents. He is divorced from his second wife but still sees her
and his children. He lost his sight five years before and lives in sheltered
accommodation.

References

Baruch, G. (1981) 'Moral Tales: Parents' Stories of Encounters with the Health
Professionals', *Sociology of Health and Illness* 3 (3): 275–95.
Batchelor, J., Dimmock, B. and Smith, D. (1994) *Understanding Stepfamilies: What
Can be Learned from Callers to the Stepfamily Telephone Counselling Service*,
London: Stepfamily.
Biggs, S. (1998) 'Mature Imaginations: Ageing and the Psychodynamic Tradition',
Ageing and Society 18 (4): 421–39.
Bohman, S. (1986) *The People's Story: On the Collection and Analysis of Auto-
biographical Materials*, Methodological Questions, no. 3, Stockholm: Nordiska
Museet.
Borland, K. (1991) '"That's Not What I Said": Interpretive Conflict in Oral
Narrative Research', in S.B. Gluck and D. Patai (eds), *Women's Words: The
Feminist Practice of Oral History*, London: Routledge, pp.63–75.
Bornat, J. (1993) 'Presenting', in P. Shakespeare, D. Atkinson and S. French
(eds), *Reflecting on Research Practice*, Buckingham: Open University Press,
pp.83–94.
—— (1994) 'Is Oral History Auto/Biography?', *Auto/Biography* 3 (1–2): 18–30.
Bornat, J., Dimmock, B., Jones, D. and Peace, S. (1996) 'Finding People to Interview: a Study of the Impact of Family Change on Older People', Paper
presented at the Fourth International Conference on Social Science Methodology, University of Essex.
—— (1999) 'The Impact of Family Change on Older People: the Case of Stepfamilies', *Ageing and Society* 19 (2).
Burgoyne, J. and Clark, D. (1984) *Making a Go of It: a Study of Stepfamilies in
Sheffield*, London: Routledge and Kegan Paul.
Carricaburu, D. and Pierret, J. (1995) 'From Biographical Disruption to Biograph-
ical Reinforcement: the Case of HIV-positive Men', *Sociology of Health and
Illness* 17 (1): 65–88.
Chamberlayne, P. and King, A. (1997) 'The Biographical Challenge of Caring',
Sociology of Health and Illness 19 (5): 601–21.
Coleman, P.G., Ivani-Chalian, C. and Robinson, M. (1993) 'Self-esteem and Its
Sources: Stability and Change in Later Life', *Ageing and Society* 13 (2):
171–92.
Echevarria-Howe, L. (1995) 'Reflections from the Participants: the Process and
Product of Life History Work', *Oral History* 23 (2): 40–6.

Erikson, E.H., Erikson, J.M. and Kivnick, H.Q. (1986) *Vital Involvement in Old Age: the Experience of Old Age in Our Time*, New York: Norton.

Gergen, K.J. and Gergen, M. (1987) 'The Self in Temporal Perspective', in R.P. Abeles (ed.), *Life Span Perspectives and Social Psychology*, New Jersey: Lawrence Erlbaum Associates.

Giddens, A. (1991) *Modernity and Self Identity*, Cambridge: Polity Press.

Goldthorpe, J.H., Lockwood, D., Bechhofer, F. and Platt, J. (1968) *The Affluent Worker: Industrial Attitudes and Behaviour*, Cambridge: Cambridge University Press.

Gorrell Barnes, G., Thompson, P., Daniel, G. and Burchardt, N. (1998) *Growing Up in Stepfamilies*, Oxford: Oxford University Press.

Grele, R. (1991) *Envelopes of Sound: the Art of Oral History*, 2nd edn, New York: Praeger.

Gubrium, J.F. and Holstein, J.A. (1995) 'Qualitative Inquiry and the Deprivatization of Experience', *Qualitative Inquiry* 1 (2): 204–22.

Haskey, J. (1996) 'The Proportion of Married Couples who Divorce: Past Patterns and Present Prospects', *Population Trends* 83: 28–36.

HMSO (1994) *National Population Projections*, Monitor PP2 96/1, London: HMSO.

Jacques, E. (1965) 'Death and the Mid-Life Crisis', *International Journal of Psychoanalysis* 46: 502–14.

Jones, D.W. (1998) 'Distressing Histories and Unhappy Interviewing', *Oral History* 26 (2): 49–56.

Levinson, D.J., Darrow, D.N., Klein, E.B., Levinson, M.H. and McKee, B. (1978) *The Seasons of a Man's Life*, New York: A.A. Knopf.

Okely, A. (1992) 'Anthropology and Autobiography: Participatory Experience and Embodied Knowledge', in J. Okely and H. Calloway (eds), *Anthropology and Autobiography*, London: Routledge.

Plummer, K. (1995) *Telling Sexual Stories: Power, Change and Social Worlds*, London: Routledge.

Portelli, A. (1991) *The Death of Luigi Trastulli and Other Stories: Form and Meaning in Oral History*, Albany, NY: SUNY Press.

Rickard, W. (1998) 'Oral History – "More Dangerous than Therapy?": Interviewees' Reflections on Recording Traumatic or Taboo Issues', *Oral History* 26 (2): 34–48.

Rodgers, B. and Pryor, J. (1998) 'Divorce and Separation: the Outcomes for Children', *Foundations*, York: Joseph Rowntree Foundation, June.

Rosenthal, G. (1993) 'Reconstruction of Life Stories: Principles of Selection in Generating Stories for Narrative Biographical Interviews', in R. Josselson and A. Lieblich (eds), *The Narrative Study of Lives*, London: Sage.

Schütze, F. (1992) 'Pressure and Guilt: War Experiences of a Young German Soldier and their Biographical Implications, Part 1', *International Sociology* 7 (2): 187–208.

Stacey, J. (1990) *Brave New Families: Stories of Domestic Upheaval in Late 20th Century America*, New York: Basic Books.

Sugarman L. (1986) *Life-Span Development: Concepts, Theories and Interventions*, London: Methuen.

14 Biography and identity

Life story work in transitions of care for people with profound learning difficulties

David Middleton and Helen Hewitt

Introduction

This chapter examines the use of biographical accounts in the lives of people with profound learning difficulties. There have been rapid changes over the past twenty years in the provision of care in Britain with the movement of people from long-term care in hospital to community-based living. The 1981 'Care in the Community' (DHSS 1981) played a large part in bringing about this change which also resulted in an eventual shift in control from health to local authority. Between 1980 and 1986 there was a large increase in the number of people with learning difficulties who were relocated from hospital to the community (Booth *et al.* 1989). Much of the research examining the impact of these changes has focused on people who are more able and can communicate their needs. However, people with profound learning difficulties are not able to represent in any direct way their own understanding of their life and their position within the care settings in which they live. We examine the way biographical accounts in the form of life story work can be used to establish continuities in the experience of people with profound learning difficulties when they are moved from hospital to community-based care. Our concern is the way that carers attend to issues of identity in their relationships with people who are unable to speak on their own behalf. We discuss how the construction of life story books contributes to the way identities are accomplished and made visible as social acts of remembering. We are interested in how social practices of remembering provide continuities of identities across changes in the provision of care from a hospital to a community base. We discuss how these identities are realised in terms of continuities of participation in the social practices that make up the conditions of living of the people who are the recipients of care and the working practices of those who provide it.

The move from hospital to community-based care raised concerns in the setting studied concerning continuities in understanding the lives of the people who were to experience such a change. For a variety of practical, financial and organisational reasons, not all the staff who were in regular contact with people with profound learning difficulties in the particular hospital setting we studied were to move their work into the community-based setting. None of the people who were users of care services could provide accounts on their own behalf about their family histories and experiences in their lives. Given that new staff were to be appointed for the community setting, this raised concerns over maintaining the depth of knowledge and understanding of service users that had been generated through long-term care relationships in hospital. The introduction of life story work was established as one way in which continuities concerning individualities in the details of their lives could be communicated as people moved into new care settings. Life story work focuses on providing biographical accounts of lived experience which can be used for this purpose.

The research focused on a major change in the provision of care for a small group of adults with profound learning difficulties (six in all over a three year period). None of these people could communicate verbally. We adopted a research strategy that provided a practical basis for being in the setting. This involved working in the setting but with an explicit brief concerned with the production of an experimental resource which it was hoped would support their transition from hospital to community-based care. Producing the biographical material for the life story books included interviewing surviving relatives and parents, nursing staff and key workers. The aim was to make available through the medium of life story books experiences of living that would not normally be part of any care plans. Access was also gained to staff meetings. These were recorded, and included meetings both before and after the transition from hospital to community-based care. All this material was transcribed and used to construct short accounts of early life; family members' experiences of home life before long-term care; transitions in care; experiences in the different provisions of long-term hospital care; changes in key workers; holidays, etc. When available, photographs were integrated into the text. Finally, additions to the life story books themselves by staff members and other people visiting the community-care setting provided further material concerning the changes in care experienced by these people.

Two forms of social remembering

Nursing-care plans

In any care setting there are numerous ways of maintaining continuities of practice. These range from informal passing on of relevant information and background on current issues and practices (see Middleton 1996), to those which address the problem of maintaining continuities of practice. For example, in this particular setting there existed a standardised method of recording and passing on the regime of care currently relevant to each resident of the hospital. These care plans were the primary source of documentation about service users (apart from medical notes). They provided information on how to 'care' for the individual person from a nursing perspective. Care plans provide information under the following categories: breathing, eating and drinking, sleeping, and personal hygiene.

The evaluation of the care plans was continuous. They were consulted on a daily basis and amended regularly. The care plans were function-oriented and focused on the here-and-now. Old action plans were removed and current ones retained. This meant that knowledge about the person's past was never available in the care plan. This oriented carers to view the person in the present. Knowledge about the person's past remained in the domain of verbal accounts only. This was problematic when carers were relatively new to the setting and no 'informants' were available to fill in details concerning the past lives and experiences of those they cared for.

In the context of a major change of care practice, these plans were not, however, an effective resource for continuity. They were not open to negotiation. They were passed on in a prescriptive format providing information about the procedures to be undertaken in the routine care of the person to whom they refer. This, of course, is their function – they were designed to inform care workers about how to look after the individual concerned. This information about the person is split into separate categories of a person's physical needs. This does not provide any real means of specifying individual differences and experiences. In theory then, it may be possible that two people could have an almost identical care plan (if, for example, they both have the same type of cerebral palsy). The construction of life story books aimed at providing a medium for representing varieties of individual experience concerning people who were to undertake this transition from hospital to community-based care.

Life story work

As we have already indicated, life story books are based on records of lived experience. There is no fixed format for such books. They can range from a scrap book to a fully electronic document stored on computer (Atwell 1993). Although many people have documented their own, and their children's lives, in the form of photograph albums and videos, life story books are a relatively new concept in institutional settings.

The use of life story books has been developed in a range of service settings in the UK. In particular they have been used to aid the transition of children who were experiencing the process of adoption (Ryan and Walker 1985). Such life story books are presented as enabling children to come to terms with their past in order to move on into the future. In addition to such claimed practical benefits, life story books are proposed as a useful research technique for practitioners within social work. For example, Harold *et al.* (1995) describe the use of open-ended story-telling in practice-based research. They applied this 'technique' to adoption practice and chemical dependency settings.

In work with older people living in institutional settings, the relevance of a life story approach to care planning and the contribution of life story books is well attested (Adams *et al.* 1998). Indeed nurses working with particularly vulnerable groups such as people with dementia have sought to develop approaches which seek to combine biographical details with clinical data (Jones and Miesen 1992; O'Donovan 1993). In doing so they are drawing attention to the importance of what Kitwood identifies as 'personhood': 'a standing or status that is bestowed upon one human being, by others, in the context of relationship and social being' (Kitwood 1997: 8).

One of the functions of life story books, according to Ryan and Walker (1985), is to provide a way of bringing together the past, the present and the future. They suggest that this enables the person to develop a better sense of who they are. If they know where they have come from, and can come to terms with things that have happened to them, then they can move on to the future. Cheston (1994) discusses life story work with people with learning disabilities arguing that a life story book 'provides an identity-enhancing account of their life' (Cheston 1994: 67). This is in contrast to the function-orientation of the nursing-care plans, described earlier, where an acknowledgement of a person's 'past' is not evident.

Although life story work has a wide application, work with people with learning disabilities is only beginning to develop its own literature (Atkinson 1997). Atwell (1993) acknowledges that practitioners within general social work settings are often reluctant to carry out life story work with people with learning disabilities. She identifies numerous reasons why life story work is not more widespread with this group of service users. The most significant reason is that life story work would appear to serve no practical purpose if the person is not in the position to understand its contents and significance. However, the focus of this research demonstrates how analysis of the talk of those who care for or who work closely with people with profound learning disabilities provides evidence of a biographical content and focus which could form the basis of individually sensitive care planning.

The social practice of remembering in life story work

We can examine the production and use of life story books as a social practice of remembering in two ways. First, it involves making the past a topic of concern. In the gathering and compilation of material, the social use of the past is the issue. The argument here is that representation of past examples of participation in life events in a life story format provides continuities of that participation across time and place. It is also a form of remembering in social practice that creates continuities in what it is to be a person who participates in particular ways across similar but different settings separated in time and space (see Middleton and Edwards 1990 and Middleton 1997 for further discussions of the social organisation of remembering).

However, we can also examine life story work as the social use of memory in a second way. Not only is the past made a topic of concern but what it is to remember is also made an explicit issue in the formulation and use of life story work. What it is to possess the past, what it is to have memories as a property of the conduct of a person's participation also features in social practices of remembering. As we shall see this is more than simply a projection of the carer's interpretation of what the person with learning disabilities has experienced.

Making visible individualities of participation

The following sequence is a transcription of a conversation with a father who describes the participation of his son in two separate incidents in his life before he came into full-time hospital care. Reference is made to remembering as part of making available to another accounts of experiences and participation in events from the past. Sequence 1 is part of an interview with a father concerning the early life of his now adult son. In this episode the past is at issue. The interviewer uses the notion of having memories as a means of accomplishing the interactional work of the interview. Memory as an issue is then taken up by the father in repre-senting continuities in the form of his son's participation across events separated in time and place. The father does more than interpret or project meaning on to the actions of his son, Lance. He formulates his son's agency in participating in the events he describes. Lance's participa-tory conduct is used to argue for his having a memory. However, what it is to have memory does not prescribe Lance's actions, it is the reasonable conclusion about the conduct of his actions. Sequence 2 is the reformula-tion of this account in the life story book for his son.

Sequence 1: The social use of memory[1]

(F: Father; I: Interviewer)

F: (....) (2) *this is basically it* (1) all I can literally *add* to it (1) or say (1) there's not much I know but (1)

I: oh no I'm sure there's a lot more rea::lly I mean (.) there's special memories that you've got of sort of (1) of isolated events that (.) you know (.) I mean I'm sure you must have a lot of photographs haven't you?

F: oh yes if you want photographs but uh (1) he was a (1) wheelchair case (or should I say pramulator) and (.) most of the time he sat in his chair (1) one of those chairs like that and he became quite (paral-ysed) but he has a memory (1) that's one thing that I would tell you (1) and the reason that I know this is becau:se in Australia (.) he used to have a chair that used to (stand) (1) and have these springs that went across (1) and he used to put his hand on one of these things and twang them (1) and of course with it being on a wooden floor (.) because there they have wooden floors (—) it was just like a double bass

I: {laughing} like a digeree-doo

F: and he used to love this (1) you know (1) he'd *really* get excited by it (1) well (3) we took him away (2) and it must have been *ten years later* that we bought a chair that was similar to that (—) and *do you know* the first thing he did his hand went straight underneath[

I: [and twanged it[

F: [*ten years later* (1) so *he's* got a memory (1) now if he thinks about that what other memories has he got about other (—) so:: (2) he wasn't a cabbage (1) there was something in there {points to head} that was (1) functioning somewhere (.) although he couldn't *express* it (1) it was there (.) but he uh (1) we were amazed he just sat in this chair (.) we sat him in this chair never never (thought of) and the first thing he did his hand went straight under (2) well he tried to do it (.) he didn't quite make it but that's what he wanted to do because he used to like (—) and that was *ten years* earlier (1) he was quite grown up then (1) so honestly he thought about this *noise* (.) or music or whatever and he wanted to do it again (1) and he knew how to make that (.) that sound so he could put pieces together to make something which was functional to to himself (3).

The point we wish to emphasise here is that what it is to have a memory is at issue in both this sequence of talk and its reformulation in the life story book (see Sequence 2 below). However, the social and rhetorical use of what a memory entails in both accounts is an outcome presented as evidence for the agency of Lance's participation. It is not presented as the psychological input that drives Lance's actions but as the reasonable conclusion concerning his participation in the events described. Lance's individuality, his personhood, is therefore made available to us as is that of his parents as people for whom such participation is a matter of concern.

Lance's twanging the springs of his chair is presented in terms of the agency of his conduct. We are presented with what he used to do ('he used to put his hand on one of these things and twang them') accounted for in terms of his preference and excitement in the conduct of his action ('he used to love this'; 'he'd really get excited by it'). This mundane feature of everyday living is worked up as a salient feature of Lance's experience. It is this that then provides the rhetorical force in the father's claim concerning Lance's participation in events some ten years later.

The crafting of this account in terms of what he did ten years later under equivalent circumstances – 'the first thing he did his hand went straight underneath' – makes available the plausible conclusion that he participated in this new setting in ways that marked the individuality of how he had participated previously. Goal, intention and mind are signalled in the description of his actions. Indeed, the interviewer completes the verbal description of the action ('and twanged it'). This then provides for the reasonable conclusion concerning the status of Lance's unexpressed mentality – 'that there was something in there that was functioning somewhere (.) although he couldn't express it'.

Interestingly, the interactively realised conclusion concerning the exact nature of his participation is subsequently modified. The shared sense of being 'amazed' is warranted in terms of this experience as being collectively shared by both Lance's father and mother – 'we were amazed he sat in this chair (.) we sat him in this chair'. Lance's actions are not reported as achieving exactly the same outcome of twanging the springs.

It was his action, his agency in participation: 'the first thing he did his hand went straight under (2) well he tried to do it (.) he didn't quite make it but that's what he wanted to do because he used to like (—) and that was ten years earlier'. Again it is what Lance's actions demonstrate in terms of the sort of conclusions that can be drawn about his mentality, what he thought of the noise, or the sound as someone who would recognise such noise as music, as something constructed out of the conduct of action in equivalent circumstances.

So the biography of the past matters to Lance's carers, not in terms of what Lance did or did not achieve as a result of his putative intentions, but in terms of what can be reported about the individuality of his conduct and the sorts of participation this entails in the future. Lance's identity as a person does not rest on whether he did or did not do these things (or whether he actually intended to do them). In the social practice of taking meaning from the reports of his actions, Lance is presented as being at the centre of those actions, as participating. The interactive organisation of this sequence makes available plausible conclusions concerning his participation.

Reformulating the conduct of participation in the life story account

Sequence 2: Life story book entry

Lance's chair

When Lance lived in Australia he had his own chair. It was an armchair that had springs that went across the bottom. Lance used to like twanging these springs and hear the noise they made. His dad described it as a noise like a double bass. He used to sit on the veranda and get very excited by the noise he was producing.

Ten years later, when he was back in England, his mum and dad bought a similar chair. The first thing Lance did was to put his hand underneath and feel for the springs. His dad suggests that he made the connection between the chair he had in Australia and the new one. This indicated to his mum and dad that he had memories.

The status of his participation is reformulated in the life story book entry. It is the framework of participation that is made the topic of concern in this reformulation. Agency in actions is used to establish the account as one where the conduct of participation is one that matters ('the first thing that Lance did was to put his hand underneath and feel for the springs'). As in the father's original account of these events it is not the possible contents of Lance's memory that are at issue but the plausible conclusions concerning the status of connections Lance may have made across the different places of participation. To understand the story as indicating possible continuities of agency in participation over time and place is to read the account as one that formulates Lance in terms of his individuality in such settings (what Dreier 1997, aptly terms 'trajectories of participation'). What is more, we also have demonstrated the forms of action that others might find it relevant to engage in in relation to Lance's conduct. The social practice of remembering makes the past matter. In both the rhetorical organisation of the father's talk and in the reformulation of his account in the life story book, memory is the logical outcome of the way that the past is made accountable.

The social practice of remembering in carer-service user interaction

We also examined the ways in which biographical material in the life story books was used. The life story books were added to and incorporated into care practice alongside the routine use of the care plans described above. This use has been the subject of separate analysis (Hewitt 1997). The life story books were also the subject of discussion in staff meetings. They provided a site for further social remembering where past events were renarrated for both the service user and members of the staff. For example, consider Sequence 3. In this sequence the life story book is reported as drawing upon carer-service user interaction. In other words, remembering as a social practice becomes an explicit part of the interactive accomplishment of care.

Sequence 3: Interacting using life story book

JACKIE: Lance liked it [
NICKY: [did he {laughing} [
JACKIE: [mm (.) he was laughing kissing (.)
          chu tuber {one of Lance's words}
HELEN: oh did you read it to him then Jackie
JACKIE: OH YEA (.) I READ IT TO HIM (.) especially the holiday bits
          he liked that:

The reading of the life story book is reported as framing the social practice of care. Lance as a person who laughs and makes sounds that are understood to indicate enjoyment ('chu tuber') is interactively accomplished in that reporting. Again it is his participation that marks his identity in these practices. The life story book calls upon a form of participation that displays Lance in one way rather than another. It is this that is marked as newsworthy at a subsequent staff meeting where these recordings were made. We do not have mere reporting that he has been happy this week. Rather, Lance is reported as displaying happiness in his participation in reading the life story book. His participation is also worked up in terms of the preferences he displayed with respect to the holiday material – 'especially the holiday bits'. The life story books are reported as being incorporated into the social practices of care. The news worthiness of doing this as a social practice is also reported in terms of his feelings and preferences. His identity is once again warranted and displayed in terms of his participatory conduct in the circumstances of engaging with others in relation to his life story book. By the same token, this carer who accompanied Lance on holiday with his father displays her position in these practices as one displaying sensitivity to Lance's individuality in terms of his participation.

Social practice of remembering in staff interactions

The life story books also provide a resource in the narration of staff experiences.

Sequence 4: Renarrating shared staff experiences

(Continuation of Sequence 3.)

JACKIE: is that the one where he's sitting with dad on the settee [
NICKY: [mm [
JACKIE: [well
    that's a typical: (.) night for Lance on holiday because its pretty late
    when we get back °in't it° {looks at Mary} but that is a typical night
    for Lance on holiday on the settee with dad and (.) happy both of
    them drop off and snore {laughs} [(1.8) you can't hear a word can you
    Mary {still laughing}
MARY: [mm {smiling}
JACKIE: you just sit there chu chu chu {laughs} [
MARY: [°we've got that on video°
                                                 [{laughs}
JACKIE: [we have we (got) said get
    that on video get Harry snoring on that video and then show him (1)

he thought you'd got something wrong with the video when you played it back didn't he?

The typicality of the night with both Lance and his father falling asleep on the settee is formulated in the book in terms of the conduct of participation in social practices of taking a holiday with them. However the discussion soon goes beyond what is directly depicted in the photographs of two people asleep on the settee. Their joint personhood as father and son is also reported as being the subject of a video. Again these retellings are framed in terms of the conduct of participation and the elaborated significances for the staff's history of experience with Lance and his father.

Social practice of remembering in defining new modes of care practice

In the transition into the care setting, discussion of the life story books also provided a basis for defining new modes of participation as professionals. Sequence 5 illustrates this. Carers discuss how they might use photographs of *their* lives to establish their identities as people who have lives beyond the care setting.

Sequence 5: The social use of remembering in redefining carers'
identities

RYAN: °I I (.) sorry (.) I was (just going) to say something° is (.) it's like when you get when you get get to know people and form relationships with people ya talking a lot of interchange of information about your background your experiences and all this sort of stuff {agreement} which is something that's difficult for us to do (.) most most of the time but its a way of getting around it isn't it it's sort of you know for us to share (.) close things I mean perhaps (1) I'm expressing my own view I don't know
        °I suppose we can talk to them about (our families)°[
NICKY: [mm
ANNA: [it's something
we really need to build on don't we and not just let them lie in the cupboard and (get) dusty
        {agreement}
RYAN: I think (.) yea I agree with that I mean (.)[
NICKY: [that would be an interesting activity to(day) to *say*: (.) you know for the next three Saturdays or the next three Fridays could everybody bring in photos

of their relatives and their holidays and show the clients (2) shall we leave that [then

ANNA: [we could have a (?) couldn't you know like having a theme party like have a photo party
                {laughs}

NICKY: for the next three Fridays then (.) shall we say that or shall we book a party

ANNA: well I must admit one of the best parties I've ever been to was like a photo party when you had to sit down and guess who (.) whose photos were whose and like everybody gets involved an gets in a look in and (.) having a good giggle {laughter} and it would be nice for the clients to be involved in something like that

The life story books are presented as 'a way of getting around' the difficulties of achieving the sort of routine 'interchange of information about your background experiences' that forms the basis of 'relationships with people'. Nicky then proposes that, in addition to using life story books, they could enhance their interaction with service users in terms of the carers' own lives, their relatives and their holidays. However this proposal is made in an interesting manner. It is not that staff might individually bring in photographs from home but that service users should become involved in the collective activity of staff discussions about their lives beyond the care setting. The issue is not whether this was realised in practice. The issue is that in discussing the impact of life story on their interaction with service users they configure it in terms of future modes or 'trajectories' of participation (Dreier 1997). Identities are once again formulated in terms of future forms of participation in social practices engendered in social remembering.

Concluding remarks

A defining feature of good quality long-term care relationships in settings of the type researched here is the way carers are able to provide detailed accounts concerning the way people with profound learning difficulties display and accomplish empathy, awareness of others and place, individual preferences and reciprocity. Bogdan and Taylor (1987, 1989) argue that such attributions are a crucial resource in the development of caring relationships based in forms of acceptance over time. They seek to provide a sociology of acceptance, explaining how people with disabilities come to be accepted by non-disabled individuals in socially organised settings of care and not identified as either 'clinical or "horror objects"' of care (Goode 1984: 231). We were interested in examining in more detail how issues of identity were engaged in by people who enter into long-term care relationships and the way identities were accomplished as part of the social practices of remembering. For example, in Sequence 1 we can see that both the father's account and its reformulation in the life story book display make apparent the sort of participatory frameworks that were of relevance to Lance's parents. These are people who note the nuances of Lance's actions: actions that would go unnoticed by those not oriented to the conduct of Lance's participation in such settings. Lance's and his parents' individualities as participants in the socially ordered conduct of that setting are interdependent. In Lance's father's reporting such incidents, he constructs his and his wife's interest and facets of their identities as carers. He makes available their stake that Lance should possess agency. Acceptance can be understood in these terms: not as some sociological category into which the parent's actions fall, but in terms of their actions as forms of participation in, and commitment to, the relevance of Lance's actions.

Life story work involves communication that makes visible individualities of participation in social practices resulting in what can count as lives. We discussed the development and use of life story work as a social practice of remembering that supported continuities of individuality in the lives of people with severe learning difficulties. Of particular analytic concern was the social use of memory in formulating the past in terms of agency in action. This was examined in the way carers make relevant issues in the lives of people who are unable to speak on their own behalf both in terms of making the past a topic of concern and what it is to possess memories of past experience. This socially accomplished remembering is also realised in terms of interdependencies between the personhood of both the recipients of care and carers themselves. We argued that such interdependencies provide a crucial resource in constituting and enabling acceptance of people with severe learning difficulties as agents in the social conduct of their lives in interactions with others. Finally, we examined how the uptake and use of life story books across the changes in care provides for forms of social practice in the care setting that are directly concerned with the social use of remembering.

Such analysis examines how what it is to be a relative, a carer, a service user, a friend, a resident, is something that can be established in the social practices of remembering engendered in the biographical material of life story work. Life story work provides for continuities of participatory identities across changes in place and time. Biographies are made to matter in life story work.

Acknowledgements

An earlier version of this work was presented at the symposium on 'The Constitution of Identity Within Social Practices: Memory and Change' at the 4th Congress of the International Society for Cultural Research and Activity Theory, Aarhus, Denmark, June 1998. Our thanks to Michael Bamberg and Allyssa McGabe, Joanna Bornat and Prue Chamberlayne for their constructive suggestions. We are also most grateful for the co-operation of all the people who participated in making this study possible. It is not possible to name them individually. However, their willingness to share their experiences of care in the production, use and research into life story work is gratefully acknowledged. This research was funded with a Loughborough University Postgraduate Scholarship.

Notes

1   Transcription conventions

°distinctly quieter than surrounding talk°

UPPERCASE: distinctly louder than surrounding talk

(.) short pause in talk < 0.5 seconds

(sounds like – guess)

. a stop with a fall in tone

emphasised

{explanatory notes}

(....) talk omitted

interruption [or spoken in unison

[or spoken in unison

(3)pause in seconds

? rising inflection

: stre:tched preceding so:und or letter

n cut off prior word or sound

(—) indecipherable

References

Adams, J., Bornat, J. and Prickett, M. (1998) '"You Wouldn't be Interested in My Life, I've Done Nothing": Care Planning and Life History Work with Frail Older Women', in J. Phillips and B. Penhale (eds), *Reviewing Care Management for Older People*, London: Jessica Kingsley Publishers, pp.102–16.

Atkinson, D. (1997) *An Auto/Biographical Approach to Learning Disability Research*, Aldershot: Ashgate.

Atwell, A. (1993) 'Working with Children With a Learning Disability', in T. Ryan and R. Walker (eds), *Life Story Work*, London: British Association of Adoption and Fostering.

Bogdan, R. and Taylor, S.J. (1987) 'Toward a Sociology of Acceptance: The Other Side of the Study of Deviance', *Social Policy* 18: 34–9.

—— (1989) 'Relationships with Severely Disabled People: The Social Construction of Humanness', *Social Problems* 36: 135–48.

Booth, T., Simons, K. and Booth, W. (1989) 'Transition Shock and the Relocation of People Form Mental Handicap Hospitals and Hostels', *Social Policy and Administration* 23: 211–28.

Cheston, R. (1994) 'The Accounts of Special Education Leavers', *Disability and Society* 9: 59–69.

Department of Health and Social Security (1981) *Care in the Community*, London: HMSO.

Dreier, O. (1997) *Subjectivity and Social Practice*, Aarhus: Centre for Health, Humanity and Culture, Department of Philosophy, University of Aarhus.

Goode, D.A. (1984) 'Socially Produced Identities, Intimacy and the Problem of Competence Among the Retarded', in S. Tomlinson and L. Barton (eds), *Special Education and Social Interests*, London and Sydney: Croom Helm, pp.228–48.

Harold, R.D., Palmiter, M.L., Lynch, S.A. and Freedman-Doan, C.R. (1995) 'Life Stories: A Practice Based Research Technique', *Journal of Sociology and Social Welfare* 22: 23–43.

Hewitt, H.L. (1997) 'Identities in Transition: Formulating Care for People with Profound Learning Difficulties', University of Loughborough, Unpublished Ph.D. thesis.

Jones, G. and Miesen, B. (eds) (1992) *Care-giving in Dementia: Research and Applications*, London: Tavistock.

Kitwood, T. (1997) *Dementia Considered: The Person Comes First*, Buckingham: Open University Press.

Middleton, D. (1996) 'Talking Work: Argument, Common Knowledge and Improvisation in Multi-disciplinary Child Development Teams', in Y. Engeström and D. Middleton (eds), *Cognition and Communication at Work*, Cambridge: Cambridge University Press, pp.233–56.

—— (1997) 'The Social Organisation of Conversational Remembering: Experience as Individual and Collective Concerns', *Mind, Culture and Activity* 4 (2): 71–85.

Middleton, D. and Edwards, D. (eds) (1990) *Collective Remembering*, London: Sage Publications.

O'Donovan, S. (1993) 'The Memory Lingers On', *Elderly Care* 5 (1): 27–31.

Ryan, T. and Walker, R. (1985) *Making Life Story Books*, London: British Association of Adoption and Fostering.

15 Understanding the carers' world

A biographical-interpretive case study

Chris Jones and Susanna Rupp

Can narratives do more than confirm our existing preconceptions? We argue that the analysis of narratives provides data and insights crucial for policy makers and practitioners. The chapter shows how the biographical-interpretive method (Breckner 1998; Rosenthal 1995) enables us to identify structuring themes in people's lives which remain dominant despite external influences, such as the subject of the research topic and the specificity of the interviewee/interviewer situation, and despite the issue of researcher bias throughout the interpretive process. We aim here also to give a flavour of how biographical-interpretive analysis works by describing a small part of the process, the thematic field analysis. We believe that such emergent themes often contradict prior and sometimes stereotypical ideas relating to, in this case, carer perspectives and concerns.

Our empirical material comes from a case from the British Cultures of Care project.[1] This focused on carers and studied two groups, one living in North London and one in East London. Some twenty-four interviews were conducted.[2] Carers were asked to talk about their caring experiences, the development of their caring situation, and the support they received. Analysing carer interviews shows that the real needs of recipients of welfare services require policies that support practices which empower practitioners, by providing them with space, time and reflective skills to obtain clear insights into the real, rather than assumed, needs of their clients.

In this chapter we concentrate on the case study of Mrs Rajan. This case showed that biographical analysis revealed neglected events and experiences and highlighted structuring themes, enabling us to understand Mrs Rajan's life and strategies. In Mrs Rajan's case we discovered that her caring needs now relate to caring for a disabled young adult, whereas previously they had related to family and cultural transformation.

First, we take Mrs Rajan's interview as an example to consider the significance of some external influences affecting the interview situation. Her lived life is then described, to provide the background for an analysis of the three main themes that emerged from the interview. Material from the stages of thematic field[3] analysis and microanalysis[4] will be used. The inter-connectedness of the themes will be explained, followed by a description of the development of her case structure.

Interviews with carers

In the Cultures of Care project a standardised approach to interviewing was adopted. Carers were encouraged to speak about difficult experiences, about their feelings and the meaning caring had for them. A number of questions were also asked concerning the political consequences of the National Health Service and Community Care Act 1990. The interviews partly followed the rules of semistructured qualitative interviews. However, other parts of the interview adopted 'narrative interview' principles aiming to elicit narratives. In a manner similar to that adopted by ethnographers, the interviewee invites the interviewer into his/her specific presentation of his/her biography. In contrast to other qualitative interview techniques, it is the interviewees' frame of reference, their gestalt or system of relevancy, which structures narrative interviewing, not the interviewer's agenda.[5]

Looking at the initial narrative question, the interviewer's conflict between initiating a narrative interview and initiating a semistructured interview is clear. The interviewees were first asked to speak generally about their experiences but were then questioned more specifically about their concerns:

> We're interested in the experiences of people caring for a family member, so I would like you to tell me about your experiences. I'm interested in how you come to take on the responsibility of caring, whether difficult decisions and choices had to be made and how the situation has developed and what kind of support or help you had? Also which aspects of caring are the most difficult ones for you? Which offers of assistance were made but were rejected by you and how you feel about being a carer and what it has meant for your life?[6]

These initial questions addressed many of the issues theoretically linked to care issues. However, from a biographical perspective we can assume that there are other life-spheres that might dominate a carer's biographical reconstruction.

Most of the interviewees picked one of the questions for response or tried to follow the interviewer's framework. However, Mrs Rajan found it very difficult to describe her caring experiences and her son's disability. She only responded to the opening question(s) after a break of seven seconds and then addressed her little son: 'Just keep dead quiet'. There followed another pause of fourteen seconds and then she blew her nose. After another eight seconds the interviewer verbalised her concerns: 'Finding it difficult to know where to start?' Mrs Rajan answered 'Yes, dear me, where do you start, I don't know'. From then on the interviewer tried to prompt the interviewee with more direct questions about being a carer and about her son who has learning difficulties. Mrs Rajan's answers were brief, and only when asked about external issues, such as the social services, did she offer to talk about the support she receives.

The beginning of this interview could easily be explained by external factors, as there were social and cultural gaps between the German-Anglo university interviewer and the Asian-British carer who had received only minimal education. Equally the methodological critique that the opening question offered too many and contradictory stimuli could apply. But what conclusions can we draw from this? Perhaps we should avoid any cultural encounters in social research or only work with methodologically perfect material. We know, however, that most of the interviews happened under similar circumstances, nearly all the interviews were a cultural and class encounter, and the interview prompts were the same in all the interviews. Rosenthal (1993: 64–5) describes the social situation of the interview as a catalyst, not as a disturbance:

> Each interview is a product of the mutual interaction between speaker and.... In our view, trying to eliminate a 'problem' such as this amounts to a quixotic fight against imagined giants, giants that in the final analysis are revealed to be not even windmills but rather the 'winds' of the everyday world...this wind is in fact the ongoing interaction between the biographer and his or her social world.

We support this view and argue that Mrs Rajan's self-presentation is not only triggered by the cultural encounter and the methodologically ambivalent interview setting but also by the type of carer she represents. In her case, caring is dominated by other aspects of her social world. Her experiences as a carer are embedded within the field of cultural diversity, conflict and transition triggered by her marriage into a family which rejected the basic cultural standards of a religious Hindu family.

We continue with a description of Mrs Rajan's lived life before elaborating on the stage of thematic field analysis and the main themes which emerged from the interview.

Mrs Rajan's lived life: from restriction to openness[7]

Mrs Rajan was born in 1958 in Kenya the third of six sisters. They lived in an overly protective extended family, unable to leave the family home or play with other children. This strategy was adopted to keep the family secret (of the mother's epilepsy) and to prevent further problems (e.g. illegitimate mixed-race babies). In 1972 the family migrated to Britain and in 1976 Mrs Rajan moved from the Midlands to East London after an arranged marriage to an unskilled worker. The couple did not live with the husband's parents but as a nuclear family. She lost the close emotional and physical support of her family members but expected to be embraced by her husband's family. However, the majority of Mr Rajan's family did not welcome Mrs Rajan wholeheartedly. This was due to a break in relations between Mr Rajan and his elder brother, with whom his mother lived.

In 1978 Mrs Rajan gave birth to a girl, Bhavini, and eighteen months later a boy, Bhavesh, was born prematurely. At twenty months Bhavesh was diagnosed as having suffered a reaction to the whooping cough vaccination. He had asthma, diarrhoea and continual fits: he was kept in hospital for eight weeks and the prognosis was very poor. Mrs Rajan discharged Bhavesh against the doctor's advice and, after taking her mother's counsel, she nursed him back to health at home. Mrs Rajan treated Bhavesh as a 'mentally retarded' boy and used the family strategy of 'staying at home' to cope with this problem. The enclosed environment fostered a symbiotic mother–son relationship. During the next ten years Mr and Mrs Rajan lived in separate worlds. He represented the world outside, and she the world inside the family. He worked long hours and often came home late at night. His domain seemed to encompass correspondence and negotiations with external agencies, including welfare agencies.

In 1990, while Bhavesh was now becoming an adolescent difficult to contain within the home, Mrs Rajan gave birth to a healthy son. These two events threatened the continuity of the symbiotic relationship. Within her cultural traditions, with the birth of her new baby, Mrs Rajan had fulfilled one of her most important roles, to be the mother of a healthy male child (Woollett 1994). Her change of attitude and biographical turning point were graphically symbolised by the active rejection of her mother-in-law's interference. Mrs Rajan now accepted an approach towards caring for her children which encompassed professional care for Bhavesh. She also began working towards a professional career. Mr and Mrs Rajan have developed a more co-operative relationship where they negotiate life issues.

Thematic field analysis: emerging themes

The thematic field analysis stage allows the researchers to see how the narrated life story is ordered, temporally and thematically. The researchers are concerned with understanding the present perspective of the biographer and discovering which structuring principles of selection, which generative structures, are guiding the choice of stories narrated and the mode of expression. Rosenthal (1993: 62) notes that it is the 'overall biographical construct [that] determines the way in which the biographer reconstructs the past and makes decisions as to which individual experiences are relevant and included'. The interviewee does not just narrate a chronological account of items they think will interest the interviewer. When reconstructing their life history they are relating and connecting experiences and events they consider as relevant from their own idiosyncratic subjective perspective. During the interview, the interviewee will be unconsciously reinterpreting past events, actions and experiences as he/she decides what and how to present the past. This process may involve him/her in a transformational experience. Mrs Rajan's case shows a mother imprisoned in the home by alien cultural and family traditions. Her perceptions and attitudes are transformed when she gives birth to a healthy male child, an Indian accolade which results ironically in her becoming more integrated into British culture.

As described previously, and as the extract below illustrates, it was difficult for Mrs Rajan to respond to the initial question:

I: Would you like to tell me about what it's like being a carer?
R: Um, well it is difficult to look after him and er (break of six seconds), I don't know (break of five seconds).
I: If you'd like to tell me about your son, he has learning difficulties?
R: Yes he's mentally retarded so he needs more care (break of four seconds).

In the context of Mrs Rajan's biography it turns out to be not surprising that she feels unable to elaborate on her caring experiences as *caring is not the theme of her life*.[8] Moreover, given her (family's) strategy of secret-keeping, we can understand this hesitation in talking about experiences. Only when the interviewer asked Mrs Rajan for her experiences with the social services was she able to answer more fluently, as she could associate this theme with the time after her turning point: 'the thing is usually – since he [the younger son, who is present at the interview] came, that is four and a half years, he [the older son] has been going to respite care – before that we never had no help'.

Mrs Rajan created a safe discourse relating to the role of the social services and implicitly introduced her problem. The comment 'we never had no help' stresses the fact that there was not only no help from social services but, even more importantly, none from her husband's family.

We now present an example of thematic field analysis relating to this text. There are two parts to this stage of analysis. First, the principle of sequentiality (Rosenthal 1991) is applied to the text. The interview text is structured to show who is speaking, the interviewer or the interviewee, what sort of text is distinguishable (the main types being narrative, evaluation, argumentation and description), and what theme is dominating. The length of each piece of text is denoted on the left-hand side of the page showing the page number and line (e.g. 11/2 means, page eleven, line two). The next stage involves the principle of abduction (Lewin 1930: 31). The intention is to develop verified hypotheses, which lead to the generation of general rules around which the actions, perceptions and understandings of the interviewee are structured.

Below is a short extract, exemplifying this second form of analysis, from Mrs Rajan's thematic field analysis. The information relating to the text is in bold letters, the capital Roman numerals refer to the segment of the sequentialisation, 'report' characterises the text-sort, and the text is a summary of the theme in the interview. Each segment of text is analysed in isolation from all other knowledge of Mrs Rajan's life. Only when all possible hypotheses ('H' numbers below) have been put forward by the analysis group is the next text segment examined and the previous hypotheses confirmed or rejected or left open on the basis of the new datum. As hypothesising progresses, thematic field hypotheses (TF) are built up and numbered. In brackets are previous TF hypotheses which have associations with the text under analysis (e.g. TF9).

XXV   page 6/l.7   report   social worker's explanation: it goes to the mums who want to foster 'it doesn't matter about the dad'

(cf TF9: *an Indian mother always has a symbiotic relationship to her son – she needs a son to have a symbiotic relationship. cf TF5: my second son and I are an identity*)

H1   children are not educated by their parents: mother is responsible

H2   father is not important, as he doesn't look after the children/the disabled son.

TF14:   the world is divided in women's and men's tasks

H3   social worker's explanation addresses her as a woman/mother, not as a carer (cf TF2, TF6)

H3.1 social worker tries to work against Mrs R's mistrust

H4   'Mum' is children's language: social worker addresses her as a child

(cf TF2: *women can't be experts (feeling of inferiority, world is divided into men=experts, women=non-experts)*, cf TF6: *I'm the person to be cared for, nobody acknowledges my needs*)

H5   'Dad' refers not to her husband but to her own Dad

H5.1 my Dad was the problem (cf TF4)

H5.2 my Dad was not important

H5.3 although my Dad was the problem I grew up and became a wife/mother

H5.4 my Dad didn't help me

TF15: my father is the biggest problem I have – but I'm not allowed to speak about him

(cf TF4 *I have a much bigger problem than caring but have to be silent about it*).

When interpreting this part of the interview the research-analysis group focused on four sets of hypotheses:

A   Mrs Rajan refers to a gendered world where roles and the division of labour are clearly defined. The children's upbringing is part of the woman's role whereas negotiating with agencies and institutions is part of the man's task.

B   The relationship between Mrs Rajan and the social services is mediated by the personal relationship to the social worker. Meetings with the social worker give her space to reflect on her situation.

C   Her notion of the 'Dad's role' is connected to her own childhood experiences of abandonment and/or to the changing gender roles in the relationship with her husband.

D   The relationship between a mother and her children, particularly her son, is special. Her problem is that she shifted the symbiotic relationship from Bhavesh to the younger son and she feels guilty, a notion which refers also to her own feelings of abandonment.

This short example of the interpretation process gives a clear hint of the circular and interwoven character of the thematic field (see Figure 15.1 below). This field structured those parts of Mrs Rajan's interview which were related to her life before the turning point, when she gave birth to a healthy second son.

This thematic field consists of three parts, keeping the family secret, the assumption of a world riven with divisions, and the symbiotic mother–son relationship. They are interrelated, often obscuring each other. Her reality has been a world divided between men and women, between inside and outside the house, between experts and non-experts. This divided world has been interwoven with the obligation to keep the family secret thereby making it difficult for Mrs Rajan to speak easily about early experiences.

The symbiotic mother–son relationship is itself a product of the divided world. It represents an attempt to overcome this division through a maximum of closeness to the 'other'. Mrs Rajan's inability to speak about her experiences before the birth of her second son is not only grounded in the obligation to keep the family secret but also in the circular character of these parts of the thematic field. The overall thematic field is probably close to the structuring principles of her childhood experiences which have remained operational throughout most of her adult life so far. This explains why it is not easy for her to bring them into a narrative form. These elements refer to her life before her younger son was born.

The text relating to the birth of her youngest son shows that Mrs Rajan constructs his birth as a turning point: she is able to speak about

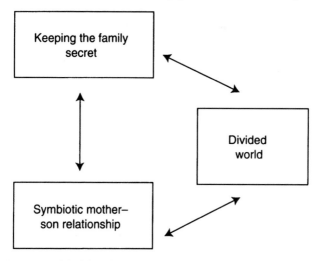

Figure 15.1 A model of the relationship between some of the themes revealed in Mrs Rajan's interview, prior to her turning point

her experiences after her younger son's birth and to bring these experiences into a narrative form. This is also exemplified later in the interview when she begins an expansive narrative that takes up about half the interview.

The overall theme: the family secret

As the description of Mrs Rajan's childhood showed, the 'divided world' thematic field was connected with the bigger problem of the 'family secret'. Her ambivalence in articulating her caring role during the interview can be understood in the context of her view that caring is not the problem, it is keeping the family secret that is the problem. As a child the stigma attached to her mother's epilepsy required her to be isolated from the wider community, and she dealt with her son's disability by the same strategy. Her understanding of 'tradition' was to care and be cared for within the family: you must not ask for support, and not look for support, outside family relationships. Mrs Rajan could not ask for help from the wider community and she felt unable to accept her husband's offer of help. She mentions the negative consequences of this strategy later in the interview recalling a situation when both children were still little:

> My husband used to work very late so sometimes I run out of milk you know, and my daughter was a baby as well so I used to keep them in the cot and quickly go in the shop you, know, quick with milk and come back, you know, but I feel really bad, I feel guilty if anything happens to them I get all the blame, yeah, 'you shouldn't have left them', so – since then they, you know, my husband found out that you been doing this and we had a good argument...so (laughter), he said you'd better stop it, if there's no milk just leave it till I come and then I'll get it for you, since that day I've stopped everything, haven't (not understandable) just staying indoors.

Apart from brief help from her sisters and telephone support from her mother, Mrs Rajan felt completely alone. She went through a horrific period during the infancy of her children when many times she had one or both children ill or in hospital, and she also had to have a hernia operation. As the example below shows, her husband's family still did not support her:

> Once they [hospital] discharged her [Bhavini] you know I took her to my in-laws. I had to pick up Bhavesh so I had two babies in my hand.

I walked from Lonsdale Avenue [a long street] up to the end and they didn't say anything, 'that's alright', you know, 'I'll come, I'll hold one baby and you can hold the other one'. I had a bag and I've got both of them.

Mrs Rajan saw her role as wife and mother as closely connected to the women in her husband's family. However, lacking this close relationship did not change her attitude towards her husband. While he made attempts to replace the help denied by his family (e.g. taking time off work to look after the children, offering to buy food, etc.) his attempts at helping were, in Mrs Rajan's eyes, not supportive, merely emphasising her inability to fulfil her expected role.

This constellation left Mrs Rajan in a situation where a close mother–son relationship was created. Mr Rajan was away doing shift work or overtime so there was no one else to care for Bhavesh. While she was stigmatised because of her son's disability, her compensation was that she was the only one able to understand and communicate with him properly. The closeness between mother and son influenced other aspects of Mrs Rajan's reality. The distance between father and son supported Mrs Rajan's belief in a gendered world and she 'kept the secret', as nobody else was able to understand her relationship with Bhavesh.

Mrs Rajan's self-presentation consists of two parts or two thematic fields which are clearly distinguishable in the construction of her reality as well as temporally. There is a time of isolation and restriction 'before', the circular or looping period, and a time 'after', when Mrs Rajan can speak in narrative form and where she presents herself as an active person.

Having introduced all the risky themes in a secure way, Mrs Rajan felt free to tell the story about the birth of her youngest son. From this moment on, the structure of the interview changed completely. Mrs Rajan, who had struggled at the beginning to say anything, and had then used oblique references to painful experiences, was now able to narrate fluently: an expansive narrative covering her life *after* the birth of her second son consists of about half the interview text. She was now able to go back in her memories and to reconnect the stream of events. She remembered the harrowing experiences at the beginning of her marriage, and linked the horrific experiences of her eldest child's near-death to the rejection of her husband's family.

Mrs Rajan spoke extensively about the problems with her disabled son. At one point it appears as if she blamed him for having caused all the problems she had experienced during the past years. This suggestion was confirmed when the thematic field analysis reflected the years of difficulty leading up to the transformation Mrs Rajan experienced on the birth of her second healthy son. It led in the thematic field analysis to the following hypothesis:

> TF 16: disabled son is the problem, other problems depend on him but it is not possible to discuss this problem with others.

This was associated with the earlier hypothesis

> TF7: We have the problem of our first (disabled) son and therefore we are not a modern family.

This small sample of analysis hopefully gives some insight into the process which led to the identification of the overall themes in Mrs Rajan's lived life.

Conclusion

The next stage in the biographical-interpretive method is a comparison of the results of the biographical data analysis and the thematic field analysis. Through this device we approach the case structure which: 'aims at formulating a structural hypothesis on the principle of how the life history (or specific lived-through experiences in the past) and the life story (or the presentation of specific experiences in the present) are connected' (Breckner 1998).

By identifying the generating principle of the life story we understand why certain events and strands of the life history were neglected. Neither Mrs Rajan's told story nor her behaviour as a carer can be understood without the knowledge and interpretation of her biography. The key experiences extracted from her biography are:

1 Her upbringing in a family with minority status which followed strictly religious and cultural rules.
2 After the family's migration into Britain, the experience that these rules were questioned, different or invalid.
3 A lack of support from both her family and from persons and agencies outside the Indian network.
4 Her feeling that she had not fulfilled the duties of an Indian wife.
5 The turning point after she had fulfilled the most important duty of an Indian wife, the birth of a healthy son. This allowed her to find solutions for her situation which satisfied the needs of her culture and religion as well as the requirements of a nuclear family.

The outcome of the biographical-interpretive method is to construct a 'carer type' which reflects the overall biographical experience of the carer. We leave the external definition of being a carer but reach an understanding grounded in the carer's experience. This overcomes the problems identified in earlier research which located a gap between carers' self-perception and the carer label (Twigg *et al.* 1990). Examining Mrs Rajan's lived life and her biographical account, we can see that the caring role does not dominate her life. She represents a 'carer type' dominated by the experience of migration and conflicting norms and role expectations. Her son's disability and her caring tasks are part of a life embedded in these defining themes. This constellation was especially marked before Mrs Rajan's second son was born. At a time when Mrs Rajan was most in need of support from the social services and the health authority she was unable to articulate such concerns, as her overwhelming problem was different. She suffered from lack of family support, but this did not mean that she was able to ask for help from external agencies.

Cultural awareness and sensitivity would have been needed by a social worker, in order to support Mrs Rajan at this time. It was during her children's youngest years that she desperately needed practical assistance but was preoccupied herself with a more overpowering concern. Now after fourteen years of living away from her family and culture she is able to accept a culturally different way of living in England. She can access support offered to care for her increasingly difficult adolescent son, and accept help to support his disability and plan for his future. The need for more varied and better provisions to support disabled children as they grow into adulthood is clear in her case and is supported by other cases in the British Cultures of Care sample (cf the case of Mrs Buckley in Jones and Rupp 1997). At a policy and practice level the lessons that this case study teaches are important for the wellbeing of carers and those they care for as well as for the effective use of public resources.

The case of Mrs Rajan has been used to answer the question set out at the beginning of this chapter. Even though this chapter has only enabled a small part of the method to be discussed, it is our strong contention that using the biographical-interpretive method does not confirm our existing preconceptions. In effect it does exactly the opposite, and demands a deconstruction of stereotypical understandings and the use of creative and critical thinking. The rigour of the method, from interview stage to case construction, is apt to educate the less fastidious and unwary researcher by ensuring that it is indeed the interviewee's real needs that are articulated. It is hoped that a better understanding of Mrs Rajan's life and needs, as well as some small knowledge about the thematic field stage of the biographical-interpretive method, has been achieved.

Notes

1 This was an extension of a study funded by the ESRC and carried out between 1992 and 1994 in East and West Germany, using a similar research design (Chamberlayne and King 1996). Twenty-four carers from two London boroughs were interviewed. They differed in age, gender, ethnicity, social status and their specific caring situation. The boroughs' demographic composition was also very different. Mrs Rajan lives in Newham, a poor, culturally diverse, inner-city borough (Rix 1997). The 1991 Census showed that Newham had a high percentage of households that included people with disability and long-term illness, as well as mortality, infant and perinatal mortality rates that were higher than the average in England and Wales by more than a third.
2 The interviewer was Frauke Ruppel.
3 The analysis of the interview text as 'thematical field analysis' aims at reconstructing the structuring principles of the life story; its 'Gestalt' (Breckner 1998; Fischer 1982; Rosenthal 1993).
4 Micro-analysis aims at analysing the interrelation between past experiences and their presentation indepth, concentrating on small selected pieces of text, and at checking previous hypothesis (Breckner 1998; Oevermann et al. 1979; Rosenthal 1993).
5 Hollway and Jefferson, in this book, highlight the problem of interviewer insensitivity to the narrator's gestalt and the value of applying the principles of the narrative interview in interviewee-centred biographical research.
6 This initial narrative was developed by the then research team, Prue Chamberlayne, Annette King and Frauke Ruppel.
7 The presentation of Mrs Rajan's life is the result of the analysis of her biographical data: information found in the interview which are not dependent on the biographer's interpretation (e.g. date of birth, educational career etc.).
8 Italics denote the authors' emphasis.

References

Breckner, R. (1998) 'The Biographical-Interpretative Method. Principles and Procedures', *SOSTRIS Working Paper 2*, London: Centre for Biography in Social Policy, University of East London, pp.91–104.

Carricaburu, D. and Pierret, J. (1995) 'From Biographical Disruption to Biographical Reinforcement: The Case of HIV-positive Men', *Sociology of Health and Illness* 17(1): 63–88.

Chamberlayne, P. and King, A. (1996) 'Biographical Approaches in Comparative Work: the Cultures of Care Project', in L. Hantrais and S. Mangen (eds), *Cross-National Methods in Social Sciences*, London: Pinter, pp.95–104.

—— (1997) 'The Biographical Challenge of Caring', *Sociology of Health and Illness*, 19(5): 601–21.

Fischer, W. (1982) *Time and Chronic Illness: A Study on Social Constitution of Temporality*, California: Berkeley.

Gurwitsch, A. (1957/1974) *Das Bewusstseinsfeld*, Berlin/New York: de Gruyter.

Jones, C. and Rupp, S. (1997) 'Coping with Caring: Lives of Informal Carers in Newham', *Rising East: The Journal of East London Studies* 1(2): 89–110.

Labov, W. and Waletsky, J. (1967) 'Narrative Analysis: Oral Versions of Personal Experience', in J. Helm (ed.), *Essays on the Verbal and Visual Arts*, Seattle, WA: University of Washington Press, pp.12–45.

Lewin, K. (1930/31) 'Der Übergang von der aristotelischen zur galileischen Denkweise in Biologie und Psychologie', *Erkenntnis* 1: 421–66.

Oevermann, U., Allert, T., Konak, E. and Krambeck, J. (1979) 'Die Methodologie einer "Objektiven Hermeneutik" und ihre allgemeine forschungslogische Bedeutung in den Sozialwissenschaften', in H.G. Soeffner (ed.) *Interpretative Verfahren in den Sozial- und Textwissenschaften*, Stuttgart: Metzler, pp.352–434.

Rix, V. (1997) 'Industrial Decline, Economic Restructuring and Social Exclusion in East London in the 1980s and 1990s', *Rising East: The Journal of East London Studies* 1(1): 118–41.

Rosenthal, G. (1991) 'German War Memories: Narratability and the Biographical and Social Functions of Remembering', in R. Josselson and A. Lieblich (eds) *The Narrative Study of Lives*, London: Sage, pp.59–91.

—— (1992) 'A Biographical Case Study of a Victimiser's Daughter', *Journal of Narrative and Life History* 2(2): 105–27.

—— (1993) 'Reconstruction of Life Stories: Principles of Selection in Generating Stories for Narrative Biographical Interviews', in R. Josselson and A. Lieblich (eds), *The Narrative Study of Lives*, London: Sage, pp.59–91.

—— (1995) *Erlebte und Erzählte Lebensgeschichte*, New York/Frankfurt: Campus.

Schütze, F. (1992) 'Pressure and Guilt: The Experience of a Young German Soldier in World War II and its Biographical Implication', *International Sociology* 7(2 and 3): 187–208, 347–467.

Twigg, J., Atkin, K. and Perring, C. (1990) *Carers and Services: A Review of Research*, London: HMSO.

Woollett, A. (1994) 'Bringing Up Children in East London: the Accounts of Asian Women', Paper presented at Annual Conference of the Society of Reproductive and Infant Psychology, Trinity College, Dublin.

16 Single mothers and Berlin life-styles

A new mode of social reproduction

Claudia Neusüss and Eva Maedje

This report aims to highlight the role of the welfare state within changing family patterns. It is concerned in particular with mothers without financial support from men, who do not initially replace such support with their own paid employment. Instead they replace the man's share of responsibility by applying for welfare state benefits. The research involves mothers in West Berlin[1] who unconventionally modify the gender hierarchy in the division of labour, in our view giving rise to a new mode of social reproduction, a new means of ensuring quality care for the next generation. Overall the recourse to social welfare in the lives of these women cannot be conceived as the result of a 'downward spiral' (Schütze 1981: 288), as passive victimhood, or as the loss of all other options.

Balance and contrast

For some of the interviewees[2] the route to the benefit office[3] has the classic character of a request for charity which they would definitely have preferred to avoid. For others it is simply an option they choose for the time being. It is not that the interviewees prefer welfare benefits. Rather, benefits have become an option within *existing* alternatives. Their ambivalence towards social assistance derives not from thinking of it in its own terms, but contrasting it with other alternatives which they have already experienced, or expect, or desire. In this process of 'contrasting', the security offered by social assistance is compared with the alternatives of labour market or partner support. Their overall attitude also depends crucially on the 'balance sheet' they draw of their lives hitherto, namely, which biographical experiences they focus on and how they deal with them.

Towards an analysis of the biographical data

The analysis of the interviews is guided by an interpretive process, which proceeds inductively towards a reconstruction of the meaning of the biographical data, including at a latent level. In the first instance single cases are examined. This has the advantage of permitting a detailed examination of individual meanings, orientations and strategies. Frequently, however, such interpretation does not clarify the differences and similarities between individual cases. Typologies, based on case comparisons, provide a better overview. For our purposes we have built our typology around characteristic or typical profiles of reconstructed meaning (Wohlrab-Sahr 1993; Brose *et al.* 1993; Giegel *et al.* 1988).

This typologising derives from a three-dimensional analysis of orientations and strategies: towards *partners, professional life* and *children*. The choice of these dimensions is as much theoretically as empirically based, and reveals the significance of social assistance in the lives of the interviewees. The question behind the analysis of the data is whether the social changes which are leading to an increase in lone mothers indicate a shift in gender relationships, and whether this shift may be rendering obsolete a system of *welfare* which is predicated on a traditional division of labour within marriage and associated forms of social protection.

The relevant literature is diverse. Some authors focus on the orientations and strategies of women towards men, while others are concerned rather with the meaning of children in women's lives or else give central importance to professional goals. The traditional 'housewife' marriage can obviously be abandoned in a great variety of ways and for a diversity of purposes. On this point our data clearly supports the following conclusion: relatively homogeneous orientations regarding children are associated with the most diverse strategies in relation to men and marriage. And it is the specific combination of orientations to partners, children and employment which decides the meaning of social assistance in the life course of the respondent. The particular combination within the individual case will reveal how the respondent assesses and comes to terms with his or her life as a recipient of welfare. And by examining these interrelationships it becomes clear that the resort to welfare is by no means felt by all interviewees as something to be passively endured in the face of overwhelming circumstances.

Our typology (see Table 16.1) incorporates the recognition that a type must be composed of more than one feature if it is to do justice to the single case. Thus the data show that a typology based on orientations and strategies towards partners, for example, brings together respondents who differ fundamentally with regard to their professional orientation, and who do not therefore constitute a single type. The data shows moreover that orientations and strategies may change and that biographical developments have a considerable influence on the assessment of a current life situation and ways of coping with it. Thus the typology demonstrates how biographical experiences have entered into present strategies and whether it is possible to talk of a change in traditional gender relationships which is now finding expression in individual biographies.

This method of constructing a typology proceeds from the empirical material and involves the reconstruction of meaning. The fundamental characteristics which provide the framework for the typology and their elaboration are extracted inductively from the material. This differs fundamentally from a procedure of classification in which the single cases are merely allocated to previously defined types (Oevermann 1983; Giegel *et al.* 1988).

The overall variance within the sample led us to distinguish six patterns of biographical life course and orientation.

Developing the typology

The starting point for our examination was the 'whole case'. At first particularly striking single cases were analysed. The initial step was to analyse just one of the three dimensions (partners, professional life, children). This analysis traced the biographical life course, looking for continuities and changes in this particular field. Proceeding from this single case we devised theoretically – like a 'virtual' experiment – a maximally contrasting case. Subsequently we looked for similarly structured cases in the sample.

This building of types crystallised commonalties and differences between cases on the basis of one dimension. Similar cases were allocated to a particular type. The next stage was to include and test a further characteristic to see if the cases analysed according to this feature fitted the existing types, or whether a changed configuration was needed. Thus it could be established whether a case characterised by the same orientation towards men, for example, was also similar with respect to strategies regarding work. In a kind of cumulative procedure all the dimensions were tested which had been involved in the forming of the types. It is no surprise that the different types are not necessarily distinguished in relation

Table 16.1 List of types

I	Consolidating Phoenix: 'I managed it'
II	Logical Continuity: 'I can make out'
III	Forced Adjustment: 'Learn, learn, learn'
IV	Legitimate Expectations: 'Victim of circumstance'
V	Struggle and Compromise: 'I've paid a high price'
VI	Conventionality: 'Everything went wrong'

to all the elaborated dimensions. In other words there are not six differing profiles for each dimension. So for example the respondents allocated to Type VI perceive their connection with social assistance as thoroughly negative. By contrast all the women allocated to Types I to V valued the fact that social welfare permitted them financial independence from men. Type V uses benefit as a resource with which to free themselves from unsatisfactory and/or violent marriages. Type IV indicates a rather instrumental attitude towards work and a latent wish to be maintained. Type III use benefits (at least unofficially) to continue their educational projects. Type II make use of benefits and family allowances to allow a temporary childrearing interruption in an otherwise continuing career. Type I uses support of the welfare system to stabilise and consolidate their situation. Of course the distinctions between types also arise from the prioritising of particular arenas of life.

Overview of the types

We present now a descriptive summary of the six reconstituted types. After that we present one case in detail. The whole field of investigation lies between the poles of: Type I – Consolidating Phoenix: '*I managed it*' and Type VI – Conventionality: '*Everything went wrong*'. Within this spectrum the dynamics of the biographical courses as well as the characteristic orientations and managing strategies show maximal contrast. These opposite types form the cornerstones of the typology.

The respondents from Type I – Consolidating Phoenix: '*I managed it*' are mostly young women with one or two children. Their educational qualifications are varied and they have little professional experience. Their life up to the birth of the first child has been shaped by the search for excitement, and during this time they have already lived off and on from benefit. Bringing up a child changes their life fundamentally. It is their first real achievement. Responsibility for the child leads them to a more responsible attitude towards their own lives and futures, and to work towards training and a stable occupation. They perceive benefit as something that allows them to bring up the child without being dependent on a man or on earnings. For some the benefit is their first independent income. With the help of benefit all these women fulfil their desire to look after their child; several of them equate motherhood with a job, perceiving the benefit as the salary for the work involved. They had found previous partners both demanding and reluctant; they felt constrained by them and hindered in their personal development. Currently they live as singles, or at any rate have no joint household with partners. This is their preferred arrangement. Marriage is out of the question and they cannot envisage being supported by a man. When the women of Type I compare their current situation with their own past experience they arrive at an apposite characterisation of: '*I managed it*'. They feel they have found a successful path through life and improved themselves.

The women of Type II – Logical Continuity: '*I can make out*' are a little older and have one or two children. They have average to advanced school-leaving certificates and middle-range professional training. They plan their lives and value security, which they primarily seek in good education and in employment. They mostly make decisions for their children independently of their partners. In relationships they confidently pursue their own ideas. Up to the birth of the child they have been continuously employed. This entitles them to maternity leave.

Proud of their professional achievements, they are more interested in stability than in promotion. They are satisfied with their position. Their priority is now for a close family life, even if returning to work is taken for granted. Initially they avoid recourse to welfare and live off savings. When all other sources of income are exhausted they take welfare benefits as a matter of course, as a means of allowing full-time care of their children for a while without needing financial support from a man.

The women of Type III – Forced Adjustment: '*Learn, learn, learn*', are now in their late twenties, never married and mothers of small children. They have intermediate school leaving certificates and training, as well as further professional qualifications. They make big demands on themselves as well as on their partners. Oriented towards promotion and training, they are constantly on the look out for new challenges, experiences and learning opportunities. They reject compromises in partnerships or in work. Motherhood cuts them off from professional, social and cultural participation and is scarcely compatible with their interests. They struggle for recognition and are bitter that society withholds the proper acknowledgement of their achievements and realisation of their aspirations. Welfare is for them the least the State can offer, and they are offended by the scale and level of benefits. For some this attitude to welfare payment alters as they recognise its potential in furthering their interests in education. Currently they have neither the energy nor time for a partner. Basically they are striving for a committed relationship or marriage, which would have to be premised on equal partnership and their own professional and financial independence.

Women of Type IV – Legitimate Expectations: '*Victim of circumstance*' are middle aged and have one or two children. They are highly qualified, academically educated, and have studied over a long period or are still studying. They have completed a practical training, but they have had scarcely any work experience. To a certain extent they have been bypassed in the labour market and only spasmodically employed. During long periods of unemployment they have gained some experience of welfare. They are politically, socially and culturally participative. On the one hand they only want to work to a limited extent, as much as is absolutely necessary; on the other hand they criticise the labour market, which makes it difficult to find the kind of job they would like. Overall they show rather little determination in utilising their academic education in the job market.

Much of their energy and effort has been consumed in disputes with partners. In their view they always invested more than they got, and partners never could or would satisfy their needs and wishes. Currently they live alone. They satisfy their emotional needs for the most part through their children. The women of this type perceive themselves as victims of a patriarchal society that hinders or denies them a life according to their ideals. They have expectations of social change, although they sense that they actually 'hide' behind their children. Their latent wish to be cared for clashes with their self-image as emancipated women. They can allow themselves to be supported by social assistance to avoid becoming dependent upon a man – at least as long as they get childcare allowance (*Erziehungsgeld*)[4] and the children are still very young.

The women of Type V – Struggle and Compromise: '*I've paid a high price*' are middle aged, and mothers of several mainly school-age children from various marriages or partnerships. They had their children young, interrupted their education, and have been able to accumulate little work experience. For long periods of time they have lived in conventional relationships in which they were responsible for bringing up the children and looking after the household, for which they were supported by their husbands. Even now they do not reject such an arrangement outright but have simply lost hope of finding a partner who corresponds to their idea of the 'good patriarch'. Their marriages were generally unsatisfactory or even violent and they were the ones who sought separation. They still, for the most part, look after the children and instead of a husband's support receive benefit. They have broken with conventional routines and their current relationships with men are at a distance. As a consequence they have moved away from conventional arrangements and developed a renewed interest in training and paid employment. Now they are aware of their needs and interests even if lingering anxieties push them into compromises when they come up against obstacles in their professional ambitions.

The women of Type VI – Conventionality: '*Everything went wrong*' are middle aged with several children of school age. They have been married, some more than once, and have had minimal schooling and almost no professional training or practice. They have lived for several years on welfare, not for the first time. The desire for a conventional marriage remains the centrepoint of their existence. Being a lone parent and living off social assistance is for them a mark of social failure. They feel over-taxed by the sole responsibility for their children. Their employment aspirations are ill-defined. All their hopes are focused on a man who will free them from this situation. But their existing relationships are not successful in achieving their aspirations.

Typical features of the three dimensions in Type II

For each type we selected an illustrative or 'clear case', which best demon-strated the features of that type. In the next section we will present such a biographical case from Type II, but first we outline the typical features of each of the three dimensions as they relate to this particular type. We deal in turn with each dimension – partners, professional life and children,[5] and discuss the significance of the welfare system for these mothers.

To remind the reader, women in Type II are between thirty and forty-five and have one or two children. Many of them were married briefly when they were young. Their children are in some cases from this marriage, others from new relationships after the break-up. They left school with medium to high certificates and most have had professional training. Unlike the other types they were all continuously employed up to the birth of the children or, at the most, interrupted work for the purposes of further education. At the time of their interview these women were already anticipating when they could turn their backs on the social assistance office.

Orientation and strategies with regard to partners

The women of Type II have as little experience of a relationship based on a shared division of labour as the women of Type I, III and IV. Many of them have been married. These marriages were embarked on early and ended, then appearing as just an episode in their lives. Many have subse-quently lived together with a partner, but have meanwhile stayed in employment and not been maintained by the partner. They feel compe-tent to bring up a child on their own, even though that is not their real wish. They would prefer a responsible father who would be involved in childcare and share responsibilities with them. They know how to assert themselves in partnerships, and have rather precise ideas of the shape they would like their lives to have and how they would like to live with a man. As they move in and out of relationships they become less and less prepared to stay in unsatisfactory ones in which tedious conflicts have to be resolved. They are self-confident and suspect that men find strong women difficult to get on with. They have abandoned any idea of 'the frog who can be turned into a prince with a kiss' and that it is just a matter of making sufficient effort to change a particular partner.

Rather they aim to change themselves. They ask themselves as to why they have attached themselves to men who cannot give them what they want, and intend to avoid such attachments in the future. They maintain a distance between themselves and potential partners, and in particular prefer separate housing. Their closeness to their children ensures and satisfies their needs for intimacy and they think that this closeness should not be disturbed by partners. If their partner proves to be responsible they will happily leave the children with him for an hour or even a day at a time. They even hope that their partner will grow into this role and assume more of the load.

Orientation and strategies with regard to professional life

Paramount within Type II is a decisive and continuing career orientation which is rarely interrupted by events in other areas of life. Its representatives have a good education, professional experience, and work in spheres that offer considerable material rewards as well as job security. This security means a lot to them. It offers them a stability which they lack in other areas of life, for example in partnerships, since even if a partner leaves, the job stays. A satisfying and fulfilling job is important to them, though without a quest for ambitious career aspirations or professional promotion. Their purpose is to maintain their position rather than to further their professional development.

Being in secure, sought-after jobs, facilitates the flexible combination of motherhood and work. The period of family life allows a certain distancing from their chosen career. With children other needs can be fulfilled. Having children is no hindrance to being employed, but children bring a certain retrenchment with regard to work in favour of time for themselves, the children, and sufficient space for family life.

Orientation and strategies with regard to children

Children belong naturally in their life scheme. The decision to have children has been theirs alone, and some have explicitly planned children. The women are glad to be mothers and they stress the importance to them of having their own family, without children becoming the whole of life. If the fathers or other adults get involved they are keen and eager to share responsibility. In the same way they rapidly organise outside child-care in order to be able to return to work, since they want their personal load reduced, and also because it makes pedagogical sense for the children. Safety and supervision are key aspects of childcare for them. Appropriate childcare must be available at the appropriate time. They apply for it early and are willing to pay in advance of really using it, in case they should need it. If it is unavoidable they will use private services, which are readily within their financial means. This guarantees them security. They make a short exit from work for the children – one or two years – provided their work position is assured. Within our sample only they are entitled to childcare leave (*Erziehungsurlaub*), since they are the only ones with tenured employment. This factor reinforces their orientation towards employment security.

The significance of welfare

Representatives of Type II acquire their first experience of social assistance as lone mothers. Initially they have no thought of turning to the benefit office, since they are still working or living off savings, but if these resources dry up they have no problem about applying for benefit. Their basic position is marked by independence, since like Types I and III, they classify themselves as in an interim period, after which they will return to work. They all get childcare allowances, have savings and sometimes financially viable fathers of their children, and are thus satisfied for the most part with their financial situation. They keep paid employment in mind, however, since their position is worse as recipients of welfare, and even part-time work brings in more than benefit. Compared with the other respondents, apart from those in Type IV, they are therefore in a privileged position. From their perspective, fathers are under obligation to pay maintenance for their children, which will naturally have to be replaced by the State in the case of default. This leaves intact their sense of independence.

Illustrative case: Klara Küsgen

Security is an important theme and motive in Klara Küsgen's life. She was born in 1959, the third child of a working-class family. With the experience of her parent's separation she learns as a young child that security in relationships does not come easily. And, even when security seems present, it may entail other dangers – as her violent father shows. Her father is a 'bad father'. Neither in or after the marriage does he take financial responsibility for his family, nor does he take any consistent care of the children. The whole family suffers the effects of his alcoholism. Occasionally, and to his daughter's disapproval, he hands out financial treats, inconsistently, for show, to preen himself with 'fatherliness'. No real interest in the children lies behind it: 'I can't find any excuse for the way he behaved towards us...and we grew up in difficult material conditions...and yet my father always earned good money'.

As a child Klara Küsgen lived alternately with her grandparents and her mother, who always demanded consideration for the father. As a young person she looks for a man who will provide the attention and warmth she has missed hitherto. She falls in love and consequently neglects school, leaving before her high-school certificate (*Abitur*). Instead she seeks vocational training. Here too her concern is security; she becomes a middle-grade civil servant.[6] She likes the work, the State as employer represents an ideal father, which unlike her real father, reliably looks after her. At nineteen she decides to marry. Security is still a guiding theme in her relationships, whose dark side she will uncover in marriage. Her husband is extremely jealous, controlling, and restricts her. Throughout this marriage Klara Küsgen is 'continually ill'. She separates, even though her husband is 'a nice bloke', and she even now maintains a friendship with him.

Shortly after the separation she meets her 'great love', a man who would like to marry her and have children. Her experience in her parental home and her own shattered marriage make her opposed to another marriage. She has no wish to live together again with a partner. The 'security' of marriage by now inspires more anxiety than confidence:

> He was prepared to give up everything just for us to be together. Only that was just what I didn't want...and he kept on about getting together...and I should give up my flat, and I said no...I said I'm with you seven days a week, but I need to know I've got my flat to go back to if I need to.

After a quarrel she leaves this man and has a number of other relationships, until she meets the man, a civil servant like herself, who will be the father of her children. She gets pregnant. He has no objection to a child and would like to live with her. But already during the pregnancy the relationship falls apart. This partner is in her words 'all reason' with 'too little feeling', and in addition 'extremely mean'. She can fit him perfectly into her childhood experiences. He has money but is loathe to spend it (on her) and expects a similarly frugal life from her. They are unable to resolve this conflict and separate before the child is born.

Shortly after the birth of the child she becomes pregnant again by this same partner. This time she decides to have the child against his wishes.

This is partly from pride and partly revenge, since her ex-partner considers a child too expensive. Like her own father, her ex-partner is not concerned with the children. Unlike her mother she has nevertheless a man who pays substantial maintenance, in line with his professional status, though probably not entirely willingly.[7]

The decision to separate from her partner is not easy at first, for she fears the strain of being a lone parent. But the idea of bringing up children in an unhappy relationship, repeating her own childhood experience, appears worse. She keeps new partners at a certain distance, also for the sake of her children:

> I'm prepared to ditch the relationship if I think it doesn't suit me, that's really the bottom line. Now I don't try to hang on by hook or by crook...it gets through to the children automatically if you're not happy in a relationship, doesn't it? Anyway I know that I felt it very clearly as a child...and I want to save my children from that.

She takes separation for granted and does not blame her partners for the fact that relationships are not always as she would like them; she takes responsibility for that herself. She realises that she is attracted by the kinds of men who will disappoint her. So although she would like to share the responsibility for the children, she accepts life as a lone parent. She has gained a new understanding of herself and of men and no longer nurtures any hope that she can transform men to conform with her image. Her concept of herself has also changed. She now no longer has the view that a woman without a man is somehow less valuable. With her present partner she has a satisfying relationship.

Basically there are now three men in her life who perform very different roles. Her newest partner is a friend and lover but hardly figures in the life of the family. The children call her ex-husband 'Daddy', unaware that he is not their biological father. There is no social relationship with the biological father, though his role as financial provider proves to be workable. Nevertheless Klara Küsgen still feels under strain. In particular she misses the full emotional support of someone who would share responsibility for the children.

After the birth of the first child Klara Küsgen does not immediately consider turning to the welfare office. She lives from her childcare allowance, maintenance and savings. She only applies for benefit when a social worker draws her attention to this option. She finds dealings with the youth service (see note 7) more difficult, especially since her financial situation is quite good; she gets considerable maintenance and has savings at her disposal. However she finds being a lone parent very stressful, because she has to carry the whole responsibility alone. 'That's really the worst time...as a lone mother. It got to be so bad that I actually toyed with the idea of giving my daughter up for adoption, just because I thought I can't take it any more'.

She would like more 'psychological and moral support'. And while she is proud of overcoming all the difficulties which crop up without a man, she actively works at finding a way out of bearing the sole responsibility for her children. She looks for professional help and applies for childcare places. Only after much effort and protest does she get a place for both of them. She emphatically rejects the suggestion of the youth service that she might look after them herself.

Until the birth of the first child she had worked continuously in the government office in which she had completed her training. She made her social contacts in the civil service and got to know all her partners there. Now she would like to be employed again in order to be with people. Nobody else in our sample was so stably situated in work. Klara Küsgen is not planning any future professional moves; she might consider further professional training, but has to keep the pressure within limits. She has given up work for the first time in her life for the sake of her children, and for their sake she wants to keep down the stress from work. Unlike her own mother, who as a lone parent had little time for her children, she sees her job as making time for them and fostering their wellbeing. She turns down a promotion in her department because she would have to take her high-school certificate and complete another three years training. In this respect she differs from her sister who is 'eaten up with ambition'. Klara Küsgen expects something else from life. She always wanted to have children and thinks she would miss her children more than professional opportunities. She prefers to invest her energy in promoting the children's development just as she wishes her own mother had. She opts for the children rather than careerism – but not at the cost of her profession:

> I can make out, because as I say: fine, as a civil servant, I mean, nowadays that is something after all, isn't it...you have a secure position...and after all you need that.... I always say if you can't get security in a relationship then at least get it from work. I know I'll always get my salary...and I'm not in the position of not knowing what'll happen tomorrow... that's for the children really.

In the near future she plans on going back to work, initially six hours a day by preference. In this way she can both improve her financial position and still find time for her children. It means much to her as an employed person to have a close relationship with her children and to enjoy the security of a family.

Women in the welfare state: the era of women's choice?

Our respondents do not conceive of all parental tasks simply accumulating in the hands of mothers. They are united in wanting a different structure of childcare. Most of them would like a shared partnership for household tasks and childcare. Even those women who prefer a traditional division of labour have specific notions of what belongs in a conventional marriage and what does not. Precisely because they have raised their expectations of men, they detach the question of children from the question of men, insofar as maintenance and a continuing relationship are concerned. For men who are simultaneously good providers, partners, and loving and responsible fathers are rarities. Since the 1980s this has been a matter of debate and research. Men are becoming transitional in the lives of women (Ehrenreich 1983) and of children. The research suggests that women are adapting their conception of relationships to the market: from 'lean production' to 'lean reproduction'.

The respondents have become choosy. The era of women's choice pushes the social state into a front row position, even though it would have preferred to serve in a subsidiary role. Their expectations of men, which are so difficult to realise, turn women towards the State and society. They expect the question of childcare to be considered a public responsibility. By de-privatising the question of children and initiating a sharing of responsibility with the State, they anticipate more room for manoeuvre within particular circumstances. Even a discriminatory social welfare policy inadvertently 'encourages' women in this outlook.

But this sharing of responsibility is not entirely satisfactory. There is a gap between existing social policy provision and women's expectations. The respondents bridge this gap between their life situation and social policy by resorting to social assistance. To allege that they are simply exchanging dependence on a 'little patriarch' for dependence on the social state, underestimates them. Employment is not the only basis for 'independence' (Fraser and Gordon 1993).

The time factor is significant, namely the accepted and actual duration of the welfare arrangement. Welfare support is less dramatic if it can be considered temporary. The respondents regard the recourse to social assistance as their right, but seldom as fair: the essential work of bringing up children is not properly acknowledged or 'paid for'. Such a judgement may conflict with common stereotypes concerning poverty and a life 'on the margins of society'.

Notes

1 As a generously subsidised leading city of West Germany situated within the territory of the German Democratic Republic (until the fall of the Wall in 1990), Berlin had a 'special status'. It was also one of the centres of radical life-styles and politics since it allowed those on a low income to participate in social and cultural life and because low incomes were less stigmatised. Even in more prosperous circles a money-based life-style was not a 'must'.

2 The presentation relates to a quantitative and qualitative investigation of lone parents receiving social assistance, which was carried out in West Berlin in 1991/92. For the qualitative part of the research thirty women were interviewed.

3 Compared with Germany's relatively generous insurance-based benefits, social assistance (*Sozialhilfe*) is considered as meagre and stigmatised. It is funded regionally and administered locally by the benefit office (*Sozialamt*). It is the bottom rung of social security, only applying in the absence of other entitlements, like sickness or unemployment related benefits and payments of maintenance. While few single father households receive social assistance, in 1991 20 per cent of single mother households depended on it. Moreover 17 per cent of all households receiving social assistance in 1991 were single mothers (Statisches Landesamt 1991; Mikro zensus 1991).

4 Parents who leave work in order to care for their children are entitled to a childcare allowance (*Erziehungsgeld*) up to 600 DM (about £250) per month, which is mean-tested after the first year. This arrangement applies for the first three years after the birth of each child, and during that time the mother or the father who stays home is allowed to work up to nineteen hours a week.

5 In a further step the other cases of each particular type and their deviations from the illustrative case were summarised (Maedje and Neusüss 1996). Due to lack of space we have omitted this stage of analysis here.

6 Civil servants in Germany have tenured positions and are relatively well-paid, according to their status, with corresponding entitlements in case of illness, care needs and old age. The civil service covers a wider range of jobs in Germany than in Britain (like teachers).

7 In the case of separation and divorce, the income-related system of maintenance is (rather intrusively) administered by the Youth Office. In this 'patriarchal' system, the child has the right to be maintained at the status of the father.

References

Brose, H.-G., Wohlrab-Sahr, M. and Corsten, M. (1993) *Soziale Zeit und Biographie*, Opladen: Westdeutscher Verlag.

Ehrenreich, B. (ed.) (1983) *The Hearts of Men. American Dreams and the Flight from Commitment*, London: Pluto.

Fraser, N. and Gordon, L. (1993) 'Dekodierung von Abhängigkeit: zur Genealogie eines Schlusselbegriffes des amerikanischen Wohlfahrtsstaates', *Kritische Justiz* 3: 306–23.

Giegel, H.-J., Frank, G. and Billerbeck, U. (1988) *Industriearbeit und Selbstbehauptung. Berufsbiografische Orientierung und Gesundheitsverhalten in gefährdeten Lebensverhälnissen*, Opladen: Leske and Budrich.

Glaser, B.G and Strauss, A.L. (1967) *The Discovery of Grounded Theory: Strategies of Qualitative Research*, Chicago: Walter de Gruyter.

Maedje, E. and Neusüss, C. (1996) *Frauen im Sozialstaat. Zur Lebenssituation alleinerziehender Sozialhileempfängerinnen*, Frankfurt, Main: Campus Verlag.

Oevermann, U. (1983) 'Kontroversen über sinnverstehende Soziologie. Einige wiederkehrende Probleme und Missverständnisse in der Rezeption der "objektiven Hermeneutik"', in S. Aufenanger and M. Lenssen (eds), *Handlung und Sinnstruktur, Bedeutung und Anwendung der objektiven Hermeneutik*, München: Kindt.

Schütze, F. (1981) 'Prozessstrukturen des Lebenslaufs', in J. Matthes, A. Pfeiffenberger and M. Stosberg (eds), *Biographie in Handlungswissenschaftlicher Perspective*, Nürnberg: Verlag der deutschen Forschungsvereinigung.

Wohlrab-Sahr, M. (1993) *Biographische Unsicherheit*, Opladen: Leske and Budrich.

17 Part of the system

The experience of home-based caring in West Germany

Annette King

Introduction

This chapter discusses the analytical shift in the 'Care Systems in Bremen' project, a qualitative study of informal caring in two districts in Bremen, a city in Germany.[1] It examines the shift in the analysis stage of the project, in which the hermeneutic case-study approach in analysing personal accounts about caring and being cared for at home is modified to examine structural features of class,[2] welfare system and family relations as emergent themes across cases. In particular, the chapter discusses the role of Giddens' structuration theory in the development of the analytical framework.

One of the continuous challenges for social researchers is to mould close, fitting links between research interest, methods used and the social theory underpinning it. This is particularly important in qualitative research, which often adopts evolving approaches to research procedures as a means to capturing the complexities of social life. It is a testimony to the richness of the qualitative research process that research methods continue to change and develop, creating new variants in research approaches.

Within the individual research project, this development often presents itself as a need to expand and modify research tools, so as to answer the research questions adequately. The following presents such a process of reassessment of research instruments, in this case through the utilisation of a theoretical perspective of social interaction offered in Anthony Giddens' structuration theory (Giddens 1984).

The research project 'Care Systems in Bremen' is qualitative research based on a series of interviews with frail older people and their carers about their personal experiences of caring and being cared for at home. The research adopted the biographical hermeneutic case-study approach for the analysis of interview data. In this approach, the case is an integral unit of analysis and the analytic process is driven through it by exploring the coherent and extensive (re)construction/interpretation of the case structure (Snow and Anderson 1991; Rosenthal 1993). In a second phase of the research, the case studies were refocused to centre on structural themes across the cases. This shifted the analysis of the individual experiences of caring to a consideration of influences of localised social systems, compromising the case studies in favour of the thematic development of structural features. In this, the research strategy departed from the methodological canon of an interpretive hermeneutic approach. A key role in the development of the research strategy in the project was played by Giddens' structuration theory, which stresses the reciprocal relationship between individual action and social structures, informing the shift in the analysis stage theoretically. In this perspective, agency and system are integral, interlocking aspects of the social world and cannot be separated. It is the interaction of agents, through which social systems are produced and reproduced; alternately patterns of interactions are bounded by the social contexts they occur in.

The chapter will briefly summarise these developments in relation to the development of the research strategy. Beginning with an introduction to the project, I go on to introduce Giddens' structuration theory and then describe the development of the research strategy with an illustration of the shift in analytic perspective. The chapter concludes by raising some wider issues of the usefulness of this process of adaptation in the research and its benefit for social policy research into caring.

Care systems in Bremen

The project investigates the experience of informal care and caring for older people in two city districts, Soltau and Weidenthal, in the north German town of Bremen. These two districts are socially distinctive: Soltau is a traditional working-class district close to the industrial heartland of the city. Weidenthal is an affluent suburban part of Bremen, close to the city centre. The fieldwork for the project was based on qualitative research, using a semi-structured interview schedule with twenty-eight dependent/frail older people and/or their informal carers. The sample was recruited via a number of welfare organisations, providing support and formal services in the localities. In addition, a number of key informants from welfare organisations and key players in welfare provision of the city were interviewed, as well as representatives of local service providers and care workers. The aim of the project was to develop a grass roots perspective at the interface of formal and informal caring within the German welfare system. It was to do this by exploring the local city-based 'system of caring' through the experiences, resources and barriers people found in organising and maintaining home-based caring in this locality.

In the case of Soltau, participants were recruited chiefly via Worker's Welfare (*Arbeiterwohlfahrt*). A significant player in the German intermediary landscape of welfare organisations providing local welfare services, Worker's Welfare maintains a strong presence in Bremen working-class districts. In Soltau, it is contracted by the city administration to organise and provide a number of welfare services, making it the most important service provider in that district for services for older people. A similar role has been assigned to the Red Cross (*Rotes Kreuz*) in Weidenthal. Both organisations are independent, but are organised according to similar structures and are fully professionalised. Their work includes advising on services and benefits, providing social work support for individual clients and organising a brokering service for home helps and clients.

The research was committed to taking personal experience and agency as its point of departure. In this approach the research follows the feminist caring research tradition, which places personal and informal aspects of caring and their meanings at the centre of analysis and relates them to their social and political context (for some of the earlier work see Ungerson 1987; Lewis and Meredith 1988; and our own work King and Chamberlayne 1996). As a piece of social policy research, the study also had to take into account the institutional and structural context of caring in Germany. Originally, this had been planned as background analysis. In the course of the study, questions of the differences between geographical location, about the *local* patterning of the welfare society, such as the impact of welfare agencies operating in the city, became of more central interest. In expanding this dimension of the research a 'system' oriented approach was required which could analyse the system of personal social services and social divisions within the city. Consequently, the research methods adopted had to match, addressing personal and experiential dimensions of caring with the specificity of local structure within one research framework and data set. The ideas in Giddens' structuration theory, which develop a view of agency, structure and system as different dimensions of social interaction, have allowed a research strategy to develop in which the case-study analysis has drawn out the social structures operating in the locality.

Giddens' structuration theory

One of the ongoing contributions to the agency versus structure debate has come from Giddens' structuration theory, which presents an ontological account of social reproduction (Giddens 1993; Cohen 1989). Rather than conceptualising social structure or agency as separate elements in producing and transforming social life, structuration theory focuses on the interrelationship between both as the key to understanding society. Society is conceived of as manifestations of social praxis, reproduced and transformed through a continuous process of social interaction (Giddens 1993: 168ff.). The development of social systems and human subjectivity and agency depend upon the process of doing, upon social interaction as social practice (Giddens 1984: 8, 9).

Structuration theory engages with a variety of theoretical problems, addressing and reformulating a number of central questions in modern social thought (Cohen 1989). These include the process of social reproduction and social change, the role of modernity and self-reflexivity, the relationship between agency and structure and between the external (institutional) and internal dimensions of social life. Social praxis as repeated interaction over time and space is understood to connect and bind agency and subjectivity with the structural, systemic relations, reproducing and transforming them continuously (Giddens 1984: 139). The basic argument is that agency and structure (here meant as the organising instances of social systems) are not constituted independently, but are part of the same process of the enactment of social practices. As such, they permeate each other. The individual is bound by the rules and resources, which are produced and reproduced through the day-to-day conduct of interaction: 'structure is not "external" to individuals: as memory traces, and as instantiated in social practices.... Structure is...both constraining and enabling' (Giddens 1984: 25).[3]

Central to the analytic framework is the understanding of structure as the organising element in social processes. Structure and the process of structuration encompass the mechanisms and rules by which interactions are produced and reproduced over time (Giddens 1984: 25). Social systems are based on concrete patterns of interaction and established through rules shared by a collective of social actors within a system. Agency is intrinsically bound up with wider social dimensions, which in different contexts act as barriers or resources, producing conditions and consequences of the pattern of everyday life. Locked into a duality of structure, agency cannot do without system and vice versa. With this conceptualisation, Giddens in effect attempts to overcome the problem of the theoretical duality of agency and system (Cohen 1989: 3).

The notion of the enabling and constraining effects in the process of structuration has been taken up by social policy writers, notably in Finch (1989) and Finch and Mason (1993). Finch and Mason explore the complexities of family support behaviour through the notion of 'negotiated responsibility' which governs patterns of support among kin in modern society. They point to the development of responsibility over time, grounded in interpersonal relationships and mediated by both moral and material patterning. These can act as restraining and enabling for the praxis of family support. Similarly, Finch's notion of 'negotiated obligations' permeates her discussion of forms of reciprocity and kin relations over time. It is the central organising principle of her inquiry (1989). This understanding of the process of structuration brings agency to the fore of social policy analysis, linking social factors, individual experiences and collective dimensions of everyday lives. In the project presented here, the concept of duality of structure has become an important device for highlighting themes of structural patterns in caring within caring experiences.

Analytically, agency and structure can be imagined as two ends of a spectrum of structuration, both implicated in social reproduction. At one end, agency manifests itself in the day-to-day management of social interaction, in everyday life. In their day-to-day dealings with each other, human agents actively participate in the structuring of their social worlds. Importantly, however, only part of the totality of social action is reflective. Many interactions are never reflected upon, they remain at a routine level. They are guided by habituated knowledge and produce intentional and unintentional consequences (Giddens 1986: 4, 5; Cohen 1989: 47ff.). At the other end of the spectrum, social systems appear as extensions and enactment of structure, as routine and institutional modes of interaction. They are limited to specific social spaces and maintained over a period of time (Cohen 1989: 87, 88).

The distinction between reflective and habituated action as knowledge shared between different agents opened up a new perspective in analysing case-study material. The accounts of different routines and habits in caring reflect the rules and patterns in a social system, pointing to the underlying structures as resource and constraints. Subjective experiences of caring appear as de-centred. They incorporate different aspects of systemic influences and feedback and express personal aspects of the experience (Cohen 1989: 47; Giddens 1986: 25). Through this perspective the systemic, institutional elements of caring in Bremen can be viewed as being part of the private and intimate experiences of caring. Shared aspects of everyday, routine encounters in the accounts are indicative of how the local system of caring works; they reproduce the system of care in the city and can be experienced as enabling and constraining (see also Finch 1989 and Finch and Mason 1993).

The case studies can be used to locate and tease out intrinsic structural elements. In as far as the 'equality of structure' diminishes the qualitative difference between agency and structure, agency and system perspectives become interchangeable. As they are grounded in the same processes of enactment of rules, the system perspective becomes accessible through the case material, as contextualised personal experiences. In this sense, the case study is a carrier of structural forms. These structures need to be worked out through further analysis of the case-study material, making the case study the starting point for this stage in the analytic process rather than the exemplary end-result. Interpretations of quite small structural dimensions operating in the caring context can be made, depicting a localised system of caring. Equally though, methods of comparing across cases and triangulating with other data, such as interviews with key informers, facilitate this process further.

Analysis

The project has drawn on two distinctive approaches to qualitative analysis. One is the techniques of hermeneutic, biographical interpretive methods, the other the analytic techniques of grounded theory (Chamberlayne and King 1997; King and Chamberlayne 1996; Strauss 1987; Rosenthal 1993). In its first phase, the analysis followed the hermeneutic approach in biographical methods. This has at its heart the exploration of subjective meanings through textual interpretive analysis. It is geared towards the interpretation of individual cases as a way of maintaining biographical experience at the core of the analytic process.

The procedures adopted follow those in the 'Cultures of Care' project, which adapted the methods of the interpretive biographical methods to the comparative social policy research field (King and Chamberlayne 1996; Rosenthal 1993). Biographical hermeneutic case reconstruction is the reconstruction of subjective meaning, as enmeshed in the presentation of the accounts. Through this, it uncovers the underlying social phenomena, which the individual case exemplifies (Chamberlayne and King 1997). The analytic process is therefore geared to the construction of 'structural types', through the uncovering of underlying structural meanings. The 'Cultures of Care' project opted for this approach precisely because it was interested in untangling the personal, social and cultural dimensions of caring in the two societies and in theorising the social encoding of personal experiences of caring. The method follows an analytical procedure, which includes text analytic steps of 'micro analysis' and 'thematic field analysis', and the interpretation of biographical data as preparatory steps for the structural reconstruction of the case (King and Chamberlayne 1996). However, for the purposes of 'Care Systems in Bremen' and its interest in specific institutional aspects of the locality, the analysis stopped short of drawing the different interpretive steps together. Rather in a second stage of the analysis, it focused on uncovering more localised structural elements across the accounts. Following the premise of structuration theory, the aim was now to disentangle common structuring principles among the individual experiences which could mark out the boundaries of the localised social system of caring.

Using case material from the previous analytic steps, which give an indication of the everyday individual structure of caring, and the interview text the material was re-examined for differences and similarities between cases. Results of case analytic procedures were investigated for reference points of defining characteristics of the social system, again using a cross case perspective. For this, the material was ordered and compared according to a number of different categories. These included comparing cases assisted by different welfare organisations, ordering cases according to locality, in relation to matters of income, welfare receipt, etc. It is at this point that different themes emerged, indicating different systemic influences operating in the local welfare system. Differences picked up on included day-to-day management of care, as well as differing perceptions, actions and aspirations which the interview participants expressed across cases. In one of the earliest exercises of this type, the cases were ordered according to the welfare agencies involved in their care. Although each case is unique in its circumstance, through comparison of cases it became clear that clients in the two districts have a different relationship with agencies.

Among the clients of the Workers Welfare home help service (*Arbeiterwohlfahrt*) in Soltau, staff and offices of the home care provider service are a local resource and advice centre which fits in with the informal care network in that community. The office of the welfare organisation is located centrally in Soltau and can be accessed easily for both carers and older people. Involvement of the staff at the centre goes well beyond that of organising home-helps. Frau Schmidt and Frau Walter, carers from the working-class district, see the centre as an important part of their support network: 'I can always ring Frau Rorsch ...' or 'Then I tell Frau Riemann about it, and that makes me less angry...'.[4] The services offered through the centre, whether practical advice on housing, or more informal modes of support, are recognised and used by clients. Home-helps (mainly women, although not exclusively) tend to take on roles of informal support – as advisers, as contacts and sometimes as friends to carers or older people. This development is facilitated in situations where home helps and clients share similar socio-economic backgrounds where both live near by.

This is different in the middle-class district of Weidenthal, where the helping agency is run by the Red Cross (Rotes Kreuz) service centre. Weidenthal serves to a larger extent middle-income clients, who often have to pay the full cost of services.[5] Home-helps seem to come from a greater variety of backgrounds, among them (female) students from the local university, which is close by. In comparison to the Soltau setting, interviewees in this district had a more formal relationship with the service centre and the services it offers. Older people and carers approached centre staff mainly with home-help and information needs. Frau Ahorn, a single woman living on her own, viewed the service centre as a form of employment agency, referring to her home-helps as 'my staff' in the interview. On the whole, services were regarded as professional assistance and, as a consequence, relationships with home-helps and in particular centre staff were quite formal. Clients took up those services, which helped in solving practical tasks, such as advice on entitlements and aids, on buying in home-help. They were reluctant to tap into some of the more psychosocial resources available, or develop the contacts in the centre as part of an informal support system. The relationship with the service centre remained very much at a formal and rather distanced level.

This practice of accepting a strictly limited intervention could lead to problems, especially in crisis situations. Asking for advice, confiding in staff, 'opening up the caring situation to others' was experienced as a difficult process and a barrier. Frau Roth junior (her case is presented in more detail further on) summed up her reluctance to discuss her problems as a carer with the social work professionals in the centre: 'I suppose I could do that.... But I don't see the point: it would not change anything, would it? I still have to carry on with it, so what's the point?' Service managers and social work staff are often aware of these barriers.

The pattern of informal support network in Soltau corresponds to that of generational proximity: children and parents tend to live close to each other, accessible for support. These living arrangements normally are not changed with the onset of caring. There is a tradition of reciprocal support in families, based on financial necessity. Asking for help as a parent or offering it to an older relative is continuing a well-established praxis. Within the working-class neighbourhood, this pattern is a resource, which maintains existing balances in family relations and living arrangements, compensating in many cases for shortfalls in services and material disadvantages. In the middle-class district of Weidenthal, older people cannot easily draw on family in the same way. Increased social mobility has tended to separate generations geographically. Children have moved away and exchanges of support between generations tend to be indirect rather than direct, involving gifts and patterns of visiting. The older interviewees in Weidenthal tended to live at a distance to their families and often lived independently. Family support was received through phone calls, arranged visits, etc. Even where geographical proximity is maintained there is still a sense in which lives are quite separate and independent. As a consequence, caring between the generations is at a distance. Increasing practical support and with it dependency has to be negotiated carefully: it changes the balance of relationships and can be intrusive. With increasing frailty in older age, the norms of relative independence, from family and other outside agencies, and of generational distance can create problems. They can isolate the older person from participating in family life or make the provision of support difficult. For carers, also bound up in this pattern, the situation can equally be overburdened when they find themselves isolated in the caring situation due to lack of support.

In developing these themes further and in integrating others and by making comparisons, the analysis began to centre on increasingly structural questions about the social institutions and system influences operating in the community. In a second phase, techniques of the grounded theory approach were used for ordering text segments in all the interviews so as to develop emergent themes in more detail. Overall, the analysis moved from an open, case oriented interpretive approach to a much more researcher oriented one, led by the research aims. The central point emerging from the analysis stresses three institutional dimensions: family relations, class and neighbourhood relations and the financial and service aspects of the welfare system. Although implicated differently in the cases, all three dimensions are part in the structuring of caring, balancing personal and institutional dimensions of care. On an individual level, the relations of class, family and welfare can be enabling and restraining in developing a sustainable pattern of informal care.

One of the advantages of operating within a case-study approach is that the analysis can be brought into a concrete, everyday life setting of individual cases. Two contrasting cases have been chosen to illustrate the pattern. They are Frau Riese and Frau Roth, two frail older women in their eighties, who have tendencies to serious blackouts and therefore require extensive support. Frau Riese has lived most of her life in the working-class district of Soltau. She used to work as a seamstress. Her daughter, who is married, lives two streets away and a son lives in another district of Bremen. Frau Riese must not exert herself, she is prone to fainting and bruising herself in falls. Nevertheless she lives alone and manages with the help of her daughter, who comes round to help her with certain aspects of her housework. As she explains, 'I can't get up to dust on top of the wardrobe. My daughter did that for me yesterday. But I can't ask her to do everything. She is glad to have holidays'. This pattern of visiting and helping has emerged over time, but is also part of an interrelationship grounded in 'doing things for each other' which has characterised

Frau Riese's family relations. She points out, 'My son has a garden. He picks me up so that I can go there as well. Or my daughter says: "Mummy, come to the garden. We'll pick you up and take you back"'. Frau Riese does not find anything unusual in this arrangement, however she will not ask for anything special 'I don't ask. You have to keep your distance'.

Frau Riese has limited additional help through social assistance (*Sozialhilfe*), which pays for a small number of hours of home-help. She is also in regular contact with the staff of her service centre (Workers' Welfare), who monitor the development of the situation closely in this way. Frau Riese feels quite supported and adequately cared for. She can also rely on her neighbours for 'keeping an eye', and in assisting her in little services, such as taking her turn in cleaning the staircase or by visiting her regularly: 'The young man [neighbour upstairs], when he comes back from work, he has a cup of coffee with me...'. Her daughter's proximity and her life-long embeddedness in the community around her allow her to remain at home. Above all, Frau Riese has maintained the greatest possible degree of independence and control over her life. And although for her there are also certain rules of intra-familial and neighbourhood support, which guide her in what she feels able to ask for, these do not stop her receiving practical assistance from her daughter or from the community she lives in.

Quite a different scenario developed for Frau Roth senior. She used to live in Hamburg (east of Bremen), where she was the wife of a shipping merchant. Widowed, she lived for many years in her flat by herself. However, when she became increasingly frail around ten years earlier and needed greater support, she reluctantly moved in with her widowed daughter to Weidenthal, the middle-class district in Bremen. Frau Roth senior still regrets leaving her hometown. At the time, her daughter saw no alternative than to move her mother to live with her in Bremen: 'We come from an old seafaring family. There was nothing else for it. I couldn't have put her in a home'.

This arrangement has been disastrous for both women. Frau Roth senior lost nearly all her social contacts and with it her independence. Socially and emotionally she is now heavily dependent on her daughter, with whom she has very little in common. She has lost most of her autonomy. She never goes out and has few people who visit. In turn, her daughter resents the restrictions on her life, especially the fact that she can no longer travel or leave the house for any length of time. She is also horrified at the prospect of having to provide personal care for her mother in the future. Being thrown together brought very difficult, long-standing personal differences and resentments to the fore, which had been kept at bay by living in different towns and having limited contact: 'My mother and I we never saw eye to eye, we never loved each other very much...I always was headstrong and so was she' (Frau Roth junior). In her turn, Frau Roth senior points out: 'My daughter is always so tidy and everything has to be in its place. I was happier by myself'. The enforced living arrangement damages the fragile balance in the personal relationships of the two women painfully developed over decades. It is affecting the caring arrangement itself, in that the emotional pressures are increasing, with little chance of change: 'the burden is getting too strong. As I said we had these conflicts years ago...' (Frau Roth junior). The situation is complicated by the fact that Frau Roth junior will not accept any form of mediating assistance by the staff of the Red Cross service centre. As social workers, they have the expertise and the experience to do some relational work with the family or point them towards alternative caring arrangements. This is not acceptable to Frau Roth junior and she keeps the service centre at arm's length. She only sporadically receives home-help services, for two or three months at a time, 'I do it when I had enough...'. In this way, home-help becomes a means of relieving periods of great emotional stress.

Discussion

The two case studies presented here illustrate how different dimensions in caring intersect to produce distinct caring constellations. Although frail, Frau Riese can still draw on a community support network in her neighbourhood and she benefits from the wider system of close neighbourhood relations (within her house, for instance) operating in the area. Informal support networks are long-standing, part of a tradition of mutual assistance in the face of material disadvantage in this traditional working-class district. Frau Riese also has her daughter nearby to organise care for her on a day-to-day basis. The service centre, offering limited practical help at this point, has the role of monitoring the situation, increasing the opportunity for supportive additional intervention when this is required. This pattern is repeated in other cases the study looked at. So the strength of the service provider in Soltau lies very much in this supervisory capacity. The ability to gain access to offer intervention at strategic points, as part of the overall community setting in the district, has strengthened its position as resource in the community setting. In Weidenthal, the links between private, informal and formal support patterns are less seamless, because caring is regarded as an essentially private, family activity and outside intervention has to be delicately negotiated. However, these norms of family care have come under conflicting pressures, brought about by social change and a distanced pattern of intergenerational assistance.

In the case of the Frau Roths, this has given rise to a caring arrangement, which does not suit either party and increases the emotional burden of the two women. There is also a lack of a developed informal support network outside the family, which Frau Roth junior could draw on. So, unlike the case of Frau Riese, formal services cannot be easily woven into the care pattern, but remain separate and somewhat inaccessible, regardless of the opportunity they may offer to positively change the caring situation.

The difference between service provision in both districts is not the consequence of management style or organisational setting, but linked to the differences in the caring constellations within middle-class and working-class settings, which intersect with and mould personal circumstances. Conceptualising caring within the framework of structuration theory shows the way in which individual circumstances of caring and aspects of the welfare system intersect and give rise to specific caring constellations. It shows local dimensions of the German welfare system to be an integral part of the fabric of informal caring, impacting and structuring informal care on an everyday basis. The difference between the reception of service provision in the two districts also shows how institutions are bounded and constrained by the individual and collective rules governing practices of support in the two districts. The system of service provision, whether it is formally organised through welfare services or informally arranged in the neighbourhood, is moulded by those who are interacting with it. In turn, this has wide-ranging consequences for the individual situation. Frau Roth senior and junior cannot move beyond the rules of privacy governing their relationships with the Red Cross service providers and so they cannot ask for additional help. This cements the *status quo* in their caring situation and makes it into the enduring characteristic of their situation. For Frau Riese, the readily available pattern of support through family, neighbourhood and services, is an extension of the patterns of support and interdependencies of the social milieu of Soltau. It is a resource, forming an enduring 'package of care', which allows her to maintain an independent life.

Using the case-study approach for this study has been an important vehicle for bringing into relief the process of interrelation between personal, social, local and institutional aspects of caring. In bringing out these features, the project had to adapt the biographical interpretive case reconstruction techniques used for analysing the case studies. In the context of this research, the close attention paid to structuration theory provides a theoretically informed background for focusing on structural elements in the case studies and for adapting the biographical hermeneutic method. With it, the analysis could be directed to the institutional dimensions of the local welfare system, the class/milieu dimension and local service provision. Acknowledging these adaptations and reflecting on methodological developments is not only important for the overall internal logic of the research process but is imperative in the context of an already sophisticated methodological approach such as biographical hermeneutic case reconstruction.

One of the costs of developing the research strategy along the lines of structural analysis has been the loss of some of the complexity and richness of the case reconstruction through the biographical interpretive method. For instance, interpretation of the two cases presented here can show only selected aspects of the undoubtedly complex personal pattern of caring. The analysis of the Frau Roths, for instance, does not draw on the role of the wider family relations in shaping the mother–daughter relationship. Nor is the family dynamics of Frau Riese's situation as a war widow in shaping her family relationships contained in this analysis. These aspects of the individual caring experience would have been considered in a full case reconstruction. In the context of the approach adopted for this research project, the individual case serves to exemplify the features of the shared system of care. This can be seen as a process of reduction and a departure from the theoretical principle of the biographical, hermeneutic method, which stresses the unity of the case. Utilising the ideas of structuration has also maintained much of the case-study approach: the analytic process of 'Care Systems in Bremen' works with the experiential accounts, and the themes developed through the analysis are grounded in the biographical and experiential subjectivity of the accounts. It has provided a focus to the research, allowing it to bring into relief the interplay between structural dimensions and individual practice.

Conclusion

I have discussed the application of structuration theory in terms of a methodological journey, as an attempt to marry potentially quite disparate research aims within a case-study approach. Central to this has been an understanding of caring as a process of enactment, in which individuals live out patterns of service provision and localised systems of care in their everyday social practices. In applying structuration theory, 'Care Systems in Bremen' has had the opportunity to draw out the institutional dimensions of welfare of service provision, neighbourhood support, class and milieu traditions and link them to the context of personal experiences of caring, as part of 'the making of social life' of caring. These social relations of caring are deeply interwoven in everyday activities and routines: they play a role in decisions about care and support, in the way assistance can be sought and care routines are carried out. They are part and parcel of a continuous, interactive process of caring and are themselves moulded and transformed in the process.

The implications for theorising caring in this way go beyond methodology. The examples of the case studies presented here have shown the significance of small-scale structural relations of caring. Feminist research methodologies into caring have successfully highlighted the relationship between the personal and social in caring (Ungerson 1987; Lewis and Meredith 1988). Gender led research interrelates social dimensions of gender, age, disability, race (Graham 1993; Morris 1993) with experiences of oppression and discrimination. So far, less work has been done in attempting to link the experiences of caring within the context of service provision and localised systems of welfare. Examples such as Daatland's (1983) ethnomethodological study of home-based carers in a rural social services department in Norway are still rare. Localised social structures and institutional relations of social welfare, such as systems of service provision, are important dimensions in the framework of home-based caring, which deserve increased attention. Analysing small-scale, localised and institutional relations of care within the structuration theory links important dimensions of the formal welfare system with the personal context of care. In this, the approach expands on existing theories of caring.

In terms of social policy development, conceptualising personal and social dimension of caring 'as part of the system' challenges perspectives of caring and care intervention, which regards recipients of intervention as passive or consumerist. The case studies show that people have an active 'relationship' to welfare intervention, that they integrate and transform services and fit them into the context of their own lives and experiences and that intervention practices are themselves shaped by this process. Theorising caring and welfare issues in this way raises issues about the relationship of welfare and individual circumstance and about addressing the complexity of welfare needs and engendering change. Finally, it raises issues about the role of providers in local settings and the need for sensitivity to local contexts. Utilising the notion of structuration along those lines may be a step forward to the more integrative social policy research advocated by social policy theorists such as Titterton (1992) and Williams (1992).

Notes

1   The research project is work for a Ph.D. project 'Care Systems in Bremen' at the University of East London. Fieldwork was conducted between 1991 and 1994 through a number of visits to the city.

2   For purposes of simplicity and ease of understanding, the research employs
      class as a generic term for socio-economic and also cultural differences in the
      two communities under investigation in the Bremen locality. While drawing
      attention to income differentials and historic differences in location of the
      middle-class and working-class districts, the term class also incorporates a
      cultural dimension, as an internalised set of social practices and modes of
      interaction, which are shared characteristics of belonging to the group. In this
      sense, the understanding of class employed for this research owes much to the
      concepts of 'habitus' and 'milieu' (Bourdieu 1991).

3   For a more critical evaluation of structuration theory, see for instance
      Mouzelis 1995 and 1997.

4   Frau Rorsch and Frau Riemann are two of the social workers in the Worker's
      Welfare Neighbourhood Centre in Soltau. All names of individuals in the
      study have been changed. The place names of the districts the research took
      place in have also been altered.

5   Fieldwork for the study was conducted before the introduction of care insur-
      ance in Germany in 1993 which created a new model of insurance cover for
      social and nursing care needs.

References

Bourdieu, P. (1991) 'The Order of Things', *Actes de la Recherche en Sciences Sociales*
    90: 7–19.

Chamberlayne, P. and King, A. (1996) 'Biographical Methods in Comparative
    Social Policy: The Cultures of Care Project', in L. Hantrais and S. Mangen
    (eds), *Methodological Approaches in Comparative Research*, London: Pinter.

—— (1997) 'The Biographical Challenge of Caring', *Sociology of Health and Illness*
    19(5): 601–21.

Cohen, I.J. (1989) *Structuration Theory Anthony Giddens and the Constitution of
    Social Life*, London: Macmillan.

Daatland, S.O. (1983) 'Care Systems', *Ageing and Society* 3(1): 1–21.

Finch, J. (1989) *Family Obligation and Social Change*, Cambridge: Polity Press.

Finch, J. and Mason, J. (1993) *Negotiating Family Responsibilities*, London:
    Routledge.

Giddens, A. (1984) *The Constitution of Society Outline of the Theory of
    Structuration*, Cambridge: Polity.

—— (1993) *New Rules in Sociological Method: A Positive Critique of Interpretative
    Sociologies*, 2nd edn, Cambridge: Polity.

Graham, H. (1993) 'Feminist Perspectives on Caring', in J. Bornat, C. Pereira,
    D. Pilgrim and F. Williams (eds) *Community Care: A Reader*, London:
    Macmillan, pp.124–33.

King, A. and Chamberlayne, P. (1996) 'Comparing the Informal Sphere: Public
    and Private Relations of Welfare in East and West Germany', *Sociology* 30(4):
    741–62.

Lewis, J. and Meredith, B. (1988) *Daughters Who Care: Daughters Caring for their
    Mothers at Home*, London: Routledge.

320   *Annette King*

Morris, J. (1993) ' "Us" and "Them"? Feminist Research and Community Care', in J. Bornat, C. Perreira, D. Pilgrim and F. Williams (eds), *Community Care: A Reader*, London: Macmillan, pp.193–206.

Mouzelis, N. (1995) *Sociological Theory What Went Wrong? Diagnosis and Remedies*, London: Routledge.

—— (1997) 'Social and System Integration: Lockwood, Habermas and Giddens', *Sociology* 31(1): 111–19.

Rosenthal, G. (1993) 'Reconstruction of Life Stories: Principles of Selection in Generating Stories for Narrative Biographical Interviews', in R. Josselson and A. Lieblich (eds), *The Narrative Study of Lives*, London: Sage.

Snow, D.A. and Anderson, L. (1991) 'Researching the Homeless: The Characteristic Features of the Case Study', see J.R. Feagin, A.M. Orum and G. Sjoberg (eds), *A Case for the Case Study*, North Carolina: University Press, pp.148–73.

Strauss, A. (1987) *Qualitative Analysis for Social Scientists*, Cambridge: Cambridge University Press.

Titterton, M. (1992) 'Managing Threats to Welfare: The Search for a New Paradigm of Welfare', *Journal of Social Policy* 21: 1–23.

Ungerson, C. (1987) *Policy is Personal*, London: Tavistock.

Williams, F. (1992) 'Diversity, Difference and Divisions in Welfare', Paper presented at University of Teeside 'Towards a Post-Fordist Welfare State?'

18 Modernisation as lived experience

Contrasting case studies from the SOSTRIS project

Prue Chamberlayne and Antonella Spanò

This chapter arises from a seven-country European project which set out to explore experiences of social change in contemporary society. The underlying thinking of the SOSTRIS research (Social Strategies in Risk Society),[1] which was funded under the EU Framework Four programme on Social Exclusion and Social Integration, was that, in the context of recent social structural and cultural change, social policy had become unhitched from the realities and strategies of people's lives. The research applicants also felt that greater emphasis in social policy on 'agency' and 'empowerment' demanded a more differentiated appreciation of subjective positionings, and a more searching understanding and recognition of informal social processes. Biographical methods were adopted as a means both of achieving a deeper and more complex understanding of social dynamics and of showing how hidden social capital might be brought into play.

In seeking to explore how the dramatic scale of change in contemporary society is played out in individual experience, the research took its bearings from the broad frame of theories of modernisation, and especially such concepts as 'individualisation', 'risk' and 'reflexivity'. The study sought to probe the validity of some of these key concepts, but also to give them a more substantive, empirical, base. The main data derived from interviews with individuals in six social categories which spanned stages in the life course (unqualified youth, unemployed graduates, ex-traditional workers, early retired), but also built in dimensions of gender (single parents) and ethnicity (ethnic minority groups). The study's focus on 'strategies' led to identifying and comparing what biographical resources individuals from particular settings might mobilise within such historic processes as de-industrialisation, democratisation and marketisation, but also what aspects of such transitions might be most paralysing or demoralising for them.

It was perhaps unusual, even pioneering, for such a large-scale comparative project to use biographical methods. Certainly the experience of the research, especially at the stage of basing cross-national comparisons on indepth case studies, was of entering methodologically uncharted waters. The initial stages of the project had focused on the twin issues of: (a) generating the case studies by means of the biographical interpretive method; and (b) discussion of 'risk' and 'social exclusion' as baseline concepts for the study. All this proceeded with considerable industry and excitement. But once the process of comparing cases began, two surprises emerged. One was the realisation that we had suddenly left the well-marked tracks of case reconstruction[2] and were in open terrain on the matter of comparing and theorising from cases. We realised not just that our own research proposal said little on the matter, but that the relevant literature seemed remarkably sparse.[3]

The second surprise was that however useful an overarching concept such as 'reflexivity' might prove to be in considering developments in contemporary society, we were also continually drawn into fascination with the *differentiated* character of modernisation processes in particular social settings. In the initial stage of making comparisons between cases we even feared that more global or 'Europeanising' processes might elude us. Yet it soon became clear that, far from leading us away from broader social structural analysis, attention to particularity at the micro-level was a powerful means of enriching macro-level conceptualisation.

The purpose of this chapter is to illustrate by means of two case studies the richness of biographical methods in capturing social structural changes. Both subjects were interviewed in the category of 'early retired'. Rita is a Neapolitan leather worker, whose working life traces shifts from craft patronage to modern managerialism, and on to flexible forms of self-employment. Tony, a London transport worker, experiences the change from Fordist working relations based on a collectivised social contract to marketised deregulation. Comparisons between the cases highlight the different resources provided by pre-modern and Fordist environments in facing postmodern conditions, the significance of gender and generational differences in the changing relationships between public and private spheres, and the deep-seated nature of meanings and values in particular work and social settings. The consideration of pre-modern, craft-based relations in Rita's early occupational career in the leather industry in Naples alerts us to the interweaving of 'pre-modern' forms in many other settings. The contrast between Rita's and Tony's emotional and moral attachment to work highlights dramatic differences in the subjective meanings of work in different modes of production. Far from restricting our focus to the single case, the contrasting of individual cases stimulated thinking about further dimensions of social change in further settings.

The chapter is divided in three sections. The first methodological section, after identifying key features of the 'case study' within the biographic-interpretive method, considers two kinds of interaction which are involved in using case studies for social structural comparisons. The first kind is that of theorising from cases, through a process of grounded theory, in which the researcher brings his/her own sociological knowledge to bear on the empirical material in the process of working through it. The second kind concerns analysis of the interaction between the subjects and the social contexts in which they are situated. The middle part of the chapter presents the case studies of Rita and Tony, both of whom had coincidentally worked for twenty-eight years in their respective work-places before their early retirement. The final section compares the biographical resources and strategies with which these workers addressed their severance, and discusses the insights which their cases bring to processes of modernisation.

From case to structure

In his consideration of case-study methods, Charles Ragin (1989) provides a useful contrast between case-oriented and variable-oriented approaches. Since, in the biographic-interpretive method, the analysis seeks to make a 'reconstruction' of the gestalt of the life and of the narra-tive (Rosenthal 1993), it follows that theorisation proceeds from the internal structure of the case rather than from its external features.

This may at first sight seem to limit the analysis to the micro-level. Inevitably the early stages of interpretation of a case are centrally concerned with personal and psychological dynamics and, however much social contexts are borne in mind, they remain somewhat marginal in the process of deriving the case structure. In the early stages of the SOSTRIS project, in which we were still mastering the techniques of biographic interpretation and discussing individual cases, this emphasis on the psychological induced considerable nervousness. This paralleled the earlier experience of using this method in the Cultures of Care project,[4] when, however inherently fascinating the analysis of individual cases, it at first seemed unlikely that the method could ever make a contribution at the level of comparative social policy. In that research, as in the SOSTRIS project, it was in the comparing of cases that structural features leapt into view (King and Chamberlayne 1996).

Whether so much time needs to be spent at the level of the 'personal' gestalt is a matter for debate, and doubtless depends on the purposes of the research and the choice of the researcher. In her research which was conducted alongside the Cultures of Care project, Annette King chose to hold back from full analysis of the case structure, in favour of more attention to context (see Chapter 17). That is one very satisfactory strategy. In the cases presented in this chapter, however, it is the deeper analysis of the latent levels of emotional meaning which reveal the key structural turning points and dilemmas in the working lives of Rita and Tony. There was, for example, much puzzlement in the case analysis of Rita as to why she still spoke with such anger about 'betrayal', ostensibly about the layoffs, when she seemed to have hated her work situation for many years before she left it. As will be shown, it was the latent structure of the text which revealed which stage and aspect of the complex and twenty year long process of work rationalisation constituted for her the key betrayal, and how that was underpinned by a strong sense of her own personal guilt. In Tony's case the analytical difficulty lay in resolving his contradictory impulses of guilt and blame – he seemed to be telling two stories. Yet the key to his case interpretation lay in this paradox, which was also pivotal in highlighting the management strategy of cooling out workers through individual 'illness'.[5]

It is thus working from the internal structure of the case rather than reverting to a 'variable-oriented' approach, which has proved particularly rewarding in the SOSTRIS project and shown that the accessing of latent levels of meaning or 'feeling states' may serve to illuminate macroprocesses. As Breckner puts it, in the family and private sphere are played out the most intimate and deep structures of social relations.[6]

If 'context' can be richly regained from an interpretation of the gestalt of the case, there remains the question of how a broader social structural analysis 'arises' from case interpretation, or rather, what forms of sociological analysis can most usefully serve such purposes. Within the tradition of phenomenology, in which the biographic-interpretive method is rooted, this is not an issue of particular significance, since biographies are themselves social constructs. In such a perspective both the lived life and the told story inherently derive from social interaction which involves both micro- and macro-levels of society. As Dorothy Smith argues, the everyday world 'is generated in its varieties by an organisation of social relations that originate "elsewhere"' (1987: 92). For the SOSTRIS project, however, with its goal of identifying strategies regarding 'risk' within specific and historically differentiated systems of power and inequality, a more structural approach to 'context' was essential. At times our emphasis on wider context has led us to refer to our method as 'socio-biography'.

As Rustin put it:

> We seek to combine and interrelate two kinds of 'thick description' –
> that of the individual biography and of the subject's own vocabulary
> of motive and self-understanding, *and* of whatever social structural
> context can be inferred to be relevant to the understanding of that
> life-history.
>
> (1998a: 114)

He distinguishes two kinds of interaction which must be heeded: 'on the one hand, between sociologists and their empirical data (the interactions involved in the "discovery of grounded theory"), and on the other hand between subjects and their own contexts of activity, decision and social survival' (1998a: 114).

While structuration theory provides a means of conceptualising the reproduction and modification of social structures and cultures through the social action of subjects, that theory itself, and how it can best be developed and utilised in empirical work, remains much debated (Healy 1998). Gottfried, in an article concerned with gender, class and patriarchy provides a useful review of theorists such as de Certeau, Bourdieu and Gramsci who have tried to theorise 'big structures from small acts' (1998: 455). But she argues that the capacity to close the gap between agency-centred and structuralist accounts remains elusive, as do the research tools to 'prise open the different dimensions of lived totality' (Gottfried quoting Pollert 1996). In the same volume of *Sociology*, and also drawing on de Certeau and Bourdieu, together with Habermas, Garfinkel and Maffesoli, Crook (1998) makes a sharp critique of the false 'purifying' of 'the social' which he sees as characterising most theorising of 'everyday life', not only that which derives from phenomenology. He does, however, reserve a particular disdain for phenomenology. While the SOSTRIS project has proceeded in parallel with and without particular reference to these debates, its relevance to them is clear.

Case study of Rita

Rita's case[7] is striking for the way her working life reflects the last forty years of economic transformation. At the same time the pre-modern aspects of her social setting are the lynch-pin in explaining both the centrality of work for her and the relatively easy way she has been able to face the loss of her job.

Born in 1950, Rita grows up in a working-class neighbourhood in the historic centre of Naples during the period of its deep transformation. In those years a myriad of small shoe and handbag factories, starting off as workshops in the underground economy and modelled on the existing handicraft industry in woodwork, become successful export firms. Many of the old artisans become entrepreneurs and the productive system of the area changes.

The youngest of four children, Rita leaves school at eleven and becomes an apprentice, moving between several small factories in the area. This is typical for girls from her milieu and generation, not least because of the close connection between work and home (the workshops are situated on the ground floors of residential blocks), and the social integration of the area (employers and workers live alongside each other and are often friends).

Rita, little more than a child, is fascinated by the vitality of the boom years. Since her father, a shop decorator all his working life, sidesteps the process of social mobility, it is understandable that she looks outside the family for a mentor. At the age of sixteen (1966) she is taken on in a small factory which she opts for as the site of her personal development. It seems to have good prospects, and over time becomes a large firm with nearly 800 employees. The owner is like an adopted father, her workmates are like friends:

> The owner helped us a lot, I must say, we got along well with him, he helped us, he was a very good person…it was a fine time, yes, we worked, but those were wonderful days, we felt well, we joked, we sang, then we girls told each other our experiences, what about your baby? My baby does this and this.

Rita's identification with 'her' factory appears very clearly in her lived life. The central axis in her life is work, but not at all in the sense of the contemporary 'career' woman who sacrifices family in the name of work. On the contrary, she marries early (meaningfully – her husband works in the same firm) and at eighteen her first child is born, perfectly in line with the social expectations of her milieu. She goes back to the factory only a month after the birth. The baby is handed over to the maternal grandmother: only at weekends does he sleep at his parents' house.

The familial and affective nature of Rita's work experience precludes a precise psychological boundary between family and work. While she devotes herself body and soul to the factory, the fruits of being 'a good worker' are dedicated to the family. By means of loans and a mortgage a house is bought (1972), where, in the future, Rita and her husband will be able to live with their son. A second pregnancy (1975) demonstrates her interest in building a solid family. In other words, the *Gemeinschaft* nature of the firm means that work is not in conflict with 'total devotion' to the family.

The importance of work for Rita is confirmed in her autobiographical construction. Rita, whose main narration focuses on her experience of the lay-offs and ends up with the loss of her job, presents herself as a betrayed worker and a victim of injustice: 'we have been working there for twenty-eight years, you grew rich at the expense of the workers, you've exploited us, and you have also got a lot of money, of support, from the government'. The emotional nature of her relation with the firm also emerges clearly, for although she gives much space to trade union questions and moral evaluations she singles out the rupture in the 'harmony' in the firm as the main source of pain: 'one against the other, this has been the worst thing we had to bear, because we were not as a family any longer'.

Yet Rita has difficulty in 'dating' the firm's betrayal. Later in the interview she suddenly remembers ('oh, I forgot!') that many years before (in 1976) she had been laid off, although after a few months the workers were taken on again, and then retained until 1990. At this later point in the interview it is the 1976 lay-off which she presents as the most dramatic episode. She underlines the terrible injustice suffered, not only by her but by her workmates: she was laid off despite being pregnant, and a friend who was put on temporary lay-off committed suicide, these being evidence of the 'cruelty' of the firm.

In Rita's interpretation of her life it is this betrayal which justifies a noticeable lowering of her devotion to work:

> after that dreadful experience I changed somewhat…to be honest I must say, I began to get a bit selfish…if my daughter gets measles I don't leave her with my mother any more, but I look after her myself, I don't go to work.

Actually it is not this period which marks her transition from a factory-centred to a family-centred life, for in spite of her pregnancy she joins the daily demonstrations for jobs, and continues to leave her older child with his grandmother.

The contradiction between the lived-life and the told-life, as well as her ambiguity in pinpointing the key moment of the firm's betrayal, lead on through deeper analysis of the text to suggest that the irremediable change in Rita's life came rather with the shift in management four years later (1980). This was when the owner, fallen ill, left the running of the firm to his sons. Rita, once feeling an appreciated and irreplaceable daughter, now becomes a stranger in her own house:

> The father loved that factory, because he'd come up from nothing, he'd been a worker like us, and knew what it was to be a worker, while he was there we were alright...he'd come by, crack a joke, he was human.... They, the sons, understood nothing about work, they'd studied in Switzerland but they don't understand anything.

What Rita experienced and still interprets as an unjust usurpation was, in reality, the rupture of *Gemeinschaft* ties in the firm and the introduction of 'cold' market relations. It is a new situation which calls for a radical reorientation, for which she lacks a script. Not knowing how to be a 'good worker' in a *Gesellschaft* context, this is the moment when she shifts her prime axis out of the firm into the family. The year of the new management is when Rita's son, now twelve, returns to live with his parents, and when a new family strategy is started, involving planning and economic investment. By loans a taxi driver's licence is bought for Rita's husband, who two years later voluntarily leaves the firm to become a taxi driver. Thus they have a proactive and positive strategy in response to the insecurity of their work situation, and as a means of improving their quality of life.

For ten years Rita continues to work in the same firm, able to sustain the anonymous and impersonal relations because the centre of her affectivity is already placed outside the factory. She is quite prepared to accept the lay-off in 1990, since her 'I' and her 'we' are both now in the private sphere:

> but my friends cried, they lived through a so awful experience, perhaps it has not been the same for me personally, because I'd already overcome...I had already bought my house, for me it has been a bit better than...but not for my friends.

Rita sells knitwear from home, now able to unite work with a central family axis. She gets the goods from a factory at which her brother works, her clients are mostly friends, her earnings pay for her daughter's education. For her son she has already bought a taxi licence. So even though she presents herself as a victim of a terrible betrayal by the firm, the final early retirement in 1994 is a relatively insignificant event. Economically protected, she is a happy mother, grandmother and worker. Her marriage is happy too – Rita and her husband are passionate and champion ballroom dancers!

The very lack of a definite border between private and public spheres (between family and work) which prevented Rita from accepting modernity, becomes her main resource in facing early retirement. If early retirement is a characteristic form of destandardisation in post-industrial society, we could say that it is her membership of a pre-modern community which eases her transition towards post-modernity.

Case study of Tony

Born in 1942, Tony grew up in the outer suburbs of the East End of London, sharing in the collectivism forged by industrialisation and war-time experience. His father was away in the forces for the first four years of Tony's life and, with the birth of a sister after his return, Tony became the middle child. His grandfather, father and brother all worked for London Transport,[8] and soon after his marriage in his early twenties, Tony also joined that labour force as 'a job for life'. He had left school at fifteen, and for ten years had moved between low-level jobs in the City, doing deliveries and shop work, possibly hoping to find his way into white-collar work. He evaluates that period as 'sort of travelling, just wanting to find my feet'. It was the era of high employment and working-class teenage rebellion, and one can perhaps picture Tony as a shiney-shoed Mod.[9] His account resonates with the 'we' culture of the East End: his wedding coincided with the famous local West Ham football team's participation in the Cup Final, and as his brother read out the telegrams, 'everyone (was) shouting out "don't worry about them, what's the score?"'.

With a mortgage, small children, and a wife at home – 'we always considered that the right way' – 'things were a little bit tight', and Tony 'settled into the railway'. He also had to combat being looked down on by his wife's family. After twelve years of alternate weekly shifts of days and nights, he moved to a permanent day shift. He worked his way up into an administrative job, but when that was computerised in the 1980s 'I ended up back on the tools'. He had a tendency to suffer from gastritis, but:

> I would go into work anyway…in the past they would have appreciated you going in and making the effort, and then they would say, 'Well, if you're finished you can go',…and the other chaps are always very good, they used to help out, and we would do the same for them if they came to work and they weren't feeling very well. But I mean tha- that was part I felt of this team work, this comradeship amongst fellow workers.

In Tony's extremely sparse initial narrative, which revolves between argumentation and evaluation,[10] the key change which led him to take voluntary severance came with the introduction of new contracts requiring shift work, which he struggled with for three years but could not tolerate physically. Counterbalancing 'system' and 'personal' factors, he also says he has not given up work entirely, since he does part-time work to make up his low pension, that he enjoys being at home, and that he was able to do some things with his lump sum payment. He has, however, been repeatedly on medication and in a very low state. His medical condition suggests that his 'fair-minded' justifications in no way resolve the situation in his mind.

By skilful questioning which keeps to Tony's frame of reference, the interviewer[11] elicits a wealth of elaboration on these issues, and interpretation of the interview shows that the case structure does indeed lie in the lack of reconciliation between social and personal factors. As in Rita's case, the core problem lies in the loss of a life world of meaning, identity and values. Yet Tony's encounter with procedures of rationalisation and early retirement denied the importance of meaning and belonging, focusing rather on a discourse of compensation, choice and illness.

The key to Tony's problem does indeed lie in the multi-dimensional effects of the new three-year contracts of the 1990s, which were introduced in a context of job cuts and newly imposed complex shift patterns. Quite as devastating as the shifting sleep patterns were the consequences of splitting up the team, of increasing lower-level responsibility by cutting back on craftsmen, the new 'wedge' between management and employees, and the loss of stability and future security. Tony elaborates on all these themes at length. Shifts meant an endless problem of 'combatting the sleeping programme'. Formerly, as in cases of illness, in the checking of trains, workers continued to help each other out. But with the job cuts, loss of craftsmen, and splitting up of teams in new shifts, despite additional training courses:

> there were – were men that were floundering, there was – there were some that weren't too sure um I know that on many occasions that – they used to come and ask me um various things...I know it was teamwork but you still had your own work to do.... And more often than not you couldn't remember you just couldn't remember back that far you just couldn't remember....

Tony participated in several seminars concerning working relationships between different sections and between management and staff, which he enjoyed, 'and yet somehow there was another system that was coming in and putting a wedge between it all'.

Underlying the technical detail is broken-heartedness at the change of values, the incomprehensible way in which contracts were broken, the loss of personal recognition, trust and reciprocity, the loss of confidence and of his role as a 'good worker'. Despite his illness, Tony clung on to his job in an attempt to hold on to this world. After a lengthy illness he goes back to work prematurely, refusing illness retirement, which would have been financially advantageous 'because I felt I still had a lot of work left in me'. He hopes to get offered a daytime job on health grounds, but this is refused, by a medical team which is itself under threat of privatisation. He stresses his popularity at work, the appreciation of the way he took trouble to explain matters in his administrative job, the affection of the young girl who came to take over his job at the end, the farewell drinks when he left, which was 'like leaving home'.

But it is the loss of the meaning of work which is most painful and which he constantly associates with his illness. With the new contracts:

> I could say my whole attitude changed um, towards work in general and in life in general and I wondered whether it was all worthwhile whether I shouldn't be like many other people and just not bother. Just don't care because nobody cares about us, or me or a – so why should I care about others, and yet I couldn't – I just couldn't bring meself to be like that because it's not in my nature. So I ended up it just made me ill.

Staff became lackadaisical and even ill with the strain. He equates the feeling with what people 'out on the streets' must feel about 'having nothing', which is 'the pits'. 'What was the point of being conscientious and hard-working when, when at the end of the day all you could see was the possibility of losing your job?'

He receives a further blow in his attempts to find new work. Having stipulated that he can only do a five-day week, his interview is broken off and benefit cut, because it turns out the particular job requires six-day working. Subsequently he appeals through a welfare rights office, but the shock effect on all his basic principles of trust, honesty and fairness make him ill again – a theme to which he returns repeatedly.

Comparison of the cases

This section compares the different biographical resources available to Tony and Rita in making the transition into the postmodern world and the management of rationalisation. The last part of the chapter returns to more methodological reflections concerning the use of case studies for social structural analysis, and especially to a more differentiated appreciation of 'models' of modernity.

For both Tony and Rita, the key problem has been their incapacity to tolerate 'modernised' and impersonal contexts of work, even though this critical change occurred at different stages of modernisation: for Rita with 'modern' managerialism, for Tony with deregulation. While they both present themselves as betrayed and angry, there are great differences in their responses. For Rita, who has in fact made a happy transition into the postmodern world, her portrayal of herself as betrayed serves to hide her own betrayal towards the firm, her own metamorphosis from a 'good worker' to happy mother and worker outside the firm. Tony, despite finding work as caretaker for a trustworthy church organisation, is still involved in the painful experience of severance. This difference in reaction is borne out by their different experiences of 'bad events' subsequent to the introduction of new managers for Rita and the new contracts for Tony. For whereas the next phase of temporary lay-off and the taking of early retirement (*mobilità*) have not been particularly significant for Rita, the refusal of a day-time job and the employment benefit stoppage have been traumatic for Tony.

The reason why re-orientation is easier for Rita lies in the greater continuity between 'old' and 'new' life worlds for her, and the greater discontinuity for Tony. The 'we' world for Tony, despite its rootedness in a working-class culture which embraces family and the East End suburban milieu, is based in a 'factory life-style', whereas Rita's 'we' overflows beyond the factory into the traditional and popular culture of her community. Tony enjoys a happy family life, but it cannot compensate for the status, camaraderie and sense of belonging of the workplace, whereas, when her identity frame collapses at work, Rita can replicate it in the community. Whatever the solidarities of London Transport, and despite his portrayal of leaving work as 'leaving home', the 'modern' conditions of Tony's work required a much greater psychological separation between work and family, which prevented him using the family as an alternative resource when he left his job. Gender and generational differences also play their part. As a woman, and as a member of the first postwar cohort of married women working (her older sisters gave up work on marriage), Rita was freer in her choice of identity as a 'good worker', whereas Tony was fulfilling an established male role. While Tony is third generation London Transport worker, Rita has diverted more individualistically from her father and her siblings, and has aligned herself with a self-made man, in the context of a particularly dramatic version of the economic miracle in her neighbourhood. Meanwhile the context of irregular work and the informal economy within her community mean that she remains socialised to precariousness and changeability, and open to flexibility and informality, whereas Tony is more conditioned to standardised life courses and stability.

Adjusting to the 'end of industrial life' is therefore made easier for Rita by the traditional or pre-modern features of her situation: the lack of rigid separation between public and private spheres, the persistence of traditional patterns of family and friendship, the pre-existence of destandardised life courses and the habits of flexibility and instability. Tony's resources are less transferable, and his case suggests how the very qualities demanded by Fordism can de-skill and un-fit workers for postmodern conditions. Routine reliability and trustworthiness which have made him a valued worker in a semi-skilled, industrialised public service, his separation between 'work' and family life, and the reciprocal and life-contractual relationships to which he is accustomed, are all obstacles in accommodating to deregulation.

While graphically illuminating the experience of economic transformation and the traumatic loss of such deeply rooted meanings of work, Tony's case also provides insights into the management of rationalisation, the 'cooling out' of severance by the attribution of 'illness' to personal responsibility, and thus the individualisation of a collective predicament, thereby feeding 'the individualistic impulses of post-industrial society' (Spanò 1997: 3). We were alerted to this by the determined 'fair-mindedness' of Tony's narrative, the importance for him and continuing difficulty in making sense of his experiences, his ambivalence between guilt and blame.

This is an example of how, as Rustin (1998b: 11) puts it, 'We moved, in our analysis, from the detail of the case, to the social context, and back again, filling out each end of this chain of connections as we did so'. In this case Tony's 'feeling state' was a critical point of interpretation, in Rita's case the latent meaning of 'betrayal'. In each case probing the most personal levels of response has extended our understanding of macro-level processes. For us as researchers, and hopefully for readers, the detail of the case studies has 'extended the lexicon of our interpretation', provoked us into new reflections on the interrelationship between context and meaning, stimulated an exercise in sociological imagination (Rustin 1998b: 14).

At the macro end of the 'chain of connections' we have 'stretched' the use of case-study methods to bring a new experiential dimension to what are often abstract categories in comparative literature. This suggests that a new case-study approach to comparative studies might engage students more imaginatively than traditional methods, making visible connections between familial, local, regional, national and global levels of analysis. Elsewhere we have discussed the search for new life paths within processes of deep social transition as 'socially pioneering', and how this extends notions of the scope for agency in structuration theory beyond 'the powerful' to 'modest positions' or 'the margins' (Rustin 1997: 10, 19; Spanò 1997).

While it is often feared that working from individual case studies will lead to false generalisations, in our experience the particularity of case studies has enriched our appreciation of complexity and differentiation, and alerted us to the interpenetration of contrasting social forms. In fact the 'single case' is not single, since it is relativised by other cases in the study,[12] and by the wide knowledge of the researchers which is brought to bear in the interpretation.[13] A distinction must also be made between generating insights into social processes and generalising about them. Neither the Rita nor the Tony case can be 'generalised' since quite opposite cases could doubtless be found in their vicinity. The biographical resources of 'pre-modernity' which are available to Rita cannot be generalised to the 'southern context' of Italy, since there are other, more fully industrialised settings, even within Naples, in which de-industrialisation is just as devastating as for Tony (Spanò 1999). Tony's 'industrialised' version of social democratic collectivism is only one of a number of 'typical East End' cultures – others are more opportunistic and individualised.

But the lack of generalisability in no way invalidates the insights which the two cases bring into processes and experiences of modernisation, insights which are helpful in generating more differentiated thinking in other as well as these particular settings. Thus the theme of the usefulness of the greater flexibility between private and public spheres in pre-modern society in adapting to postmodern conditions, and the more difficult transition arising from the greater separation between the two spheres in 'modern' societies, suggests a rich seam of investigation concerning the re-balancing of private and public spheres in postmodernity. In her critique of 'binary' thinking in the theorisation of de-traditionalisation, Adam (1996) advocates a focus on 'interpenetration', warning that: 'The prefixes of de- and post-...transform ongoing and embedded processes into disembedded, static states' (p.143). Her argument might be taken to suggest the need to abolish such terms: however we find them essential in making social structural comparisons. Our argument is that with the help of case studies, the 'abstract' terms of structural analysis can be given new experiential meaning and complexity.

Notes

1   The SOSTRIS project was funded under the EU Targeted Socio-Economic programme for three years, 1996–9. It included teams in Britain (London),

France (Paris), Germany (Halle), Greece (Athens), Italy (Naples), Spain (Barcelona) and Sweden (Gothenburg).

2 The research followed the procedures of case reconstruction as developed by Rosenthal (1993). See also Breckner (1998).

3 Project discussion on issues of comparison is reflected in Rustin (1997, 1998) and Wengraf (1998).

4 The ESRC-funded Cultures of Care project (1992–6) was based on narrative interviews with home carers in East and West Germany and Britain (King and Chamberlayne 1996).

5 These are examples of the interpretation understanding the subject 'better than they know themselves', going beyond the person's self-understanding, for research purposes. To some researchers it may seem unwarranted, even 'disempowering', to go beyond 'giving voice'. Hopefully the value of doing so is clear from these cases.

6 A point made during discussions within the SOSTRIS project. Roswita Breckner (University of Halle, Germany) was initially research methods consultant for project, and then joined the German team.

7 Both the interview and the analysis of the case were carried out jointly by Paola Caniglia and Antonella Spanò.

8 Before privatisation in the 1990s, London Transport operated an integrated system of underground travel and buses in the metropolitan area.

9 In the mid-1960s there was a sharp division among youths between neatly suited office-worker Mods and leather-jacketed motorbike Rockers, who were more usually from manual occupations.

10 The method of interpretation distinguishes between key sorts of text (such as description, argumentation and narrative) which involve different time perspectives in the construction of the account.

11 The interview and main analysis of the case were conducted by Susanna Rupp, the main researcher for the British SOSTRIS team.

12 The first stage of the SOSTRIS project (1996–8) was based on six to eight interviews in each of the six different categories in seven countries i.e. about 300 interviews, of which at least fifty were analysed indepth, the others being used as background profiles.

13 Key stages of the analysis indepth were conducted in group workshops. In the SOSTRIS projects workshops were held both within the national teams and at cross-national meetings.

References

Adam, B. (1996) 'Detraditionalization and the Certainty of Uncertain Futures', in P. Heelas, S. Lash and P. Morris (eds), *Detraditionalization: Critical Reflections on Authority and Identity*, Oxford: Blackwell.

Breckner, R. (1998) 'The Biographical-Interpretive Method – Principles and Procedures', *SOSTRIS Working Paper 2, Case Study Materials: the Early Retired*, London: Centre for Biography in Social Policy, University of East London.

Crook, S. (1998) 'Minotaurs and Other Monsters: "Everyday Life" in Recent Social Theory', *Sociology* 32(3): 523–40.

Gottfried, H. (1998) 'Beyond Patriarchy? Theorising Gender and Class', *Sociology* 32(3): 451–68.

Healy, K. (1998) 'Conceptualising Constraint: Mouzelis, Archer and the Concept of Social Structure', *Sociology* 32(3): 509–22.

King, A. and Chamberlayne, P. (1996) 'Comparing the Informal Sphere: Public and Private Relations and Welfare in East and West Germany', *Sociology* 30(4): 741–61.

Pollert, A. (1996) 'Gender and Class Revisited: the Poverty of "Patriarchy"', *Sociology* 30(3): 639–59.

Ragin, C. (1989) 'New Directions in Comparative Research', in M.L. Kohn (ed.), *Cross-National Research in Sociology*, London: Sage.

Rosenthal, G. (1993) 'Reconstructon of Life Stories. Principles of Selection in Generating Stories for Narrative Biographical Interviews', *The Narrative Study of Lives* 1(1): 59–91.

Rustin, M. (1998a) 'From Individual Life Histories to Sociological Understanding', *SOSTRIS Working Paper 3, Case Study Materials: Lone Parents*, London: Centre for Biography in Social Policy, University of East London.

—— (1998b) 'From Individual Life-Stories to Sociological Understanding', Paper at the Conference on Biographical Methods in the Social Sciences, Tavistock Centre, London, September.

Smith, D. (1987) *The Everyday World as Problematic: a Feminist Sociology*, Milton Keynes: Open University Press.

Spanò, A. (1997) 'Personal and Social Effects of De-Institutionalisation of Life Courses. The Case of Early Retired', Composite Report in *SOSTRIS Working Paper 2, Case Study Materials: the Early Retired*, London: Centre for Biography in Social Policy, University of East London.

—— (1999) 'Structural and Cultural Dimensions of Poverty in Italy: The Implications for Social Policies', in P. Chamberlayne, A. Cooper, R. Freeman and M. Rustin (eds), *Welfare and Culture*, London: Jessica Kingsley Publishers.

Wengraf, T. (1998) 'Representations of Interpreted Biographies in Contexts: General Concepts and Unique Cases', Paper presented in the Biography and Society strand at the ISA Conference, Montreal.

Index

Lightning Source UK Ltd.
Milton Keynes UK
07 September 2010
159558UK00001B/15/A